LAWYERS ON TRIAL

Lawyers are universally unpopular, but is that justified? Aren't lawyers necessary for justice? This book uses real-world examples, case studies, and commentary from practitioners to answer this question and to reveal the many and varied strategies American and English lawyers use to protect clients. It shows how lawyers tackle their conflicting duties, and highlights the choices lawyers everywhere routinely make through their power of decision.

What emerges are new ways of understanding the critical role lawyers play in society – and their professional responsibilities. This new edition considers the litigation surrounding Donald Trump and the role played by his lawyers. It includes a new chapter on SLAPPs and the way the law is used to advance clients' interests.

This book presents a unique and fascinating account of what happens when lawyers' duties to clients conflict with their duties to the legal system, and looks in detail at the ethical codes and laws that regulate their conduct.

Lawyers on Trial

Hired Guns or Heroes?

Christopher Whelan

•HART•

OXFORD • LONDON • NEW YORK • NEW DELHI • SYDNEY

HART PUBLISHING

Bloomsbury Publishing Plc

Kemp House, Chawley Park, Cumnor Hill, Oxford, OX2 9PH, UK

1385 Broadway, New York, NY 10018, USA

29 Earlsfort Terrace, Dublin 2, Ireland

HART PUBLISHING, the Hart/Stag logo, BLOOMSBURY and the Diana logo are
trademarks of Bloomsbury Publishing Plc

First published in Great Britain 2024

A catalogue record for this book is available from the British Library.

A catalogue record for this book is available from the Library of Congress.

Library of Congress Control Number: 2024944065

ISBN: PB: 978-1-50997-760-4
        ePDF: 978-1-50997-762-8
        ePub: 978-1-50997-761-1

Typeset by Compuscript Ltd, Shannon

To find out more about our authors and books visit www.hartpublishing.co.uk.
Here you will find extracts, author information, details of forthcoming events
and the option to sign up for our newsletters.

FOREWORD

This new edition of Christopher Whelan's already classic work *Bodyguard of Lies*, primarily designed for an academic and professional audience, has now mutated into a revised paperback whose still more striking title signifies a justifiable aspiration for wider readership.

The words Shakespeare put into Jack Cade's mouth, 'The first thing we do, let's kill all the lawyers', may be an exaggerated summary of the popular view of lawyers' appropriate destiny, but indisputably, as a group, they do not rank high in the public esteem.

Against this backcloth, the author with a wealth of research has developed two major themes, enlivened by tales of trials (and tribulations) on both sides of the Atlantic: the first is that qualified lawyers are subject to codes of ethical conduct of varying intensity; and the second is that their duty to comply with those codes is often in tension with their mandate to win for their clients. The professional obligations of the English Bar are more demanding than those of solicitors in the same jurisdiction – most importantly, the latter are not subject to the cab-rank rule, which prevents a barrister from refusing to provide his services because of an aversion to his client or the client's cause. Among his many insights, Dr Whelan shows that the statement of Henry Brougham justifying his defence of Queen Caroline in her divorce from King George 1V, sometimes cited as the paradigm example of the rule in action, has been interpreted in the US (where the codes are generally more relaxed), with some contextual underpinning, as the vindication of the concept of the advocate as hired gun.

The issues which this book explores remain real and recurrent. In a practice which has extended into its sixth decade as recorded in my own memoir, I have had to explain to one client why I was obliged to act in an wholly unconnected matter for another client whose long-term enemy he was, and to explain in a separate matter why I could not continue to act if my client would not disclose to the judge a document that was significantly unhelpful to its position.

The justice system is the Cinderella of our social services, always last in the queue for public monies with no Chancellor of the Exchequer willing to play the Prince Charming to rescue it from its plight. Unless lawyers, players in that system, whether in the civil or criminal spheres, act themselves with a forcefulness which is always subordinate to fairness, the system will no longer sustain the rule of law. And in an era when what was once a profession has increasingly changed into a business, and lawyer activists are assailing the cab-rank rule, this important book should serve as an admonition as well as an education.

Michael J Beloff KC
Former President of Trinity College, Oxford and Treasurer of Grays Inn

PREFACE

What should lawyers do for clients and should you care? Would you expect *your* lawyer to use all the tricks of their trade – like a hired gun? But if you're a lawyer, should you use those tricks? Would that make you a hero? What about your other duties: to the court, to the administration of justice, and to the public? Lawyers who protect clients may be *their* heroes, but what about the rest of us?

This book is aimed at anyone interested in what lawyers do and, more importantly, what they ought to do. The purpose is to explain lawyers' 'tricks' and then invite *you* to judge the tragic choices they face. What do you think about what lawyers have done; what should they have done; what would you have done and why?

This is a new, revised, edition of *The Bodyguards of Lies: Lawyers' Power and Professional Responsibility* (2022). That book was aimed primarily at *specialists* – academics and practitioners. The title came from a Churchill quote: 'in wartime, truth is so precious it should always be protected by a bodyguard of lies'. Lawyers are 'bodyguards of lies' when they conceal clients' inconvenient truths or create versions of reality that are far from real. As such, they're very *powerful*, so their ethical *responsibilities* are very important too.

Lawyers are generally unpopular, but is this justified? Aren't they necessary for justice? If their role and responsibility were better understood, would that help their image?

ACKNOWLEDGEMENTS

Thanks to the many lawyers who've generously contributed to the research. Special thanks to 3PB for offering me a pupillage and tenancy after (despite?) many years as an academic. Practising provided further opportunity for ethnography, participant observation, discussion and debate about lawyers in diverse fields of advocacy practice. Particular thanks to 3PB's Peter Kent and Russell Porter.

I'm grateful to Rick Abel (UCLA). Preparing to teach Professional Responsibility (PR) for the first time at the University of Texas (Austin) in 1982, he generously gave me the structure and readings for his course. Since then, I've taught PR over 10 times at three US law schools, and many more times at the Universities of Warwick and Oxford, all inspired by that first outing.

The support provided by the Frances Lewis Law Center at Washington & Lee University has been invaluable. Thanks to Blake Morant for inviting me to be Scholar-in-Residence in 2005, and to David Partlett for the offer to return each year. The Center provided student assistance – Penn Clarke, now of Longleaf Law Partners, was the star! He arranged and conducted several interviews in the early days which whetted the appetite to delve deeper into the subject.

Most of all, though, I'm grateful to Jane, a storytelling genius, for her unwavering support – definitely a heroine!

CONTENTS

PART II
TRICKS OF THE TRADE

ABBREVIATIONS

ABA	American Bar Association
ACCA	Association of Chartered Certified Accountants (EW)
ACLU	American Civil Liberties Union
AML	Anti-Money Laundering
BMJ	British Medical Journal
BSB	Bar Standards Board (EW)
CCRC	Criminal Cases Review Commission (EW)
CD	Core Duty (BSB)
CPS	Crown Prosecution Service (EW)
CPR	Civil Procedure Rules 1998 (EW)
DA	District Attorney (US)
DPP	Director of Public Prosecutions (EW)
DR	Disciplinary Rule (ABA Model Code)
EAT	Employment Appeal Tribunal (EW)
EC	Ethical Consideration (ABA Model Code)
ECJ	Court of Justice of the European Union
EPA	Environmental Protection Agency (US)
ET	Employment Tribunal (EW)
EU	European Union
EW	England and Wales
FBI	Federal Bureau of Investigation (US)
FCA	Financial Conduct Authority (UK)
FPC	Foreign Policy Centre (UK)
FRC	Financial Reporting Council (EW)

FRE	Federal Rules of Evidence (US)
FRCP	Federal Rules of Civil Procedure (US)
GAAR	General Anti-Abuse Rule (EW)
GJLE	Georgetown Journal of Legal Ethics
GM	General Motors
HMRC	Her Majesty's Revenue and Customs (EW)
IRS	Internal Revenue Service (US)
ITV	Independent Television (UK)
KC	King's Counsel (EW)
LJ	Law Journal
LPP	Legal Professional Privilege (EW)
LRev	Law Review
LSA	Legal Services Act 2007 (EW)
LSB	Legal Services Board (UK)
LS4CA	Law Students for Climate Accountability (US)
MC	Model Code of Professional Responsibility (ABA)
MP	Member of Parliament (UK)
MR	Model Rules of Professional Conduct (ABA)
NAS	National Academy of Sciences (US)
NCA	National Crime Agency (EW)
NDA	Non-Disclosure Agreement
NRA	National Rifle Association (US)
OBSF	Off-Balance Sheet Financing
OLC	Office of Legal Counsel (US)
ONS	Office of National Statistics (UK)
PACE	Police and Criminal Evidence Act 1984 (EW)
PD	Public Defender
PO	Post Office
POL	Post Office Ltd (EW)
POST	Parliamentary Office of Science and Technology (EW)

QC	Queen's Counsel (EW)
SAR	Suspicious Activity Report (EW)
SDT	Solicitors Disciplinary Tribunal (EW)
SFO	Serious Fraud Office (UK)
SRA	Solicitors Regulation Authority
TUC	Trades Union Congress (EW)
UK	United Kingdom
US	United States
USC	United States Code

TABLE OF CASES

PART I

Hired Guns or Heroes:
The Ethical Conundrum

If there were no bad people, there would be no good lawyers.

— Charles Dickens (1841)

1

Lawyers' Ethics

Oxymoron or Heart of the Matter?

There is a vague popular belief that lawyers are necessarily dishonest.

— Abraham Lincoln (1850)

Lawyers are generally unpopular, even a laughing stock (Galanter 2005). One reason for 'a cynical and sometimes hostile public opinion' might be the perception that lawyers are 'no more than "guns for hire"' (Boon 2023: 36).

But aren't lawyers necessary for justice? When a law student or lawyer is asked by an old friend 'what do you do now?', should they answer proudly or defensively, as in: 'I *am* a member of the legal profession, but I'm not a lawyer in the pejorative sense' (Lorenz nd)? There are many 'sinners' in the legal profession: the bad (Abel 2011) – nearly 30 lawyers in the Watergate scandal (Dean 2000; Graff 2022) – the greedy (Dillon and Cannon 2011; Wilkie 2011), and those who've 'lost their soul' (Kronman 1993). Some drum up business in questionable ways, like divorce solicitors Brookman's posters in City of London wine bars inviting prospective clients to 'ditch the bitch' and proclaiming 'all men are bastards' (*Law Society Gazette* 2001), or divorce lawyer Corri Fetman's billboard proclaiming 'Life's Short. Get a Divorce', placed in a Chicago location with many nightclubs known locally as the 'Viagra Triangle'. Others are accused of creating a litigation explosion via a kind of 'lawsuit lotto' where people sue at the drop of a hat or, more famously, a McDonald's coffee cup. After all, didn't that McDonald's woman win $2.9 million in 1994 after spilling her coffee?

But aren't there 'saints' too? One lawyer, Sir Thomas More, literally was a saint. And what about you? If you needed a lawyer, what would you expect of them – probably use all the 'tricks of their trade' for you – like a hired gun? But if you were a lawyer, should you use those tricks – or not? What does it take to be a lawyer-hero – like Atticus Finch?

I. Heroes?

A. Atticus Finch

Finch was fictional, created in Harper Lee's 1960 classic *To Kill a Mockingbird*. But his plaque in Harper Lee's hometown, Old Monroeville Alabama, is real. It says he was 'a great and noble lawyer'; a 'lawyer-hero who knows how to see and tell the truth, knowing the price the community, which Atticus loves, will pay for that truth'; a 'lawyer-hero who knows how to use power and advantage for moral purposes, and who is willing to stand alone as the conscience of the community'. The truth in *Mockingbird* was that, although the biased jury found him guilty, Finch's client was innocent (Dare 2001; Symposium 1993–94), like the 3,524 others, exonerated in the US since 1989 (up to June 2024). Which is why Innocence Project co-founder Barry Scheck was inducted into the American Academy of Achievement. Other lawyers, though, have paid a heavy price – and some the ultimate price – for following their professional consciences and doing their duty.

B. Sir Thomas More

More became England's Lord Chancellor in 1529, when King Henry VIII was about to get rid of his first wife, Catherine of Aragon. Henry split from the Roman Catholic Church and declared himself Supreme Head of the Church of England. But More refused to repudiate the Pope or recognise the marriage annulment. In 1532, he resigned, but two years later, after refusing to take the oath to recognise Anne Boleyn as Henry's lawful wife, he was arrested, imprisoned in the Tower of London and, in 1535, convicted of treason.

More refused to lie, to say he believed something he didn't. Ironically, he was convicted based on the (almost certainly) perjured testimony of the Solicitor-General Richard Rich. More was executed on Tower Hill. Exactly 400 years later, in 1935, he was made a saint and became the patron saint of lawyers, judges and politicians. No wonder More is praised as a lawyer-hero, a man with a conscience: 'A Man for All Seasons' (Bolt 1960).

C. 'Let's Kill All the Lawyers'

Not long after the death of More – perhaps 1591 – 'Dick the Butcher' said those famous words, written by Shakespeare (*Henry VI, Part 2*): 'The First Thing We Do, Let's Kill All the Lawyers'. Fictional words perhaps, but being killed has been an occupational reality: 'Around the world hundreds of lawyers are killed or jailed for simply doing their jobs' (Baroness Kennedy of the Shaws KC, quoted in Baksi (2024)).

In Colombia, between 1991 and 2009, over 400 lawyers were murdered – over one a month (Rayner 2009). In Iraq, three of Saddam Hussein's lawyers were killed, two of them after being abducted and tortured. In Mexico, lawyers involved in drug turf wars have been killed. Silvia Raquenel Villanueva defended not the drug lords but low-level drug traffickers: 'I'm a lawyer for people who really need me'. There were four attempts on her life, including one when she was shot eight times. Her luck ran out in 2009 (Lacey 2009). In Italy, Giorgio Ambrosili investigated a bank controlled by a Sicilian banker. Hours after Ambrosili spoke with US authorities, he was shot dead by three Mafia hitmen commissioned by the banker. In South Africa, lawyers in the Western Cape were 'under siege from criminals who have killed two prominent legal eagles since November [2018]' (Hyman and Nombembe 2019). In Northern Ireland in 1989, a human rights lawyer, Pat Finucane, who'd represented paramilitaries on both sides of the Irish 'troubles', was shot 14 times by two masked gunmen in his own home with his wife and three children present (O'Neill 2020). In Ukraine in 2015, some Russian special forces officers were charged with terrorism. In 2016, their lawyer, Yuri Hrabovsky, was drugged, abducted and murdered (Zmina 2016). In Amsterdam, Derk Wiersum represented a drug gang member who turned state witness in March 2018. One week later, the witness's brother was murdered; in September 2019, Wiersum was shot 10 times and killed. Another lawyer, Omno de Jong, who represents the key prosecution witness, is under permanent police protection (Parrock 2024). The Dutch Justice Minister called the shooting of the lawyer 'an attack on our rule of law' (BBC 2019).

Shakespeare's words were fictional, but killing and threatening lawyers has been – and remains – a fact. Which is ironic because Shakespeare was praising lawyers not condemning them. Dick the Butcher was a member of Jack Cade's gang. Cade was a real person who led a rebellion against the King on behalf of Richard Duke of York, who aspired to the throne. Were the words a joke, a vision of the utopia life would be under Cade or, most likely, an acknowledgement that lawyers might threaten the absolute power of the King? Because that's how real-life dictators see the threat independent lawyers pose to them. Just 50 years after Shakespeare wrote those words, Oliver Cromwell had King Charles I executed after winning the English Civil War. A Republic was created and Cromwell, a military dictator (Churchill 1956: 314), decreed that no more than three lawyers could congregate together outside of court because of the threat he thought lawyers posed to his dictatorship. Three hundred years after, Adolf Hitler, before the Reichstag in April 1942, was quoted as saying he would not rest until 'every German sees that it a shameful thing to be a lawyer'.

Sadly, while some lawyers are threatened by autocrats – in 2023, five Iranian lawyers were murdered, 10 injured in assassination attempts, and many more arrested for defending anti-government protesters – others are embraced by them (Abel 2024a, 2024b, 2024c). No wonder lawyers are harassed all the time.

D. Harassment

In 1995, a 7,000 lb bomb blew up a Federal building in Oklahoma, killing 168 people. Timothy McVeigh was charged with the crime and Terry Nichols with being an accomplice. Also charged was Michael Fortier. He knew about the plans but didn't warn the authorities. He pleaded guilty to four counts involving transporting stolen weapons and concealing the conspiracy. He also became a key witness in securing the conviction of both McVeigh (who was executed) and Nichols (who was sentenced to life in prison). Despite all this, it was Fortier's lawyer, Mike Maguire, who was harassed so much he left Oklahoma City for Tulsa in 1996.

In Iran, the punishment for adultery is not just death, but death by stoning. So, when Sakinah Mohammedi Ashtiani was convicted in 2005, she was put on death row. She was released in March 2014, but by then, her original lawyer had fled Iran, leaving behind his wife – held in solitary confinement in a tiny cell – and his seven-year-old daughter (Watson 2010). Another of her lawyers fled to Turkey.

In London, fake bombs were placed at chambers in Gray's Inn to intimidate two barristers investigating 'one of the UK's biggest [suspected] gangland money launderers' (Brown 2023). Intimidating notes had been left, including one threatening to rape a daughter. Barristers representing Jimmy Lai, a Hong Kong newspaper publisher charged with offences under the National Security Law, have also suffered a campaign of intimidation, including rape and death threats (*The Times* 2023a).

E. John Demjanjuk

Israeli lawyers can refuse a case for any reason (National Council of the Bar Association 1986: Rule 12), which makes Yoram Sheftel's bravery and determination even more heroic. Demjanjuk was sentenced to death in 1987 for being 'Ivan the Terrible', the nickname given to the Nazi guard responsible for 900,000 counts of murder at Treblinka concentration camp. His appeal, however, was delayed because of what happened to his lawyers. Just days before the appeal, Dov Eitan, in unclear circumstances, died after falling from the fifteenth floor of a Jerusalem building. Then, at his funeral, Sheftel, another of Demjanjuk's lawyers, had hydrochloric acid thrown on his face by a 77-year-old Treblinka survivor.

Both events led to the appeal's delay – over a year – while operations repaired Sheftel's face and eyes. Undeterred, and with Demjanjuk spending seven and a half years in prison – over five on death row – Sheftel exposed the miscarriage of justice. When the appeal was eventually heard, the Berlin Wall had fallen and Sheftel presented convincing new evidence from 33 Soviet prisoners of war that Demjanjuk definitely wasn't 'Ivan the Terrible' and shouldn't have been executed – as he would've been had it not been for what happened to his lawyers. Sheftel, and possibly Eitan, paid dearly for doing their duty as lawyers. After Demjanjuk was freed, Sheftel said he was 'the most hated man in the country, more than my client' (Geiger 2019).

F. Fact is Stranger than Fiction

In 1967, when Georgia prosecutor Floyd Hoard started his car, 12 sticks of dynamite exploded (Buffington 2018). Since the 1960s, at least 13 American prosecutors have been killed. In 2013, in Kaufman County Texas, two DAs were murdered. In January, assistant DA Mark Hasse was gunned down walking to the courthouse. Then, a few weeks later, the DA, Mike McLelland, and his wife Cynthia, were killed in their home. Aryan Brotherhood members, being investigated for racketeering, were suspected, which was why Federal prosecutor Jay Hileman quit after explaining his 'security concerns'. That's why Judge Erleigh Norville Wiley is another lawyer-hero – she took McLelland's place in Kaufman County. It turned out the murders were committed by another lawyer and justice of the peace, Eric Williams, who had been prosecuted by Hasse and McLelland, and convicted of stealing $600 worth of computers from his courthouse (Allen 2019).

Lawyers are never safe. William Weissich was murdered in 1986, 31 years after he'd prosecuted the person who killed him (*Los Angeles Times* Archives 1986). In 2011, five people were murdered by 73-year-old Carey Hal Dyess, including a lawyer, Jerrold Shelley. He'd represented Dyess' (fifth) wife in their divorce. Shelley was killed as he was packing up his office on, literally, his last day before retirement (Lee Myers and Christie 2011).

G. Historical Heroes

When citizens pay tribute to a nation's 'founding fathers', they're often praising lawyers. People remember Mahatma Gandhi helping India win independence from Britain dressed in his loincloth and making his clothes at the spinning wheel, but he practised as a barrister in South Africa. Gandhi trained at Inner Temple, one of the four Inns of Court in London where barristers are called to the Bar. Another founding father, Pandit Nehru, the first Indian Prime Minister, was a barrister in India. In the US, 25/56 who signed the Declaration of Independence, and 32/55 who framed and 22/39 who signed the US Constitution were lawyers – like John Adams.

Prior to the American Revolution, Adams represented British soldiers who fired on, and killed, five American colonists in the Boston Massacre of March 1770. The soldiers needed representation, but several lawyers refused. The captain asked for Adams. Even though he was a revolutionary already looking to stand for public office, he agreed (and Josiah Quincy II, another Boston lawyer, joined him). Adams got six out of eight acquitted; two were found guilty not of murder but of manslaughter. The trial 'cemented Adams's reputation as the archetypal lawyer-as-hero, a man willing to be hated in order to give individuals the chance to have their cause fairly heard' (Peterson 2018).

Adams wrote in his diary about his defence of the soldiers: 'It was … one of the most gallant, generous, manly and disinterested Actions of my whole Life, and one of the best Pieces of Service I ever rendered my Country' (Adams and Butterfield 1962: 79). Admittedly this was written before Adams became the first American Vice-President and the second President. He also became Chief Justice of the Massachusetts Supreme Court and was a signatory to the Declaration of Independence. But how many non-lawyers would think this would be rendering the best service to their country? Many probably believe lawyers are nothing more than 'hired guns'.

II. Hired Guns?

The best-known American advocate of a hired gun – client-first (and last) – approach was Monroe Freedman. So controversial were Freedman's views about supporting clients committing perjury that Judge Warren Burger – later Supreme Court Chief Justice – and two other federal judges sought to have him disbarred (Freedman 2008). But Freedman was probably right to claim: 'Client-centered adversarial lawyering [is] the traditional American approach to law practice' (Freedman and Smith 2010: 355). Abel (1989: 247) agrees: 'Lawyers are hired guns: they know they are, their clients demand that they be, and the public sees them that way.' Hodes (1996: 1077) regarded 'the label of "hired gun" as a badge of honor rather than an invitation to a fistfight, at least in the context of a seriously contested criminal trial'.

The most often-quoted 'defence' of this 'duty to client' position is the early nineteenth-century speech by Lord Henry Brougham, Lord Chancellor and barrister. He defended Queen Caroline, the estranged wife of King George IV, in their divorce. She returned to the UK in 1820 to claim her share of the Crown after George ascended the throne. He accused her of adultery, but, when heir to the throne, he'd contracted a secret marriage with Mrs Fitzherbert, a Roman Catholic. Being married to a Catholic meant the King would have to give up the Crown, 'perhaps with his head still attached to it' (Hodes 1996: 1106). This would also mean Caroline hadn't committed adultery, nor could she be 'divorced', since there wasn't a lawful marriage in the first place: the King was a bigamist.

The case was extremely controversial; George was unpopular. If Caroline was found to have committed adultery, divorce would follow, and she would lose her claim. Many supported her; there were demonstrations and army mutinies. The dispute even threatened the monarchy itself. It was in this context that Brougham explained his role:

> An advocate, in the discharge of his duty, knows but one person in all the world, and that person is his client. To save that client by all means and expedients, and at all hazards and costs to other persons, and, amongst them, to himself, is his first and only duty; and in performing this duty he must not regard the alarm, the torments, the destruction which he may bring upon others. Separating the duty of a patriot from that of an advocate, he must go on reckless of the consequences, though it should be his unhappy fate to involve his country in confusion. (Nightingale 1821)

Brougham intended this statement to be regarded not as an opinion, but as a 'menace' addressed mainly to the King (quoted in Curtis 1951: 4 and Forsyth 1875: 380). In essence, Brougham was threatening to expose his secret marriage to a Catholic widow – and make the disorder worse – if the King proceeded with the adultery claim. This was the 'fearless discharge' of his 'paramount duty' as a defence advocate (Brougham 1871: 309 note *). If he carried out the threat, there could be civil war. The charges against Caroline were dropped.

Brougham's statement 'constituted the ultimate in zealous advocacy' (Freedman 2011: 406). It was actually 'a nation-shaking act of blackmail' (Luban 1988: 55), and later, Brougham substituted 'highest and most unquestioned of his duties' for 'first and only duty' (Brougham 1871: 308–09). But it appears 'many [American] lawyers have taken it as the ultimate expression of the ideal of zealous advocacy' (Luban 2006: 4). Indeed, there has developed an 'uncontrolled expansion of libertarian ideology into lawyers' common consciousness' that 'privatizes the lawyer's role' where

> lawyers have come to feel genuinely affronted and indignant when any authority tries to articulate a public obligation of lawyers that may end up putting them at odds with clients. Lawyers claim to be 'private agents for private parties' … our loyalties to clients must be absolute and undivided. (Gordon 1988: 320)

It's an 'image of the adversarial advocate who places [the] client's cause above every other consideration' (Boon and Levin 1999: 107), and it has a long American history. Berle (1933: 342) wrote almost 100 years ago that the historic view was that a lawyer was an officer of the court and therefore an integral part of the scheme of justice. But the conception of the lawyer now obtaining is that he is the paid servant of his client, justified in using any technical lever that the law supplies in order to forward the latter's interest.

Michael Katz, 'who operate[d] an eviction mill for Los Angeles landlords … boasted "I'm a hired gun, bottom line. Somebody pays me money to go out there and fight their battle with this tenant. I like the fight"' (Abel 1995a: 15).

But it's not just an American image. Brougham's statement 'continues to be the dominant standard of lawyerly excellence among lawyers in both Canada and the United States' (Freedman 2011). In EW, it's been claimed lawyers are 'hired guns' (Nicolson and Webb 1999: 165) and 'adversarialism' 'casts a long shadow over the legal system' (ibid: 55). Lawyers instructed by the Post Office 'boasted of how one individual was a "steamroller that crushes anything that gets in his way"' (Richard Moorhead, quoted in Hyde 2024). Another KC was said to be able to 'turn a pile of refuse into something that looks great' (ibid).

No wonder 'cadres of lawyers', using 'their learned skills' in the context of lawfare (Comaroff 2023), have been accused of 'chasing the money', pursuing cases for their 'own financial reasons', being 'ambulance-chasing scoundrels', 'leeches', 'bloodsuckers', 'bad and egregious', as well as manipulating 'victims' grief' and making 'vexatious claims' (Schulenburg 2021). In 2019, Stephen Pound MP claimed lawyers came up with 'trumped-up cases to embarrass, and in many cases threaten and terrify, people who had served with distinction and honour. I have no time for these leeches, those bloodsuckers, those ambulance-chasing scumbags' (HC Debs, vol 660, col 245). UK law firms named by Bob Seely MP as 'acting as a "fifth column" for criminals include Carter-Ruck, Schillings, Harbottle & Lewis and Mishcon de Reya', though they 'deny breaking the rules'. We're looking at 'legalised intimidation … effectively legal gangsterism' (*The Times*, 2023b).

Robin Tolson KC sums it up. Lawyers, he says, 'are not do-gooders'. He continues: 'The right concept of a lawyer is as his client's champion. For the barrister … dedicates himself to the client's cause. I make no apology for putting the point shortly: a lawyer is a hired gun and not a healer' (Symposium 2008: 55, 56).

III. Conclusions

If lawyers are necessary, both for clients and for the justice system, should they be 'hired guns' or 'heroes'? More importantly, should you care? Michael Tigar, one of the 100 'great lawyers in American history' (Vile 2001), said the following about Lynne Stewart representing a convicted terrorist client, Sheik Omar Abdel Rahman: 'If a lawyer is sworn to represent somebody who is despised, neglected, hated, it is a mark of pride and a badge of honor to pay attention to that client's needs' (quoted in Preston 2005). Unsurprisingly, 'There will never be a Nobel prize for defense attorneys who succeed in freeing the guilty' (Dershowitz 1982: 417). But would the image – and popularity – of lawyers improve if their role and their 'tragic choices' were better understood (Haskell 1998), like the infamous McDonald's coffee case?

A. 'Spill Hot Coffee and Win Millions'

This case is folklore's prime example of how to win big at 'litigation lotto'. Jurors were sceptical and thought the claim ridiculous: a coffee spill, her fault, why are we here? So how come they awarded her $2.9 million and some wanted to give her $9.6 million?

Answer: the victim wasn't a 'money-grabbing opportunist', nor did a greedy lawyer approach her. Stella Liebeck, a 79-year old retired schoolteacher, had never filed a lawsuit before and didn't want to now. She wasn't driving, nor was the car moving when she spilled the coffee. Nearly four minutes after getting the coffee, with the car parked, she placed the cup between her legs to add cream and sugar. When she tried to get the lid off the Styrofoam cup, it tipped, spilling all the coffee onto her lap, drenching her sweatpants. Within seconds, Liebeck had third-degree burns (destroying the first three layers of skin and fatty tissue) on about 6 per cent of her body and other burns over 16 per cent. She was in hospital for over a week getting several skin grafts. She was partially disabled and permanently disfigured. After losing 20 lbs she weighed just 80 lbs.

Two weeks after the incident, she wrote to McDonald's. She admitted the spilling, didn't intend to sue or demand unreasonable compensation, but said it was unreasonable that the coffee was so hot that it would cause such severe damage when there'd been no warning. She asked McDonald's to check their coffee-making processes to see if they were faulty, to re-evaluate the temperature standards and to cover the less than $20,000 medical costs not covered by Medicare.

McDonald's offered $800 but refused to change their policy. After six months, she went to a lawyer who asked for $90,000. Just before trial, the judge ordered mediation and the mediator recommended $225,000. At the trial, the jury heard the coffee was served at extremely high temperatures, higher than other fast food restaurants and McDonald's knew it was a hazard with a risk of serious harm. How did they know? They'd already had 700 complaints.

The jury said it was Liebeck's fault she spilled the cup, but it was McDonald's responsibility that the coffee was so hazardous because of the extreme heat. The failure of McDonald's to respond to something they knew about meant they should be punished to make them change and to protect future coffee drinkers. Liebeck's lawyer asked for two days' coffee revenues which, at $1.35 million per day, came to $2.7 million. The $9.6 million figure was one week's coffee revenues. Liebeck was awarded $2.7 million in punitive damages plus $200,000 in compensation.

The case entered legal history, but the true story is very different from the myth. In the end, no one knows how much Liebeck actually won. The punitive damages were reduced to $480,000 and the parties agreed a confidential settlement.

B. The Heart of the Matter

Some lawyers are rightly unpopular, but surely Liebeck's shouldn't be criticised. Because now we're getting to the heart of the matter. Maybe the fundamental reason why lawyers will never be popular is not only because of what they do, but, more importantly, what they're supposed to do. But what exactly is that? What are – or should be – their essential qualities (Haskins 2013)?

This book takes us 'inside lawyers' ethics' (Parker and Evans 2018; Holmes and Bartlett 2023), to get a better understanding of lawyers' professional responsibilities. Lawyers '[c]onsciously or unconsciously … are part of a complex legal culture' (Bellow and Moulton 1981: 36). They work within a 'culture of deception, manipulation and power' (Barnhizer 2015). Understanding that 'culture' has implications not only for lawyers and clients, but also for the operation of law and the administration of justice in society. Lawyers can employ the tricks of the trade as clients' *bodyguards of lies*. The next chapter explains this metaphor and how it will be used, putting lawyers on trial for *you* to judge: hired guns or heroes?

2

Bodyguards of Lies

'All warfare is based on deception.'
— Sun Tzu (c 400–320 BCE) (1910)

I. 'The Truth, the Whole Truth, and Nothing But the Truth'

So says a person in court promising their evidence will be true. The promise is 'designed to impress that duty on the witness's conscience' (FRE 2023: 603). But what if they want to hide truth, whatever it is, whether in or out of court, or create a version of reality that is far from real? And if they must reveal, or admit to anything, how can it be *not* the truth; not even a bit of the truth; in fact, everything but the truth? Who can help them and, more importantly, get away with it? A hired gun? Or a hero, like in wartime?

II. Operation Mincemeat

A supreme example of wartime deception was Operation Mincemeat (Macintyre 2010). The plan involved 'plot and counterplot, stealth and treachery, lies and deceits' (Cave Brown 1975). In 1943, the body of a supposed British Royal Marine officer, Captain William Martin – apparently drowned after a fictitious plane crash but actually released from a submarine – floated ashore on the Spanish coast. In fact, the corpse was 34-year-old homeless drifter Glyndwr Michael, who'd ingested rat poison. The body carried many items designed to deceive the Nazis – a threatening letter from a bank, nightclub bills, love letters and an engagement ring receipt, and London theatre ticket stubs – even underwear from a deceased Oxford history professor: 'No upper-class corpse would be convincing without appropriate underwear' (Macintyre 2010: 357; see also Letter to *The Times* 2010).

The purpose, however, wasn't only to convince the Nazis the body was Captain Martin (whose death on active duty was announced in *The Times* newspaper),[1] but

---

[1] Macintyre (2010: 269–70) describes *The Times* newspaper as 'the place all important people wanted to be seen dead in. And it is not possible to be deader than in the death columns of Britain's most venerable newspaper'. However, it was also 'the first time in the newspaper's history that a person was formally announced dead without having been alive' (ibid: 270).

to *conceal a truth*: the location of an invasion. Sealed letters, including one from the Vice Chief of the Imperial General Staff Sir Archie Nye addressed to General Alexander in North Africa, stated the Allies intended to invade Greece and Sardinia. In fact, they intended to invade Sicily. Alan Hillgarth, whose pre-war 'adventure stories' included *The Princess and the Perjurer*, played a prominent role in Operation Mincemeat (Hart-Davis 2012). He was simultaneously trying to retrieve the documents *before* the Nazis saw them, while making sure they *did* see them, all without arousing suspicion.

The deception worked; Nazi military intelligence fell for it and Hitler was convinced. He sent reinforcements away from Sicily to the Balkans and put General Rommel in command. There were only two divisions in Sicily when a huge Allied invasion was launched. A total of 160,000 troops took Sicily in July 1943 in 38 days, with a loss of 7,000. This compared favourably with the estimate: a 90-day campaign with much higher losses. After Sicily, the Allies 'rolled up Italy' (Llewellyn 2014: 734), Mussolini resigned, and Hitler sent his panzer units from the Eastern Front to Italy.

How powerful was the deception? Churchill commented: 'Everyone but a bloody fool would *know* it was Sicily' (Macintyre 2010: 34; Montagu 1978: 143). Whether or not the deception did 'change the course of World War II' (Boyd 2010), historians concluded that it had a 'profound impact' (Macintyre 2010: 34). Ian Fleming, the creator of James Bond who was also involved in Operation Mincemeat, referred to Hillgarth as a 'good war-winner' (ibid: 148). Through a 'feat of imagination', the framers of Operation Mincemeat had

> dreamed up the most unlikely concatenation of events, rendered them believable, and sent them off to war, changing reality through lateral thinking, and proving that it is possible to win a battle fought in the mind, from behind a desk, and from beyond the grave. (ibid: 307)

Churchill was told the Nazis took the bait: 'Mincemeat swallowed rod, line and sinker' (ibid: 308).

In November 1943, the Allied leaders – Churchill, Roosevelt and Stalin – met in Tehran. They approved another deception plan: the 'D-Day' landings in Normandy (Stafford 1999). It was named 'Operation Bodyguard' because of Churchill's remark to Stalin: 'In wartime, truth is so precious it should always be protected by a bodyguard of lies' (Macintyre 2010: 4).

III. 'Corkscrew' Minds

In Operation Mincemeat, the 'bodyguard of lies' included 'both a false real plan, and a false cover plan – which would actually be the real plan' (Macintyre 2010: 58). There was the 'bare-faced' lie: the body was not Captain Martin but Glyndwr Michael; misleading the enemy: supporting the lie by the unexplained – and fictitious – plane crash, the paperwork placed on the body, and the body dressed up as an upper-class Briton; and deception: where the invasion would take place. The success of Operations Mincemeat and Bodyguard was the result of unconventional thinking by people who, Churchill said, had 'corkscrew minds' (Macintyre 2010: Chapter 2). Charles Cholmondeley devised the plan and then teamed up with barrister Ewen Montagu KC to develop it.

Many lawyers have 'corkscrew minds' too and clients may want these skills to protect them. After all, their truth is 'precious, not something they part with often, or easily' (Feige 2001). Wartime metaphors work in adversary legal systems because:

> the adversarial process is likely to encourage an adversarial *culture* and to degenerate into an environment in which the litigation process is too often seen as a *battlefield* where no rules apply ... This situation arises precisely because the conduct, pace and extent of litigation are left almost completely to the parties. (Lord Chancellor's Department 1995, emphasis added)

As a result, 'the elusive and essentially fatuous concept of "the whole truth" is always lost in the fog of adversarial combat' (Hodes 2002: 58). One of the 'most contentious parts of civil litigation' – the handing over of documents ('discovery' (US) or 'disclosure' (EW)) is 'like a game of Battleship' (Luban 2000: 106). A criminal defence lawyer is a 'warrior for justice' (Klein 2012), and one 'warrior' said a trial is 'less a search for truth than a battle to be won' (Wishman 1981: 223). 'Warrior' language was used by New York's Jeffrey Lichtman, who represented the Mexican drugs lord 'El Chapo'. His approach in court was as follows: 'We fought like complete savages and left it all on the battlefield ... This was balls to the wall, and that's how we fight cases' (Pullman 2019). Similarly, the cases of Roy Black, a member of the Trial Lawyer Hall of Fame (celebrating the best American trial lawyers), his cases 'are World War III to me. I don't take prisoners when I go to trial' (Boyd 1998). So, it comes as little surprise that, in most criminal trials, 'discovery of truth is the *last* thing a defense lawyer desires' (van Kessel 1992: 436).

IV. A Hippocratic Oath for Lawyers?

But lawyers owe duties not only to clients; they're 'officers of the court', and in EW, the duty to the court and the administration of justice is 'overriding' (BSB 2024: CD 1, 22). Adversary justice systems emphasise just how precious truth is, both in and out of court. The US Supreme Court regards 'the very nature of a trial as a search for truth' (*Nix*: 166) and 'arriving at the truth is a fundamental goal of our legal system' (*Oregon*: 722). It says: 'A fundamental premise of our criminal justice system is that the jury is the lie detector' (*US v Scheffer*: 313). Some courts believe 'the adversary system ordinarily can be trusted to separate the liars from the truthful' (*US v Rhynes*: 322).

Ethical and legal rules also seek to regulate and constrain lawyers' conduct. For hundreds of years, English lawyers swore an oath, upon admission to the bar, to 'do no falsehood, nor consent to any to be done to the court' (Goodman 1967: 406; see also Andrews 2009; 4; Symposium 2008). Was this pledge of truth a kind of 'Hippocratic Oath' for lawyers (Jessup 1922)? Is the 'bedrock' cab rank obligation – barristers must generally take a case offered – their 'equivalent of the doctors' oath (Vineall 2023a)? Simpson says no: 'lawyers possess no equivalent to the Hippocratic Oath' (1988: 29). Most US states require lawyers to swear an oath to support the Constitution, and some require them to defend it (Levin 2022: 174-75). But Economides (2007) wonders if lawyers now possess what he calls a 'Hippocritical Oath'. Gerson (1980: viii) notes that 'at the core of the public's ambivalence about the legal profession is the suspicion that, as often as not, the lawyer is attempting to obfuscate the truth'. So, what might the relationship between lawyers, truth and justice look like?

V. Lawyers, Truth and Justice

The judge and former attorney Marvin E. Frankel (1975: 1032) says 'the adversary system rates truth too low among the values that institutions of justice are meant to serve'. He added, 'we know that many of the rules and devices of adversary litigation as we conduct it are not geared for, but are often aptly suited to defeat, the development of the truth' (ibid: 1036). Indeed, 'it is the rare case in which either side yearns to have the witnesses, or anyone, give *the whole truth*' (ibid: 1038). No wonder lawyers 'are engaged very often in helping to obstruct and divert the search for truth' (Frankel 1980: 75). The adversary system 'seems to license lawyers to trample on the truth, and legal rights, and morality' (Luban 1988: 89). An estate planning attorney told us: 'The system is designed in an adversarial fashion – in a litigation setting, the person on the other side is not your friend – that person is also concealing the truth.' He added that 'when you sign up, so to speak, to be a lawyer, you take on the responsibility of representing your client in a zealous manner. Part of this is concealing the truth – not lying – but keeping parts of the truth out'.

Luban (1988: 13) went further, 'the lawyer's art is to manipulate arguments about law and fact ... to bend, fold, and spindle, if not mutilate, the facts and the law'. In other words, 'lawyers learn that they are not responsible for truth in any absolute sense, but rather are responsible for their clients' interests' (Perrin 2007: 1720). In criminal defence, this means the lawyer's main function is to control 'what the court will learn about what the client knows' (Hazard Jr 1997: 1048). As Shargel wrote (2007: 1267), 'a trial may be a search for the truth but I – as a defense attorney – am not part of the search party'. Even US Supreme Court Justice Byron White acknowledged: 'defense counsel has no ... obligation to ascertain or present the truth'. He went on: '[as] part of the duty imposed on the most honorable defense counsel, we countenance or require conduct which in many instances has little, if any, relation to the search for truth' (*US v Wade*: 258). Dershowitz (1996: 166) agreed:

> A criminal trial is anything but a pure search for truth. When defense attorneys represent guilty clients – as most do, most of the time – their responsibility is to try, by all fair and ethical means, to *prevent the truth* about their client's guilt from emerging.

He believed: 'It is fair to say the American justice system is built on a foundation of *not* telling the whole truth' (Dershowitz 1982: xix). George Bernard Shaw was more cynical. The search for truth, he said, was based on '[t]he theory ... that if you set two liars to exposing each other, eventually the truth will come out' (quoted in Boon 2014: 682, referring to Saks 1987). In any case, 'whose "truth" are we searching for, whose "truth" has been revealed and whose "truth" do we accept? Is it the lawyer's truth? The plaintiff's truth? The defendant's truth? The judge's truth? The public's truth? The media's truth?' (Facher 1999: xvii). In the OJ Simpson trial, the phrase 'the search for truth' was invoked by both sides more than 70 times (Dershowitz 1996: 34). In short: 'The administration of justice is no more designed to elicit the truth than the scientific approach is designed to extract justice from an atom' (Curtis 1951: 12).

So, what about lawyers? Frankel (1975: 1035) acknowledged that: 'The advocate's prime loyalty is to his client, not to truth as such'. In other words: 'In a competition between candor and zealous advocacy, advocacy usually wins hands down' (Mason III 1997). Luban (1988: xvii) claims that lawyers 'are professionally concerned with the interests of their clients, not the interests of justice'. One general practitioner told us: 'all attorneys are exaggerating facts, concealing facts and evidence in order to paint their clients in the best possible light'. A small-town estate attorney said that 'in most situations, lawyers conceal the truth because they are arguing for their client's best interests, and at times, concealing the truth falls into the category of zealous advocacy'. In short, 'victory, not veracity, is the ultimate goal' (Hazard Jr 2000: 75), just like in war. But there *is* a better wartime image: lawyers 'crusading for truth in an unjust world, and suddenly there is nobility in it' (Siegel 2006). Many would agree that '[j]ustice cannot exist anywhere without lawyers to champion it and laws to enforce it' (Ervin Jr 1980:11).

But what's the reality? US lawyer Alan Dershowitz's son is a professional magician. He said they both do the same thing: 'sleight of hand – making things appear to be what they are not' (Nebo-lit nd). Jeremy Bentham, referring to a person who helped a criminal escape commits a crime, noted that 'what the non-advocate is hanged for, the advocate is paid for, and admired' (Pannick 2015). Benthan thought defence of the guilty made the lawyer an accessory after the fact (Rogers 1899: 260). John Stuart Mill (quoted in Nicolson 2005: 601, fn 2) said the lawyer 'hires himself out to do injustice or frustrate justice with his tongue'. So, instead of crusading *for* truth and championing justice, the 'corkscrew minds' of lawyers crusade to *protect* the truth and 'the craft of lawyering inevitably overwhelms the justice of it' (Siegel 2006: 31). As a result:

> gradually, imperceptibly, we [lawyers] transfer our admiration to the supreme tacticians: the litigators and trial mavens [experts or connoisseurs] whose mastery of the tricks of our trade produce stupendous victories, for which they are celebrated among lawyers far and wide. (ibid)

Michael Beloff KC (2017) recalls how:

> As a baby junior I learnt the tricks of the trade the hard way in magistrates' and county courts, in front of tough eggs at the Newington causeway sessions, or doing undefended divorces of which I managed to lose one by mispronouncing the petitioner's name.

After a while, it seems, '[e]very lawyer knows tricks of the trade' (Luban 1983a: 75).

VI. Tricks of the Trade

Lawyers develop tricks for many reasons. Markovits' claim that 'lawyers are *professionally obligated* to lie and cheat' (2008: 39) has been strongly contested, but Markovits was referring to 'various activities that are common in law practice and that most practicing lawyers consider perfectly ethical' (Freedman and Smith 2010: 930). Lawyers 'are licensed, and at times are obligated, to speak insincerely' (Solan 2012: 524) and, it appears, have always done so. Aristotle said that the advocate 'must render the audience well-disposed to yourself, and ill-disposed to your opponent; you must magnify and depreciate' (Barnhizer 2015: 2, referring to Aristotle 1932: 19). Plato observed that the advocate's role is inherently deceptive rather than truth-directed; the advocate 'enchants the minds' of the courts of law: '[H]e who would be a skillful rhetorician has no need of truth – for that in the courts of law literally care nothing about truth, but only about conviction' (Barnhizer 2015: 2, referring to Edman 1928: 306).

Lawyers rationalise that developing tricks is their role. They take pride in creativity and ingenuity. For many lawyers, the thrill – or the sport – of litigation includes making arguments they don't personally believe. As the barrister and academic Sir Rupert Cross (1973) said: 'I have seldom felt more pleased with myself than when I persuaded three out of five law lords to come to a conclusion I was convinced was wrong'. The culture of the adversary system, along with legal practice, support and reinforce lawyers' confidence in what they do. In short, '[e]very lawyer knows tricks of the trade that can be used to do opponents out of their legal deserts' (Luban 1988: 75), and it would be viewed as falling short if they didn't use them. Clients benefit – often to protect an inconvenient truth.

VII. An Inconvenient Truth

Protecting a client's inconvenient truth might also be a kind of nobility and has a long history. The English Court of Exchequer summed it up in 1743:

> (i) a 'gentleman of character' does not disclose his client's secrets; (ii) an attorney identifies with his client and it would be 'contrary to the rules of natural justice and equity' for an individual to betray himself; and (iii) attorneys are necessary for the conduct of business, and business would be destroyed if attorneys were to disclose their communications with their clients. (*Annesley*, quoted in Boon 2023: 84–85)

No wonder one thing that 'makes lawyers special' is the 'extraordinary' duty of confidentiality: 'a code of silence that seals their lips in a way that other employees' lips are not sealed' (Luban 1988: 180). Keeping client confidentiality is a 'fundamental ethical duty imposed on the legal profession' (Boon and Levin 2008: 219). The English

> Courts have stated that the duty of confidentiality is *unqualified*, in that is a duty to keep the information confidential, not merely to take all reasonable steps to do so. It is not limited to the *duty not to communicate the information to a third party*. It is a *wider duty* not to misuse it, i.e. … to make any use of it or to cause any use to be made of it by others otherwise than for the client's benefit. (SRA 2019c, emphasis added, referring to *Prince Jeffrey*)

Lawyers in the common law world share this duty: to protect clients' secrets, including embarrassing or otherwise detrimental information which, if disclosed, would be to their clients' disadvantage (DR 4-101(A)). Hodes (2010) explains: 'a lawyer representing a client should not be seeking the truth, but rather obscuring it, if the truth may be inconvenient to the client's cause'. So, there may be a difference between truth as commonly understood and what might be called legal truth. One litigation associate we interviewed said: 'As a lawyer you have to figure out what facts are important to your client's case and construct your legal truth.'

VIII. Why Tricks Matter

This book is about strategies lawyers can employ in the day-to-day representation of clients. The word 'tricks' may imply that 'justice' is being undermined. In fact, many 'tricks may promote justice. What's at stake though cannot be exaggerated because: 'One of the most brutal clashes between competing values is that between "truth" and "justice", with implications for the very nature of the legal system itself' (Hodes 2002: 57). In adversary systems, lawyers must resolve these clashes, and how they do so has profound implications: 'the ethical problems of lawyers are social and political problems for the rest of us' (Luban 1988: xviii). As Karl Llewellyn (1952: 23) put it: 'technique without ideals is a menace; ideals without techniques are a mess'. Chief Justice Warren Burger (1971: 215) agreed: 'Lawyers who know how to think but have not learned how to behave are a menace and a liability … to the administration of justice'. Even an American law student saw the potential problem if 'Law schools create people who are smart without a purpose' (Sullivan et al 2007: 142).

Many strategies share this feature: 'a great deal of what goes on between lawyers and clients is shielded by the attorney-client privilege and the ethical duty of confidentiality, and never sees the light of day' (Luban 2006: 1). No wonder the choice of tactics relies on the exercise of professional judgment. When opinions differ on what is 'ethical', it can be hard to tell if a lawyer has misbehaved. But maybe *you* can answer this: how far *should* an ethical lawyer go to assist a client who wants – or needs – to protect their truth?

3

Virtuous Lying?

> Your honour, I swore to tell the truth, the whole truth and nothing but the truth,
> but every time I try, that barrister over there complains.
>
> — Apocryphal quote in Goldsmith P 2007

Lawyers shouldn't lie, should they? But if lying can be justified, maybe they should.

I. Defining 'Lying'

The best analysis of 'lying' was by psychologist and ethicist Sissela Bok. Her books –
Lying (1979), Chapter 1 of which asks 'Is the "Whole Truth" Attainable?', and *Secrets*
(1983) – show lying is complex, nuanced and contextual. A lie is 'any intentionally
deceptive message which is stated' (Bok 1979: 13). Fallis asks 'What is Lying?' and
defines 'deceptive lying': an 'intent to deceive' condition (2009: 56). Ekman states: 'There
are two primary ways to lie: to conceal and to falsify' (1985: 28). Bok also referred to
lying as 'falsification' and keeping secrets as 'concealment'. Putting these definitions
together – 'intentionally deceptive message', 'intent to deceive', but, especially, 'conceal
and falsify' – we see why lawyers can be 'bodyguards of lies'. Lawyers conceal by keeping
clients' secrets and falsify (broadly defined) by helping them create a reality that's often
far from real.

II. Defining 'Truth'

'Truth' is also 'surprisingly difficult to define' (Pardi 2019). A simple definition is 'a
statement about the way the world actually is' (ibid) – a 'realist' approach. However,
there's another approach: all truth is relative and not absolute. Hence a more widely held
definition of truth – the 'correspondence theory of truth':

> there are a set of 'truth-bearing' representations (or propositions) about the world that align
> to or *correspond* with reality or states of affairs in the world. … When a proposition aligns to
> the world, the proposition is said to be true. Truth, on this view, is that correspondence rela-
> tion. (ibid, emphasis in original)

III. Clients' 'Truths'

Using a variation of correspondence theory, clients' 'truths' are the representation or proposition that corresponds or aligns with clients' 'reality or states of affairs'. Clients' propositions about their reality are 'said [by lawyers] to be true'. In criminal defence, for example, the truth is 'what the client says happened and what he asserts the truth to be ... the advocate is bound to advance the defendant's case on the basis that what his client tells him is the truth' (Lord Judge, *R v Farooqi*: 107–08). So, a client's 'truth' may be the 'realist's truth', but may also be a lie, a myth or even a conspiracy theory. It may change over the course of representation, and be difficult to identify and pin down. Truth in this sense is what clients perceive it to be and what lawyers believes clients' perceptions to be. There's no absolute truth, only clients' truths. As Sir Ivor Judge put it (*R v Ulcay*: 27):

> the client's instructions encompass whatever the client ... asserts to be the truth about the facts ... Those instructions represent the client's case, and that is the case which the advocate should advance.

IV. Truth Decay

Some argue that when a client's 'truth' is so far removed from reality, lawyers shouldn't protect it. On the other hand:

> The indeterminacy of language, and even of 'truth', means the advocate is striving for a decision-maker to adhere to the advocate's 'version' of reality constructed through the discourse she is creating. ... the advocate has a wonderful breadth of opportunity in which to construct reality through discourse. (Murray and DeSanctis 2013: Chapter 2)

In this sense, there's no 'objective truth' at all, which is why lawyers such as Rudy Giuliani, one of former President Trump's lawyers, could proclaim 'truth isn't truth' and 'nowadays' facts are 'in the eye of the beholder' (Morin and Cohen 2018). This led to references to George Orwell's *1984* (Orwell, 1949) and 'doublethink', where 'war is peace', 'freedom is slavery' and 'ignorance is strength'. In January 2017, Trump's senior adviser, Kellyanne Conway, described White House Press Secretary Sean Spicer's claim that Trump's inauguration crowd was the 'largest ever' as 'alternative facts'. Similarly, in reporting the size of his Trump Tower apartment as 30,000 square feet when, objectively, it was 11,000, Trump's lawyer argued 'square footage can be subjective' (Ferran 2022).

This has been called 'truth decay' (Kavanagh and Rich 2018). In a 2023 cartoon in *The Times*, Prince Harry was in a witness box, his hand on his autobiography *Spare*, swearing to tell 'my truth, my whole truth and nothing but my truth ... so help you God' (*The Times* 2023d). In *Spare*, Harry claimed: 'There's just as much truth in what I remember and how I remember it as there is in so-called objective facts.' But is there? In which section of the bookshop should *Spare* be placed: non-fiction or fiction? More seriously, 'How is a democracy to survive if people are unable to discern truth from untruth?' and 'More disturbing still, what if a class of experts and professionals lead the way?' (Green and Roiphe 2021: 38).

V. Detecting Lies

In the Middle Ages, torturers poured boiling water over 'suspects' believing virtuous truth-tellers would hold out longer than sinful liars. Women accused of witchcraft in the sixteenth and seventeenth centuries suffered the ordeal of being submerged in water, despite a fundamental flaw: the innocent drowned while the guilty (witches) floated, so they could be executed! Are polygraphs an improvement? America deploys lie detection as a systematic tool of government. Applicants for federal government posts and many of those employed take tests. Former CIA director Richard Helms claimed 'lie detection worked best on Americans because foreigners were more natural liars and more able to fool the machine' (Macintyre 2019). But it was an American CIA Officer, Aldrich Ames, who passed two polygraph tests in 1986 and 1991 – and continued spying for the KGB. In 1988, the US Supreme Court said the results of lie detector tests were 'little better than could be obtained by the toss of a coin' (ibid). Currently, a Deception and Analysis and Reasoning Engine is gathering data from courtroom trial videos to create a system that can spot perjury through body language.

VI. Lying: Good or Bad?

Philosophically, there are two approaches to lying: absolutist and contextual. Absolutists – 'do not lie under any circumstances' – say there are no exceptions. This is a Kantian view justified by the 'slippery slope': one 'good' lie can justify another and another (Kant 1959 [1785]). Kant regarded lying as 'the greatest violation of a human being's duty to himself regarded merely as a moral being' (quoted in Williams 2002: 102). Contextualists – 'it all depends' – hold that a simple universal rule is impractical. This is a Confucian view; morality depends on context (Puett and Gross-Loh 2016).

Absolutists would prohibit lying to Nazis who asked: 'are there any Jews in your house?' Kant's example (1799) was the 'murderer at the door'. The lie outweighs any benefit from lying; the end doesn't justify the means. Contextualists would weigh up the pros and cons of lying – on balance, lying might be justified. The absolutist view is easy to comply with, but unrealistic – there can be 'virtuous lying' such as Operation Mincemeat. The contextual view is practical, but requires the exercise of judgement – and who decides what is the 'right' decision? If lying is contextual and complex, then morality and ethics are too.

A. The Judgement of Solomon

King Solomon's custody dispute involved two mothers and two babies. One baby was dead, and both mothers claimed the live one. To protect the truth, Solomon was about to cut the live baby in half when one mother stopped him and said the baby should be given to the other mother. Solomon declared her to be the true mother. But was he bluffing about killing the baby? If so, the lie's success depended on his skills as a liar: his words, authority and poker face. Solomon was a 'bodyguard of lies' protecting the truth – and is applauded – but virtuous lying is not without risks.

B. Placebos

Doctors need poker faces when they lie too. Half of American and 97% of UK doctors routinely prescribe placebos (Harris 2008; Howick 2013). They include headache pills, vitamins, and even sedatives and antibiotics. In 'placebo surgery' the surgical procedure imitates the active intervention (Wartolowska et al 2014). A scope is inserted under a general anaesthetic, nothing is done, but the patient doesn't know that. Medical ethicists are troubled – how can the patient give 'informed consent' and what if the experiment goes wrong?

People who suffered a heart attack were routinely given adrenaline (epinephrine) to help resuscitate them. In 2014, the University of Oxford Ethics Committee approved giving a placebo – a saltwater dummy drug – to see if adrenaline was effective (*The Times*, 13 August 2014). The results showed the 30-day survival rate was 'significantly higher' with the adrenaline than the placebo (Perkins et al 2018). The Committee had made a 'tragic choice', but believed the falsification and concealment was justified. So, if doctors can engage in virtuous lying' (Simon 1999), why shouldn't lawyers?

C. Daniel Gatti

MR 8.4(c) says they shouldn't: it's professional misconduct for a lawyer to engage in conduct involving dishonesty, fraud, deceit or misrepresentation. But how about deception to uncover discrimination or other unlawful conduct – what Hodes (2002) called 'lying with an explanation'? Contextualists might argue MR 8.4(c) is intended to apply 'only to conduct of so grave a character as to call into question the lawyer's fitness to practice law' (Isbell and Salvi 1995; see also Temkin 2008).

Chiropractors suspected that an insurance company was using non-medical personnel to review medical records and then improperly denying benefits (*In Re Conduct*: 521). Gatti called personnel at the company posing as a chiropractor and doctor who saw patients, performed independent medical examinations and was looking to work for the company. When he sued the company, his deceit came to light and the company filed a disciplinary complaint under MR 8.4(c).

Gatti argued there should be an exception for misrepresentations made 'solely for purposes of discovering information' to allow lawyers to 'root out evil' (ibid: 529). The Oregon Supreme Court agreed 'there are circumstances in which misrepresentations, often in the form of false statements of fact by those who investigate violations of the law, are useful means for uncovering unlawful and unfair practices' (ibid: 532), but, preferring 'Faithful adherence to the wording' of the Rule, it issued Gatti with a public reprimand and called on rule makers to carve out any exception – which they did. Oregon Code DR 1-102(D) now states it shall *not* be professional misconduct for lawyers to supervise lawful covert activity in the investigation of violations of civil and criminal law or constitutional rights. Other states have adopted this contextual approach.

D. Operation Greylord

Rooting out evil was also the aim of Operation Greylord. Over a three-year period in the early 1980s in Cook County, Illinois, several lawyers and the FBI conducted an undercover investigation into corruption in the judiciary. To obtain evidence, Terrence Hake posed as a corrupt prosecutor and then as a bribe-paying criminal defence attorney (Hake 2015). One lawyer had a judge's chambers bugged, and other judges also helped by engaging in deceitful conduct. Lawyers lied to the judges, in open court, and even gave false testimony in the witness box under oath. Fake tort suits and drunk-driving cases were brought – good enough to be credible but weak enough to need a crooked judge. More serious felony charges were also involved and one lawyer was heard on tape bragging 'even a murder case can be fixed if the judge is given something to hang his hat on' (Possley 2014).

Did the end – exposing and prosecuting judicial corruption – justify the means – lying and perjury? The Court of Appeals thought so in upholding the conviction of one judge. In the end, 93 were indicted, including 17 judges (15 of whom were convicted), 48 lawyers, 10 deputy sheriffs, eight police officers, eight court officials and a state representative. Judge Reginald Holzer received the longest sentence – 18 years. He was prosecuted by Scott Turow, whose book *Personal Injuries* is based on Operation Greylord.

E. Mark Pautler

You might think lying to capture an axe murderer on the loose would be justified. You'd be right if police lied, but what about a lawyer?

In 1998, William Cody Neal raped and murdered three women (Jackson 2022). Mark Pautler, a Chief Deputy DA, witnessed 'the gruesome crime scene' (*In Re Pautler*) and was present when contact was made with Neal by a deputy sheriff. A three-and-a-half-hour mobile phone conversation followed. Neal made clear he wouldn't surrender without legal representation and asked the sheriff to contact his former attorney. Pautler telephoned, but the office number was no longer in service. The sheriff agreed with Neal to secure a PD. Instead of so doing, however, Pautler offered to impersonate a PD. The sheriff introduced Pautler to Neal as 'Mark Palmer', a PD. Neal sought three guarantees before he would surrender: isolation from other detainees, cigarettes, and 'his lawyer' present at the surrender. Neal then surrendered. Pautler had no further contact with Neal. A PD undertook Neal's defence, but 'had difficulty establishing a trusting relationship' after he told Neal no Mark Palmer existed within the PD's office. Later, Neal dismissed the PD and represented himself. He was convicted and received the death penalty.

Pautler, charged with violating MR 8.4(c), argued deception was justified under the circumstances. The Colorado Supreme Court disagreed: 'purposeful deception by an attorney ... is intolerable ... even a noble motive does not warrant departure from the Rules' (ibid: 1176). Pautler also argued an exception should be made in situations constituting a threat of 'imminent public harm'. Again, the Court disagreed: Pautler had 'several choices'. He could've called another PD or explored with Neal the possibility that no attorney would be called until after he surrendered. In short, 'we are adamant that when presented with choices, at least one of which conforms with the Rules, an attorney must not select an option that involves deceit or misrepresentation'. The Court added: 'Until a sufficiently compelling scenario presents itself and convinces us our interpretation of [MR 8.4(c)] is too rigid, we stand resolute against any suggestion that licensed attorneys in our state may deceive or lie or misrepresent, regardless of their reasons for doing so.'

In 1999, Pautler was a prosecutor in the Columbine school shooting incident, but his lying to Neal led, in 2002, to a three-month suspension, stayed for one year of probation, during which he had to retake the MultiState Professional Responsibility Exam.

4

The Ethical Conundrum

> The time is always right to do what is right.
>
> Martin Luther King (1964)

How lawyers behave isn't just about clients, but law, the legal system and the administration of justice. Lawyers represent clients, are officers of the legal system, and public
citizens having special responsibility for the quality of justice (MR Preamble: 1). As
Lord Hoffmann said: 'Lawyers conducting litigation owe a divided loyalty. They have a
duty to their clients, but they may not win by whatever means. They also owe a duty to
the court and the administration of justice' (*JS Hall*: 686E). Lawyers are bound to strive
to win a case but must do so without in any way seeking to evade the rules intended to
safeguard the administration of justice (*Ridehalgh*, Lord Bingham). Duties to the court
reflect the public interest in the administration of justice (*Medcalf*: 54, Lord Hobhouse).

US authorities acknowledge this divided loyalty:

> An attorney's duty to a client can never outweigh his or her responsibility to see that our
> system of justice functions smoothly. Too many attorneys have forgotten the exhortations
> of these century-old canons. Too many attorneys ... have allowed the objectives of the
> client to override their ancient duties as officers of the court. In short, they have sold out
> to the client. We must return to the original principle that, as officers of the court, attor-
> neys are servants of the law rather than servants of the highest bidder. We must rediscover
> the old values of our profession. The integrity of our system depends on it. (*Malautea*:
> 1546–47)

Lawyers' representation of clients is so important that it's strongly *supported* by both
law and ethics. But there are also constraints because, in the very nature of law practice, 'conflicting responsibilities are encountered' (MR Preamble [9]). Indeed: 'Virtually
all difficult ethical problems arise from conflict between a lawyer's responsibilities to
clients, to the legal system and to the lawyer's own interest in remaining an ethical
person while earning a satisfactory living'; lawyers must 'balance the interests of their
clients with their duties to the court, third parties and the public interest' (ibid). Does
their divided loyalty create just an ethical conundrum – what is the right thing to do – or
a 'bigamous relationship' as well?

I. Virtuous Lawyering

What lawyers do for clients is so essential to the 'effective and efficient running' of a legal system (BSB 2014) that they 'play a vital role in the preservation of society' (MR Preamble: 13):

> [O]ur society is based on a rule of law. Everyone needs to be able to seek expert advice on their legal rights and obligations and to have access to skilled representation in the event of a dispute or litigation.
>
> Our system of justice depends on those who provide these services acting fearlessly, independently, and competently, so as to further their clients' best interests, subject always to their duty to the court. (BSB 2014)

These are social values. When lawyers provide representation, they act in the public interest as well as clients' interests. But what if the interests of others outweigh those of clients? Why protect the relationship and prefer the client – despite potentially tragic consequences?

A. Protecting the Relationship

Protecting clients' secrets comes at a heavy price. Concealing information detracts from a trial's fairness by denying access to relevant documents or keeping even key facts out of court: 'Communications seeking professional legal advice … are absolutely and permanently privileged even though, in consequence, the communications will not be available in court proceedings in which they might be important evidence' (*R v Derby*: 74, Lord Nicholls). Indeed:

> So long as we have an adversary system a party is entitled not to produce documents which are properly protected by privilege if it is not to his advantage to produce them and even though their production might assist his adversary if he or his solicitor were aware of their contents or might lead the court to a different conclusion from that to which the court would come in ignorance of their existence, (*Causton*: 460).

It 'may thus impede the proper administration of justice in the individual case' (*Three Rivers*: 61, Baroness Hale). Privilege is an exception to the rule that all relevant evidence lawfully obtained is admissible in court unless its exclusion can be justified (Twining 2006: 203–04). Privilege and confidentiality impede the investigation and discovery of truth, and may harm third parties. There *needs* to be a strong justification.

i. Privilege

Privilege is a 'fundamental human right long established in the common law' (*R v Special Commissioner*, Lord Hoffmann). It is 'firmly established judge-made law dating from the sixteenth century abolition of the Star Chamber' (*Bishopsgate*). The Star Chamber was set up in the fifteenth century to be relatively free from the corruption and influence to which regular courts were subjected. But later, kings used it to enforce their policies relatively easily because of the lack of 'due process' – no juries, the accused required to answer questions under oath, and the court used directly upon the petition of individuals instead of their using the regular courts. Star Chamber abuses explain the protections against self-incrimination in the US Constitution Fifth Amendment:

> Historically, the privilege was intended to prevent the use of legal compulsion to extract from the accused a sworn communication of facts which would incriminate him. Such was the process of the ecclesiastical courts and the Star Chamber – the inquisitorial method of putting the accused upon his oath and compelling him to answer questions designed to uncover uncharged offenses, without evidence from another source. The major thrust of the policies undergirding the privilege is to prevent such compulsion. (*Doe*: 212)

The US Supreme Court had earlier stated:

> The Star Chamber has, for centuries, symbolized disregard of basic individual rights. [It] not merely allowed, but required, defendants to have counsel. The defendant's answer to an indictment was not accepted unless it was signed by counsel. When counsel refused to sign the answer, for whatever reason, the defendant was considered to have confessed. (*Faretta*: 821–22)

Thus, privilege is an extension of the client's morally and legally based rights against self-incrimination. It derives from the law of evidence which determines what client information can be protected. It's a principle whose 'centrality to the professional relationship between lawyer and client is recognised throughout the world' (LSAG 2023: 154). The classic formulation is that of Wigmore (1905: §3204): privilege can be invoked by a client (or prospective client) with respect to a communication, made between privileged persons – a lawyer acting as such and their client – in confidence, for the purpose of obtaining or providing legal advice or assistance of any kind for the client. This formulation mirrors 'Legal Advice Privilege' which, with 'Litigation Privilege' constitute 'LPP' in EW law (Thanki 2018).[1]

Privilege belongs to clients and attaches to what they tell their lawyers and what lawyers advise them to do. It can be invoked or waived only by clients. Privileged information cannot be disclosed without clients' consent. If not waived, lawyers are professionally obliged to assert privilege for clients (*Prince Jeffrey*). Clients may prevent lawyers from making a disclosure in court in breach of their privilege (*Harmony*).

No wonder some believe, wrongly, that privilege is designed to benefit clients. In fact, it's a 'fundamental condition upon which the administration of justice as a whole rests' (*Al Sadeq*: 509). Why? Because, on balance, without effective legal representation, the system fails. If the rule didn't exist, people wouldn't trust lawyers and 'everyone would be thrown upon his own legal resources' (*Greenough*, Lord Brougham). So, 'the purpose is to encourage full and frank communications between attorneys and their clients and *thereby promote* broader public interests in the observance of law and the administration of justice' (*Upjohn*: 389, emphasis added). Privilege is therefore a

> necessary corollary of the right of any person to obtain skilled advice about the law. Such advice cannot be effectively obtained unless the client is able to put all the facts before the adviser without fear that they may afterwards be disclosed and used to his prejudice (*R v Special Commissioner*, Lord Hoffmann).

---

[1] Important technical differences between these types are beyond the scope (and length) of this book.

It protects the privacy of the lawyer–client relationship by preventing the compulsory disclosure of protected information, a so-called 'safe space' rationale. It's 'inviolable, and its loss, irremediable' (*Al Sadeq*). Courts won't balance conflicting policy or justice arguments to override privilege (*R v Derby*, Lord Taylor of Gosforth). It cannot be over-ridden except by statute (*Bowman*; see also *Three Rivers*). And for lawyers? Privilege 'is one of the few occasions when you can suppress unhelpful information with a totally clear conscience' (Smith 2021).

ii. Confidentiality

Lawyers mustn't reveal confidential client information unless clients or the law require disclosure (BSB 2024: CD6; rC15.5; SRA Code 2023: 6.3; MR 1.6(a)). Unlike privilege, it can be overridden, but the justifications are similar: 'the public interest is usually best served by a strict rule' of confidentiality (MR 1.6, Comment [6]). Lawyers are the means to achieving the goals of the legal system – resolving disputes, protecting constitutional and legal rights, and so on. Therefore, 'lawyer-client confidentiality is the foundation of orderly and effective adversarial justice' (Zacharias 1989: 358).

For clients, lawyers perform several functions: adviser, advocate, negotiator and evaluator (MR Preamble: 2). Advisers provide an informed understanding of clients' rights and legal obligations. Advocates zealously assert their client's position under the rules of the adversary system. Negotiators seek results that are advantageous to clients, but are consistent with the requirements of honest dealings with others. Evaluators act by examining clients' legal affairs and reporting about them to their clients and others. In all these functions, confidentiality means: 'The client is encouraged to seek legal assistance and to communicate fully and frankly with the lawyer even as to embarrassing or legally damaging subject matter. The lawyer needs this information to represent the client effectively' (MR 1.6, Comment [2]; see also *Upjohn*: 389). Thus:

> The duty of confidentiality (CD6) is central to the administration of justice. Clients who put their confidence in their legal adviser must be able to do so in the knowledge that the information they give, or which is given on their behalf, will stay confidential. In normal circumstances, this information will be privileged and not disclosed to a court. (BSB 2024: gC42)

Full and frank communications benefit the system in several ways. Clients who fear their information might be revealed may lead to them lying, or withholding or filtering information, perhaps due to ignorance of the law. Indeed, they may not use lawyers at all unless confident of lawyer–client secrecy. Confidentiality helps lawyers discover improprieties and dissuade clients from illegal or unlawful actions (Levin LC 1994). Lawyers can 'advise the client to refrain from wrongful conduct' (MR 1.6, Comment [2]). It's therefore in clients' interests to obtain effective legal services through fully informed counsel. Indeed:

> the emphasis in all the case law had been on the importance as a matter of public policy of the client being able to speak frankly to his legal adviser in the knowledge that the legal adviser could not reveal those communications even if at some point in the future it became convenient for the legal adviser to do so. (*FRC*, Lady Justice Rose)

In short, the duty of confidentiality is 'a fundamental principle in the lawyer-client relationship' because it contributes to the 'trust that is the hallmark' of the relationship (MR 1.6, Comment [2]).

B. Preferring Clients

There are many other reasons – powerful but more controversial – to prefer clients over others.

i. *Legal*

Lawyers are agents for clients and agency law provides that agents should do nothing adverse to the principal (client's) interests (DeMott 1998). This model 'reinforced the impression of the lawyer as a "hired gun" or client's mouthpiece' (Boon 2023: 32) – though the 'mouthpiece' metaphor was refuted by the Lord Chief Justice, Lord Judge (*R v Farooqi*: 108). Indeed, the agency model must be reconciled with lawyers' duties to non-clients.

The lawyer–client relationship is based on contract which implies an exchange whereby, in return for a fee (the 'retainer'), parties agree the scope of the representation (the 'instructions'). Lawyers also have fiduciary relationships with clients (Luban 2020). The trust clients place in lawyers implies they'll use their superior knowledge for their clients' benefit. Usually, fiduciary responsibilities concern the holding of clients' money or property. However, it extends to the holding of client information and the duty not to disclose unless authorised. The duty of confidentiality is 'fundamental to the fiduciary relationship that exists between a solicitor and client. It extends to matters divulged to you by a client or on their behalf, from whatever source' (Law Society 2015: 3.3). These legal bases constitute a promise: clients can have trust and confidence that lawyers will use all lawful and ethical means to advance their interests in all aspects of their relationship.

Of course, there may be a less noble reason for preferring clients: lawyer self-interest. Helping clients 'win' may be necessary to receive higher fees or indeed any fees in 'no win, no fee' cases. One lawyer we interviewed was clear: 'Just like every other profession, money is a motivation for lawyers. Money is a huge driver. They want more money for their client for two reasons: their client gets more money; they get more money.' It's also arguable 'The legal profession, not clients or society as a whole, is the primary beneficiary of confidentiality rules' (Fischel 1998: 3). Giving lawyers a 'unique' competitive advantage over other professions such as accountants increases 'the value of legal advice and hence the demand for legal services' (ibid: 5).

C. Adversary System Ethics 101: The Standard Conception

Lawyers justify or 'excuse' their role via 'the ethics of the adversary system' (Luban 1988; see also Luban 2007; Abel 1997: 3). Luban criticises the adversary system but argues it should be kept, 'not because it is a mighty engine of truth and justice ... but simply the alternatives to it are not significantly better' (Luban 2007: 104). The adversary system makes parties responsible for presenting their cases. It then assumes a kind of 'three-legged stool' model where the parties' lawyers and a judge (all independent) are required to perform a specific role. If just one fails to perform their role, the system fails. This 'Standard Conception' of the lawyer's role has two basic principles: 'neutrality' (non-accountability) and 'partisanship'.

i. Neutrality

Lawyers must put aside personal views on clients and their objectives. If they don't, their competence and ability to perform the tasks expected are suspect. MR 1.2, Comment [5] declares 'representing a client does not constitute approval of the client's views or activities' and MR 1.2(b) confirms: 'A lawyer's representation of a client, including representation by appointment, does not constitute an endorsement of the client's political, economic, social or moral views or activities'. Ethically, Timothy McVeigh's lawyers were representing an alleged terrorist, not terrorism.

After all, it's the client's, not the lawyer's, case; lawyers should put forward their case. If what clients want is lawful, lawyers shouldn't substitute their opinions. Doing so risks an 'oligarchy of lawyers' where it's lawyers not clients who determine the rights and wrongs based on their individual views (Wasserstrom 1975; Pepper 1986: 617).

It's a principle of 'non-accountability': lawyers shouldn't be held accountable, personally, legally or morally, for what clients want. This principle is symbolised by barristers and solicitor-advocates wearing wigs and gowns. They not only emphasise their professional rather than personal role, but 'lend a dignity and solemnity to the proceedings', 'anonymise the judge or barrister' and add 'gravitas and demonstrating the independence of the profession by putting the focus on the case rather than the barrister's appearance' (Lord Burnett of Maldon, Lord Chief Justice, quoted in Baksi 2021). When Thomas Erskine defended Thomas Paine in 1792, he told the jury 'I will now lay aside the role of the advocate and address you as a man', at which point the judge interrupted: 'You will do nothing of the sort. The only right or licence you have to appear in this court is as an advocate' (quoted in Leggatt 1998/99: 77).

In practice, solicitors and attorneys can choose who to represent, meaning they have to justify representing unpopular clients. By contrast, barristers have the cab-rank rule. As Pannick (2021) put it: 'If barristers were to act only for those of whom we approve, we would be associated with our clients and unpopular litigants would then find it much more difficult to obtain competent representation'. Indeed, 'if I had confined my advocacy to those clients I loved, I would have been unemployed for large parts of each year' (Pannick 2023: 72).

ii. The Cab-Rank Rule

Barristers must take on cases 'irrespective of the identity of the client; the nature of the case to which the instructions relate; and any belief or opinion which you may have formed as to the character, reputation, cause, conduct, guilt or innocence of the client' (BSB 2024: rC29.3a, b, d). They mustn't withhold their services or permit them to be withheld on any of the following grounds:

that the nature of the case is objectionable to you or to any section of the public; that the conduct, opinions, or beliefs of the prospective client are unacceptable to you or to any section of the public; or relating to the source of any financial support which may properly be given to the prospective client for the proceedings in question. (ibid: rC28)

The cab-rank rule makes it the advocate's duty

to appear for the Yorkshire Ripper or any other defendant against whom there may be a hostile climate of public opinion. In civil cases, it is also his duty to appear not only for a particular interest group with which he might prefer to identify, but for every interest group; for plaintiffs or insurers in personal injury cases; for employers or trade unions on labour law cases; for the citizen or the State in judicial review cases. (Lord Irvine of Lairg, quoted in Leggatt 1998/99: 76)

According to Sam Townend KC, 2024 Bar Council Chair, the cab-rank rule is 'the expression of the Bar's commitment to neutrality' (Boon 2014: 62). It's 'there for a very good reason – it protects the Bar. If you undermine that with particularly strong views, you undermine the whole set-up – ultimately the rule of law and the role of lawyers' (*The Times* 2024a). As Baroness Kennedy KC put it: 'A fundamental element of the rule of law is that lawyers are independent. The lawyer must not be confused with the client. Their role in acting for a client should not be interpreted as the sharing of a world view' (Hamilton 2023).

iii. Partisanship

The principle of partisanship means lawyers should do for clients what clients would do for themselves if they had the knowledge, skills, experience, detachment and so on (Royal Commission on Legal Services 1979: 3.18(e)). As one EW judge put it, 'the very word "represent" means to "re-present" the client's case' (Hunter et al 2018: 13). Therefore, lawyers should be everything they can, lawfully and ethically, to vindicate clients' causes. This means: 'The lawyer's function as advocate is *openly and necessarily partisan*' (Federation of Law Societies of Canada 2019: r 5-1-1, Comment [3], emphasis added). Partisanship 'requires lawyers to use such tricks [of the trade] if they can advance their clients' interests by doing so' (Dare 2004: 33).

iv. Rationale

Codes and courts endorse the standard conception. The duty to act in the best interests of clients means barristers must 'promote fearlessly and by all proper and lawful means the client's best interests … without regard to your own interests or to any consequences to you … to any other person' (BSB 2024: rC15.1, 2. 3; see also gC22). Solicitors must also act in the best interests of clients (SRA 2019d: Principle 7). Lord Chief Justice Burnett explained:

The vitality and independence of the legal profession is an essential hallmark of a society governed by the rule of law. Lawyers have a duty to act fearlessly for their clients, subject always to their overriding professional obligations and duties to the courts. *They shouldn't be subject to criticism for doing so.* (Evidence before the House of Commons Justice Committee, 10 November 2020, emphasis added)

In the US, there's a similar emphasis. The first ABA Canon of Ethics (1908: C 15) stated: lawyers owe 'entire devotion to the interest of the client, warm zeal in the maintenance and defense of his rights and the exertion of his utmost learning and ability'. Lawyers have several duties: 'to represent his client zealously within the bounds of the law' (MC Canon 7, EC7-1), to 'abide by a client's decisions concerning the objectives of representation' (MR 1.2(a)) and as an advocate, 'a lawyer zealously asserts the client's position under the rules of the adversary system' (MR Preamble: 2). Lawyers must act with 'commitment and dedication to the interests of the client and with zeal in advocacy upon the client's behalf' (MR 1.3, Comment [1]). In other words, the 'ultimate authority to determine the purposes to be served by legal representation' is conferred on clients (MR 1.2(a), Comment [1]). Lawyers in civil matters must abide by clients' decisions whether to settle and in criminal matters what to plead and whether the client will testify (MR 1.2(a)).

v. Amoral Technicians?

The standard conception has been criticised. It understates the importance of 'morality'. If lawyers act as 'amoral technicians' (Wasserstrom 1975: 6), this 'alters, if not eliminates, the significance of moral considerations that would obtain were it not for the presence of the role' (ibid: 4). What characterises the lawyer's role is the 'required indifference to a wide variety of ends and consequences that in other contexts would be of undeniable moral significance' (ibid: 5). Some believe the standard conception 'must be abandoned, to be replaced by a conception that better allows the lawyer to bring his full moral sensibilities to play in his professional role' (Postema 1980: 64). Clients who want to achieve goals that lawyers – and maybe others – regard as immoral undermine not only morality itself but also the morality of lawyers. Lawyers are in danger not only of harming clients' adversaries but also of 'losing their soul' (Kronman 1993: 2).

Dare (2004) argues not that it should be abandoned, but a 'fragile' distinction should be drawn between 'mere-zeal' and 'hyper-zeal', with the former and not the latter being the requirement of the standard conception. Mere-zeal means lawyers 'must zealously pursue their clients' legal entitlements, but need not zealously pursue every advantage … that the law can be made to provide'. This distinction is unsustainable. As MC EC 7-1 stated, every client is entitled 'to seek any lawful objective through legally permissible means' and a lawyer 'shall not intentionally (1) fail to seek the lawful objectives of his client through reasonably available means' (DR 7-101(A)(1)). In any case, isn't 'zeal' an all-or-nothing word – like 'pregnancy'? You are either zealous – pregnant – or you're not.

Boon (2014: 31) concludes that the 'main argument in justification of the standard conception is that it is better than any alternative'. Some argue the model may be valid in the criminal justice context but not elsewhere (Schwartz 1983), and certainly not outside the advocacy required in the courtroom (Luban 1988; Eekelaar et al 2000; Menkel-Meadow 2000: 123; Boon 2014: 26). I concluded in the first edition that it should be modified (Whelan 2022). That said, Luban (1988: 11) believed the 'principle of partisanship is generally taken as a credo by lawyers in non-advocate roles just as much as by courtroom lawyers'. Pepper (1986: 615) believed there *was* a 'far broader moral justification for the amoral professional role of the lawyer' than the adversary system: respect for client autonomy.

D. Respect for Client Autonomy

There's strong support for the value of autonomy: the idea that individuals should be as free as possible to make their own choices about how to live. John Stuart Mill (1978: 9) argued that individuals should enjoy maximum freedom to make choices about their lives subject to not impinging on others' similar degree of autonomy. The constraints on autonomy should be based on the 'no-harm' principle: 'The only purpose for which power can be rightfully exercised over a member of a civilised community, against his will, is to prevent harm to others' (Mill 1978: 13). Clients' autonomy is enhanced by their being able to resist, with the assistance of lawyers sworn to fidelity, the state and others. Bok (1983: 120) argued that keeping secrets is generally justified because of concern for 'human autonomy regarding personal information, respect for relationships, respect for the bonds and promises that protect shared information'.

i. First-Class Citizenship

Pepper's (1986) first-class citizenship model has several steps. First, law is a public good and, if available to all, increases an individual's ability to successfully attain goals. It increases individual autonomy. Societies like the US have an in-principle commitment to it. Liberty and autonomy are morally good; free choice is better than constraint; having choices is good. Thus, increasing autonomy is morally good. The next step is acknowledging that in a highly legalised society, autonomy is dependent on access to law. Without access, 'first-class' citizenship may be denied to individuals, like a disabled person seeking to have their disability accommodated or getting access to education via the Individuals with Disabilities Act 2004. Fulfilling goals may be difficult, or even impossible, without legal assistance. Denying access to law is denying access to justice, thereby undermining 'equal justice under law'. The idea that a society is based on 'the rule of law' becomes suspect if access to law is denied.

So, 'first-class citizenship is dependent on access to the law' which, in practice, means dependent on access to lawyers. Simpson (1988: 162) explained:

> the pursuit of the ideal of the rule of law, the subjection of government to law, can have little chance of even a modest degree of success unless there are lawyers who can, through their expertise, make the law, in spite of its mystification, available to citizens.

The 'primary job of the lawyer is to give the client access to the law in its multitude of facets'. The lawyer is 'the means to first-class citizenship, to meaningful autonomy, for the client' (Pepper 1986: 617).

Another significant value supporting first-class citizenship is equality: 'If law is a public good, access to which increases autonomy, then equality of access is important' (ibid: 618). Pepper is aware some individuals are denied access to justice for reasons such as lack of funding, but his idea of equality of access is that access shouldn't be 'filtered unequally'. When individuals seeks legal representation, lawyers shouldn't let their own moral views impinge on clients in ways that undermine their autonomy. If lawyers did so, given the wide variety of moral views they hold, there wouldn't be equality of access, but disparate access depending on individual lawyer's moral views. It's inequality because there's inequality of lawyers' consciences. If lawyers had moral responsibility for each of the acts they facilitated on behalf of clients, or if lawyers had a moral obligation to refuse to represent clients whose objectives were immoral, then lawyers would be substituting their beliefs for individual autonomy and diversity. There would be the dreaded oligarchy of lawyers.

Pepper's model is powerful. Access to the law is good; access to justice is good; access to both increases individual autonomy; thus, lawyers are good too. Being a good lawyer – by putting aside personal views – *is* being a good citizen because it promotes first-class citizenship. Pepper's justification for the lawyer's role goes beyond the adversary system justification, which depends heavily on criminal defence and the use of which in civil law scenarios is troubling. The principle of autonomy suggests a person should be able to pursue *any* lawful objective. Pepper's probably right that access to the legal system often requires a lawyer (ibid: 617). As the saying goes, people who represent themselves have a fool for a client! But his conclusion that a lawyer can be a good lawyer and a good person is founded on two questionable assumptions: individual autonomy is good, and access to the law is good because it enhances individual autonomy.

Is enhancing individual autonomy 'good' if it means helping clients do 'bad'? If a person murders someone, that's bad. If they use a hired gun, they're still bad, but so's the hired gun! Using lawyers doesn't make bad things good. So lawyers have to take responsibility – justify – what they do for clients. Enhancing autonomy may infringe Mill's 'no-harm' principle if the objective adversely affects others. That's why Raz (1986: 417) argued: 'Autonomous life is valuable only if it is spent in the pursuit of acceptable and valuable projects and relationships.'

E. Respect for Dignity and Liberty

In a way, autonomy is 'positive' – to achieve goals a person needs to act. Another value, liberty, is 'negative' – a person has a wish (or a right) to be left alone. The idea that a person should be free to do what they want with their life is different from autonomy. A person might want medical treatment – autonomy – but be refused, whereas they can refuse treatment others might want to give them. This idea is expressed as *Whose Life is it Anyway?* (Clark 1978) In a legal context, however, there may not be freedom to refuse 'legal treatment': if a person is prosecuted or sued, or their rights threatened, they may need legal representation. Their secrets may be exposed; their liberty – and property – at risk.

A system that doesn't allow (or restricts) citizens making cases effectively – via lawyers if necessary – 'fails in honoring human dignity' (Luban 1988: 86). Indeed, for Luban (2007: 66), 'what makes the practice of law worthwhile is upholding human dignity'. This reinforces the value of autonomy and the need for access to the law. As Rhode (2000b: 53) put it: 'In a highly legalistic society, preservation of personal dignity and autonomy requires preservation of access to law.'

F. The Pervasiveness of Law

The 'access to justice' problem for many citizens is they live in a 'law-thick' world but encounter barriers in gaining access to lawyers and legal services (Galanter 1974;

Mayhew 1975). It's been called 'hyperlexis' – the 'condition of overwhelming proliferation of law' (Chao 2021: 130). This 'law-thick' world points to another justification for the lawyer's role: the pervasiveness of law in everyday life. Arthur Baer is quoted as saying that: 'If you laid all our laws end to end there would be no end'! After setting out the 'superabundance of laws' that affect everyone on a daily basis, Simpson (1988: 3, 7) noted a 'puzzling phenomenon: the pervasiveness of law in a society in which there is widespread ignorance of law'. The explanation was 'the existence of experts' (ibid: 7); in other words, lawyers (and others who 'practise' in the legal world). The pervasiveness and complexity of law reinforce Pepper's argument that first-class citizenship requires access to the law – and lawyers who perform their role faithfully.

G. 'Everyone Deserves Legal Advice'

But what about this 'commonly held belief' within the legal profession (Vaughan 2023: 1)? It's an argument 'practising lawyers like to put forward about access to justice' (ibid: 4, 29), supported by the right to counsel for serious criminal offences, the (dwindling) availability of civil legal aid, pro bono services and other attempts to provide access to justice, including the cab-rank rule. Many highlight the pervasive problem of unequal access to justice and unequal distribution of legal services (Sandefur 2019) – a 'justice crisis' (Knake Jefferson 2024). As former ABA President Robert Grey Jr powerfully put it: 'There is no justice as long as millions lack meaningful access to it' (Grey Jr 2018; see also Abel 1979). MR Preamble [6] acknowledges 'the fact that the poor, and sometimes persons who are not poor, cannot afford adequate legal assistance', so lawyers should be 'mindful of deficiencies' and 'devote professional time and resources … to ensure equal access to our system of justice'.

Many also regard the vindication by lawyers of individual rights – especially of unpopular clients – as protecting the rights of all (Goldberger 1995), like the ACLU's representation of the NRA in the Supreme Court in 2024 (*NRA*). Despite disagreeing vehemently with the NRA's 'goals, strategies or tactics' (Enloe 2023), when a New York State official attempted to discourage banks and insurance companies doing business with the NRA after the 2018 Parkland Florida mass shooting, 'the ACLU has long stood for the proposition that we may disagree with what you say but will defend to the death your right to say it' (David Cole, ACLU national legal director, quoted in ibid).

So far, so good, but there's generally no *right* to counsel in non-criminal cases. There's 'no moral or political claim to legal assistance in every exercise of a legal right, let alone to the zealous assistance of a lawyer who has qualms about what the citizen proposes … because not every exercise of a legal right has a moral justification' (Schneyer 1984: 1540). Attorneys may refuse to represent if they find clients or their cause 'so repugnant' it's likely to impair their ability (MR 6.2(c)), and may withdraw from representation if clients insist on taking action their lawyers consider repugnant or with which they have a 'fundamental disagreement' (MR 1.16(b)(4)). Perhaps a distinction should also be made between human and non-human clients (Luban 2007). After all, on what basis does an organisational client have autonomy or *deserve* legal advice? Why should lawyers who opposes smoking help tobacco companies (Wasserstrom 1975: 8)?

So this 'everyone deserves' justification becomes 'problematic' (Vaughan 2023: 33). It 'often masks a simple ethical choice, where lawyers prioritise commercial concerns over [other] considerations, unburdened by more complex ethical constraints' (ibid: 1). This is why law firms have been criticised for disproportionately representing companies whose activities contribute to climate change or cause environmental harms (Baksi 2023a; Vaughan 2023): 'lawful but awful' (Vaughan 2023, referring to Passas 2005). The LS4CA hopes its '[Law Firm Climate Change] Scorecard will push firms to move away from the fossil fuel industry and toward a livable future' (LS4CA 2023).

This is also why Michael Mansfield KC and others have called for an end to the cab-rank rule (Baksi 2023b), arguing that lawyers should decide for themselves which clients they're willing to represent. In 2023, the 'Lawyers are Responsible' group declared they'll not act for new fossil fuel projects or prosecute protesters campaigning against them. Mansfield also claimed the rule is 'more honoured in the breach than adherence' (ibid). Bar Council Chairman Vineall KC (2023b) distinguished between contentious and non-contentious work. Everyone, he said, should be able to vindicate their legal rights. That's what barristers do – hence the cab-rank rule and the 'greater public interests served'. By contrast, non-contentious advisory work had no compelling public interest requiring this legal need to be met. Schneyer (1984: 1540) also argued that there's 'no moral or political claim to legal assistance in every exercise of a legal right, let alone the zealous assistance of a lawyer who has qualms about what the client proposes'.

Patrick O'Connor KC (2023: 32) argued that representing 'the worst of the worst' in a serious criminal case is a 'noble mission for the legal profession', which is why the Bar Council strongly discouraging barristers in 1945 from defending Nazis at Nuremberg was a 'blemish'. Beyond personal 'liberty' cases, however, he argued that the rule fails to further the public interest, for three reasons. First, the rule has limitations: solicitors can ethically decline to represent clients and some large City firms have done so; also, the rule doesn't apply to barristers' 'direct access' or 'conditional fee' cases, or if the fee is not 'adequate'. It's 'easily evaded' and more 'symbol than substance'. Secondly, the rule has 'no practical impact' upon the 'justice crisis' – restrictions on access to justice. Thirdly, the rule 'is the 'handmaid of the very market forces which create inequality of access to justice'. Those with resources are more likely to instruct barristers and to do so before others, and barristers, according to the rule, must accept them. This 'positively reinforces inequality in access to justice'. He concludes that in civil cases the public interest necessary to justify the rule cannot be demonstrated.

In short, autonomy may not be valuable if it undermines the autonomy of others. The problem for all lawyers not bound or abiding by the cab-rank rule is their representation implies they do *not* find the client *or* their cause repugnant, *nor* have a fundamental disagreement with the client's actions.

II. Divided Loyalties

All the virtues for preferring clients incorporate constraints, leaving lawyers to resolve conflicts in duty. Legal requirements to *reveal* rather than *conceal* client information are discussed in Chapter 5. Here, we look at limits – crime-fraud, statutory, ethical and moral – on putting clients first.

A. The Crime-Fraud 'Exception'

If lawyers' services are being sought to further crime or fraud, then the 'seal of secrecy' is broken, and neither privilege nor the duty of confidentiality exists. As Justice Cardozo famously put it: 'The privilege takes flight if the relation is abused. A client who consults an attorney for advice that will serve him in the commission of a fraud will have no help from the law. *He must let the truth be told*' (*Clark*, emphasis added).

If lawyers *know* legal services are being abused, communications aren't privileged. If lawyers *suspect* it, it's more complex. Courts require prima facie evidence of crime/fraud before displacing privilege (*O'Rourke*). Otherwise, privilege could be 'avoided' simply by alleging crime/fraud, in the expectation the communication would have to be disclosed to see if the allegation was correct (see ibid; *Bullivant*). If there's prima facie evidence, then even if the suspicion turns out to be mistaken, solicitors may rely on the 'reasonable excuse' defence if they disclose (CPS Guidance 2022).

Privilege normally still applies to legal communications after the commission of a crime. However, the exception may extend to those communications or if crime/fraud is ongoing, for example, relating to the proceeds of crime/fraud. Under section 10(2) PACE 1984, 'items held with an intention of furthering a criminal purpose' are excluded from the ambit of LPP.

i. Donald Trump and Mar-a-Lago

Trump was suspected of unlawfully retaining classified documents and blocking efforts to retrieve them at Mar-a-Lago. In May 2022, a subpoena required the production of all classified documents and in June, one of his lawyers, Evan Corcoran, claimed a 'diligent search' led to all documents being returned. A later FBI search found 102 more classified documents in Trump's office and a storage room, 17 of which were marked 'Top Secret' and 54 'Secret' (*US v Donald J Trump*).

In January 2023, Corcoran refused to answer questions at the grand jury regarding events leading up to the search. Prosecutors then argued successfully that the crime-fraud exception applied. Chief Judge Howell found they'd presented compelling evidence that Corcoran was misled by Trump by intentionally concealing the existence of additional classified documents. As a result, Corcoran gave evidence in March and released his notes. The subsequent indictment of Trump revealed the Trump–Corcoran communications, including Trump's implied hint for Corcoran to remove – 'pluck' – 'anything really bad' (ibid: 25) from the documents. They showed how Trump sought to avoid anybody looking through the boxes of documents.

ii. 'Iniquity'

In EW, the 'iniquity exception' is broader than the crime-fraud exception. Courts focus closely on the purpose of advice rather than whether there was a crime or fraud. Iniquity is 'an old-fashioned word meaning something like gross injustice' (Boon 2005: 244). The approach was explained in the nineteenth century:

> there is no confidence as to the disclosure of an iniquity. You cannot make me the confident of a crime or fraud and be entitled to close my lips upon any secret which you have the audacity to disclose to me relating to any fraudulent *intention* on your part. (*Gartside*, emphasis added)

If there's abuse of the lawyer–client relationship and iniquity exists more likely than not (a prima facie or balance of probabilities test), then privilege doesn't apply (*Al Sadeq*). There have been concerns privilege protection might be weakened, for example, if clients sought legal advice about crimes they planned to commit. As the Court of Appeal noted, regarding

> those wishing to engage in sharp practice ... the effect of the present decision may well be to discourage them from going to their lawyers. This has the arguable public disadvantage that the lawyers might have dissuaded them from the sharp practice. However, it has the undoubted public advantage that the absence of lawyers will make it more difficult for them to carry out their sharp practice. (*Barclays*)

Critically, though, for the iniquity exception to apply, there must be abuse of the relationship. If clients seek legal advice on whether something was lawful, it would not be disclosable even if it revealed an iniquity.

B. Statutory Exceptions

The Regulation of Investigatory Powers Act 2000 permits covert surveillance of communications between legal advisers and persons in custody. Although the Act makes no reference to LPP, the Act's Code of Practice states surveillance of LPP communications can be authorised so as to be 'lawful for all purposes'. The House of Lords (now the Supreme Court) held in 2009 that Part 2 of the Act did permit the targeting of privileged information for the purposes of gathering intelligence (*Re McE*) – including covert surveillance of defendants and their lawyers in virtually any setting. Surveillance of this kind, the Court said, required enhanced authorisation and additional procedures in order for it to be lawful. Further Codes of Practice were issued after this case to 'safeguard' LPP. LPP should be violated only in 'exceptional and compelling circumstances'. Authorisation should only be granted where there is a threat to national security or to 'life and limb'. This statutory 'exception' to LPP has been challenged, partly because there already is the crime-fraud 'exception' (Griffin and Nardell 2021: 30).

C. Ethical Constraints

There are SRA codes for solicitors and law firms (SRA 2023a, 2023b). The solicitors' code 'describes the standards of professionalism that we, the SRA, and the public expect of individuals ... authorised by us to provide legal services'. The SRA (2019d) also has a set of principles – the 'fundamental tenets of ethical behaviour' – that all solicitors are expected to uphold. The firms' code requires them to have a 'Compliance Officer for Legal Practice' who must take all reasonable steps to ensure compliance by the firm and its employees or interest holders with the SRA. They must also promptly inform the SRA

> of any facts or matters that you reasonably believe should be brought to its attention in order that it may investigate whether a serious breach of its regulatory arrangements has occurred or otherwise exercise its regulatory powers. (SRA 2023b: 9.1(e))

Barristers are regulated by the BSB. Its *Handbook* (2024) includes a Code of Conduct which sets out 'Core Duties', 'Guidance to the Core Duties', as well as Rules, Guidance and Outcomes. Each US State has its own professional conduct rules. Virtually all, however, to a greater or lesser extent, adhere to the ABA's MR – the MC has been mostly superseded. Some States impose responsibilities on firms to regulate the attorney members, but most don't have a separate code for firms (see generally Schneyer 1991; Chambliss and Wilkins 2003).

All codes acknowledge ethical and legal constraints on lawyers putting clients first. MR principles include 'the lawyer's *obligation* zealously to *protect* and pursue a *client's legitimate interests*, within the bounds of the law, while maintaining a professional, courteous and civil attitude toward all persons involved in the legal system' (MR Preamble: 9, emphasis added). MR 1.3, Comment [1] states that a lawyer 'is not bound to press for every advantage that might be realized for a client'. The duty to act with reasonable diligence 'does not require the use of offensive tactics or preclude the treating of all persons involved in the legal process with courtesy and respect'.

SRA Principles expect solicitors to act 'with honesty ... integrity ... in the best interests of each client', but also to promote the rule of law, the administration of justice, and public trust and confidence in the profession, as well as the client's best interests. Solicitors are also subject to a duty of fairness towards third parties, and integrity means they mustn't 'take advantage of third parties in either their professional or personal capacity' (SRA 2011, Outcome 11.1). They mustn't use their position as solicitors to take unfair advantage by, for example, writing offensive letters to third parties. The courts also impose a general obligation of fairness on lawyers, particularly in litigation or other conflict situations.

In short, what's ethical may *not* always be what's in clients' interests. The SRA's rules 'clearly cover impropriety arising from behaviour that was in the best interests of the client' (SRA 2015: 5). Excessive zeal has led to solicitors 'improperly prioritising the client's interest over their other duties' (SRA 2018: 5). The SDT even stated: 'A solicitor ... must and should on occasion be prepared to say to [their] client 'what you seek to do may be legal but I am not prepared to help you do it' (SRA 2018: 7, referring to *In the Matter of Paul Francis Simms*). Attorneys have been similarly advised. They 'should not be deterred from giving candid advice by the prospect that the advice will be unpalatable to the client' (MR 2.1 [1]) and could 'refuse to aid a client in conduct they believe to be unlawful even though it is arguably legal' (DR 7-101A).

So which loyalties should 'win'? Authorities agree conflicts should be resolved in ways which 'safeguard the wider public interest' (SRA 2023a); the attorney 'must give precedence to his duty to the public' (*Van Berkel*: 1251, District Judge Devitt). The 'public interest' is the constitutional principle of the rule of law, the proper administration of justice, and upholding the public's trust and confidence in the solicitors' profession and in legal services provided by persons authorised to offer 'reserved' legal services (litigation, advocacy, probate and so on). This principle 'takes precedence over an individual client's interests' (SRA 2023a). As Judge Devitt put it: 'Any other view would run counter to a principled system of justice' (*Van Berkel*: 1251).

The precedence EW lawyers should give to the administration of justice is enshrined in the Administration of Justice Act 1999. Section 42(2) states that in both criminal and civil procedure, there's an overriding objective imposed on lawyer behaviour: 'doing justice'. The Courts and Legal Services Act 1990 specifies the duty is to act with independence in the interests of justice. This mirrors the special responsibilities placed on American prosecutors as 'ministers of justice and not simply that of an advocate' (MR 3.8, Comment [1]). The Supreme Court stated that the interest of a US attorney 'is not that it shall win a case, but that justice shall be done' (*Berger*: 88).

D. Moral Qualms

Many commentators believe the predominant duty of lawyers ought *not* to be to clients. Simon (2000: Chapter 6) advocated: 'Lawyers should take those actions that, considering the relevant circumstances of the particular case, seem likely to promote justice'. Wendel (2010, 2012) argued that lawyers' 'obligation of fidelity to law' is the approach to be preferred. Luban (1988: xxii) believed lawyers should pursue morally worthy ends using morally justifiable means. In other words, representing a client effectively should *not* mean 'doing whatever one may get away with as long as it is in the client's interests' (Wendel 2011: 1). The professional responsibility of all American lawyers is their responsibility for the legal system as a whole (Luban 1988).

III. A Bigamous Relationship?

So, the authorities resist the 'hired gun' metaphor. In litigation, although 'solicitors must fearlessly advance their clients' cases, they are not "hired guns" whose only duty is to the client' (SRA 2015: 3). Justifications for preferring clients mean loyalty 'is important, but is not an absolute value for lawyers' (Boon 2023: 55). A 'Lawyer's loyalty to client wishes is therefore conditional at best' (Boon 2014: 31). No wonder ethical challenges are 'the most difficult' (*People v Belge*: 800) and 'the excruciating difficulty of law practice is [their] *pervasiveness*' (Hodes 2000: 978). Resolving the ethical conundrum is correspondingly complicated.

Criminal defence counsel 'have the difficult task of serving both as officers of the court and as loyal and zealous advocates for their clients'. However, one way to reconcile the conflict is to prioritise the client:

> the *primary* duties that defense counsel owe to their clients, to the administration of justice, and as officers of the court, are to serve as their *clients'* counsellor and advocate with courage and devotion. (ABA 2017: 4-1.2(b), emphasis added)

Robin Tolson KC made 'no apology' for saying a lawyer is a 'hired gun', and acknowledged they're 'bound by a variety of duties'. He concluded: 'Above all ... the Code of Conduct is clear that my primary duty is to the lay client' (Symposium 2008: 57). He even argued that there was 'real danger in imposing on a lawyer's mind any other higher duty' than 'championing the client' (ibid: 56). But then he referred to section 188(2) LSA 2007 giving advocates and litigators 'a duty to the court ... to act with independence in the interests of justice'. Its purpose may be to 'warn of the dangers of binding lawyers too closely to their clients. It attempts to water down the duty to the client', and he added: 'I agree that it is right to do so. An oath to act only in the client's interests would be dangerous'.

No wonder Curtis (1951: 11) characterised 'the relations which a lawyer has with his client on the one hand and his court on the other [as] somewhat bigamous'. If this is so, it also begs the question posed by Frankel (1975: 1056): 'How and why should the client pay for loyalties divided between himself and the truth?' It's in this context that lawyers have available a bag of tricks to protect clients – if they choose to use them.

PART II

Tricks of the Trade

Lawyers do tricks even I cannot figure out.
— Harry Houdini (attributed)

5

Squelching Truth

Truth is the most valuable thing. Let us economize it

— Mark Twain (1897)

Lawyers instinctively – and ethically – do not reveal information about clients unless given informed consent or required by law (MR 1.6(a); BSB 2024: CD6, rC15.5, gC42; SRA 2023a: Rule 6.3). Confidentiality is a 'core professional principle' (section 1(3)(e) LSA 2007), a 'fundamental principle in the client-lawyer relationship' (MR 1.6, Comment [2]). Clients' information must be used only for their benefit, irrespective of the source (MR 1.6, Comment [3]). Confidentiality, however, isn't 'merely a subset of secrecy'; it's also 'a euphemistic label for squelching truth' (Stevenson 2014: 341).

But why should lawyers squelch truth? Wolfram (1995: 150, emphasis added) claims there's a 'U.S. *cult* of confidentiality' and 'legal rhetoric' about it 'is expansive, grandiose, and one-dimensional, quite misleadingly so' (ibid: 157). That's because 'the doctrine of confidentiality is rather determinedly multifaceted, issue sensitive, and policy responsive'. If so, the hard question is *not* whether lawyers should keep confidentiality, but when, if ever, they should *break* it. There are bound to be 'costs' – something 'bad' – as well as 'benefits' – something 'good' – either way.

I. Ghostly Metaphors: Silence Can Kill

A. Buried Bodies

Frank Armani was appointed by a New York State court to represent Robert Garrow, accused in August 1973 of killing a young man in July (Alibrandi and Armani 1984; Zitrin and Langford 1999a: Chapter 1; Hobin and Jensen 1980; Callahan and Pitkow 1980). After Armani hypnotised Garrow, Garrow told Francis Belge, who'd joined the defence team, he'd also killed two young women – Susan Petz and Alicia Hauck, both missing in July – and where their bodies were, which the lawyers confirmed. Garrow was suspected, so their parents pleaded with the lawyers for information. Armani's daughter, Dorina, was a classmate of Alicia Hauck's sister, and Alicia's father worked at the courthouse where Armani knew him; the Haucks lived in Armani's neighbourhood and went to his church (Lerman et al 2007: 27). When Mr Hauck tried to meet at Armani's office, Armani would 'sneak out the back door. ... I knew ... I couldn't trust myself with him' (ibid).

It took five months to find Alicia's body and two more weeks to find that of Susan. Armani and Belge became hated figures. Armani's office was broken into several times; his wife and daughter received numerous obscene and threatening phone calls; his health, marriage and law practice all suffered disastrously. The lawyers 'were both armed all the time' because of gun threats (ibid: 28). Armani's trauma was heightened because in 1962 his brother had been lost on an air force reconnaissance mission, his body never being recovered.

The lawyers kept confidentiality. Armani explained: the parents' suffering was 'not worth justifying the breach of my sworn duty and the Constitution' (WETA 1988). Interestingly, a court agreed. A law requiring the reporting of dead bodies for burial did *not* override their duty of confidentiality – a rare example of ethical duties overriding legal duties.

B. Patrick T Beall

Beall represented William 'Pop' Campbell. Campbell and Henry Drake were charged with murdering, in rural Georgia in 1975, 74-year-old barber CE Eberhart, who was bludgeoned to death with his own claw hammer (and $300 was also stolen). Both denied it. Drake admitted helping Campbell, who told him of the murder, escape to Virginia. Campbell was arrested and blamed Drake, thinking he'd turned him in.

Campbell claimed he was having his hair cut when Drake came in and 'killed the barber'. Drake claimed he'd dropped off Campbell at the barber's and picked him up later that day with no knowledge or involvement in the crime. The jury believed neither of them and both were convicted of first-degree murder, sentenced to death and placed on death row. This was despite the 'lack of any physical evidence implicating [Drake], despite the fact that he had an alibi, and despite the medical examiner's testimony that Mr Eberhart could not have been killed by more than one person' (Blank and Jensen 2005: 107).

Held at the same prison, Campbell told Drake he'd confessed to Rev Murphy Davis of Atlanta's Clifton Presbyterian Church. Davis persuaded Campbell to sign an affidavit in 1981 stating:

> I lied at his trial. I said Henry was the one who killed the barber, Mr Eberhart, and that I tried to stop Henry from killing him. But what I said were lies. I was the one who killed Mr Eberhart. Henry wasn't even there. He had nothing to do with it. (ibid: 107–08)

Campbell handed the affidavit to Beall, telling him he'd got a bad haircut, beaten the barber to death and walked away with the money. The story was consistent internally and with what both Drake and his girlfriend had said. Beall, trying to get Campbell's sentence reduced, advised him not to repeat his admissions in court. Beall said: 'I had my job. My job is to be Campbell's attorney, to do the best that I could for him.' It would not be 'in the interests of the client' to reveal the information – Campbell wouldn't get off death row and could also be charged with perjury. Meanwhile, Drake was on death row – for eight years. As Drake said in 2001, each day: 'All day long, when the door opens, you're going to die. That's it.'

The affidavit was given to Drake's attorney, Mary Wilkes. She filed an extraordinary motion for a new trial, but the trial judge, William Grant, denied it, despite Campbell giving evidence on Drake's behalf, as did Beall, corroborating Campbell's story. The Georgia Supreme Court affirmed. After Campbell died, Beall broke confidentiality, despite the duty persisting after death (MR 1.9(c)(2); see also SRA 2023a: Rule 6.3). In 1984 and 1985, 11th Circuit decisions overturned Drake's death sentence and conviction – not because of Campbell's confession, but because of the prosecutor's inflammatory references in closing arguments and Judge Grant's misleading and imprecise instructions to the jury.

At Drake's first new trial in 1987, Beall had 'no qualms' about testifying. There was a hung jury: 10-2 for acquittal. At the second, he was reconvicted and sentenced to life imprisonment. By now, he was eligible for parole. The parole board released him *not* on time served, but 'on the grounds that he was actually innocent' (Blank and Jensen 2005: 108). Drake's view of Beall was: 'He was wrong. He was wrong. He was a wrong man.' However, he was *not* wrong ethically – *until* he broke confidentiality after Campbell's death. Even had Drake been at risk of imminent execution, Beall's disclosure would have been unethical because the old MR 1.6 permitted disclosure only to prevent clients committing *crimes*. The new MR (below) would have given Beall discretion to disclose, but should he? He'd called the Georgia State Bar Ethics 'hotline' for guidance and was told to

> represent the client solely … But do not let him tell any further lies. As long as your client has not told lies while you've been representing him, you are under no ethical obligation to make things square with the courts about a lie he told in the past. (Siegel 1988b; see also Siegel 1988a)

Beall (and his associate lawyer Floyd W Keeble Jr) helped keep Drake on death row for years, despite Campbell wanting to do the 'right thing': 'I've thought it over and I know it was wrong to lie and I can't go on living like this … I know what I'm saying might hurt my own appeals but I'm not going to worry about it. I want to get this off my conscience' (Siegel 1988b). Beall later said he 'should have been relieved and walked away after they got the affidavit. But maybe by then I was wrapped up in the game' (ibid). Campbell had emphysema. If he died, Drake might never be released. Sadly, Henry Drake was not the only innocent person at risk of being executed (Kaplan 1988: 35–38; Symposium 1996).

C. Leslie P Smith

Atkins v Virginia is the landmark ruling banning executions of 'mentally retarded' inmates. Daryl Atkins' case also involved two people accused of the same murder. Atkins, William A Jones and the victim, 21-year-old Air Force mechanic Eric Nesbitt, were seen in photos taken by a car surveillance camera. Atkins was also seen forcing Nesbitt to withdraw cash from a bank machine. Atkins and Jones blamed each other, but in Virginia only the 'triggerman' gets the death penalty.

Smith, representing Jones, attended interviews with his client and prosecutors, the first in August 1997. If Jones proved to be credible, prosecutors offered to drop several charges and use his statements to convict Atkins. At one interview, however, Jones' statements were at odds with the forensic evidence. Prosecutors turned off the tape recorder and told Smith: 'Do you see we've got a problem here?' Smith informed them Jones sometimes confused left with right; prosecutors then created a mock crime scene so he could show them what happened. Law enforcement officers then coaxed Jones to give answers that fitted the facts. The tape recorder was turned back on about 16 minutes later.

Atkins was convicted and put on death row. Smith also called his State Ethics 'hotline'. Again he was told his first obligation was to his client and it might harm Jones' interests by giving Atkins' attorneys the exculpatory evidence (Olive 2014: 377). Smith accepted this advice but wrestled with the knowledge: it bothered him. After 10 years, he wrote a letter to the Virginia Bar outlining what had happened and whether he could reveal what he knew (ibid). This time, he got a different answer – the Bar said 'Yes'. Atkins' sentence was 'commuted' to life imprisonment and the Virginia Supreme Court upheld this decision (*In re Commonwealth*).

D. Dale Coventry and Jamie Kunz

For over 25 years, Coventry and Kunz kept secret Andrew Wilson's confession to the murder of a security guard at a McDonald's restaurant in Chicago in January 1982. Wilson asked them to keep the secret until after his death. When the lawyers confronted Wilson, he 'kind of chuckled over the fact that someone else was charged with something he did'. But they agreed and in March 1982 swore an affidavit, signed by a witness and a notary public, and stored it away. Meanwhile in 1983, Alton Logan was sentenced to 25 years for this crime. As Kunz said: 'It hurts to know somebody is in prison all these years and is innocent.' In 2009, Logan was finally declared innocent.

E. Darrel Parker

In 1955, Nancy Parker was raped and murdered. After a 12-hour interrogation by John Reid, her husband Darrel confessed but immediately recanted. In 1956, he was convicted, based almost entirely on the confession. Wesley Peery had also been questioned and 20 years later was convicted of another murder. On death row, Peery told his lawyers about 13 murders he'd committed, including that of Nancy Parker, but told them to keep this confidential until he died – which they did … until 1988. After his lawyers revealed the confession, Parker was granted parole in 1991 and in 2012, Nebraska declared him innocent and paid $500,000 (National Registry of Exonerations, nd).

F. *Spaulding v Zimmerman*

Spaulding, a passenger in Ledermann's car, was injured when it collided with Zimmerman's car. Doctors concluded Spaulding's injuries had healed. However, the defendant's lawyer learned from his neurologist that Spaulding – a minor – had an aorta aneurysm, 'a serious matter' that might rupture and cause death (Cramton 2005; Joy 2004). The accident might have caused the aneurysm (Joy 2004: 3). None of Spaulding's experts detected the aneurysm and his lawyer didn't ask to see the neurologist's report. The neurologist, at the time, wasn't obliged to reveal the information, so the defence lawyer had to decide what to do. He kept quiet.

Since the aneurysm could be attributed to the accident, the case settled 'far below what the case would have been worth if the plaintiff's lawyer had been informed of the plaintiff's true condition' (Wendel 1999: 22). Spaulding's aneurysm was discovered two years later when examined as part of his military army reserve obligations. It was repaired after surgery, but he suffered permanent and severe speech loss possibly 'as a consequence of the delayed treatment of his aneurysm' (Cramton 2005: 201; Cramton and Knowles 1998: 127). Cramton called the case 'a ghostly metaphor for the silence of lawyers, judges and the organized bar on the moral issues presented by lawyer secrecy' (Cramton 2005: 200). Yet the trial court and the Minnesota Supreme Court stated the defence lawyers were correct to keep confidentiality, even in this extreme case where an innocent human life was at stake. As we saw, MR 1.6 then permitted disclosure only to prevent the client committing a crime – no matter how many 'Spauldings' could die.

G. Corporate Wrongdoing

Corporate wrongdoing is far from uncommon (Faulkner 2011; Markham 2006; Markkula Center nd), but most lawyers probably keep quiet, even in life and death scenarios.

i. Ford Pinto

Ford Motor Company developed the Pinto from 1967 under Lee Iacocca's direction. He wanted a car weighing under 2,000 lbs and $2,000 to compete with Japanese imports. His decision anticipated the 1973 oil crisis which persuaded many to buy smaller, more fuel-efficient cars. Ford put the fuel tank behind the rear axle, despite safety implications: vulnerable in rear-end collisions; only nine inches of 'crash space'; ornamental, not safety. bumper; no reinforcement in the rear structure (no cross- or side members); and several bolts protruded, threatening the tank in a collision.

An internal memorandum stated the tanks could be pierced when struck from behind at speeds as low as 21 mph, fuel would leak, and sparks would ignite it, followed by an explosion. At 40 mph, Pinto doors would jam, trapping passengers inside. The memo explained the tank's location. First: above rather than behind the rear axle, there'd be very small trunk/boot space; secondly: a cost-benefit analysis, the leak of which made the Pinto case (in)famous, showed a safer tank location cost between $5.08 and $11 per car (Luban 1988: 207); 12.5 million cars at $11 per car equalled $137 million. That would result in an estimated 180 fewer deaths, 180 fewer serious burns and 2,100 fewer cars wrecked. The less safe location would cost an estimated $200,000 per death, $67,000 per injury and $700 per vehicle, a total of $49.5 million. So, the tank's location saved Ford over $85 million.

In 1972, Lily Gray drove a new Pinto with her 13-year-old grandson Richard Grimshaw when it stalled in a freeway's middle lane and was struck by a car travelling at 30 mph upon impact. The rear-end fire killed Gray and left Grimshaw with disastrous injuries: burns on 80 per cent of his body; nose, left ear and much of his left hand lost; face scarred and burned beyond recognition; and 68 instances of surgery. At the 1978 trial, the jury, after eight hours, awarded the Gray family $560,000 for wrongful death and Grimshaw $2.5 million in compensation and $125 million in punitive damages. The trial judge reduced the punitive award to $3.5 million as a condition for denying a new trial; the Court of Appeals affirmed (*Grimshaw*). The Supreme Court denied a hearing.

Ford engineers and executives were aware of the design issues; one Ford executive said Ford lawyers 'definitely knew'. No lawyer went public on the dangers or, it seems, sought to get Pintos recalled, the design decision reversed or threaten to blow the whistle. As we saw, the MR on breaking confidentiality referred to a 'criminal act', but did Ford commit a crime? In 1978, after the *Grimshaw* case, Ford was prosecuted for reckless homicide on the basis of a 1977 statute. Ford's Pinto design pre-dated 1977 so the charge wasn't reckless design but reckless failure, post-1977, to repair or warn – a more difficult charge to sustain: a narrow issue and 50 mph collisions would rupture almost any car. The prosecution also failed to secure admission of Ford internal documents to build its case. Ford defended with significantly more effort than the *Grimshaw* case. In 1980, the jury found Ford not guilty – so there was no crime.

ii. General Motors

GM failed to notify regulators about ignition switch defects that led to several deaths (Basu 2014). The faulty switch could suddenly cut engine power and disable airbags. GM itself linked 13 deaths and 54 crashes to the defect, which vehicles had had for over 10 years (Vlasic 2014b). Why so long? A GM internal investigation attributed one reason to the role played by GM's legal department. It 'took actions to obscure the deadly flaw, both inside and outside the company' (ibid). GM lawyers 'even kept their knowledge of fatal accidents related to a defective ignition switch from GM's general counsel, Michael P. Millken' (ibid).

William Kemp had 'been orchestrating GM's legal strategy and in-house investigations'. He was one of four lawyers on the company's 'settlement review committee'. They agreed a $5 million settlement involving GM's chief switch engineer because it was a 'very poor trial candidate … it needs to be settled' (ibid). $5 million was the maximum amount that could be settled without involving Millken. This and several other settlements were confidential. Fears that information might come out led company lawyers to advise employees not to take notes in safety meetings and to audit emails that could be used as evidence against the company (ibid). The audits were described as 'information life-cycle management'. As the then Transportation Secretary Anthony R Foxx put it: 'Literally, silence can kill' (Vlasic 2014a).

II. For the Greater Good?

When should confidentiality 'costs' outweigh disclosure 'benefits', and who should decide – lawyers, ethics or legislature?

A. Lawyer Disobedience

Some lawyers decide on 'moral' grounds to break confidentiality.

i. Mecca v McClure

In Oregon in 1984, Christopher Mecca represented Robert A McClure, who was accused of killing Carol Jones. Her two children, Michael aged 14 and Tanya aged 10, were missing. McClure drew a map and told Mecca where the children were: remote, deserted and wooded areas, 60 miles apart. By then they'd been missing for eight days. Mecca 'felt in his own mind that the children were dead but, of course, I wasn't sure'. His conversations with McClure were neither simple nor straightforward. McClure originally denied killing anyone, saying he was 'framed'; he talked about his hallucinations and fantasies, and rambled, often bizarrely. In one conversation, McClure said 'Satan killed Carol Jones'; in another 'Jesus saved the kids'. Mecca wondered whether the children could be alive.

Mecca tried to reveal the information via a plea bargain. He told prosecutors 'I may have information that would be of interest to the State', referring to the missing children. The 'Buried Bodies' lawyers also offered information on the missing girls in exchange for prosecutors accepting an insanity plea. The DA (later judge) William Intemann rejected the bargain, describing the tactic as 'despicable' (WETA 1986). Mecca's attempt also failed. So, he got his secretary to telephone the police anonymously with the children's location. They were found; both had been shot dead. Mecca withdrew from the representation and the disclosure was revealed. At McClure's trial, the prosecution presented extensive evidence stemming from the discovery of the children's bodies and introduced testimony regarding the anonymous telephone call. This helped procure McCure's conviction and three consecutive life sentences with a 30-year minimum term. After losing his appeal against conviction, McClure appealed, claiming Mecca's disclosure violated his 6th Amendment right to effective assistance of counsel. The question was whether Mecca's disclosure of confidential information was ethical.

The confidentiality rule MR 1.6(b)(1) at the time stated: 'A lawyer may reveal such information to the extent the lawyer reasonably believes necessary to *prevent the client from committing a criminal act* that the lawyer believes is likely to result in imminent death or substantial bodily harm'. But how could Mecca 'prevent' McClure from committing a criminal act, as McClure was in police custody? However, a majority in the Ninth Circuit concluded he didn't break the rule because Mecca couldn't have *known* if the children were dead or alive. By disclosing the location, Mecca prevented an *earlier* criminal act – kidnapping – being transformed (escalated) into a later *more serious* one – murder. That triggered the ethical exception.

The dissenting judge – Ferguson – was outraged. Mecca had 'breached one of the *most sacred obligations* of the attorney-client relationship, the duty of confidentiality' (emphasis added), a duty embodied in the 6th Amendment right to counsel. Moreover, he added, Mecca could have got the facts either from the client – he never directly asked whether the children were alive or dead – or he or his private investigator could have gone to the locations, rather than relying on 'wishful thinking', before taking the 'extreme step' of breaching confidentiality. Ferguson's conclusion was powerful:

> It seems to me that the time has come for Mecca to *take responsibility* for the choice he made to breach his client's confidence and for a court, *this court*, to recognize that, whether or not Mecca did the 'right thing' does not diminish the fact that his doing so constituted an abdication of his professional responsibilities and rendered his performance as McClure's defense attorney deficient under the Sixth Amendment. Mecca's concern for the children is certainly understandable and laudable, however, it does not negate the infirmity of McClure's conviction. (Emphasis added)

This view has been endorsed by an Ethics Opinion (2002), which stated that the ethical Code does *not* permit disclosure of client's confidences and secrets based on the client's 'continuing crime' when the client has already completed conduct which satisfies all elements of the crime and the client has sought to engage the lawyer to defend the client against criminal charges relating to that conduct. Frank Armani, one of the 'Buried Bodies' lawyers, sums it up best. He justified looking for the bodies for three reasons: 'One, as defense counsel, I always feel I should know all the facts. But the main reason we searched was that the Petz girl might still have been alive … Third, we went to see/make sure what Garrow had said was true' (Lerman et al 2007).

ii. Nicola Gobbo

Gobbo, an Australian barrister who was 'top of her legal ethics class at university' (Maynard 2020), secretly provided police with over 1,000 intelligence reports on clients and their associates (Lagan 2020). 'Gang wars' between 1998 and 2010 had claimed as many as 40 lives (Maynard 2020) and it appears she sometimes warned police about crimes before they happened. Her information is thought to have helped convict 350 people (Lagan 2020). She claimed police threatened to blow the whistle and 'effectively feed [her] to the wolves' if she didn't continue. She told the Royal Commission into the Management of Police Informants:

> When … people you are either acting for or … to whom you have been introduced are being shot and murdered on a weekly basis, and you're being pre-warned about those things taking place, to not do anything when you have that knowledge is something that I morally had an issue with – and that … in part, is one explanation why I assisted the police. (Maynard 2020)

The High Court and the Victoria Supreme Court Appeals Court disagreed. Gobbo's 'actions in purporting to act as counsel for the Convicted Persons [seven clients who were convicted of serious offences] while covertly informing against them were fundamental and appalling breaches of [her] obligations as counsel to her clients and of [her] duties to the court' (*AB*). The Commission's conclusion (Royal Commission 2020: 17) 'whether Gobbo breached legal privilege' was damning:

> After a rigorous analysis of the evidence, including all relevant submissions, the Commission has concluded that the convictions or findings of guilt of 1,011 people may have been affected by Victoria Police's use of Ms Gobbo as a human source. This includes people who were deprived of the opportunity to be represented by an independent lawyer acting in their best interests, and those who may have been affected by Ms Gobbo's conflicts of interest and/or

tainted evidence arising from her conduct as a human source. It includes cases where she was acting as the person's lawyer, and cases where she was not; for example, where the person was a co-accused of one of her clients.

Placed under police protection, she was in hiding from her 'gangland clients'. She was struck off the Supreme Court's Roll of Legal Practitioners (ibid: 18).

iii. Stephen Chittenden

Shortly after qualifying as a solicitor, Chittenden represented 15-year-old Roy Brooks, who had been charged with the murder of 16-year-old Lynn Siddons in 1978. Roy was acquitted, but before and during the court case, evidence emerged that Roy's stepfather, Michael, was involved (Sears 2017). He was arrested but not prosecuted. In 1991, the Siddons family began a civil case. An MP asked Chittenden if he could help them. Chittenden released confidential papers to the Siddons' law firm. They revealed Roy had been put up by Michael to take part in the killing, was frightened of Michael, and Michael would cut out pictures of women from magazines and stab them with a knife. The Siddons family won and Mr Justice Rougier was 'in no reasonable doubt' Michael was the killer (ibid). The police then charged Michael and in 1996, helped by his client's information about his stepfather, Michael was sentenced to life imprisonment.

No one complained about Chittenden until 2016, when he admitted what he'd done to a local newspaper. He said he risked 'being struck off as a solicitor' and 'it could have lost me my career' – and it did. In 2017, the SRA declared 'Mr Chittenden admits that these actions … constituted conduct that is completely unacceptable on the part of a solicitor' and being struck off would 'properly reflect the gravity of his misconduct'. To avoid this, Chittenden agreed to have his name removed from the roll of solicitors. He stated: 'Of course I accept it is a serious matter that I breached client confidentiality, but I thought everyone understood my concerns were with a wider sense of justice' (ibid). Sadly for him, trying to prevent a miscarriage of justice is not an 'ethical' exception.

B. Ethical Exceptions

Many argue that ethical exceptions to confidentiality are too narrow, which was why the criminal element was removed. Disclosure is now permitted to 'prevent reasonably certain death or substantial bodily injury' (MR 1.6(b)(1)). MR 1.6(b)(2), (3) also permits disclosure to prevent clients committing a crime or fraud that's reasonably certain to result in substantial injury to someone's financial interests, or to prevent, mitigate or rectify such injury resulting from the client's crime or fraud if the client has used the lawyer's services to further the crime/fraud. Some American jurisdictions make no mention of 'using the lawyer's services'. Lawyers 'may', not 'must', so lawyers can choose whether or not to reveal.

If lawyers are asked to advise on 'past' criminal or fraudulent conduct but suspect the conduct will continue, 'the lawyer's responsibility is especially delicate' (MR 1.2, Comment [10]). A solicitor learnt of an allegation his client had been systematically defrauding the insurance company he ran in Louisiana. Upon investigation, the solicitor realised fraud may have occurred and he had unwittingly facilitated it. He sought court approval to disclose the information to the Louisiana liquidator. The client claimed he'd sought legal advice after the fraud had been committed, not on how to commit it. The court determined the solicitor had probably been consulted to guide and help the client cover up or stifle a fraud. Therefore, privilege didn't attach to the advice. The solicitor could seek to set aside privilege since that would amount to the solicitor aiding and abetting the client's fraudulently covering up the original fraud (*Finers*).

However, clients seeking guidance on how to commit crime or fraud doesn't automatically remove privilege and confidentiality – lawyers may persuade them not to go ahead. If persuaded, the communication remains confidential and privileged (*Bullivant*), perhaps even if they seek advice on the prospects of prosecution (*Butler*). If not persuaded, lawyers may not ethically assist clients and should withdraw, and may, in the US, find it 'necessary … to give notice of the fact of the withdrawal and to disaffirm any opinion, document, affirmation or the like' (MR 1.2, Comment [10]). This is an exception to the duty of confidentiality 'through the back door' (Wendel 2004: 240). It allows the lawyer to withdraw '"noisily", waving all kinds of red flags, ringing bells and blowing whistles' (ibid: 244).

Even if clients engage in crime/fraud, it's up to lawyers what to do. They may try to persuade clients to disclose the fraud or take corrective action. Failing that, they may feel compelled to reveal information. That's because by failing to warn potential victims, they and their law firm are at risk of civil liability. In 2000, Locke, Liddell and Sapp, a Texas law firm, was accused of having 'aided a client in defrauding investors' (Class Action Reporter 2000). It denied liability but settled for $22 million. The client, Russell Erxleben, ran a foreign currency trading company, Austin Forex International (AFI), that defrauded investors of $34 million in an alleged Ponzi scheme (ibid). Erxleben pleaded guilty in 1999 to federal conspiracy and securities-fraud charges. Locke may have had 'credible defenses' (ibid), but was accused of allowing AFI to sell unregistered securities, signing off on brochures and promotional materials that contained misrepresentations, and knowing about the company's growing losses months before state securities regulators began investigating.

Texas lawyers' malpractice insurance companies reported seeing several cases of lawyers being sued for failing to blow the whistle, but none where lawyers have been sued for blowing the whistle erroneously. In-house lawyers, economically tied to one client, may be fearful of whistleblowing and retaliatory discharge. It appears that while the 'gatekeeper role remains intact', the 'specter of liability' for corporate counsel in the US who negligently or knowingly fail as gatekeepers has 'dramatically decreased in recent years' (Steinberg 2020). There are, however, incentives to 'blow the whistle'.

EW ethical codes provide no exceptions to confidentiality, regardless of the consequences. SRA Guidance (2019c), however, accepts disclosure might be justified (before an event but never after): 'from a disciplinary point of view, the justification will be taken into account and is likely to mitigate against regulatory action by the SRA'. If solicitors believe clients intend to commit suicide or seriously self-harm, and they don't consent to disclosure, 'you may decide, to protect the client or another, to disclose that information without consent'. Where the harm involves 'children or vulnerable adults' and clients refuse to allow disclosure, but solicitors have reason to be concerned about the risk of future harm: 'You are not required by law to disclose this information. You must therefore consider whether the threat to the person's life or health is sufficiently serious to justify a breach of the duty of confidentiality.'

So, disclosure may be *both* prohibited *and* justified – talk about tragic choices! Note the language 'breach of the duty', not 'exception' to it. Surely this creates an incentive on solicitors to cite the absolute rule and not disclose – despite the consequences? This may be why some American States provide lawyers 'must' reveal information in certain circumstances. Virginia State Bar Rule 1.6(c) declares:

> A lawyer shall promptly reveal (1) the intention of a client, as stated by the client, to commit a crime reasonably certain to result in death or substantial bodily harm to another or substantial injury to the financial interests or property of another and the information necessary to prevent the crime.

The Rule requires lawyers, where feasible, to 'advise the client of the possible legal consequences of the action, urge the client not to commit the crime, and advise the client that the attorney must reveal the client's criminal intention unless thereupon abandoned'. If the client doesn't abandon it, lawyers must reveal it. Florida State Bar Rule 4-1.6(b) goes further: 'When Lawyer Must Reveal Information. A lawyer must reveal confidential information to the extent the lawyer reasonably believes necessary: (1) to prevent a client from committing a crime; or (2) to prevent a death or substantial bodily harm to another.' Arguably, these rules remain underinclusive ('crime'), but Florida's is overinclusive ('any crime'). No wonder there's a growing trend for legislatures to set out mandatory disclosure requirements in a variety of contexts.

C. Legislative Override

i. EW

A suspicious activity regime (SAR) for money laundering and terrorist financing has been created because the

> intelligence that law enforcement receives from SARs is vital to tackling crime and to gain an insight into emerging and current threats to the UK. Legal practices have a key role in providing quality intelligence … information that can prevent and disrupt criminal activities. (LSAG 2023: 136)

Where lawyers know or suspect clients are involved in money laundering or terrorist financing, their information must be disclosed to the UK Financial Intelligence Unit, which sits within the NCA.

Applying these laws is technical and complex, which is why the LSAG published a 217-page guidance which courts must consider 'in assessing whether a person committed an offence or took all reasonable steps and exercised all due diligence to avoid committing the offence' (2023: 14). An offence is committed when lawyers know or suspect, or have reasonable grounds for knowledge or suspicion that a person has engaged in money laundering. Disclosure should be made 'as soon as reasonably practicable' via the SAR Portal.

The threshold for suspicion is low. A suspicion is reportable if lawyers think there's a more than fanciful possibility that the relevant facts exist, a 'vague feeling of unease would not suffice' (*R v Da Silva*). Solicitors may have 'reasonable excuse' not to report: the information's in the public domain; the suspicion's based on privileged information and the crime-fraud exception doesn't apply; or the suspected offending takes place entirely outside the UK and there is no UK connection to the suspected criminal property. Privilege isn't breached by lawyers making suspicious activity reports to their 'nominated officers' – who are responsible for being aware of and reporting suspicious activities – or seeking advice as to whether a report should be made. However, the nominated officer cannot include privileged information (and the Law Society (2020) reminds solicitors they need strong prima facie evidence they're being involved in a criminal offence for the crime-fraud exemption to apply (*O'Rourke*)). Barristers are less likely to be suspicious as they don't handle client money, though the Bar Council (2024) offered advice on this.

So, why the conundrum? The LSAG guidance explains: 'every situation is different and … legal practitioners and practices themselves are best placed to understand the risks and deal with them proportionately' (LSAG 2023: 16). There's a 'tension between the professional duties of the lawyer' (ibid: 153) – the 'all-encompassing duties of client confidentiality and the duty to protect LPP' (ibid: 163) – and the legal requirements to disclose. The 'burden of making the decision falls on the lawyer … If the lawyer discloses, without good reason, there is a breach of client confidentiality and LPP … Conversely, a failure to disclose may result in criminal sanction' (ibid). Maximum sentences range from two years' imprisonment for breach of the Regulations to 14 years for breach of the substantive offences. However, making a SAR will be a defence. It's also an offence to tip off the person being reported. These obligations override the duty of confidentiality (but not privilege). That said, lawyers may disclose to clients 'for the purpose of dissuading them from engaging in criminal conduct' (ibid: 139, 191, 192). Also, if they get it right, they won't be in breach of their duty of confidentiality (ibid: 169).

In 2017, the SDT fined three partners of Clyde & Co £10,000 each and the firm £50,000 for accounting failures and breach of AML rules. In 2024, it fined a former partner £11,900 and the firm £500,000 for failing to carry out due diligence over a period of four years on a shipping company client incorporated in Liberia (Hyde and Castro 2024).

ii. The US

Several State statutes impact the duty of confidentiality. 'Most common' are those relating to child abuse (Bernabe 2017: 25). Some make disclosure mandatory if attorneys suspect abuse. To avoid legislative intervention, the ABA in 2023 amended MR 1.16 to combat money laundering and terrorist financing (though the amendment affects all scenarios). Lawyers must 'inquire into and assess the facts and circumstances of each representation' to determine whether they may accept or continue the representation. However, they may still not break confidentiality if they discover information. The Corporate Transparency Act, in effect from 2024, makes it harder to benefit from financial crimes via shell companies or other ownership structures. Information about beneficial ownership must be reported by lawyers and others to a database that's accessible to law enforcement agencies.

6

The Lecture

The trouble with Law is Lawyers.

— Clarence Darrow (attributed)

A lawyer should provide clients with 'an informed understanding of their legal rights and obligations and explains their practical implications' (MR Preamble: [2]). Clients should have sufficient information to participate intelligently in decisions concerning the objectives of representation (MR 1.4, Comment [5]). So, lawyers must 'explain a matter to the extent reasonably necessary to permit the client to make informed decisions regarding the representation' (MR 1.4(b)).

However, 'Knowledge of the law … is two-edged' – it can be used 'to follow the law or to avoid it' (Pepper 1995: 1547). While MR 1.2(d) states

> a lawyer may discuss the legal consequences of any proposed course of conduct with a client and may counsel or assist a client to make a good faith effort to determine the validity, scope, meaning or application of the law,

MR 1.2 Comment [10] prohibits 'a lawyer from knowingly counselling or assisting a client to commit a crime or fraud' or 'suggesting how the wrongdoing might be concealed'. Comment [9] provides more guidance. The prohibition

> does *not* preclude a lawyer from giving an honest opinion about the actual consequences that appear likely to result from a client's conduct. Nor does the fact that a client uses advice in a course of action that is criminal or fraudulent of itself make a lawyer party to the course of conduct. *There is a critical distinction between presenting an analysis of legal aspects of questionable conduct and recommending the means by which a crime or fraud might be committed with impunity.* (Emphasis added)

So what should a lawyer do with Lord Chief Justice Goddard's client? Goddard asked the client: 'Now, my man, what is your story?' The client replied firmly: 'That's rather up to you guvnor' (Simpson 1988: 149). The ABA, in its original 1971 section of the 'The Defense Function' on 'Interviewing the Client', states that 'the lawyer should seek to determine all the relevant facts known to the accused'. However: 'In so doing, the lawyer should probe for all legally relevant information without seeking to influence the direction of the client's responses' (ABA 1971: 3.2). The most recent version puts it differently. Counsel 'may seek information from the client as to the facts', discuss and 'determine in depth the client's view of the facts', and 'the range of potential outcomes and alternatives' (ABA 2017: Standard 4-3.3(a), (c) (i), (vi)). It concludes: 'When asking the client for information and discussing possible options and strategies with the client, defense counsel should not seek to induce the client to make factual responses that are not true' (ibid: 4-3.3(4)).

The rules raise – but don't resolve – the challenge lawyers face: how to discuss the legal consequences of a proposed course of conduct *without* counselling or assisting clients in criminal or fraudulent conduct? It's improper for lawyers to construct versions of events for clients that would amount to perjury (Blake and Ashworth 2004: 176), but drawing the line between permissible and impermissible advice may be difficult. The classic illustration is the film *Anatomy of a Murder*.

I. *Anatomy of a Murder*

This film (Columbia Pictures, 1959) was based on a book by 'Traver' (1958), the pseudonym of Michigan Supreme Court judge, John D Voelker. The story was semi-autobiographical: a 1952 case in which Voelker was a defence attorney. Army Officer Lieutenant Frederick Manion admitted shooting and killing Barney Quill, one hour after Quill allegedly raped Manion's second wife Laura. Manion is jealous and violent; his first wife divorced him claiming cruelty. Laura is constantly flirting with men – including, eventually, Paul Biegler – so there was plenty of factual ambiguity.

Biegler is a defence attorney. He'd been a DA, got 'kicked out' and now has his own law practice, but with little work – and money – coming in. In his police cell, Manion tells Biegler he has the 'unwritten law' on his side – a husband has a right to kill his wife's rapist. Biegler tells Manion this 'law' is a myth. He asks Manion how much time elapsed from learning of the alleged rape before shooting Quill. Manion says 'about one hour'. Biegler is visibly disappointed by the answer and is unsure whether or not to take Manion's case. He concludes the interview knowing that 'a few wrong answers to a few right questions' could mean first degree murder because he would be 'legally defenceless'. Biegler then meets his associate McCarthy – I have italicised and under-lined the key words/phrases:

> **McCarthy**: Did you give the Lieutenant the well-known *lecture*?
>
> **Biegler**: Well, if you mean *did I coach him into a phony story*, no.
>
> **McCarthy**: Maybe you're *too pure* for him. Too pure for the *natural impurities of the law*. Could be that you owe the Lieutenant a *chance to find a defense*. Could also be that you might *guide him a little, show him the way and let him decide if he wants to take it …*
>
> **Biegler**: … I'm not the lawyer for this boy. He's insolent, hostile.
>
> **McCarthy**: You don't have to love him, just defend him.

Biegler returns to the cell and gives Manion 'The Lecture':

> **Biegler**: Now, Lieutenant there are four ways I could defend murder: number one, it wasn't murder – suicide or accidental; number two, you didn't do it; number three, you were legally justified, like the protection of your home or self-defense; number four, the killing was excusable.
>
> **Manion**: *Where do I fit* into this rosy picture?
>
> **Biegler**: I'll tell you where *you don't fit in. You don't fit in any of the first three.*
>
> **Manion**: But why? Why wouldn't I be legally justified in killing a man who raped my wife?

Biegler: Time element. Now, if you'd caught him in the act, the shooting might have been justified. But you didn't catch him in the act. And you had time to bring in the police. You didn't do that either. *You're guilty of murder. Premeditated and with vengeance. That's first degree murder in any court of law.*

Manion: Are you telling me to plead guilty?

Biegler: When I advise you to cop-out, you'll know.

Manion: Cop-out?

Biegler: That's plead guilty and ask for mercy.

Manion: Well, if you're not telling me to cop out, *what are you telling me to do?*

Biegler: *I'm not telling you to do anything. I just want you to understand the* <u>letter of the law</u>.

Manion: Go on.

Biegler: Go on with what?

Manion: Whatever it is you're getting at.

Biegler: You're very bright Lieutenant. Now, *let's see how really bright you can be.*

Manion: Well, I'm working at it.

Biegler: All right. Now because your wife was raped, you'll have favorable atmosphere in the courtroom. The sympathy will be with you, if all the facts are true. *What you need is a legal peg* so that the jury can hang up their sympathy on your behalf. Do you follow me?

Manion: Uh-huh.

Biegler: What's your *legal excuse* Lieutenant? What's your legal excuse for killing Barney Quill?

Manion: Not justification, huh?

Biegler: Not justification.

Manion: Excuse. Just excuse. Well, *what excuses are there?*

Biegler: How should I know? You're the one that plugged Quill.

Manion: I must have been mad.

Biegler: How's that?

Manion: I said *I must have been mad.*

Biegler: Well, *bad temper's no excuse.*

Manion: I mean I must have been crazy. *Am I getting warmer? Am I getting warmer?*

Biegler: Well, I'll tell you that after I talk to your wife. In the meantime, *see if you can remember just how crazy you were.*

Biegler returns to his office:

McCarthy: You're gonna take the case, huh?

Biegler: Well, I don't know. That *depends on what Manion has to tell me tomorrow.* He's thinking things out.

McCarthy: Oh. Well, *that's more like it.*

Biegler visits Manion the next day:

Manion: I tried remembering; there was still some pieces missing. I remember going to Quill's bar with a gun and remember Quill's face behind the bar. But I don't remember anything else, not even going home.

Biegler: But don't you remember firing the gun? That's five shots. That's a lot of noise to forget.

Manion: Yeah. I remember five shots, but *they don't seem to be connected with me*. They seem far away, *like somebody else was doing the shooting*.

Biegler: Lieutenant Manion, I'll take your case.

Manion: Thank you Mr Biegler.

A. Analysis

Was the 'lecture' ethical? Note, first, how Manion's original response to the murder allegation was 'the unwritten law': the right to kill his wife's rapist. Then, note how Biegler sets out the only possible defence – the killing was excusable because of temporary insanity. When Manion offers one legal excuse – he must have been mad – Biegler rejects it. Manion offers another – he must have been crazy and asks: 'Am I getting warmer?' Eventually, Manion sets out a defence Biegler deems sufficient to take the case. Biegler later finds an Army psychiatrist who diagnoses 'dissociative disorder' and 'irresistible impulse', a defence available when Traver was in practice.

I've asked hundreds of law students whether 'The Lecture' and the dialogue were ethical. Was Biegler waiting to see if Manion would come up with a lie – he was 'crazy' – or doing what a lawyer should do – mount a defence of irresistible impulse? Some believe 'communicating "the law" is always acceptable, and by itself not to be considered suggestion or otherwise' (Hazard Jr and Hodes 2008: 37-6–37-8). But they acknowledge that 'educating the client about the law may function as the equivalent of suggesting or assisting in its violation' (ibid: 5-37–5-38). If context matters, 'The Lecture' is clearly unethical. Biegler is writing the defence for the client. He will *not* take the case on what Manion began with, but will if he understands what defence has the only chance of success. Biegler was saying to Manion: given your facts, you have no defence but if you acted in a blind rage, that would be a defence. When Manion asks 'Am I getting warmer?', Biegler tells him 'see if you can remember just how crazy you were'.

I show 'The Lecture' a second time asking students to examine Biegler's face – which changes as Manion slowly understands – and absorbs – what's being proposed. Biegler ends smiling: 'I'll take your case'. Biegler was hoping knowledge of the law would tempt Manion to colour his version of the facts. I emphasise Biegler's key words and phrases:

- I'm not telling you to do anything, I just want you to understand the *letter of the law.*
- You're very bright Lieutenant. Now, *let's see how really bright you can be.*
- What you need is a *legal peg* so that the jury can hang up their sympathy on your behalf, *do you follow me?*
- What's your *legal excuse* for killing Barney Quill?
- After Manion asks '*Am I getting warmer?*', Biegler says: *see if you can remember just how crazy you were.*

The insanity defence is 'the best, if not the only, legal defense the man had' (Traver 1958: 35). When Manion asks about this, Biegler says: 'insanity, where proven, is a complete defense to murder. It does not legally justify the killing, like self defense, but rather excuses it'. Manion replies: 'Maybe I was insane ... when I shot Barney Quill.' Traver's book has more:

> The Lecture is an ancient device that lawyers use to coach their clients so that the client won't quite know he has been coached and his lawyer can still preserve the face-saving illusion that he hasn't done any coaching. For coaching clients, like robbing them, is frowned upon, it is downright unethical and bad, very bad. Hence the Lecture, an artful device as old as the law itself, and one used constantly by some of the nicest and most ethical lawyers in the land. 'Who me? I didn't tell him what to say', the lawyer can later comfort himself. 'I merely explained the law, see.' It is good practice to scowl and shrug and add virtuously: 'that's my duty isn't it?' (ibid: 35)

Does the 'Lecture' in *Anatomy* violate MR 3.4(b), which prohibits a lawyer from coun- selling or assisting a witness to testify falsely (Salmi 1999; Tanford 2002)? The practice of explaining the law before hearing the client or witness's version of events has been approved by some US courts (*State v McCormick*) and Bar Association ethics commit- tees (Bar Association of Nassau County Committee on Professional Ethics Opinion 94-6, 1994), as long as the lawyer in good faith doesn't believe they're participating in the creation of false evidence. Courts have held it not improper not only to discuss facts with clients before asking the client what they recalled (*Hamdi*), but to try and persuade a witness that their recollection is faulty (*RTC*). This approach has somewhat surprising implications if we vary the *Anatomy* scenario.

B. The Perfect Murder?

Suppose Manion found Quill raping – or committing adultery with – his wife, then immediately telephoned Biegler asking for legal analysis of his proposed question- able conduct – killing! 'The Lecture' reveals there are *two* possible defences: 'excuse' as before via temporary insanity, but also justification – the so-called 'crime passionelle' – but only if he shoots Barney Quill immediately. Texas law, until 1973, confirmed: 'homicide is justifiable when committed by the husband upon one taken in the act of adultery with the wife'. To the argument that giving this advice constitutes assisting a client in criminal conduct, the answer is simple – there is no crime! Indeed, Manion was acquitted (as was Voelker's client in 1952 on identical grounds – 'irresistible impulse' and insanity. A day or two later, an expert declared Voelker's client to be sane). The perfect 'murder' is not murder!

There are four interrelated ways of giving 'The Lecture': legal advice; answering questions; law enforcement advice; and evidence advice – coaching. We know *where* the ethical line should be drawn – the rules do that – but, critically, *how do we identify* which side of the line the advice falls?

II. Legal Advice

Unethical advice 'turns the lawyer into an accomplice of sorts, helping to make the client's socially harmful conduct more effective and harder to detect' (Yablon 2019).

In 2011, Denise N Slavin, an American immigration judge and Vice President of the National Association of Immigration Judges, called fraud in immigration asylum cases 'a huge issue and a major problem' (Dolnick 2011). To qualify for asylum, applicants had to show a well-founded fear of persecution on account of race, religion, nationality, political opinion or membership of a particular social group – including gay people or abused women. Judges would err on the side of caution given the consequences of a mistake, which would be far less disastrous than denying a genuine claim.

A. James Christo

Ninety per cent of Manhattan immigration attorney Christo's practice consisted of immigration work and many clients were ethnic Albanians, as was his wife Remila. His firm assisted Albanians seeking political asylum (FBI 2009). In 2004, he helped a 'client' – an undercover FBI agent posing as an Albanian immigrant – to create and document a fake story of persecution in support of an asylum application. Christo gave this 'lecture': 'In order to obtain asylum, you must demonstrate political problems and provide those examples of persecution in the application' (*In re James D Christo*). He provided examples. Although the 'lecture' accurately reflected the legal requirements, the FBI agent specifically *denied* suffering persecution, yet Christo went on to say: 'Maybe you had to leave [Albania] because someone threatened to kill you, because of something your father did to somebody else, or something to do with the land. You understand? That can be a way to get asylum' (Dolnick 2011). In 2009, Christo and Remila were found guilty of conspiracy to commit immigration fraud and sentenced to five years' probation. Despite it being a 'serious crime', Christo was only suspended from practice for the same five-year probation period.

B. Syed Naqvi

According to a former immigration judge, James Hanratty (2020),

> when I was sitting, a few lawyers had coached appellants to lie about their age, to say they were gay, to engage in sham marriages and, in asylum cases, to say they had come from, say, Afghanistan when in reality they had come over the border from Pakistan. (Ellery and Ames 2020)

An undercover reporter was told by Naqvi ways to circumvent immigration procedures and how to pass off fake marriages as genuine. The ITV programme in 2015 was called *Exposure UK: The Sham Marriage Racket*. The SDT struck off Naqvi in 2019, stating it

> did not consider there was anything objectionable in itself in advising the client on the type of questions the Home Office may ask, but doing so when the client had discussed paying to 'get the girl' and asked about 'the risk of getting caught' made it so' (*Naqvi*).

Several other solicitors have been struck off over misconduct in immigration cases. In 2021–22, seven lawyers were convicted of assisting unlawful immigration; in 2023, the SRA suspended three law firms caught offering to submit false asylum claims

(Dathan 2023). In 2024, a Church of England priest revealed he'd been repeatedly asked by immigration lawyers to make up evidence saying asylum claimants had converted to Christianity (Dathan 2024).

III. Answering Questions

But if clients directly ask legal questions, shouldn't lawyers answer? An alleged rapist asks: 'will it go bad for me if I say I had a knife?' – 'yes'. Then he asks, 'will it go worse for me if I say I held it to her neck?' – 'your case is getting weaker'. Answers to these questions may 'teach' clients what's best to say. Lawyers are again in danger of 'writing the defence' for clients.

A. Eileen Hongisto

In 2007, Vermont police obtained a warrant, approved by judge Katherine Hayes, to allow undercover detective Mark Carignan to attempt a 'sting' on attorney Hongisto, who was suspected of obstruction of justice (*Brattleboro Reformer* 2007). Hongisto represented Terry E Russ in a domestic violence assault case. Police recorded phone calls between Russ, his mother and his girlfriend. They talked about comments allegedly made by Hongisto to Russ to the effect that the State would drop its case if witnesses failed to come to court. Russ, apparently, was attempting to discourage the alleged victim from testifying. He plea bargained and admitted guilt on a variety of charges, including obstruction of justice.[1]

The sting 'failed'. Carignan, saying he wanted to help Russ, asked Hongisto whether he should try to avoid police efforts to serve him a subpoena or whether, if served, he should fail to show up in court. Advising the 'witness' to take those steps would be an obstruction of justice. In fact, Hongisto told Carignan she wasn't his lawyer and that if he got a subpoena, he would need to go to court.

What should lawyers tell clients? In a domestic violence scenario, David Sleigh, representing Hongisto, 'claimed there is nothing wrong with telling your client if the witness don't show up, you win' (*Times Argus* 2007). He said it was a simple statement of fact: 'This hits at the *absolute core* of the defense function. If you can't tell your client about the state's burden of proof, your ability to do your job is not just chilled, it's frozen' (*Brattleboro Reformer* 2007, emphasis added). Local lawyer David Silver posed the question: 'Your client asks you, "What will happen if the complainant does not testify at trial?" Must you respond, "I cannot answer that question"?' (ibid).

Perhaps ethical lawyers should ask questions *before* answering or answer but then add 'do not contact them yourself, do not obstruct justice, do not get your friends to put the frighteners on her – you will be asked lots of questions and may face another

---

[1] In 2014, Russ was sentenced to two and half to five years for stealing guns from a house; in 2019, he was arrested for an alleged violation of an abuse prevention order according to the Brattleboro Police Department.

charge if a key witness, known to be about to give evidence, does not appear'. If clients say to lawyers 'maybe she won't turn up', is that something the lawyer should pursue? It could be a `jokey remark` – 'maybe we'll get lucky'. But if lawyers ask why and clients say they'll 'send a friend out to warn her off' – 'put the frighteners on her' – that might put lawyers in a position where not only can they withdraw from representation, but they can also break confidentiality to prevent bodily harm. This example illustrates vividly the 'critical distinction between presenting an analysis of legal aspects of questionable conduct and recommending the means by which a crime or fraud might be committed with impunity' (MR 1.2(d), Comment [9]).

So what are possible responses to suspicious questions like: 'we'll win if she doesn't show up right?' Lawyers could avoid answering and plead ignorance; answer 'yes'; answer 'yes' with a wink; ask what they have in mind; warn clients, emphasising they don't want to be surprised when further allegations are made; warn clients they might break confidentiality. If an inevitable witness didn't show up, questions would be asked and it could make their situation worse.

How should lawyers respond to: 'What are the legal consequences of having child pornography images on my computer?' 'It's a serious crime'. 'So, what should I do with the images?' Not only may lawyers answer, but they may also, assuming there's no current proceeding, advise clients to destroy them. Gillers (2012) believes the advice remains confidential and if clients are prosecuted for destroying the images, lawyers could be called as witnesses to confirm the clients acted on legal advice, in 'good faith' and without criminal intent. This is justified because clients should be encouraged to seek legal advice, confident of confidentiality. Lawyers can then counsel compliance with the law. The opportunity to turn people away from crime should be encouraged. But this does depend on the choices lawyers make. Paradoxically, law-abiding clients seeking legal advice may end up with incentives *not* to comply.

IV. Law Enforcement Advice

Law enforcement is a dynamic process with many challenges. Lawyers may be experts in how enforcement plays out in particular contexts. They can make effective enforcement difficult. In 2014, 372 Fortune 500 companies had 7,827 subsidiaries in tax haven countries (Norris 2014). Suppose clients ask: 'What's the speed limit?' Lawyers could answer with a number and quote West Mercia Chief Constable Anthony Bangham: drivers should face penalties for going just 1 mph over the limit (Freeman 2018). But should lawyers answer the question: 'How fast can I go?' If lawyers know police don't stop or prosecute drivers who exceed the speed limit slightly, should they tell clients about the 'outcry' that followed Bangham's comment, that advocating the strictest application of the law was 'not, perhaps, the wisest' (ibid)? If police are known not to arrest marijuana smokers – a crime – unless convinced they're dealing, might lawyers be facilitating criminal conduct? Questions and answers about Sunday trading laws might be: 'what is the law?' – 'don't trade'; 'is it enforced?' – 'rarely'; 'what's the fine?' – '£25'.

A. Weak Enforcement

i. Stephen Pepper

Pepper gave the example of polluted water discharge from a rural plant. A client asking about the law is told the EPA limit is 0.05 grams of ammonia per litre of effluent. Should the lawyer then inform the client, correctly, that inspection in rural areas is rare; enforcement officials invariably issue a warning for a first (discovered) offence – giving a 'second chance' to comply; and violations up to 0.075 grams per litre or less are ignored (Pepper 1986: 628). It might turn out that: 'Access to an amoral, "legal realist" lawyer leads to violation of the law.' The client has an incentive, in the interests of the company and its shareholders, *not* to comply with the law and discharge up to 0.075 grams – or even more. The lawyer may be aware that removing ammonia is an expensive process; fines are relatively small; the budget of the company is stretched; and so on.

ii. Erin Brockovich

Pepper's fictional example is not unlike events in Hinkley, in California's Mojave Desert, made famous by Brockovich. Between 1952 and 1966 Hinkley groundwater was turned toxic by a carcinogen used to prevent rust in the cooling tower at the natural gas compression station nearby. The run-off from towers ended up in unlined holding pools. Toxic chemicals leached from pools into the town's drinking water. Brockovich brought a class action suit, and Pacific Gas & Electricity (PGE) was ordered to contain the toxic plume to prevent it spreading into the town's second and deeper aquifer. Despite the order, the second aquifer reported having high levels of carcinogen, and the plume was 208 miles long and 1.5 miles wide and spreading at one foot per day. Hinkley became a ghost town. In 1993, Brockovich won $333 million in a settlement from PGE.

iii. The UK

Water companies pollute rivers and beaches. In 2021, Southern Water was fined £90 million. It admitted 6,971 illegal spills of raw sewage between 2010 and 2015, and a cover-up. The judge said the company 'flagrantly disregarded the law' (Ball 2021). Many companies were repeat offenders. Thames Water has been fined over 20 times for pollution spillages, including £20 million in 2017 and £3.3 million in 2023. Judge Francis Sheridan said: 'It should not be cheaper to offend than to take appropriate action' (*BBC News* 2017). Judge Christine Laing KC said the company had shown a 'deliberate attempt' to mislead the Environment Agency (*BBC News* 2023).

iv. Fracking

Hydraulic fracturing is a method of drilling for natural gas by injecting huge amounts of water, mixed with sand and chemicals, at high pressure to break up rock formations and release gas. The fracking industry expanded rapidly, especially in the US: Pennsylvania was called the 'Saudi Arabia of natural gas'. It is, however,

> linked to higher levels of exposure to toxic air pollutants and poor water quality … Numerous studies have suggested elevated rates of congenital heart defects, childhood leukaemia, asthma, and premature deaths in neighbourhoods close to fracking sites. (Lakhani and Milman 2022)

Fracking uses vast quantities of water, raising concerns about endangering aquifers as well as how the tons of wastewater, often with corrosive salts, carcinogens and radioactive elements from underground, are disposed of. In 2022, a doctors' group revealed the use of PFAs – known as forever chemicals because they take centuries to break down, accumulate in humans and are linked to serious health conditions – in over 12,000 wells. The industry had 'hidden the use … by claiming them as trade secrets' (ibid).

So, what about law enforcement? In 2012, a review of scientific and engineering advice was that 'the health, safety and environmental risks … [of fracking] … can be managed effectively in the UK as long as operational best practices are implemented and enforced through regulation' (Royal Society 2012). It reported 'widespread concern in the USA about the environmental impact … One cause for concern has been improper operational practices' (ibid). In the past, State and federal regulators were allowing the sewage plants to not test for radioactivity, and drinking water plants to test only once every six to nine years. In 2008, local officials advised people in Pittsburgh to drink bottled water, because waste released during a drought overwhelmed the Monongahela River. In Texas, which had 93,000 natural gas wells, a hospital system where some of the heaviest drilling occurred reported a 25 per cent asthma rate for young children, more than three times the state average of 7 per cent. In Pennsylvania, there were 31 inspectors for 125,000 oils and gas wells. One inspector said: 'If we're too hard on them, the companies might just stop reporting their mistakes.' Inspectors don't perform unannounced inspections for spills or accidents; instead, gas producers 'police themselves'. From October 2008 to October 2010, regulators were more than twice as likely to issue a written warning as to levy a fine. Fifteen companies were fined an average of $44,000 each – less than half what some companies earned in a day, and a tiny fraction of the $2 million plus some of them paid to haul and treat waste. Governor Tom Corbett, who took political donations from the gas industry, said industry regulation had been 'too aggressive'. In 2020, the 43rd Statewide Grand Jury found 'repeated and systematic violation of Pennsylvania environmental law' and Pennsylvania had failed to protect citizens during the fracking boom.

B. Disobeying 'Law'

Pepper's conclusion is that unless lawyers receive strong moral guidance from somewhere, clients will be under no pressure to obey the law. They may even feel bound to disobey – shareholder profit, competition, career and so on. Indeed, it becomes economically 'rational' to break the law (Shavell 1988). Lawyers may reason: is disobeying the law so bad when it's not enforced or the sanctions minimal? In any case, 'law' is not monotypic. Some crimes are 'minor' – smoking marijuana at home, for example. Others are 'stupid' (O'Mara (2000) – it being illegal to kiss in front of a church in Boston, Massachusetts; naming your pig Napoleon in France; throwing snowballs in Oklahoma City; lending a vacuum cleaner to your next-door neighbour in Denver, Colorado. Many are ignored: adultery is a felony in Michigan and several other states. As for the law requiring the reporting of dead bodies, it didn't override the ethical duty of confidentiality in the 'Buried Bodies' case.

Should advice on criminal law enforcement be different from regulatory law enforcement? It's a fine distinction and sometimes they overlap (Law Commission 2010). Canada's Supreme Court explained: 'criminal offences are usually designed to condemn and punish past, inherently wrongful conduct, regulatory measures are generally directed to the prevention of future harm through the enforcement of minimum standards of conduct and care'. There are fundamental differences between the criminal justice system and regulatory regimes (*R v Wholesale*). Should lawyers advise clients there's a 'right' to break 'civil law – a tort or breach of contract – but a potential 'duty' to remedy the breach?

V. Coaching: A Dark Little Secret

Effective witness preparation 'is perhaps the single most important component of successful trial advocacy' (Hays and Tulle 2000: 1). It's 'unethical to fail to prepare a witness, and it is cruel to subject anyone to cross-examination without preparation. The unrehearsed witness can deal a lethal blow to an otherwise winnable case' (Berg 1987: 14). Hodes (1999: 1350) agrees: failure to engage in witness preparation would be 'unethical and unprofessional, bordering on legal malpractice to boot'. On the other hand, some believe the way lawyers prepare witnesses 'more than almost anything else, gives trial lawyers their reputations as purveyors of falsehoods' (Luban 1988: 96).

In the old days, 'horse-shedding the witness' referred to attorneys who lingered in horse carriage sheds near courthouses to rehearse their witnesses. But today, one American lawyer asked: 'who among us has not warned the client, "Before you tell me your side of the story, let me tell you what the law is in this area", or "if you say that, you'll lose"' (Berg 1987: 13)? How should lawyers advise on how to present evidence?

Lawyers typically advise clients to 'give answers that will not be unresponsive, but that also won't open up areas of inquiry' (Sarat 2003:149). The effect of this is to reinforce

> adversarialism – the truth, but not the whole truth until and unless asked. This is, of course, the lawyer's skill, namely to know what has to be said to be responsive, and, at the same time, to say that and nothing more. (ibid)

According to Applegate (1989: 279): 'American litigators regularly use witness preparation, and virtually all would, upon reflection, consider it a fundamental duty of representation, and a basic element of effective advocacy.' The obligation arises from duties of competence and zealousness (ibid: 289), but is also the profession's 'dark little secret' (ibid: 309).

A. Coaching Rules

Barristers must 'not encourage a witness to give evidence which is misleading or untruthful; you must not rehearse, practise with or coach a witness in respect of their evidence' (BSB 2024: rC9.3, .4). They shouldn't 'devise facts which would assist in advancing a lay client's case' (Boon 2014: 318), nor should they draft documents not supported by the client or their instructions (BSB 2024: rC9.2). Solicitors similarly must not 'construct facts supporting your client's case' (SRA 2013, Indicative Behaviour 5.7) or 'seek to influence the substance of evidence, including generating false evidence or persuading witnesses to change their evidence' (SRA 2023a: 2.2). Witness statements – presented as evidence in court – declare:

> This statement is true to the best of my knowledge and belief and I make it knowing that, if tendered in evidence, I shall be liable to prosecution if I have wilfully stated in it anything which I know to be false or do not believe to be true. (Criminal Justice Act 1967, s 9)

The Court of Appeal explained the rule against coaching:

> The witness should give his or her own evidence, so far as practicable uninfluenced by what anyone else has said, whether in formal discussions or informal conversations. The rule reduces, indeed hopefully avoids any possibility, that one witness may tailor his evidence in the light of what anyone else said, and equally, avoids any unfounded perception that he may have done so. These risks are inherent in witness training. An honest witness may alter the emphasis of his evidence to accommodate what he thinks may be a different, more accurate, or simply better remembered perception of events. A dishonest witness will very rapidly calculate how his testimony might be 'improved' ... the risk that training or coaching may adversely affect the accuracy of the evidence of the individual witness is constant. So we repeat, witness training for criminal trials is prohibited. (*R v Momodou*: 61)

The Court distinguished between training/coaching and 'familiarisation' – the 'sensible preparation of the experience of giving evidence, which assists the witness to give of his or her best at the forthcoming trial'. Familiarisation is permissible: the 'evidence remains the witness's own uncontaminated evidence' (ibid: 62).

American lawyers can suggest a choice of words (Restatement of the Law Third 2000: §116, Comment (b)). However, MR 3.4(b) states 'a lawyer must not counsel or assist a witness to testify falsely'. It's also professional misconduct for a lawyer to 'engage in conduct involving dishonesty, fraud, deceit or misrepresentation' or is 'prejudicial to the administration of justice' (MR 8.4(c), (d)). MR 3.4, Comment [1] states: 'fair competition in the adversary system is secured by prohibitions against ... improperly coaching witnesses'.

B. Guidance

However, lawyers have freedom to decide what is improper. That's because lawyer–client communications are private, privileged and confidential. So, the boundaries of witness preparation are 'controlled by a lawyer's own informed conscience' (Wydick 1995: 3). The ethical line between 'developing testimony so it will be effective and suborning perjury by telling the witness what to say' (McElhaney 2005: 108) is fuzzy, so it can be 'difficult to distinguish between legitimate witness preparation and unlawful coaching' (ABA 2023), There's 'relatively sparse authority' on witness preparation (Restatement of the Law Third 2000: §116).

Applegate (1989: 280) sets out seven witness preparation methods, any of which might be entirely appropriate, improper coaching or perjury: (1) general advice and moulding personality; (2) providing a legal background to the witness; (3) providing a factual context; (4) providing factual details; (5) the use of perhaps privileged documents in witness preparation; (6) the use of non-privileged documents to refresh recollection; and (7) rehearsals. He notes 'witness preparation can also have a distorting effect on the accuracy of the testimony. The possibility of distortion interferes with the judicial system's attempt to reach the truth' (ibid: 282). Wydick (1995: 26) divides witness coaching into three grades: (1) when the lawyer knowingly and overtly induces the witness to testify to something that the lawyer knows is false; (2) when the lawyer does so covertly; (3) when the lawyer does not knowingly induce the witness to testify to something that the lawyer knows is false, but the lawyer's conversation with the witness nevertheless alters the witness' story. Guidance has also been provided by the District of Columbia Bar (1979: Opinion No 79):

> A lawyer may not prepare, or assist in preparing, testimony that he or she knows, or ought to know, is false or misleading. So long as this prohibition is not transgressed, a lawyer may suggest language, as well as the substance of the testimony, and may – indeed, should – do whatever is feasible to prepare his or her witness for examination.

C. Contrasting Approaches

Coaching is more accepted and 'thorough' by some lawyers than others.

i. Outsourcing

In EW, 'assurety', a firm owned by three KCs, comprising 'leading barristers and trainers', offers what it calls 'witness familiarisation training'. This seems to conflict with the Court of Appeal's prohibition, but the key word is 'familiarisation' rather than 'training' or 'coaching'. The company's website claims to 'transform communication skills' and focus not just on what participants say, but 'how they say it ... While at all times emphasizing that the duty of the witness is to tell the truth'.

By contrast, an American outsourcing company, On Trial Associates, claimed its input can make all the difference: 'After coaching with On Trial Associates, witnesses take the offensive, control the spotlight, and win the jury's trust'.[2] It now uses slightly more modest language:

> On Trial cuts the costs of litigation by helping companies and law firms achieve favorable settlements and better results at trial. By optimizing testimony at depositions, identifying influential jury issues, and shaping the trial narrative, our clients have had cases dropped after deposition and verdicts rendered in cases with million-dollar expenses.

---

[2] An earlier version of the website is on file with the author.

The company offers not only individual witness preparation but also 'Group witness development' for pending company-wide litigation: 'Send your witness to "Witness College" for a group preparation session with On Trial.'

ii. Public Defenders

In California, a 'standard probation condition' imposed upon those convicted of alcohol-related crimes is participation in Alcoholics Anonymous (AA). Participation, however, cannot be verified; individuals might sign in and then leave. To tackle this 'loophole', judges would 'quiz' individuals to test whether they'd in fact completed the probation terms.

Zacharias and Martin (1999) asked public defenders – repeat players who knew the judges' strategy – how they should 'prepare' clients for the judge's anticipated questions. Should they 'remind' clients of the various 'steps' in the AA programme and inform them of the 'usual questions' asked and the 'permissible answers'? As the authors note, lawyers owe a duty of loyalty to clients, but must not suborn perjury.

Assuming lawyers didn't 'know' whether or not individuals had attended the AA session, it turned out their answers depended on how they viewed the ethics rules: 'Public defenders who looked exclusively at the rules seemed inexorably to conclude that they were *not only allowed* to so coach their clients, but perhaps were even *ethically required* to do so' (ibid: 1013, emphasis added). It seems some didn't 'know' because they 'took care not to inquire into any of these elements'. Other public defenders 'responded differently'. They 'examined not only the terms of the ethics rules, but also their goals, the reasons for the contemplated coaching, and the conduct the system expects of a reasonable, objective lawyer'. They concluded coaching was 'intended, improperly, to put words into a witness's mouth that did not, in fact, accurately convey reality'; it 'would facilitate perjury' (ibid: 1014).

D. Getting Away with it?

A rare example of witness preparation being disclosed was the 'Script Memo' inadvertently disclosed by a novice lawyer at Baron & Budd. The firm represented plaintiffs in asbestos claims, but the memo, entitled 'Preparing for Your Deposition', was disclosed to defence counsel. Brickman's (2002: 1) analysis of 'Asbestos Litigation Land' puts the memo in context. Asbestos-related diseases develop after substantial exposure, but take between 10 and 40 years to manifest themselves. Around 1970, the manufacture of asbestos products ceased after knowledge of the hazards became widespread. Asbestos litigation 'took off' when it emerged several asbestos corporations had 'conspired decades earlier to suppress information on the hazards of inhaling asbestos in the course of mining and manufacturing asbestos-containing materials' (ibid, referring to Brodeur 1985).

By 1982, Johns-Manville, 'by far, the leading manufacturer of asbestos-containing materials' (ibid) had 16,000 claims against it and declared bankruptcy. Consequently, claimants would receive only a few cents of any dollars compensated. So, 'Almost overnight, plaintiffs changed their testimony' saying that Manville's share of the relevant market was far less than had been the case in earlier claims: 'It is reasonably clear that this altered testimony was procured by plaintiff lawyers as part of their re-tooling of asbestos litigation' (ibid). That 'retooling' continued: 'As each asbestos defendant goes bankrupt, there is an immediate and uncanny change in claimant and witness testimony as to the percentage of that company's product as particular work sites' (ibid).

Most litigation involved claims of exposure 15, 20, 30 or more years earlier at multiple work sites where many different asbestos-containing products were used. Proving causation was therefore difficult, but the 'proximate cause obstacle was swept aside by creative lawyering'. Claimants only had to show one company's products were used at their work site and that exposure could cause their significant injury. The 'retooling' paid off – at least for the lawyers. According to an estimate, Baron & Budd had, by 1994, grossed more than $800 million from asbestos litigation (Biederman et al 1998).

i. The Memo

The first half of the 20-page memo provided detailed descriptions of the uses of different asbestos products: insulating cement, refractory cement, gin mix, pre-cut gaskets, sheet gaskets, rope packing, pipe covering, block insulation, plastic cement, fireproofing, asbestos boards and panels joint compound, cloth and felt, and firebrick. For each of them the memo gave a detailed account of which type of workers used it, for what purposes, in what places, how it was mixed and supplied, and what types of containers held the products. The memo reminded clients – and emphasised – 'Insulating cement is NOT like sidewalk concrete … it was typically used to insulate steampipes'. It repeatedly emphasised the importance of memorising the information about the products: 'How well you know the name of each product and how you were exposed to it will determine whether that defendant will want to offer you a settlement.' It went on:

> Your responses to questions about asbestos products and how you were exposed to them is the most important part of your deposition. You must PROVE you worked with or around the products listed on your Work History Sheets. You must be CONFIDENT about the NAMES of each product, what type of product it was, how it was PACKAGED, who used it and HOW it was used. You must be able to show that you were close to it often enough while it was being applied to have inhaled the fibers given off while it was being mixed, sanded, sawed, compressed, drilled or cut, etc. You will be required to do all this from MEMORY which is why you MUST start studying your Work History Sheets NOW! … It is best to MEMORIZE all your products and where you saw them BEFORE your deposition. … Have a family member quiz you until you know ALL the product names listed on your Work History Sheets by heart.

It instructed clients as follows:

> You will be asked if you ever saw any WARNING labels on containers of asbestos. It is important to maintain that you NEVER saw any labels on asbestos products that said WARNING or DANGER … You will be asked if you ever used respiratory equipment to protect you from asbestos. Listen carefully to the question. If you did wear a mask for welding or other fumes, that does NOT mean you wore it for protection from asbestos! The answer is still 'NO'! … Do NOT mention product names that are not listed on your

Work History Sheets. The defense attorneys will jump at the chance to blame your asbestos exposure on companies that were not sued in your case. Do NOT say you saw more of one brand than another, or that one brand was more commonly used than another. At some jobs there may have been more of another brand, so throughout your career you were probably exposed equally to ALL the brands. You NEVER want to give specific quantities or percentages of any product names. The reason for this is that the other manufacturers can say you were exposed more to another brand than to theirs, and so they are NOT as responsible for your illness! Be CONFIDENT that you saw just as much of one brand as all the others. All the manufacturers sued in your case should share the blame equally! … Any other notes, such as what you are reading right now, are 'privileged' and should never be mentioned.[3]

It also tried to deflect any suspicion that clients were coached:

You may be asked how you were able to recall so many product names. The best answer is to say that you recall seeing the names on the containers or on the product itself. The more you thought about it, the more you remembered! If the defense attorney asks you if you were shown pictures of products, wait for your attorney to advise you to answer, then say that a girl from Baron & Budd showed you pictures of MANY products, and you picked out the ones you remembered.

Was this memo helping individuals remember or creating a false memory? Lawyers should discuss a witness' memory of an event many years earlier (as in asbestos cases), but it becomes easy to reconstruct the memory to benefit the case. 'False memory' – memories individuals truly believe to be accurate but are false – is a well-known phenomenon, especially in historical child abuse cases (see, eg, Loftus and Ketcham 2013). Baron & Budd, however, defended the memo. Fred Baron argued it didn't counsel anything improper, especially in the context of other materials the firm provided to plaintiffs which advised them to 'tell the truth'. The firm also argued that the memo, labelled 'Attorney Work-Product', was protected by attorney–client privilege. This enabled the firm to block investigations into the use of the memo, the knowledge of its use by the firm's lawyers, and inquiries of other clients as to whether they had seen the memo. Brickman's conclusion, however, was unequivocal: it was 'subornation of perjury' (Brickman 2002: 6).

---

[3] Reprinted in S Rep No 108-118 (21 July 1993), Fairness in Asbestos Injury Resolution Act, at 85–95 (Script Memo reprinted at 109–31). See also 'The Fairness in Asbestos Injury Resolution Act of 2003, Senate Judiciary Committee.

7

Turning a Blind Eye

I am the wisest man alive, for I know one thing, and that is that I know nothing.

— Plato, *The Republic*

Senator Howard Baker's famous question about Richard Nixon's involvement in Watergate – 'What did the President know and when did he know it?' (Bassetti 2018) – could be asked of lawyers because it's 'one of the most fundamental issues in legal ethics' (Hodes 2002: fn 16). On the one hand, the duty to provide competent representation to clients 'includes inquiry into the factual and legal elements of the problem' (MR 3.1, Comment [2]). To avoid bringing or defending 'frivolous' proceedings, lawyers must 'inform themselves about the facts of their clients' cases and the applicable law and determine that they can make good faith arguments in support of their clients' positions' (ibid). Criminal defence lawyers 'should encourage candid disclosure by the client to counsel and not seek to maintain a calculated ignorance' (ABA 2017: Standard 4-3.3(4)). In EW, the Privy Council (Supreme Court judges) suggested lawyers aren't permitted to fail to investigate the facts of the case properly without sacrificing the duty of competence and diligence to the client (*Sankar*).

On the other hand, 'selective ignorance' enables lawyers to provide more, not less, competent representation if they can do 'what is otherwise forbidden by the ethical rules' (Roiphe 2011: 206). That's because some rules are triggered by 'knowledge'. The prohibition against offering false evidence 'only applies if the lawyer knows that the evidence is false' (MR 3.3, Comment [8]); a lawyer must not 'counsel … or assist a client … in conduct that the lawyer knows is criminal or fraudulent' (MR 1.2(d)); reporting requirements are triggered when a lawyer 'knows' a corporate employee has violated certain legal obligations (MR 1.13). By avoiding knowledge, lawyers can allow clients to testify falsely – in apparent compliance with the rules (Freedman 2008: 143). No wonder the MR provide a definition: '"Knowingly", "known", or "knows" denotes actual knowledge of the fact in question' (1.0(f)), although knowledge may also be 'inferred from circumstances' (ibid: 3.3, Comment [8]).

There's a commonly held view that lawyers 'know', hence the question: 'how can you defend someone you know is guilty?' But Blackstone (2006) asks 'self-righteous' individuals under what conditions does defence counsel

> know whether the prosecution's witnesses are lying or mistaken … that the … confession was voluntary … that the defendant was sane or acted under a form of diminished capacity … that the defendant's defense or alibi … are false? Should defense counsel not proceed … when DNA evidence incriminates … without consulting a DNA expert … When a Medical

Examiner determines that a baby's cause of death was 'Shaken Baby Syndrome' ... should defense counsel not investigate to determine whether some other care provider previously mishandled the child?

Lawyers who learn 'truth is elusive' (Sward 1989: 317) learn knowledge is too. By giving the knowing requirement a 'highly restrictive meaning', lawyers can avoid concluding that clients are lying (Freedman 2008: 135). Clients can be protected by 'not knowing' and what lawyers 'know' can be hidden. Confidentiality and privilege create 'powerful obstacles' and 'shield attorneys from public scrutiny' (Fischel 1998: 9). The challenges, complexity and implications of turning a blind eye were vividly illustrated in the film of Grisham's *A Time to Kill* (1989).

I. *A Time to Kill*

The film opens with the horrific rape and torture of a 10-year-old African-American girl by two 'white' racists. Her father, Carl Lee Hailey, has seen his daughter in hospital, has held her in his arms and been told she will never bear children because of the injuries. Lawyer Jake Brigance has just learnt of the incident when Carl Lee visits his office:

Carl Lee: You remember them four white boys that raped that little black girl over in the Delta last year?

Jake: Yeah.

Carl Lee: They got off, didn't they?

Jake: Yeah.

Carl Lee: Jake, er, if I was in a jam, you'd help me out wouldn't you?

Jake: Sure Carl Lee, what kind of jam you talkin' about?

Carl Lee: You got a daughter Jake ... what would you do?

Was Carl Lee planning to kill the two men and asking Jake to be his lawyer? When Jake asks 'what kind of jam?' Carl Lee doesn't answer. Given that conversations with 'prospective clients' are privileged and confidential (MR 1.18(b)), what should Jake do, if anything? Jake didn't alert Sheriff Ozzie Walls and Carl Lee killed the men. Charged with first-degree murder, Carl Lee tells Jake: 'You didn't think I'd do it did you?' Jake replies: 'I hoped not.'

The critical scene is a conversation between Jake and his wife, Carla. Jake agreed to defend Carl Lee and Jake's family is being threatened: a Ku Klux Klan cross was left burning at their house; threatening phone calls have been made to Jake and his secretary; riots are expected. Carla is very angry and Jake is apologetic:

Carla: What exactly you sorry about Jake?

Jake: Remember the other night, I told you Carl Lee came out to the office ... you remember we talked about me calling Ozzie.

Carla: You never called him, did you? You never called Sheriff Walls?

Jake: I didn't call him Babe.

Carla: Lord have mercy Jake – you had a *responsibility*; Carl Lee chose you. He told you what he was thinking.

Jake: Yeah, he told me what he was thinking but I didn't *KNOW* what he was gonna do.

Carla (interrupting): Jake Tyler Brigance: we agreed, you were going to call the sheriff. Now look it, everything that has happened, I am sorry to tell you this darling, but those two boys are in the ground, and *you were in a position to prevent every bit of this*.

Carla says Jake had a responsibility; but did he have a *professional* responsibility? He had tragic choices: do nothing; find out what Carl Lee was planning; persuade Carl Lee not to kill; and if he failed, break confidentiality and tell the sheriff. Carla's point is: he was in a 'position to prevent every bit of this'.

We've seen how questionable questions might arouse suspicions. Freedman's example is extradition treaties and terrorist offences questions (Freedman 1990: 143). A lawyer turning a blind eye may be like a flight instructor not asking why a person wanted to know how to 'control an aircraft in flight but took no interest in takeoffs and landing' (National Commission on Terrorist Attacks upon the United States, nd). A client might ask: 'is it true the law says: if the police cannot prove which member of a group of people responsible for causing physical harm to a child or a vulnerable adult, then *all* the suspects avoid justice?' Should lawyers answer – it was EW law until 2011 – or be 'on enquiry'? Does it depend on what clients look like, although the 'prudent paedophile' might preface the question with: 'I'm writing a crime thriller and want to make sure the information is correct.' Ironically, lawyers representing one member of a group involved in child abuse are then in 'The Lecture' scenario. After giving 'The Lecture' the individual can blame others in the group and escape 'justice'.

Unless lawyers make enquiries, they don't *know* whether clients are paedophiles or terrorists. Is that just 'selective ignorance' and 'wilful blindness', or can there be 'blind-eye knowledge'?

A. 'Blind-Eye Knowledge'

In EW, this approximates to actual knowledge in certain scenarios, including breach of trust cases and uberrimae fidei (utmost good faith) contracts such as insurance contracts. They require good faith and the full declaration of material facts. Lord Scott explained by reference to Lord Horatio Nelson (*Manifest*). Nelson, at the Battle of Copenhagen, made a deliberate decision to place the telescope to his blind eye in order to avoid seeing what he knew he'd see if he placed it to his good eye. The test is as follows: a firmly grounded suspicion that certain facts may exist and a conscious decision to refrain from taking steps to confirm their existence (negligent failing to investigate will not suffice). It remains to be seen whether EW courts will expand this concept to other areas, although it has been used in a breach of trust case involving a multidisciplinary law firm where the perpetrator was an accountant (*Group Seven*). However, judges consider suspicions which fall short of the blind-eye knowledge test will still be relevant to an individual's subjective beliefs. They may lead to a determination of dishonesty (*Ivey*).

Sometimes, knowledge is staring a lawyer in the face. Earl Rogers[1] – said to be the model for Erle Stanley Gardner's Perry Mason – told a 'true story'. A Chinese man came into his office and asked Rogers how much he'd charge to defend him for murder. After Rogers told him, the man pulled little bags out of his pockets and counted out the money in gold. When he finished counting, he got up, bowed and started to leave the office. 'Hey! Come back here. What's all this? Where are you going?' Rogers asked. 'I go kill the man now, then I be back' (Cohn and Chisholm 1934: ix; the words were spoken by Adela Rogers St Johns, daughter of Earl). Rogers told Charles Mootry, after successfully defending him of murdering his wife, 'Get away from me, you slimy pimp. You're guilty as hell and you know it' (Trope 2001: 63; Snow 1987). Knowledge can make lawyers' choices tragic for all concerned.

II. Perjury

Perjury is so serious that the Romans threw perjurers from the Tarpeian Rock and Greeks branded them with the mark of infamy. Perjury was first criminalised in EW in 1563. Under section 1 of the Perjury Act 1911, it's defined as a person wilfully making a material statement in a judicial proceeding which they know to be false or do not believe to be true. However, detecting it isn't easy and prosecutions are rare – there were only 96 offences recorded in the UK in 2014. Prosecutors have to prove that the evidence was material to the case, the defendant realised the lie was material, and the lie might have affected the trial outcome.

Lawyers are 'precluded from taking steps or in any way assisting the client in presenting false evidence or otherwise violating the law' (*Nix*: 166), but how do they *know* it is false? In the landmark *Nix* case, the client told his lawyer – which was inconsistent with his previous accounts – he saw 'something metallic' in the victim's hand before stabbing him to death, and 'If I don't say I saw a gun, I'm dead' (ibid: 161). In both the US and EW, criminal defendants have a right to testify but not a right to testify falsely. The right against self-incrimination is a right to silence, not a right to lie (*Nix*: 173). Equally, clients don't have a 6th Amendment right to lawyers who will aid and abet them to testify falsely (*Rock*).

Lawyers have a MR duty *not* to offer false evidence when they have actual knowledge of clients' intention to perjure. They *may* present evidence even if they reasonably believe it's false. As a result:

> Defense lawyers who view their role solely in terms of winning and/or who resist any sense of obligation or responsibility for truth or justice, can avoid their client's perjury by rationalizing that they do not have sufficient certainty of the falsity of the defendant's testimony. (Perrin 2007: 1725)

---

[1] Clarence Darrow, famous for several cases including the Loeb and Leopold murder trial which included his twelve-hour appeal against the death penalty, and the Scopes evolution trial, said he would almost certainly have been disbarred had not Earl Rogers defended him when he was accused of witness-tampering.

Thus: 'The distinction between knowledge and belief is a rather fine one, a chasm in which any reasonably intelligent person could find shelter' (Henning 2006: 263). The Massachusetts Supreme Court

> acknowledged the myriad approaches in the case law, including: 'good cause to believe' a client intends to testify falsely; 'compelling support' for such a conclusion; 'knowledge beyond a reasonable doubt'; 'firm factual basis'; 'good-faith determination'; and 'actual knowledge'. (*Commonwealth*)

However, the general view is that unless clients tell lawyers directly, it would be unusual for them to 'know'. There are good reasons for this (*State v McDowell*). First, it's not the lawyers' job to decide the facts: 'except in the rarest of cases, attorneys who adopt "the role of judge and jury to determine the facts" pose a danger of depriving their clients of the zealous and loyal advocacy required by the Sixth Amendment' (*Nix*: 189). Secondly, a less-than-stringent standard threatens to undermine the lawyer–client relationship. If lawyers conclude clients are lying, they may break confidentiality, reject their duties of loyalty and 'zeal in advocacy' (see *Strickland*: 688). Luban (1999) also argues, recognising defence counsel's duty of loyalty and the 'overarching duty to advocate the defendant's cause', that lawyers must be allowed to avoid the truth to preserve the integrity of, and to protect, the lawyer–client relationship. The third reason is perhaps the strongest. A less-than-stringent standard is practically unwork-able. Upon what can lawyers base knowledge? The prosecution case? Would lawyers always have to investigate the veracity – or otherwise – of the client's position? A duty to do so would 'submerge' the lawyer and, potentially, the courts to determine whether or not there was sufficient corroborating evidence to justify the conclusion that the client intended to commit perjury.

By contrast, if clients admit to a fact, there's usually no need for lawyers to corrob-orate. Actual knowledge therefore must come from clients, one way or another: 'Without a client's clear admission of intent to testify falsely, counsel sails swirling seas, changeable from one moment to the next, without a single star by which to chart a course' (*State v McDowell*). It's 'far more realistic for counsel to maintain the unique humility of "not knowing," absent an admission by the client' (*Strickland*).

In *State v McDowell*, the lawyer became sceptical about the client's defence, which had changed as the power of the prosecution evidence became obvious. There were inconsistencies between what the client and Sunshine, his girlfriend, said. The client then asked the lawyer: 'What if Sunshine and I get together and we say ... I'll say what I need to say to help myself out and if I have to say something untruthful, I'll say that. I need to help myself out.' If the client went ahead with that plan, the lawyer concluded, he would be presenting perjured testimony, giving the lawyer an ethical dilemma. But the Wisconsin Supreme Court determined the attorney had been deficient:

> Short of 'knowing' that one's client intends to testify falsely, counsel must proceed as a zeal-ous advocate. Regardless of suspicions about a defendant's account, counsel must assist the defendant in presenting it if the defendant desires to do so and maintains that the account is true.

Critics argue that requiring 'actual knowledge' may 'promote duties to the public on the surface while allowing lawyers to ignore them in reality' (Roiphe 2011: 187).

There are inconsistent principles in the rules. A main justification for confidentiality and privilege is the need for full and frank disclosure: 'communication, knowledge, and truthfulness are the cornerstone of a productive attorney-client relationship' (ibid: 190). Permitting 'willful ignorance' by definition, therefore, 'undermines the efficacy of the attorney-client relationship' (ibid: 187). That said, we saw that some California public defenders avoided 'knowing' whether clients were telling the truth by taking 'care not to inquire into any of these elements' (Zacharias and Martin 1999: 1013). Such ignorance increases the efficacy of the lawyer–client relationship, but is it ethical – or 'none of the lawyer's business'?

III. 'None of My Business'

Some lawyers may decide this to be the case. Attorneys representing immigrants and asylum seekers may suspect many are working when they shouldn't, so 'have to decide whether to protect or disclose a client's immigration status' (Cimini 2008: 360) – but only if they 'know'. In EW, a 2013 survey estimated there were over 200,000 renters facing 'revenge evictions'. Asking landlords why they want to evict tenants risks lawyers learning of unlawful motives such as retaliation. Giving landlords 'The Lecture' may result in them presenting lawful reasons. Should lawyers challenge landlords to *prove* their 'reason' is true?

In Massapequa Park, New York, the Murtha Law Firm LLC specialises in landlord/tenant law. As Murtha & Murtha LLC it advertised 'Fast and Effective Tenant Evictions', with a picture of James D Murtha and the words: 'Using my Skill and Expertise, I can get the money you are owed, and I can get your tenant out!' If tenants fail to pay rent, they're liable to eviction. In Queens, in New York City, in September 2010, a landlord of Romanian Jewish descent claimed his tenant owed $22,000 rent and when asked for it painted symbols of swastikas, the KKK and other profanities on the walls. Based on this information, lawyers would have few qualms about helping to evict.

But what about 'getting the tenant out' for an unlawful reason? Tenants may be forced to leave because landlords fail to repair or maintain a healthy living environment. Turning a blind eye liberates lawyers from accusations of unethical conduct while enabling clients to get tenants out – like that landlord in Queens. He was a 'slum landlord' who'd painted the offensive remarks on the walls himself to create the pretext for a justifiable eviction.

A. Collusion

For some, 'the suspicions of an advocate as to the story told by their client can be so well-based as to justify an (objective) allegation of *collusion* on the part of the advocate' (Evans 2011: 78, emphasis added). A 'lawyer's silence in such circumstances may be practically indistinguishable from an actual *conspiracy* with the client' (ibid).

When the only ground for divorce was adultery, collusion was common. New York lawyers probably *knew* of the collusion because it appears there was a 'cottage industry' of imitation adultery. Some women made a living out of being the 'other woman', as a magazine article title in 1934 suggested 'I was the Unknown Blonde in 100 NY Divorces' (Woo 2010). Judges knew about the collusion – or at least strongly suspected it – but also turned a blind eye. In EW recently, High Court Judge Moor rejected divorce applications after an online service, iDivorce, 'submitted "absolutely identical" reasons for 28 marriages failing' (Hyde 2021).

IV. Inferences

In the US, lawyers cannot disclose upon *mere suspicion* that clients intend to commit crimes; they must have a reasonable basis for believing it (Opinion No 2002). However, 'a lawyer cannot ignore the obvious' when corporate employees are violating certain legal obligations (MR 1.13, Comment [3]). Similarly, an EW criminal defence lawyer's 'suspicion may harden into a belief that the client is guilty. There may come a point where this is a certainty' (Boon 2015: 128). The ABA tells criminal defence counsel they should 'encourage candid disclosure by the client to counsel and *not seek to maintain a calculated ignorance*' (2017: Standard 4-3.3(d), emphasis added).

Thus, a lawyer may 'know' of a client's lies even if the client is silent. A client was accused of driving while his driving licence was suspended (*In the Matter of Paul J Page*). His lawyer used a procedural defence: the records failed to show a notice of suspension had been sent to the client's proper address, as legally required. The suspension was technically invalid; the client couldn't be found guilty, regardless of whether he was driving. Before this verdict, however, the client sought a probationary licence. At the hearing, which the lawyer attended, the presiding commissioner asked the client whether he'd driven a car in the previous nine years. He answered, under oath, 'no'. The lawyer didn't remonstrate with the client or raise the accusation about driving while suspended. The client never told the lawyer directly he'd driven a car. Did that mean the lawyer didn't 'know'? The Indiana Supreme Court said no – for obvious reasons. If a person is accused of driving a car unlawfully, 'a minimally-competent defense lawyer would ferret out the defense: I didn't drive the car'. The lawyer, the court said, 'knew of credible evidence that his client had driven'.

There may be many scenarios where ignorance does exonerate lawyer behaviour. Whether that ignorance is selective may be hard to prove. The conduct of Vinson & Elkins, the private law firm used most by the giant energy corporation Enron, is an example. (Whelan 2007).

A. Enron

Lawyers regularly give important opinions. As Judge Henry Friendly put it: 'In our complex society the accountant's certificate and the lawyer's opinion can be instruments for inflicting pecuniary loss more potent than the chisel or the crowbar'

(*US v Benjamin*). Investors and others rely upon them, which is why a 'selective ignorance' strategy is regarded as suspect:

> When the opinion is based on underlying materials which … suggest that they cannot be relied on without further inquiry, then the failure to investigate further may support an inference that when the [lawyer] expressed an opinion it had no genuine belief that it had the information on which it could predicate that opinion. (*Eisenberg*)

Enron was the seventh-largest corporation in the US, the largest contributor to President George W Bush's presidential campaign as well as a contributor to many prominent Democrats. Enron retained hundreds of outside law firms, including Vinson & Elkins, then a global law firm with over 800 attorneys. When Enron filed for bankruptcy in 2001, so did its 13 affiliates which had over 4,000 direct and indirect subsidiaries. In a corporate context, 'abiding by a client's decisions' means taking instructions from 'its duly authorized constituents' (MR 1.13(a)). These constituents are the corporation's officers, directors, employees and shareholders (ibid: Comment [1]); when they make decisions on behalf of the corporation, they 'ordinarily must be accepted by the lawyer *even if their utility or prudence is doubtful*' (ibid: Comment [3], emphasis added). The 'top-notch' Enron Board of Directors included Kenneth Lay – Economics PhD – and Jeffrey Skilling – Harvard MBA and in the top five per cent of his class. Outside directors included four PhDs, one honorary doctorate, two medical doctors, two other law school graduates, 12 Chief Executive Officers, the Dean of the Stanford School of Business, a Member of the British House of Lords, and the Former Chair of the Commodity Futures Trading Commission. The in-house legal team was also regarded as 'world-class'.

From Vinson & Elkins' point of view, Enron was an extremely complex, sophisticated and knowledgeable client whose instructions would clearly define the objectives of representation and the lawyers' responsibilities. The client would closely monitor and evaluate performance, so exercising independent professional judgment may appear to lawyers to be superfluous. But the constituents might be freer to manipulate the lawyers, to conceal wrongdoing and to enlist the support of lawyers – unwittingly – in that enterprise.

Indeed, when an ABA Task Force (ABA 2002: 208) looked at the Enron and other corporate scandals, it noted there'd been 'criticism of corporate lawyers for turning a blind eye to the natural consequences of what they observe and claiming that they did not "know" that the corporate officers they were advising were engaged in misconduct'. It found lawyers were prone to 'accept management's instructions and limit their advice and/or services to a narrowly defined scope, ignoring the context or implications of the advice they gave' (ibid: 207). It observed that 'while lawyers should not be subject to discipline for simple negligence, they should not be permitted to ignore the obvious' (ibid: 208). Indeed, some lawyers might 'shut their eyes to what was plainly to be seen' (*US v Benjamin*: 863, Judge Henry Friendly).

My analysis (Whelan 2007) suggests Vinson & Elkins didn't 'shut their eyes' and shouldn't be held responsible. Not only was the client highly sophisticated and knowledgeable, the lawyers were involved in discrete tasks, separated from the overall strategy of the corporation, and therefore ignorant of the fuller picture. They worked in teams, and individual lawyers had little or no knowledge of that picture. Senior Vinson & Elkins lawyers did, on several occasions, raise questions and express concerns about what they were being asked to do. These were addressed, each time, by Enron officers. It's true vital information was hidden from public view or distorted and Enron was the largest bankruptcy in American corporate history at the time. But wrongdoings were unsurprisingly missed, violations were understandably overlooked and the suspicions or beliefs that something might be amiss were insufficiently evident to justify 'blowing the whistle' or taking more action than the law firm actually did. The 'Enron' problem was not a failure by lawyers as such, but the tendency of all lawyers – particularly lawyers of clients like Enron – to *defer* to the client. The deference was inevitable given the sophistication and expertise of Enron.

Another of Enron's professional advisers was Arthur Anderson, then one of the world's largest accountancy firms. It had directed employees to destroy documents. The Supreme Court reversed its conviction for so doing stating that 'A "knowingly" … "corrup[t] persuade[r]"' – referring to the language of the statute – 'cannot be someone who persuades others to shred documents under a document retention policy when he does not have in contemplation any particular official proceeding in which those documents might be material (*Arthur Andersen*: 707–08). The statute required proof of consciousness of wrongdoing (ibid: 704–07). Vinson & Elkins lacked the expertise to 'know' one way or the other. Indeed, sometimes, for this reason, lawyer ignorance may be inevitable.

V. Expertise

How do lawyers determine whether 'reasonably certain death or substantial bodily harm' will be prevented if they break confidentiality? How is 'reasonable belief' to be assessed? Should lawyers who are not medically or scientifically equipped seek expert advice?

A. HIV/AIDS

In the 1980s, a diagnosis of HIV/AIDS was virtually a death sentence. If clients disclosed their intention to deliberately infect others, the exception to the duty of confidentiality would apply. Today, the diagnosis no longer means 'reasonably certain death', so does infecting others constitute 'substantial bodily harm' (MR 1.6(b)(1))? What's the threshold for lawyers' disclosure?

B. Toxic Waste

In 2014, a Texas family was awarded $3 million after a range of ailments were linked to contaminated ground water, solid toxic waste, and airborne chemicals generated by natural gas fracking operations run by Aruba Petroleum. According to the family's lawyer, David Matthews, up to 600 chemicals were used in making fracking fluid, including several known carcinogens and other toxins (Blakely 2014). MR 1.6, Comment [6] states lawyers may reveal information to the authorities 'if there is a present and substantial risk that a person who drinks the water will contract a life-threatening or debilitating disease and the lawyer's disclosure is necessary to eliminate the threat or reduce the number of victims'.

But only experts on toxic waste could 'reasonably believe it is necessary to disclose'. Is there – or should there be – an ethical duty on lawyers to find out? Some lawyers may choose *not* to know, *not* to have full and frank disclosure, just communication on a 'need to know' basis. In practice, lawyers will be uncertain on whether disclosure is necessary and might refer to the Opinion of the Bar of the City of New York (2002): the lawyer should not disclose on 'mere suspicion'; the lawyer needs a reasonable basis for believing.

8

Contracts of Silence

Most of lawyers' work is 'in the shadows', meaning there's little or no oversight. Most civil cases settle; most criminal cases are disposed of via plea bargaining or guilty pleas. So the 'rules' may be far from the minds – and practices – of lawyers: 'during the heat of the moment in a negotiation, most people do not engage in thoughtful analysis of the ethicality of their actions' (Hinshaw 2019). The same goes for 'contracts of silence' (Dean 2018): secret settlements and NDAs. Secrecy may encourage deviance from ethics. Indeed, 'in negotiation, more than in other contexts, ethical norms can probably be violated with greater confidence that there will be no discovery and punishment' (White 1980: 926). As one attorney told us: 'Ethical is what I can get away with.' He wished to remain anonymous!

I. Plea Bargaining

In plea bargaining, a client pleads guilty in exchange for some perceived benefit – 'the first to squeal gets a better deal'. In the US system, Johnson (2022) describes the regular use of lying about facts, law and process in plea bargaining. One 'lying' scenario is the client who insists on their innocence yet pleads guilty. There's 'the disturbing reality that such incentives do actually motivate innocent people to plead guilty' (Joy and McMunigal 2020: 3). The National Registry of Exonerations found that 18 per cent of known exonerees pleaded guilty (ibid). In EW, lawyers reckon around 10 per cent of those who plead guilty are innocent (Zander and Henderson 1993: 146, cited in Boon 2023: 224). Many innocent subpostmasters pleaded guilty in the UK 'Post Office Scandal' to avoid the risk of prison.

A. The 'Alford' Plea (*North Carolina v Alford*)

In most American States, the 'Alford' plea enables clients to plead guilty *and* assert their innocence at the same time. In EW, by contrast, if clients assert innocence to lawyers but plead guilty, lawyers must proceed on the basis that the client is, in fact, guilty.

At the sentencing hearing, lawyers must declare they are guilty; mitigating evidence based on a claim of 'innocence' cannot be presented. Is this not a 'lie' or 'misleading the court'? As Freedman (1966) notes, not only might the lawyer be 'prompting his client to lie' by conveying the plea bargain, but the lawyer also cannot inform the court the client is innocent because that would compel the client to stand trial and risk a heavier sentence.

B. The Consequences

If innocent clients plead guilty, the consequences can be dire: loss of liberty; harshness and indignities of prison life; loss of livelihood and future employment prospects; loss of one's home and other personal property; break-up of family; loss of children and other personal relationships; and stigmatisation and damage to reputation (New Zealand Law Commission 1998: 1). The 'Post Office Scandal' confirmed these huge consequences for individuals. Some of the 39 convicted subpostmasters and subpostmistresses were imprisoned, went bankrupt or lost their homes; at least one suicide was connected to the scandal (*The Times*, 2021b). All were exonerated but 35 had pleaded guilty.

C. The Role of Lawyers

The role of lawyers when innocent clients plead guilty is important (Alschuler 1975). It's also 'complicated' because it's

> not clear whether attorneys should be (and are) advising clients on the decision that they should make, based on an assessment of their best interests, or whether the proper role of the attorney is just to provide the relevant information to a client and leave them to make the best decision for themselves. (Helm et al 2018: 916)

As Blake and Ashworth (2004: 189) note, 'the defence advocate represents more than the client – she or he is simultaneously responsible for maintaining fundamental guarantees central to the justice system'. That said, perhaps the system 'can reproduce the ideology of justice while denying it' – conviction being the routine outcome (McBarnet 1981: 167). Also, some lawyers who feel overworked and underpaid may see plea bargaining as a solution that benefits them as well (McConville et al 1994).

An EW study found defendants were often persuaded to plead guilty even when the lawyers were convinced of their innocence (McConville 1998). An American study that interviewed 189 criminal defence attorneys in several States also found that even when attorneys thought their client was innocent, 'they may encourage them to plead guilty' (Helm et al 2018: 929). However, it also found that 'attorneys are more reluctant to encourage defendants who they believe are innocent to plead guilty'. The authors acknowledge there are cases where 'from a practical perspective, innocent defendants *should* plead guilty, even when the chances they will be convicted at trial are not high' (ibid: 930).

Innocent clients plead guilty for several reasons. They may be protecting the actual guilty party. Many falsely confess in the US, resulting in wrongful convictions (Kassin and Gudjonsson 2004; Gudjonsson 2018), possibly because of the 'Reid Technique' of police interviewing. Challenging a confession's 'falsity' might be difficult and, in the lawyer's opinion, unlikely to succeed. The evidence might be strong, or the client someone unlikely to receive sympathy from the judge or the jury. A sentencing discount is routinely given to those pleading guilty, perhaps a non-custodial sentence rather than prison. Defendants may have to make 'Monte Carlo' calculations – assess the risk of bringing a case to trial and losing it (Blackstone 2006).

II. Negotiations

White (1980: 927–28) noted that: 'To conceal one's true position, to mislead an opponent about one's true settling point, is the essence of negotiations.' To achieve client objectives, 'lawyers usually employ some deceptive tactics' (Craver 1997; see also Craver 2010; Menkel-Meadow and Wheeler 2004; Rubin 1995). Wetlaufer (1990) goes even further: 'effectiveness in negotiations is central to the business of lawyering and a willingness to lie is central to one's effectiveness in negotiations'. Yet 'deceptive negotiation tactics can be – and frequently are – described as "ethical"' (Hinshaw 2020). But doesn't MR 4.1 prohibit lawyers from knowingly making false statements of material fact or law to third persons, and requiring them to be truthful when dealing with others on a client's behalf (Comment [1])? Yes, but lawyers are also told they 'generally have no affirmative duty to inform an opposing party of relevant facts'. In any case: 'Whether a particular statement should be regarded as one of fact can depend on the circumstances.' In negotiations it adds: 'Under generally accepted conventions … certain types of statements ordinarily are not to be taken as statements of material fact.' This would include a statement about 'a party's intentions as to an acceptable settlement' (MR 4.1, Comment [2]).

All the tools of lying – bluffing, deception, false promises, threats, demands and other statements – play a part in negotiations. Craver (1997) calls this the 'schizophrenic character of the ethical conundrum', and White (1980: 927) explains the paradox: 'On the one hand the negotiator must be fair and truthful; on the other he must mislead his opponent … The crucial difference between those who are successful negotiators and those who are not lies in this capacity both to mislead and not be misled.'

Misrepresentation by lawyers is generally unacceptable, but in negotiations it's acceptable. MR 4.1 does 'little more than prohibiting lawyers from engaging in fraudulent misrepresentations' (Hinshaw 2020). If there's a power imbalance between clients and adversaries, opportunities for deception are greater. Opponents may not know the 'generally accepted conventions in negotiation'. A threat in a labour dispute to close the plant 'if you vote for union representation' or claim more money might be a bluff, but do workers understand the 'rules of the game'? How can a statement *not* be a material fact when it may directly affect the outcome?

III. Secret Settlements and NDAs

Many civil cases settle with a confidentiality clause or NDA; liability, fault or reputation are concealed and protected. Persons signing NDAs risk losing their compensation and incurring penalties if they breach them. Some NDAs even prohibit them from speaking to their families about the deal. NDAs originated in the context of maritime law in the 1940s, but they 'began to creep in to contracts of all kinds' in the 1980s (Dean 2018). They're frequently used in US product liability, employment, medical negligence and abuse cases (Drahozal and Hines 2006; Sefarian and Wakley 2003). From claimed that 'most attorneys [for corporate defendants and insurance companies] insist on secrecy provisions' (2001: 675–76); an estimated 85–95 per cent of employment discrimination settlements have confidentiality agreements (Kotkin 2007); and 'it is almost impossible to settle mass tort cases without a secrecy agreement' (Weinstein 1994: 511). In the UK, Bloomberg analysed a government database of ET sex discrimination decisions and found that 2,195 out of 3,585 suits were dropped before court rulings in a period of two and a half years from 2017 – 'lawsuits vanished into the ether' (Wiggins and Browning 2019). Cases involved major banks, the police and multinational corporations. Settlements 'overwhelmingly include confidentiality clauses and non-disclosure agreements' (ibid).

NDAs have 'emerged as a critical element in explaining why so many of these cases remained secret for so long' (Garrahan 2017). They've been linked to concealing 'the dangers of silicone implants, the flaws in a kind of side-mounted gas tank by GM, and toxic-waste leaks into rivers across America' (Dean 2018). In the US, lawyers have been accused of being part of a 'culture of extreme bullying'; in EW there have also been allegations of 'unfair pressure' put on claimants by lawyers to sign NDAs.

A. Tiger Woods and Rachel Uchitel

Days after a relationship with Woods was revealed in 2009, Uchitel signed a 30-page NDA. She was offered $5 million plus $1 million annually for three years. The NDA not only prohibited Uchitel from discussing anything to do with Woods with anyone, but also from saying she'd signed it. So she was continually referred to as 'a tramp, a mistress, a home wrecker and a "hooker"', but couldn't respond. She fell out with her lawyer, 'the famed Hollywood lawyer Gloria Allred' (Rosman 2021). Allred's firm was representing between five and 10 other women in matters involving Woods and negotiating settlements so frequently that the lawyers 'developed a written protocol'. As Uchitel put it: 'At every level, I was up against these big-shot lawyers' (ibid).

B. Harvey Weinstein and Zelda Perkins

Perkins was Weinstein's personal assistant in London. She quit and, with Rowena Chiu, brought a claim against Weinstein for sexual harassment (Perkins) and attempted rape (Chiu). They settled in October 1998 for £250,000, to be shared equally, and signed an NDA. After hearing of the many allegations of harassment and assault levelled against Weinstein in the US, Perkins broke the agreement in 2017 because: 'Unless somebody does this there won't be a debate about how egregious these agreements are and the amount of duress that victims are put under' (Garrahan 2017). NDAs also 'allowed the sexual abuse to continue' (Kim 2023: 466).

The agreement was partly published in 2018 (written submission from Zelda Perkins to the House of Commons Women and Equalities Committee, March). It contained several attempts to prevent disclosure or to limit its potential impact on Weinstein. One clause referred to 'any criminal process involving' Weinstein or Miramax, the entertainment company he and his brother founded. If Perkins was asked to provide testimony, she had, 'where reasonably practicable', to give 48 hours' notice to Mark Mansell, a lawyer at Allen & Overy, 'before making any disclosure'. Perkins was also required to 'use all reasonable endeavours to limit the scope of the disclosure as far as possible' and to give 'reasonable assistance' to Miramax 'if it elects to contest such process'. Perkins claims the lawyers negotiating the agreement warned her they 'would try to destroy my credibility if I went to court. They told me he would try to destroy me and my family' (Garrahan 2017). As she later put it, lawyers think the NDA 'is a good solution. The aggrieved person gets a bunch of money and off they go, and the problem person doesn't get their reputation ruined. What they don't understand is the real evil of NDAs starts when you sign it' (Rumbelow 2021). She also said her 'bigger trauma was what happened with the lawyers … what broke my heart is what happened when I went to the lawyers' (Kantor and Twohey: 68).

C. The Law and Ethics of NDAs

Secrecy means that even if the dispute is known, the outcome is not. Sometimes, the dispute's existence itself might be concealed, thereby reducing the potential for future lawsuits. Some settlements include a requirement not to 'assist any person who files a lawsuit … against [the defendant] unless … required pursuant to a lawful subpoena or other legal obligation' (Bauer 2008: 484). Bauer argued that this violates MR 3.4(f), which generally prohibits a lawyer from requesting a non-client refrain from voluntarily giving information to another party.

In both countries, the legality and ethicality of NDAs have been questioned (see, for example, Centre for Ethics and Law 2018; Lobel 2018; Mishcon de Reya 2018). AH Robins hid the safety risks of its contraceptive device, Dalkon Shield, with secret settlements while continuing to market the product (Givelbar and Robbins 2006: 134). Cover-ups led to a vigorous debate on whether secret settlements should be prohibited. About 20 American States have introduced 'sunshine in litigation' laws to restrict their use where a 'public hazard' (Florida Statute 69.081(2)), the general public health or safety (Texas Rules of Civil Procedure 76a(1)(a)(2)) or an environmental hazard is involved (Arkansas Code Annotated 2009: 16-55-122). Whether these provisions are effective or not – they can probably be bargained around – they do reflect concerns with client secrecy. As Zitrin (1999: 115) put it:

> Because the rules of ethics generally require putting the interests of the client ahead of those of society, lawyers are bound to settle cases in ways which serve the needs of specific clients while potentially harming the interests of society as a whole.

In EW, NDAs have been called 'a weapon used by powerful bullies, racists, abusers and dangerous incompetents' (Rumbelow 2021). Archbishop of Canterbury Justin Welby banned their use in the Church of England, calling them 'unacceptable' after victims of racist abuse were paid off to 'buy their silence' (Burgess 2021). Philip Davies MP questioned the ethicality of lawyers if NDAs stopped individuals disclosing details of the perpetrators of unlawful conduct. He said: 'I was always brought up to tell the truth, the whole truth and nothing but the truth … [the use of these clauses in NDAs] *flies in the face of telling the truth*' (Botsford 2018, emphasis added). Partly as a result of this session and the release of part of Perkins' NDA, the SRA investigated, and proceedings were brought against Mark Mansell before the SDT.

i. Mark Mansell

The SRA's argument was that

> in the context of a serious allegation of sexual assault, a solicitor acting for an employer was guilty of misconduct because the NDA, on the SRA's interpretation, purported to restrict the women's ability to report the alleged crime to the police, co-operate fully with criminal proceedings and obtain medical treatment. (Rose 2021)

The SDT agreed the SRA's case 'at its highest – that Mr Mansell knew or suspected that the NDA was improper – was "reasonably tenable"' and should not be summarily dismissed, as Mansell had argued. In other words, there was a 'case to answer' that Mansell breached his professional duties. For his part, Mansell argued that, properly constructed, the agreement did not prevent Perkins from reporting or co-operating (ibid). The SDT ultimately stayed the proceedings because of Mansell's ill health, despite his continuing to practise. Perkins was 'furious' (Ames and Baksi 2021). At the end of August 2020, Mansell stepped down as co-head of corporate responsibility at Allen & Overy.

ii. Warning Notice

The aim of the SRA's updated 'Warning notice' on NDAs (2020) is to ensure they don't prevent reporting to the SRA and law enforcement or making disclosures protected by law. It's also 'to ensure that those we regulate do not take unfair advantage of the other party when dealing with NDAs', as Perkins claimed happened to her. In fact, there are already rules to achieve this. Solicitors are told not to abuse their position by taking advantage of others (SRA 2023a: 2); to cooperate with regulators (ibid: 5); not to attempt to prevent anyone from providing information to the SRA or any other regulator or law enforcement agency (ibid: 7.5); and to promptly report to the SRA or other regulator any facts or matters they reasonably believe are capable of amounting to a serious breach of their regulatory arrangements, including those involving the solicitor themselves (ibid: 7.7).

The Notice reminds solicitors they should consider withdrawing if their client's instructions are to act in a way that is inconsistent with these requirements. Examples of 'taking unfair advantage' include exploiting an opposing party's lack of knowledge or limited access to legal representation; applying undue pressure or using aggressive or oppressive tactics, such as imposing oppressive or artificial time limits on a vulnerable, opposing party to agree to the terms of the NDA; or preventing someone entering into an NDA from keeping or receiving a copy (as happened to Perkins).

iii. Thematic Review

In 2023, the SRA (2023c) published its review on the use of NDAs in workplace complaints about 'inappropriate behaviour' such as sexual misconduct, discrimination and criminality. It surveyed 150 law firms and held on-site visits and interviews with 25. It found 'the vast majority' of NDAs were 'legitimate means of protecting interests' that 'operate to the mutual benefit of both parties'. It found 'no direct evidence' of solicitors deliberately intending to prevent reporting of inappropriate behaviour. However, it did find a number of 'common trends or practices which inadvertently might contribute to this happening'. In particular, it found that the 'risks posed by NDAs are routinely underestimated and rarely explored'. It concluded that 'solicitors must acknowledge the ethical considerations' when advising clients.

iv. Ongoing Concerns

In EW, signing an NDA doesn't prevent a person from making a 'whistleblowing' disclosure under the Public Interest Disclosure Act 1998 (section 43J of the Employment Rights Act 1996). In 2023, the Higher Education (Freedom of Speech) Act prevents universities from using NDAs for complaints of sexual abuse, harassment and bullying. In 2024, the LSB published its summary of evidence on the misuse of NDAs. It highlighted examples of legal professionals' conduct that gave it 'cause for concern' (LSB 2024: 37), but felt it better to determine how existing regulation ensures adherence to ethical standards.

9

Private Law-Making

> The power of the lawyer is in the uncertainty of the law.
>
> — Jeremy Bentham (1843: 429)

Lawyers give legal advice and pursue clients' lawful objectives, but their zealous advocacy should be 'within the bounds of law'. What *are* 'the bounds' of law when they 'in any given case are difficult to ascertain … Certainty of law ranges from the well-settled rules through areas of conflicting authority to areas without precedent' (MC EC7-2). MR 3.1, Comment [1] confirms: 'the law is not always clear and never is static. Accordingly, in determining the proper scope of advocacy, account must be taken of the *law's ambiguities and potential for change*' (emphasis added). As Bentham suggests, uncertainty of the law gives lawyers extraordinary power (and responsibility). But why is the law uncertain?

I. Legal Realism and Indeterminacy

In many cases, adversaries believe the 'law is – or should be – on their side'. As Lord Alexander of Weedon QC noted in a lecture on the 'Art of Advocacy' (Alexander 1991), 'the canvas is wide, thrillingly wide, for the variety and the evolution of the problems of the law creates genuine and legitimate choice for the Court between rival contentions. There is often no absolutely right, or totally logical, answer'. Pannick (1996) adopted the 'Legal Realist' view:

> When they take themselves seriously, lawyers and judges like to pretend that the legal system is based on objective rules that regulate what we may or may not do to each other and to ourselves. In fact, litigation is, to a surprisingly large extent, a game of chance determined by good fortune as much as by good judgment, occasionally influenced, as the school of American realists taught in the 1930s, by what the judge had for breakfast.

In the US, legal realism has been called 'the ordinary religion of the law school class-room' (Cramton 1978). Legal realists stress the open-textured, vague nature of law over its perceived precision; its manipulability over its certainty; and its instrumental qualities over its normative content (Pepper 1986: 624; Wilkins 1990). Hart (1961) emphasised the 'open texture of law'. He noted that there are areas of conduct where much must be left to the development of the courts striking a balance, in the light of circumstances, between competing interests which vary in weight from case to case.

A. The 'Bed of Procrustes'

Sir Stephen Sedley (2008: 52) was aware of a

> very important dichotomy. The laws and usages of this realm are not fixed and immutable. They change. But all judges spend their lives – their nights anyway – on the bed of Procrustes, being stretched or cramped. Law either has to be stretched to meet the demands of justice, or justice has to be cramped to stay within the law. That is the titanic struggle which adjudication involves.

This 'dichotomy' means 'unpredictability is at the essence of litigation' (Pannick 1996) and law is merely 'prophecies of what courts will do in fact' (Holmes 1897: 460–61). One solicitor told us that he seeks a barrister's opinion not 'for technical advice. *We're* the specialists. We go to counsel because he'll tell you how a court will react' (McBarnet and Whelan 1999: 216). Even if judges have consistently found against the position being argued, it's always possible they'll find things have changed to justify a new approach, despite common law systems being based on 'stare decisis'.

II. Stare Decisis

This is the theory that there are authoritative precedents which inferior courts must follow. It's designed 'to provide legal certainty which was a foundation stone of the administration of justice and the rule of law. They ensured order and predictability while allowing the development of the law in well-understood circumstances' (*R v Barton*, Lord Burnett). However, this system 'had to be capable of flexibility' (ibid). No wonder stare decisis has been said 'to be more a rule of thumb than an iron-fisted command' (Eskridge Jr 1988).

A. Rule of Thumb or Iron-Fisted Command?

Treating stare decisis as a rule of thumb enables lawyers to present arguments that might be regarded as frivolous or otherwise improper. In *Lawrence*, the US Supreme Court accepted a legal argument – state legislation prohibiting private, consensual, homosexual activity was unconstitutional – that 17 years earlier had been described by the same Court as 'at best, facetious' (*Bowers*: 194). As Freedman and Smith (2010: 95) point out: 'Since the dictionary definition of "facetious" is "not meant to be taken seriously or literally", the Court was characterizing that argument in a way that was perhaps even more pejorative than the word "frivolous"'. Similarly, in the UK Supreme Court, Lords Hamblen and Leggatt acknowledged they were reaching a 'different conclusion now to that which we both reached over ten years ago' (*FCA*: 311). In a case involving the construction of 21 samples of insurance policy, the Court determined that a decision of the Commercial Court had been wrongly decided. They justified the departure from their earlier views by quoting the brilliant summary by US Supreme Court Justice Robert Jackson:

Precedent, however, is not lacking for ways by which a judge may recede from a prior opinion that has proven untenable and perhaps misled others. See Chief Justice Taney … recanting views he had pressed upon the Court as Attorney General of Maryland in *Brown v Maryland*, … Baron Bramwell extricated himself from a somewhat similar embarrassment by saying, 'The matter does not appear to me now as it appears to have appeared to me then' … And Mr Justice Story, accounting for his contradiction of his own former opinion, quite properly put the matter: 'My own error, however, can furnish no ground for its being adopted by this Court. …' Perhaps Dr Johnson really went to the heart of the matter when he explained a blunder in his dictionary – 'Ignorance, sir, ignorance.' But an escape less self-deprecating was taken by Lord Westbury, who, it is said, rebuffed a barrister's reliance upon an earlier opinion of his Lordship: 'I can only say that I am amazed that a man of my intelligence should have been guilty of giving such an opinion.' If there are other ways of gracefully and good naturedly surrendering former views to a better considered position, I invoke them all. (*McGrath*: 177–78, citations omitted)

These examples show lawyers cannot know for sure whether arguments are frivolous until they've been so held. The issue is therefore whether the argument is made 'in good faith' (MR 3.1), which means there are few, if any, constraints on lawyers because

clients are free to reject advice and insist that cases be litigated. It is rarely safe for a court to assume that a hopeless case is being litigated on the advice of the lawyers involved. They are there to present the case; it is … for the judge and not the lawyers to judge it. (*Ridehalgh*, Sir Thomas Bingham)

This isn't condoning frivolous lawsuits, but trying to identify what's ethical:

It is … one thing for a legal representative to present, on instructions, a case which he regards as bound to fail; it is quite another to lend his assistance to proceedings which are an abuse of the process of the court … It is not entirely easy to distinguish by definition between the hopeless case and the case which amounts to an abuse of process, but in practice it is not hard to say which is which and if there is doubt the legal representative is entitled to the benefit of it. (ibid)

Some judges invite speculative lawsuits. Concurring in *Dobbs*, a decision overturning the 'precedent' of *Roe*, Justice Clarence Thomas urged reconsideration of several other precedents, including *Griswold* (1965 – contraception), *Obergefell* (2015 – gay marriage) and, ironically, *Lawrence*. Clearly, he doesn't regard those precedents as 'foreclosing' lawsuits, otherwise how could they reach the Supreme Court?

B. The 'Genius of the Common Law'

One central characteristic of the common law that 'few would disagree on … is its casuistic character' (Simpson 1988: 70). Civil law system lawyers look to texts as the foundations for law; common law lawyers look to cases. It's the 'case method' that predominates in American law schools: students study cases to 'tease out the deep principles of the law' (ibid: 71). The common law 'is not a text, and there is a sense in which, because it is always on the move from case to case, you never quite know from case to case what it is' (ibid: 73).

Simpson has called this dynamism 'the genius of our common law'. It changes through subtle distinctions or, less subtly, through judges overtly adopting a new approach. There may be contradictory pulls in law, each justifying reasonable, but different outcomes – principles and rules to draw on, and different cases with which to draw analogies and from which to draw different conclusions. Every rule can have its exception. No wonder judges disagree. They have different personalities or political persuasions. Nowhere is this more obvious than the US Supreme Court – hence the importance attached to making the 'right' choice of Justice. And even though UK judges aren't appointed politically (or elected), they also adopt different approaches. Some are literalists, while others are more interested in law's purposes or goals. A literalist judge interpreting a law requiring 'drug shops' be closed 'by 10 pm' would allow them to re-open a few minutes later. The actual judge said 'no one but a lawyer would ever have thought of imputing such a meaning' to the law (Cross: 1976: 60). Or as Justice Scalia (2018: 24) put it, a 'good textualist is not a literalist'.

C. *Citizens United*

Judges have a wide discretion. In *Citizens*, the US Supreme Court held that the Constitution prohibited government restrictions on political campaign financing by corporations. In so holding, it overturned one precedent (*Austin*), reversed another (*McConnell*) and invalidated part of the 63-year-old Labor Relations Management Act it had previously upheld that banned corporate financing in elections. As Justice Kennedy pointed out, there were also other conflicting cases which the Court had to consider: 'The Court is thus confronted with conflicted lines of precedent: a pre-Austin line that forbids restrictions on political speech based on the speakers corporate identity and a post-Austin line that permits them.'

D. The Verdict

If judges can choose different interpretations of the law, so can lawyers. As Singer (1988: 467) put it: 'We are all legal realists now.' Simon (1996: 237–38; 1998: 100–01) used an incident in *The Verdict* to show how. The book (Reed 1980) and film were inspired by events Reed witnessed as a trial lawyer. An attorney, Frank Galvin, is acting in a wrongful death case. The victim was given the incorrect anaesthetic and died horribly. The 'medical establishment's powerful lawyers are using 'dirty tricks', so Galvin is up against it. They've driven the key witness – a nurse – out of town by threatening her career if she co-operates. The case hinges on Galvin finding her.

Galvin's exhausted conventional ways of finding the witness. Her best friend is deposed, but probably lies by saying she doesn't know where she is. So, Galvin breaks into her mailbox on the day phone bills are mailed. He finds an out-of-town number he suspects is the key witness'. Through this method he finds her, the case is turned around and justice is done. But did Galvin commit a *crime*? A federal statute makes it a crime to intercept mail addressed to someone else. State statutes make it criminal trespass to enter on someone else's property for the purpose of larceny; larceny is to take someone's mail from their mailbox, even if the mail is returned.

Simon sets out the following arguments to legally justify taking the mail. First, there may be a 'necessity' defence, such as the Model Penal Code 1985 § 3.02(1), which states that otherwise criminal conduct – taking the mail – is justified if 'necessary to avoid a harm or evil' where the 'harm of evil sought to be avoided' – the injustice to the plaintiff – 'is greater than that sought to be prevented by the law defining the offence charged'. The evil or harm of taking and returning the mail is negligible compared with the injustice. Even if a statute expressly rejected a necessity defence, a court might still find the statute unconstitutional, or a prosecutor or a jury might nullify its application. Even if there's no statutory necessity defence, the courts might imply one and even if courts have rejected such a defence before, they might accept it in another case if the circumstances have changed. His final point is that even if the lawyer is certain the 'positive law' forbids taking the phone bill, the prosecutor will prosecute, the trial judge will instruct the jury it's a crime, the jury will convict and the highest court will affirm, the lawyer might claim they're all wrong – like Roy Moore did.

E. Roy Moore

Moore was the 27th Alabama Supreme Court Chief Justice until he was removed, and the 31st, until he was removed again! His first removal in 2003 stemmed from his refusal to accept a US Federal Court order to remove a marble monument of the Ten Commandments that he placed in the rotunda of the Alabama Judicial Building. He said: 'I believe this order is unlawful, and that compliance with such an order is unenforceable'. He was re-elected in 2013 but removed a few years later, this time for defying a US Supreme Court decision about same-sex marriage. Bearing in mind that he was twice Alabama Chief Justice, we can see Simon's arguments are far from unprecedented or 'beyond belief'. Maybe there's no such thing as 'positive law', only 'non-positive law'.

III. Non-positive Law

Yablon looked at 'the problem of counselling firms with business models involving deliberate and repeated violations of the law'. He cited Uber, which avoided being treated as a taxi company – subject to licencing and other regulatory restrictions – by calling itself an app, and Airbnb, which avoided regulations on hotel booking services by claiming it merely enables home sharing. He argued '[t]hese claims are often legally dubious and have been rejected by courts and regulatory bodies', but the companies continue with them 'hoping their popularity among consumers will lead to little or no sanctions for their violations or, better yet, changes in the law' (2019: 1). To avoid falling foul of MR 1.2(d), a good faith interpretation will have to be constructed or lawyers may be at risk not only of ethical discipline but also criminal liability. However, finding a good faith argument may not be a major hurdle.

A. Playing with Words

Lawyers' work is 'founded upon the use of language. Words and their nuances and subtleties, and their shades of composition, are all important' (Alexander 1991: 10). Legal words can be abstract, their meaning dependent on context. Is it 'murder' or 'manslaughter'? 'Affirmative action' or 'discrimination'? 'Equality' or 'United in diversity'? As Justice Oliver Wendell Holmes said: 'A word is not a crystal, transparent and unchanged; it is the skin of a living thought and may vary greatly in color and content according to the circumstances and time in which it is used' (*Towne*).

i. *Bill Clinton*

Clinton provided testimony in a deposition. Paula Jones accused Clinton of sexual harassment when he was Arkansas Governor. Later, Clinton was investigated by Kenneth Starr, a Special Prosecutor, concerning Whitewater, a real estate investment. Starr convened a grand jury to determine whether Clinton committed perjury or obstructed justice in that deposition. Clinton had been questioned about whether he had sexual relations with White House intern Monica Lewinsky. He said no. He argued that his statement that 'there is nothing going on' between himself and Lewinsky was truthful because he had no ongoing sexual relationship with her when he was questioned. He said: 'it depends on what the meaning of the word "is" is. If ... "is" means "is and never has been" ... that's one thing, if it means "there is none", that was a completely true statement' (Starr Report: Narrative 2004). He also argued there were no sexual relations because that term is applicable only to sexual intercourse. Clinton told the public media: 'I did not have sexual relations with that woman, Ms Monica Lewinsky.'

   According to Clinton's lawyers during his disbarment proceedings in Arkansas, this and other answers he gave were evasive, incomplete and misleading but 'not legally false'. In other words, Clinton didn't commit perjury. Clinton accepted a five-year voluntary suspension from the State Bar for having provided false and misleading testimony during the deposition.

ii. *'One'*

ConvaTec Technologies had a patent which stated its wound dressing should have between 1 per cent and 25 per cent sodium chloride. Smith & Nephew produced a dressing with 0.77 per cent sodium chloride. Had ConvaTec's patent been infringed?

   The English High Court said no. The Court of Appeal (*Smith & Nephew*) disagreed: 0.77 per cent was as close to 1 per cent as makes no difference – 0.77 per cent should be rounded up to one. Lord Justice Christopher Clarke referred to the 'skilled person', that is, a person who possessed average knowledge and ability in the relevant field of technology and is aware of what was common general knowledge in the art: 'A linguist may regard the word "one" as meaning "one" – no more and no less. To those skilled in the art it may, however, in context, imply a range of values extending beyond the integer.' In this patent, he said, the words 'between 1 per cent and 25 per cent' extend to all values greater than 0.5 per cent and less than 25.5 per cent. His words are reminiscent of Humpty Dumpty:

> **Humpty Dumpty**: When I use a word, it means just what I choose it to mean – neither more nor less.
>
> **Alice**: The question is: whether you can make words mean so many different things.
>
> **Humpty Dumpty**: 'The question is, which is to be master – that's all. (Carroll 1871: Chapter 6)

iii. 'After the Date'

A bank was robbed on a Saturday and later that same day the proceeds were given to the robber's wife. Could the proceeds be recovered from her? The law stated that only proceeds given 'after the date on which the offence was committed' could be recovered. 'Date' literally means the day, so 'after the date' means the days *after* the Saturday. The Court of Appeal held that 'date' meant 'time'. In effect, the court rewrote the law as 'after the time the offence was committed' (*R v Lehair*).

iv. 'Any'

Many US Supreme Court opinions 'turn on the word "any"' which 'seems to be an essential element of statutory drafting' (Brudney and Leib 2023). A barrister, cross-examining an expert witness in a criminal trial, asked a question 'imputing dishonesty' without reasonable grounds for so doing (*Walker*). The Code of Conduct at the time stated: 'Any failure … to comply with any provision … shall constitute professional misconduct.' On appeal from a finding of misconduct, the Inns of Court Visitors (who heard appeals at the time) quashed the finding. Sir Anthony May said the word 'any' should not be taken literally; the 'stigma and sanctions attached to the concept of professional misconduct … only arises if the misconduct is properly regarded as serious'. Indeed, 'the authorities … require[s] us to modify the literal effect'.

v. 'A'

Under a 1996 federal law (8 USC §1229b(b)(1)), immigrants subject to deportation could apply to remain if they met certain criteria. One criterion was that they had been continually present for at least 10 years. The accrual of time, however, stopped once immigrants received 'a notice to appear' for a deportation hearing. 'A notice to appear' is defined as 'written notice … specifying' certain information.

Niz-Chavez received the information in two documents, sent two months apart. In 2021, the US Supreme Court had to interpret the meaning of 'a' (*Niz-Chavez*). Did 'a' notice comprise a single document containing all the required information – the nature of the proceedings, the charges against the immigrant, when and where the hearing would take place – or was 'a' not a 'one-size-fits-all word' so that its meaning depended on the circumstances? Six justices held 'a' notice to appear meant 'a single document containing the required information, not a mishmash of pieces with some assembly required'. The article 'a', they said, suggests 'a' single notice rather than a series of notices – a 'mishmash' (ibid: 5). Therefore, according to the majority, Niz-Chavez had plainly not received 'a' notice.

So, even when the words of law appear clear, 'context matters' (ibid: 6). Justice Gorsuch, writing for the majority, acknowledged: 'today's dispute may seem semantic, focused on a single word, a small one at that. But words are how law *constrains* power' (ibid: 16). The words of law and the indeterminacy of language, however, are what gives *lawyers* power as well. They can use 'language euphemisms'. Words can convey not only a misleading impression but also: 'Through renaming actions … and relabelling decisions … we turn what may be unacceptable into socially approved behaviors' (Tenbrunsel and Messick 2004: 226). An example of 'Euphemistic language [that] can make harmful conduct respectable' (ibid) was the briefing note co-written by Susan Crichton, the Post Office's most senior lawyer. In July 2013, Post Office executives 'swapped "bug" for "exception"' to 'soften criticism of the Horizon IT system' (Witherow 2024). The power of language gives lawyers great flexibility to present an arguable case.

IV. An Arguable Case

EW lawyers generally must only make submissions which are 'properly arguable' (SRA 2023a: Rule 2.4; BSB 2024: rC9.2b). If they consider they are, they should argue them 'without reservation', but if not, they should refuse, and may withdraw if the client insists (*Buxton*: 45). The US Supreme Court said a claim is frivolous if it lacks an arguable basis in either fact or law (*Neitze*). MR 3.1, Comment [2] states an 'action is not frivolous even though the lawyer believes that the client's position ultimately will not prevail'. These 'rules' leave lawyers with a surprisingly wide discretion.

A. The IRS

If attorneys, signing tax returns, do not alert the IRS to a particular tax position, the IRS may not know of its existence, which is why the Code of Federal Regulations (31: §10.34 (2024)) requires practitioners meet the 'Realistic Possibility Standard'. It is met 'if a reasonable and well-informed analysis of the law and the facts by a person knowledgeable in the tax law would lead such a person to conclude the position has approximately a one in three, or greater, likelihood of being sustained on its merits'. To put it another way, if practitioners believe there's a two in three chance of it *not* being sustained, that's acceptable, and lawyers needn't alert the IRS.

B. The Torture Memos

Lawyers in OLC issued opinions that waterboarding and other interrogation techniques were not torture under domestic and international law. They claimed the words 'specifically intended to inflict severe physical or mental pain or suffering' (18 USC § 2340–2340A (2001)) meant asking what was the 'principal goal' of the 'waterboarder'?

If it wasn't to inflict pain or suffering but to get information, there wasn't the required intention to constitute torture (Memo 2003: 37; see also Memo 2002a). They also claimed the words 'severe pain' triggered the torture prohibition only when the physical condition or injury inflicted was sufficiently serious that it would result in death, organ failure or serious impairment of bodily functions (ibid: 39). The memo omitted any reference to how American law had treated waterboarding in the past (Wallach 2007).

In 1947, at the Tokyo War Crimes Tribunal, a Japanese officer, Yukio Asano, was convicted of war crimes for waterboarding a US civilian and sentenced to 15 years' hard labour. During the Vietnam War, American soldiers were 'caught on camera' waterboarding a captured North Vietnamese soldier; the photograph was published in the *Washington Post*. After an Army investigation, one soldier was court martialled and discharged from the army. In 1983, a Texas sheriff, James Parker, together with three colleagues, used waterboarding to coerce confessions from suspects. They were all sentenced to four years in prison. On a technical issue relating to this case, the 5th Circuit in 1984 referred to waterboarding as 'water torture' (*US v Lee*).

The memo acknowledged reasonable persons might disagree on these issues, but 'we have applied our best reading of the law' (Memo 2002b: 19). The author of the torture memo, Professor John Yoo, claimed it was 'an abstract analysis of the meaning of a treaty and a statute' (2006; see also Yoo 2005). Others agreed it was 'standard lawyerly fare, routine stuff' (Posner and Vermeule 2004). Critics described it as like 'the advice of a mob lawyer to a mafia don on how to skirt the law and stay out of prison' (Lewis 2004) and 'contriving legal arguments to legitimize … torture' (Luban 2010). Jack Goldsmith, who resigned as head of the OLC in 2004, described the memo as 'tendentious, overly broad and legally flawed' (Rosen 2007) and 'more an exercise in sheer power than reasoned analysis' (Goldsmith J 2007: 150). The most damning critique came from Professor Jordan J Paust, a former military lawyer and faculty member of the US Army Judge Advocate General's School. He said 'not since the Nazi era have so many lawyers been so clearly involved in international crimes concerning the treatment and interrogation of persons detained during war'. The memo on 'Standards of Conduct for Interrogation' was withdrawn and replaced by another in 2004 (Levin 2004). This explicitly rejected the defence of 'good motive' to permit or threaten 'torture'.

V. 'Hard' Cases

Whether 'hard cases may be apt to introduce bad law' (*Winterbottom*, Baron Rolfe) or even 'good law' (Corbin 1923), they definitely make *law*.

A. Dr Death: Jack Kevorkian

In 1987, after retiring, pathologist Dr Jack Kevorkian, known as Dr Death, referred to himself as a 'death consultant' in newspapers adverts, telling readers he'd assist their suicide. He developed two machines – 'Thanatron' and 'Mercitron' or Mercy

Machine – whereby individuals would push a button which released drugs intravenously. It's estimated Kevorkian participated in over 100 deaths. In the 1990s, Kevorkian was tried four times in Michigan. Three times he was acquitted and the fourth ended in a mistrial. He'd been represented by Geoffrey Fieger.

Kevorkian's fame – or infamy – stemmed from the death of Thomas Youk. He had 'Lou Gehrig's disease' (amyotrophic lateral sclerosis), a progressive nervous system disease that affects nerve cells in the brain and spinal cord causing loss of muscle control. In a letter to the judge, Youk's wife, Melody Haskin Youk, wrote that Thomas could only control his thumb and first two forefingers on his right hand and was losing the ability to speak, having trouble swallowing and choking (Youk nd). His lung capacity dropped to 25 per cent of normal but he didn't want to be put on a ventilator, or be completely dependent on others, 'in a totally paralyzed body ... [He] was not depressed, nor was he a victim'. His brother said Thomas was 'caught in hell'. Youk asked Kevorkian to assist.

Could Fieger advise Kevorkian ethically by citing cases arguing the right to commit suicide is guaranteed by the US Constitution? In Michigan, two lower courts accepted this argument, but the Appeals and Supreme Courts rejected it. In 2014, the New Mexico Second Judicial District Judge Nan Nash dealt with a physician prescribing a medication that a patient might self-administer for the purpose of suicide. Would self-administration protect the physician from criminal liability? Nash ruled that physician-assisted dying is a right under the New Mexico Constitution (*Morris*). An Appeals Court rejected this. In 2016 the New Mexico Supreme Court stated that if the court answered no, the alternatives for the patient would be to: '(1) endure the prolonged physical and psychological consequences of a terminal medical condition that the patient finds intolerable; or (2) take his or her own life, possibly by violent or dangerous means'. Despite this, it declined to hold that there was an absolute and fundamental right and said 'the matter should be resolved in the executive and legislative branches' (ibid).

Kevorkian carried out Youk's wishes, but administered the drugs himself, Youk being unable to do so. At his murder trial, Kevorkian represented himself after the judge ensured he was fully aware of the risks – the charge could lead to life without parole. Kevorkian clearly wanted a change in the law:

> If I'm convicted, Your Honor, we get a shot at the Supreme Court. Not that they'll accept it, but we get a shot at it with what they want, *a particularized case*. They said that, we got their quotes. *They want a particularized case.* Four of them said we want to *revisit the issue*. Now two or three years may be too quick, but when you've got someone starving to death in prison who you know is *not a criminal* and you know what he's doing is *not a crime*, maybe they'll look at it – maybe. But if not, who cares. In 15, 20 years, they'll say well, *he was right.* He's dead now, but *he was right.* I've got to do what I know is right and I can't let the law, which is often immoral, block me. If Margaret Sanger did that, if Susan B. Anthony[1] did that – look at Martin [Luther King] – look at all these people. I'm not saying I'm like

---

[1] In 1872, Susan B Anthony was convicted for voting at a time when women didn't have the vote. She refused to pay the fine, but the authorities declined to take further action. In 1878, a constitutional amendment was presented by Senator Aaron A Sargent giving women the right to vote. It later became known as the Susan B Anthony Amendment. It was ratified in the 19th Amendment in 1920.

them, but they certainly – I'm certainly going to act like them. I mean, I know this is *not a crime. So do you. Everybody with sense does.* Your religion may say it's a sin, but that doesn't make it a crime. All these people broke the law and went to jail. I'm willing to do the same. But the Supreme Court has got to decide this on the Ninth Amendment where there is no equivocation, there is no stretching due process. They've got to do that. And if they do and *break all these laws down*, then we can have a better society, an honest society. I'm willing to risk that. Because at the age of 71, I cannot go on living a hypocritical life when I can't do what I know is right, and the world knows I'm right. Everybody does. Every nation the majority is for what I'm doing. *How come it's illegal?* That's why I'm doing this. (Kevorkian nd, emphasis added)

In a letter to the judge, Youk's wife wrote (nd): 'Tom was not a victim, and to his mind this was not a crime, and most certainly not murder.' The Coroner, Ljubisa Dragovic, commented 'there are only three categories as relates to death cause: natural, by your own hand and homicide. Clearly there needs to be another category, as in Tom's situation' (Roscoe et al 2000). Youk's tragic case was just the kind where a new legal rule might be created. If a judge were to agree it wasn't a crime, then, by definition, what Kevorkian did would be 'perfectly legal'.

However, after a two-day trial, Kevorkian was found guilty of second-degree homicide. Judge Jessica Cooper told Kevorkian:

This is a court of law and you said you invited yourself here to take a final stand. But this trial was not an opportunity for a referendum. The law prohibiting euthanasia was specifically reviewed and clarified by the Michigan Supreme Court several years ago in a decision involving your very own cases, sir. So the charge here should come as no surprise to you. You invited yourself to the wrong forum. So, we are a nation of laws, and we are a nation that tolerates differences of opinion because we have a civilized and a nonviolent way of resolving our conflicts that weighs the law and adheres to the laws and we have the means. We have the means and the methods to protest the laws with which we disagree. You can criticize the law, you can write or lecture about the law, you can speak to the media or petition the voters, but you must *always stay within the limits provided by the law.* You may not break the law. You may not take the law into your own hands ... When you purposely inject another human being with what you know to be a lethal dosage of poison, that, sir, is murder ... No one, sir, is above the law. No one. (www.courttv.com/title/11-mi-v-kevorkian-1999-sentencing, emphasis added)

She sentenced him to 10–25 years. He served eight years and was released on parole in 2007 on condition he wouldn't offer advice, participate or be present in any type of suicide or talk about the procedure of assisted suicide (Davey 2007). He died in 2011.

B. Margaret Sanger

Sanger also used the judicial system to promote a social change she believed was just a matter of time: birth control and contraception. Landmark decisions that transform society – or the law's approach to social issues – occur frequently and sometimes unexpectedly. But they *can* take time.

Several laws obstructed Sanger's campaign, including the 'Comstock' laws, a series of federal statutes, effectively making birth control and contraception criminal offences.

In 1914, Sanger challenged the anti-contraception position and was charged with 'depositing non-malleable matter for mail and delivery' (Indictment of Margaret Sanger). She was sentenced to 30 days in the workhouse and her appeal that the law was unconstitutional failed. As the Court of Appeals – including future Supreme Court Justice Cardozo – put it: 'Much of the argument put to us by the appellant touching social conditions and sociological questions are *matters for the legislature and not for the courts*' (*People v Sanger*, emphasis added).

While Sanger tried to get the legislature to amend the statutes, she also, with her attorney Morris Ernst, 'began searching for a test case to challenge the 1873 Comstock Act and related anti-obscenity laws, which prohibited the circulation of contraceptives and contraceptive information through the mails' (Margaret Sanger Papers Project 2011). In fact, they created one. They targeted 'a direct descendent of the Comstock Law', the Tariff Act, which prohibited the importation of contraceptives and contraceptive information. Ernst wished to 'frame a test case argument on the medical legitimacy of contraception' (ibid). He ordered a package of diaphragm contraceptive devices from the Japanese doctor (who'd developed them) to be delivered to a doctor at Margaret Sanger's Birth Control Clinical Research Bureau. The devices were detained by US Customs under the Tariff Act as articles for the prevention of conception. Customs claimed that 'the articles in question cannot be legally imported even where the same are addressed to a duly qualified physician *since the law makes no exception*' (ibid, emphasis added).

Sanger secured funding for the case and Ernst asked the court to address Cardozo's sociological questions in a way that defied a literal reading of the law. They wanted a decision that had the effect of restricting the reach of the Comstock laws. Witnesses for both the government and the clamant testified that the use of contraceptives was in many cases 'necessary for the health of women' and the court accepted '[t]here was no dispute as to the truth of these statements' (*US v One Package*). Judge Augustus Noble Hand, giving the judgment of the court, noted that:

> It is true that in 1873, when the Comstock Act was passed, information now available as to the evils resulting in many cases from conception was most limited, and accordingly it is argued that the language prohibiting the sale or mailing of contraceptives should be taken *literally* and that Congress intended to bar the use of such articles completely. (ibid, emphasis added)

However, the court rejected this literal approach because times had changed, and the law now covered 'only such articles as Congress would have denounced as immoral if it had understood all the conditions under which they were used' (ibid). The 'radicalism' of what the court had actually done was acknowledged by Judge Learned Hand, the judicial philosopher (and younger first cousin of Augustus). He concurred, but with some reluctance:

> If the decision had been left to me alone, I would have felt more strongly than my brothers the force of the Senate amendment in the original act, and of the use of the word, '*unlawful*', as it passed. There seems to me *substantial reason* for saying that contraconceptives [sic] were *meant to be forbidden*, whether or not prescribed by physicians, and that *no lawful use of them was contemplated*. Many people have changed their minds about such matters in sixty years, but *the act forbids the same conduct now as then*; a statute stands until public feeling

gets enough momentum to change it, which may be long after a majority would repeal it, if a poll were taken. Nevertheless, I am not prepared to dissent ... I am content ... to accept my brothers' judgment, whatever might have been, and indeed still are, my doubts. (ibid, emphasis added)

An article setting out in full the background to the case states it was an

historic decision that effectively disabled the Comstock laws and legalized doctor-prescribed contraception ... the *One Package* case still reverberates today through its influence on subsequent court decisions. Orchestrated by Margaret Sanger and her celebrated attorney, Morris Ernst, One Package secured the legal foundation for groundbreaking rulings on reproductive and privacy rights. (Margaret Sanger Papers Project 2011)

Sanger had to wait until she was 81, in 1965, for the law to be completely transformed by another landmark Supreme Court decision. In *Griswold*, a majority (7-2) held a Connecticut Comstock law prohibiting all contraception to be unconstitutional. Justice William O Douglas wrote for the majority: there was a right to marital privacy. This right hadn't been previously recognised, but the Supreme Court 'discovered' it on the 'penumbra' and 'emanation' of other constitutional protections, such as the self-incrimination clause of the 5th Amendment (Justice Douglas), the 9th Amendment (Justice Goldberg) and the due process clause of the 14th Amendment (Justices White and Marshall Harlan III).

VI. Fidelity to Law

So far, we've discussed 'law in the books'. However, law is, in practice, 'operationalised' by the 'actors' in the legal system – officials, regulators, police, lawyers and others. This is 'the law in action' lawyers deal with routinely: 'In a lawyer's worklife, every legal concept and proposition is automatically operationalized; and realism is nothing more than a philosophy that insists on operationalizing legal concepts and propositions' (Luban 1988: 19).

A. Lehman Brothers

Lehman Brothers, a global financing services firm, filed for bankruptcy in the US in 2008. It had used so-called 'repo' financing, a kind of short-term banking loan. 'Repo 105', 'a type of loophole in accounting' (Kenton 2020), was an attempt by Lehman Brothers to claim it gave up effective control – a 'sale' – because it received only $100 for each $105 in posted collateral (hence the '105'). In substance, however, the arrangement could also be viewed as a loan – paying 5 per cent interest. If it were a financing transaction – borrowings – it would have to be disclosed on the balance sheet; if not, it would be off-balance sheet. Linklaters lawyers were asked to provide an opinion as to whether the repo financing amounted to a sale and repurchase agreement or a secured loan. The opinion enabled Lehman Brothers 'to hide the fact that it was highly leveraged during the financial crisis' (ibid). More importantly: 'Without the opinion the accounting practices and the alleged securities law violations could not have taken place' (Kershaw and Moorhead 2013: 27).

Kershaw and Moorhead analysed the role of Linklaters and concluded the opinion given was 'accurate and unlikely to raise ethical questions or a threat of any sanction under current professional regulations'. They believed: 'As a matter of English law, its opinion that a repo involved a legal sale and repurchase is clearly correct' (ibid: 36). Despite this, they argued law firms should bear 'consequential responsibility' for unlawful client activity *'facilitated* by their legal advice and counsel, *even when such advice is accurate and competently provided'* if their zealous pursuit of client interests 'generate a *real, substantial and foreseeable risk* of client action that is unlawful or "probably unlawful"' (ibid: 27, emphasis added). They regard this as a way of 'ensuring lawyerly *fidelity to the rule of law'* (ibid: 48). As they put it: 'Zeal must operate *within* the parameters of such fidelity.'

Kershaw and Moorhead echo Wendel's arguments (2010: 177) about fidelity to law. He claims 'law is always aimed at some end – that is, it is a purposive activity'. But this and the following chapters call into question the viability of their proposals, regardless of any intrinsic merits. Their approach assumes the true purpose – or spirit – of law can be readily identified by lawyers objectively, but that's an approach 'lawyers are likely to deride' (Luban 1988: 18). In fact, the spirit of the law is elusive (McBarnet and Whelan 1991) and, as we've seen, law is wide open to interpretations made with sufficiently good faith to pass muster.

10

Creative Compliance

Lawyer definition: One skilled in circumvention of the law.

— Ambrose Bierce (1906)

Creative compliance manipulates the law and legal form, treating law as material to be worked upon. It challenges law's 'enforceability' because law's being used both to regulate – it's the regulators policy tool – but also to escape regulation. The problem for enforcement is not 'non-compliance' – the flagrant breach of regulation – but 'creative compliance' – what's been done is 'perfectly legal'. Consequently, there's a struggle for legal control (McBarnet and Whelan 1991). Can creative compliance survive if challenged, and is it ethical?

This chapter draws on research which used OBSF to analyse the challenge of creative compliance (McBarnet and Whelan 1992, 1997a, 1997b, 1998, 1999). Clients disguised their financial position by removing liabilities from the balance sheet. Many complex OBSF arrangements were developed and, if accounted for in accordance with their *legal* form, resulted in accounts that did not reflect their *commercial* reality. The reward for such creative accounting: 'How to make your profits what you want them to be' (Griffiths 1986).

OBSF hid large-scale financial risk and defeated the purpose of financial reporting law. Regulators, aware of the challenge, realised what was needed was not stronger enforcement, but a new regulatory regime to capture creativity, pre-empt the 'perfectly legal' claim and thereby combat creative compliance. By targeting artificial structures and improbable interpretations, they hoped to limit the scope for manipulation. In particular, regulators wanted the reporting of economic substance rather than legal form.

The new regime undoubtedly had an impact; there were improvements in disclosures and some clear successes. However, opportunities for creative compliance remained for those motivated or undeterred. We set out what could happen if there was a renewed search for 'perfectly legal' routes for enhancing accounts. While there was no guarantee any carefully constructed creative device would work, nor would any carefully constructed regulation succeed to control it.

I. Techniques of Creative Compliance

A. Find the Gap or the 'Ex-Files: The Truth is Out There

Looking for gaps, exemptions, exclusions and limits in rules facilitates the claim: 'where does it say I cannot do that?' If gaps in the law exist – or can be found – lawyers may feel duty-bound to use them. Creative lawyers can structure activities to locate them within these express gaps.

B. Safe Havens

Similarly, structures or transactions can be created, after careful scrutiny of legal definitions and criteria, that fall beyond the reach of law. Creative compliance tries to find safe havens beyond the letter of the law. One example is forum-shopping – finding favourable laws or legal regimes – to escape specific domestic laws and regulations, or unwelcome scrutiny.

i. Dr Death: Philip Nitschke

Nitschke, like Kevorkian, was nicknamed Dr Death and assisted suicide – 'patients' activated a syringe using a computer. He did this lawfully four times when the Rights of the Terminally Ill Act 1995 came into force in the Northern Territory of Australia in 1996. But it was no longer lawful after the Australian Parliament's Euthanasia Laws Act 1997. So, Nitschke formed 'Exit International' with plans to launch a 'death ship' to circumvent national law by enabling euthanasia to be performed at sea in international waters, beyond the reach of Australian law.

ii. Women on Waves

Similarly, the Dutch Dr Rebecca Gomperts founded 'Women on Waves' to assist women with unwanted pregnancies. One plan was to sail an 'abortion ship' to countries where abortion was illegal. It flew a Dutch flag so it could legally dock (although two Portuguese warships prevented it from entering their waters), pick up women and retreat into international waters. The project 'espoused a kind of radical pragmatism – clever in its evasion of the law' (Donegan 2021; see also Rumbelow 2014).

iii. Blackwater USA

Founded by Erik Prince, Blackwater was named because the training ground was at the Great Dismal Swamp on the Virginia/North Carolina border. It became the world's most powerful mercenary army (Scahill 2007). In 2007, in Baghdad, Blackwater employees, using heavy machine guns and grenade launchers, mistakenly shot dead 17 Iraqi civilians and seriously wounded another 20. The incident and other alleged abuses led to criminal and Congressional investigations, and in 2014 four employees were convicted: three of manslaughter, one of first-degree murder. It led to Blackwater losing valuable security contracts with the State Department.

To get new government contracts, the company apparently created a web of 30 shell companies or subsidiaries. Paravant, a shell company, won a government contract to train Afghan troops. Army officials at a Senate hearing in 2010 said, when they awarded it, they had no idea Paravant was part of Blackwater: 'Paravant had never performed any services and was simply a shell company established to avoid what one Blackwater executive called the "baggage" associated with the Blackwater name as the company pursued government business' (Ackerman 2010, quoting Carl Levin, Senate Armed Services Committee Chairman). Blackwater was renamed Xe Services in 2009 and Academi in 2011, and merged with Triple Canopy in 2014 to form Constellis.

C. Working to Rule

Focusing literally and narrowly on the words of a rule, especially a clear rule, enables lawyers to claim compliance: 'where does it say I can't do this?' As we saw, this strategy may fail when it turns out the definition of 'one' in a patent is less than one!

i. Ramsey Barreto

In 2019, Barreto was driving his car when he used his mobile phone to video record a serious accident. It was in video mode when the police stopped him. He was convicted under the Road Traffic Act 1988: it is an offence to drive 'while using a hand-held mobile telephone'. His appeal was upheld after the High Court considered the law. Lady Justice Thirlwall referred to another case where a motorist was using his phone to listen to music while driving. That driver changed tracks on his phone, which he held in his hand, with his thumb. There was no definition of 'mobile telephone' in the Act, and the Court agreed the ban applied only to use of the phone for the purpose of a call or other interactive communication, not all uses of the phone (*DPP*). As the judge said, whether a review of the law was needed to take account of advances in technology and other uses of mobile phones 'was a matter for Parliament, not the courts (ibid: 52). Ames (2019) described Barreto's 'escape' as being saved by a 'loophole'.

ii. Mr Loophole

Solicitor Nick Freeman was given this nickname – which he later trademarked. His list of 'celebrities' acquitted using 'technicalities' can be found on Wikipedia. When asked how does he 'square that with his conscience' he said: 'Morally I can't but ethically I can. I am a lawyer and my job is to give my clients the best defence I can' (Broggan 2006).

D. The Regulatory Response

Law-makers who understand the challenge of creative compliance have responded in a couple of ways. One is deliberately to leave terms undefined because: 'Any definition of the term will encourage attempts to avoid the provision by artificial constructions with the intention of escaping from the letter of the definition' (Lord Strathclyde, HL Deb, vol 503, col 1018). Another is to emphasise principles rather than rules – the 'spirit' of the law. There are 'catch-all' laws which might apply to these facts – 'careless' or 'dangerous' driving for example. But catch-all laws also pose a challenge to law enforcement. Finding the 'spirit' can be elusive; sustaining it can be hard, especially when efforts are made to construct rules instead. Catch-all laws can be challenged as ill-defined, vague or even arbitrary. Lawyers can choose: they can argue both for – or against – an interpretation on the basis of the 'rule of law': the need for legal certainty and the idea that rules cannot be made retrospectively (McBarnet and Whelan 1991).

E. In My Opinion

No wonder there's a market for opinions by expert lawyers. Much of barristers' work involves giving opinions about the merits and prospects of a case. Getting an endorsement from the 'right lawyer' can be invaluable; 'opinion-shopping' is not uncommon. One in-house corporate lawyer we interviewed noted his 'big mistake' in 'not getting to leading silk [KC] first' for an opinion (McBarnet and Whelan 1999: 216). Recall how Enron's in-house team sought out Vinson & Elkins and Lehman Brothers sought out Linklaters for their opinions. For clients, opinions lend credibility to their conduct, help hide facts and protect against intrusion. They also provide 'insurance': clients can point to opinions as evidence of their 'good faith' and a defence to claims they acted unlawfully (Pepper 1995; Pollman and Barry 2017). In the tax field, this defence has been called 'tax avoision' (Seldon et al 1979).

II. Enforceability

Law enforcement is a *process* and many factors influence outcomes in individual cases. Choices have to be made, strategies followed and resources allocated – or not. There can be competing interpretations of law and how it should be applied. In short, there's the problem of 'enforceability'.

A. Substance Over Form?

A transaction may be understood in several ways. Its commercial purpose might be called its economic substance; its legal substance might be a sale or a loan; its legal form might be corporate, trust, contract and so on. The legal form may conceal the commercial reality, which is why some seek to 'pierce the corporate veil'. Lawyers generally focus less on the ends of the transaction – the economic substance – than the means – the legal form, legal rights and obligations. This approach was challenged to tackle artificial tax avoidance schemes. In 1981, the highest UK court declared that 'the true nature of a *legal* obligation and nothing else is the "substance"' (*Ramsay*, Lord Wright, emphasis added). It was described as the 'new approach' of substance over form (*Furniss*).

B. Economic or Legal Substance?

However, 'when the law is looking for the substance of a matter, it is normally looking for its legal substance, not its economic substance (if different)' (*In re Polly Peck*: 444, Mr Justice Robert Walker). This changed in the Finance Act 2013. Parliament decided:

'Taxation is not to be treated as a game where taxpayers can indulge in inventive schemes in order to eliminate or reduce their tax liability' (HMRC 2020: B2.2). HMRC, the UK tax authority, was given a new 'new approach', a 'general anti-abuse rule (GAAR)', focusing on economic rather than legal substance:

> [It] rejects the approach taken by the Courts ... to the effect that taxpayers are free to use their ingenuity to reduce their tax bills by any lawful means, however contrived those means might be and however far the tax consequences might differ from the real economic position. (ibid: B2.1)

The 'rule' limits how taxpayers can reduce their tax bill: 'when the arrangements put in place ... go beyond anything which could reasonably be regarded as a reasonable course of action' (ibid: B2.3, referring to section 207(2) of the Finance Act 2013). This 'double reasonableness' test is the 'crux of the GAAR test' (ibid: C5.10.1). It's an 'anti-abuse', not an 'anti-avoidance' rule. Taxpayers have a choice as to how transactions can be carried out and differing tax consequences ensue. Only 'abusive' choices are liable to challenge under the GAAR. HMRC Guidance suggests abuse would arise

> only ... when the course of action taken by the taxpayer aims to achieve a favourable tax result that Parliament did not anticipate when it introduced the tax rules in question and, critically, where that course of action cannot reasonably be regarded as reasonable. (ibid: B11.1)

This book doesn't explore the ramifications of the GAAR (for an overview, see Seely (2021)), but the GAAR acknowledges the challenge creative compliance poses and attempts to control it. It's an approach that 'rejects the proposition that taxpayers [and others potentially] have unlimited freedom to use their ingenuity to reduce their tax bills by any lawful means' (HMRC 2020: C5.6.7). It also appears to reject what might be termed a 'rule of law' response – but can it?

C. The Rule of Law

A central feature of the rule of law is that people can rely on rules they can know in advance 'as a guide to their practical reasoning' (Chao 2021: 126) – 'the planning conception of the rule of law' (ibid: 127). The implication for tax planning was explained by Lord Cairns:

> If the person sought to be taxed comes within the letter of the law he must be taxed, however great the hardship may appear to the judicial mind to be. On the other hand, if the Crown seeking to recover the tax, cannot bring the subject within the letter of the law, the subject is free, however within the spirit of the law the case might otherwise appear to be. (*Partington*: 122)

In contrast, the basic purpose of the GAAR is to 'deter or counteract the deliberate exploitation of shortcomings in the legislation'. Exploiting 'defects' in the law is inconsistent with this purpose and 'would not be regarded as reasonable for the purposes of GAAR' (HMRC 2020: C5.10.5).

Patrick Way KC (2013) analysed the GAAR. He showed Parliament's rejection of the 'game ... where taxpayers set out to exploit some loophole in the tax laws' is in danger of conflicting with the basic principles of the rule of law: 'The law is sacrosanct, and an individual is entitled to govern his or her affairs exclusively by reference to the law in force, particularly as far as is concerned the citizen's obligation to pay tax.' He referred to the Bill of Rights 1688, which established that 'the levying of money to or for the use of the Crown without grant of Parliament was illegal'.

i. *The Elusive Spirit of the Law*

In any case, capturing the spirit is easier said than done. This is 'anti-formalism', and sustaining it is difficult, especially if there is resistance (McBarnet and Whelan 1991). Formalism is the dominant approach in legal thinking: law should be clearly defined, uniform, consistent and predictable; it's the legal rule which should be followed, regardless of its purpose. Legalism is the 'operative outlook of the legal profession' (Shklar 1964: 1). Lawyers generally adopt an ethical attitude that views moral conduct to be a matter of rule following, and moral relationships to consist of rights and duties determined by rules. As a social outlook, legalism is: 'The dislike of vague generalities, the preference for case-by-case treatment of all social issues, the structuring of all possible human relations into the form of claims and counter-claims under established rules, and the belief that the rules are 'there'" (ibid). This is why lawyers 'will fight to the death to defend legal rights against persuasive arguments based on expediency or the public interest or the social good' (ibid: 9).

Creative compliance highlights both the limits of formalism as a strategy of regulation and the 'dangers' of legalism in defeating its purpose. The anti-abuse rule and the regulatory response to creative accounting both seek to control by focusing on the overall 'purpose of the law'. They wanted those subjected to regulation to reflect the spirit of the law rather than the legal form. In the context of tax and financial reporting, this would be to focus on economic or commercial substance. But avoiding the disclosure of substance may be the reason to engage in creative compliance in the first place. Clients – and their lawyers – can resist the new 'new approach'.

D. Resistance

Resistance to anti-formalism, anti-avoidance and anti-abuse can occur at many levels. Lawyers can mobilise the 'rule of law' defence. Citizens have a right to know what the law is, what it prohibits and what it allows; law should be pre-stated not retrospective; and there should be legal limits on state discretion and on the exercise of arbitrary state action. Indeed, the fundamental premise of common law systems, perhaps in contrast to civil law systems, is that whatever is *not* prohibited expressly by law leaves citizens *free* to act as they choose.

The GAAR anticipates this 'rule of law' defence by setting a 'much higher threshold' for tax arrangements which are 'abusive' (HMRC 2020: B10.2). It's akin to a criminal law standard of 'reasonable doubt'. To ensure taxpayers are 'given the benefit of any reasonable doubt when determining whether arrangements are abusive', several safeguards have been built into the GAAR (B2.1). They include the double reasonableness test: the giving of an independent advisory panel opinion on whether an arrangement constituted a reasonable course of action before HMRC would apply the GAAR; and placing the burden of proof on HMRC.

Commenting on the 'deficiencies' in the GAAR, the TUC (2013a, 2013b) noted that while the panel might be 'independent' of HMRC and comprise tax experts, those experts would be 'drawn heavily from the tax avoidance industry'. It described the 'double reasonableness' test as 'Orwellian' and 'intensely subjective'. It noted that placing the burden of proof on HMRC rather than taxpayers is not only a 'reversal of normal practice', but will also be a 'difficult standard to meet given that the taxpayer will hold all the evidence'. In short, the TUC concluded that the GAAR 'will be hard to use' and will 'allow 99% of tax avoidance to continue'. Even if it is used, it added, there's no penalty regime attached to it, so there's 'little or no disincentive to tax avoiders'.

These 'deficiencies' reveal the *power* of the rule of law defence. If the TUC is correct, the GAAR will not deter lawyers or clients. The defence also provides a strong foundation for a retreat away from all anti-formalist law – whether anti-abuse or anti-avoidance – and towards the formulation of the tighter, narrower rules upon which many creative compliance techniques thrive. This retreat can take the form of guidelines issued by the regulator, clarification in the courts, legal opinions or clearances. The struggle for legal control between regulators and regulated will continue.

E. 'Cat-and-Mouse'

The 'cat-and-mouse' struggle can be seen in HMRC guidance. Regarding legal opinions, HMRC state (2020: C5.10.4, emphasis added) that 'some person's view that the tax arrangements are a reasonable course of action (whether the view of Queen's Counsel (QC), an accountant, a solicitor or anyone else) will *not* inevitably lead to the conclusion that the arrangement is not abusive'. Regarding clearances, HMRC seeks to avoid the struggle by not providing a clearance system for the GAAR (ibid: B17.1), although it adds that the GAAR 'cannot be invoked to override' a clearance in respect of a particular transaction (B17.2). The TUC (2013a) also criticised the lack of a clearance system because it would create uncertainty – another example of the 'rule of law' critique.

III. Will Creative Compliance Survive?

Wendel (2010: 69) and Luban (1988: 15) quote King Louis XII of France's complaint: 'Lawyers use the law as shoemakers use leather; rubbing it, pressing it, stretching it with their teeth, all to the end of making it fit their purposes.' Wendel wishes lawyers weren't 'just sophists' – people who reason with clever but false arguments. He takes issue with legal realist and 'indeterminacy of law' scholars, and claims that law is in fact relatively stable and determinate. The position Wendel defends is that

> the law is not fully determinate, in the sense that in any given situation there is only one view a reasonable lawyer could reach about the content of a citizen's legal entitlements, *but* it possesses sufficient determinacy to ground ethical evaluation of lawyer's advising on the basis of whether their advice is adequately supported by legal reasons (2011: 2).

Regardless of the merits of his argument (see Wendel 2012), I predict that lawyers and clients who have the motivation (and resources) will continue to 'use law as shoemakers', whether one calls their lawyers sophists or not. Many law firm websites boast about their legal creativity (Whelan 2007). Corporate lawyers, 'once seen as arbiters of appropriate business conduct for their clients, had their role narrowed to that of legal technician, solving legal problems to advance client interests' (Yablon 2019: 4).

In short, creative compliance is here to stay, despite attempts to control it. This reflects the manipulability of the legal system and the indeterminacy of law, and poses a difficult challenge to regulators. Wendel (2010) is surely right though – if the law can essentially be manipulated out of existence, there *is* a problem. That's why underpinning the GAAR is the claim that the 'intention' of Parliament can sometimes override the laws Parliament enacts. In practice, however, not only is 'intention' open to interpretation, but formalism and legalism also provide the ideological framework for lawyers to manage the risks for clients. The definition of tax avoidance reinforces this point: 'Tax avoidance is legal in that it incorporates *no wrongful concealment of relevant facts*' (*Simon's Taxes* 1988: 117, emphasis added). The IRS (nd) declares succinctly and starkly: 'tax avoidance is perfectly legal'. Even post-GAAR, the definition remains the same: 'tax avoidance is compliant with the law, though aggressive or abusive avoidance, as opposed to simple tax planning, will seek to comply with the letter of the law, but to subvert its purpose' (Seely 2021: 3).

IV. Creative Compliance: Ethical or Not?

The SRA (2019f) issued a warning notice to solicitors facilitating tax avoidance schemes that are 'aggressive in ways that go beyond the intentions of Parliament'. Doing so, the SRA claimed, shows a 'want of integrity and a failure to act with independence. They also compel a conclusion [solicitors] so acted as to diminish the trust the public would place in [solicitors] and the provision of legal services' (*SRA v Chan*). The SRA warned that solicitors involved in such arrangements are at risk of disciplinary proceedings. In these circumstances, solicitors should advise clients they cannot comply with their instructions and unless they change them, they should terminate the retainer. The same goes for the promotion or implementation of abusive arrangements. If solicitors consider that a scheme is likely to be found abusive, they can advise clients to this effect. That said, the SRA (2019f) also tells solicitors:

> Where a scheme can reasonably be argued not to be abusive, you can advise a client to that effect, facilitate the scheme where so instructed by a client, properly advised as to the risks, and litigate on behalf of a client as to the legality of the scheme where you can do so in a manner consistent with your duty to the court.

Is there a contradiction here? While the SRA is concerned about 'aggressive schemes', it leaves open the extent to which solicitors can be aggressive or zealous. Solicitors may be investigated where they have facilitated schemes which are found to be abusive, or where schemes contain indicators of abuse. But if one adopts the 'zealous within the bounds of law' mantra, solicitors can help clients if a scheme can reasonably be argued not to be abusive. As the SRA confirm, '[i]t is for the relevant courts and tribunals to adjudicate on the legality of tax avoidance schemes', not solicitors.

Lawyers are duty-bound to present clients with all legal options – including ways to reduce tax – so isn't it for the client to decide whether to adopt them? As McBarnet (1991: 324) notes: 'There is a spectrum of greys at the boundaries of lawful and deviant behaviour.' It's unlikely, but not inconceivable, that lawyers could be held to be negligent *not* to advise on a tax avoidance scheme that other competent lawyers would have advised (*Hossein*). Once again, 'good faith' is critical in determining the ethicality of advising clients on the bounds of law. The problem for regulators is simple: how can it *not* be ethical if it *is* legal?

Creative compliance strategies are perceived by many lawyers as not only perfectly legal but also perfectly ethical – despite the consequences. That's why creative compliance – using the *law* as material to be worked upon – is so powerful: *endorsing* rather than *limiting* the *zealousness* for clients. Creative compliance equates legality with permissibility. If it's lawful, it's acceptable, and clients can claim compliance. Meanwhile, lawyers can claim to be 'perfectly ethical'. It's a 'rule of law' justification – even if inescapably immoral actions have been 'laundered' by the amoral technician lawyer into an amoral construct (McBarnet 1991), or even into 'lawfare'.

11

Lawfare

Gaming the System

The broad mass of a nation ... will more easily fall victim to a big lie than a small one,
— Adolf Hitler (1925: vol 1, Chapter 10)

Lawfare also uses 'rights and law' strategically for clients, but the objective is to 'advance their political goals' (Gloppen 2023). This '"domestic lawfare" is perhaps the most potentially pernicious variant of lawfare for liberal democratic systems' (ibid). That's because it uses law strategically 'to obtain illegitimate purposes of a geopolitical, political, financial or commercial nature' (Lawfare Institute 2021). It entails 'using – and often misusing – legal instruments to undermine their political opponents' (Gloppen 2023). Tactics include abuse of laws to 'harm an adversary's public image', an abuse of legal procedure to 'restrain their freedom, to intimidate opponents, to silence them, influence public opinion negatively to anticipate judgments and curtail their right to an unbiased defence' (Lawfare Institute 2021). No wonder lawfare is viewed as 'a pejorative and polemical word' and 'doing something sneaky' (Luban 2010) and there's been vociferous criticism of lawyers who employ lawfare. Indeed, by 'inventing cockamamie theories ... it's clear we in the legal profession have come to a crisis point' (Conway, Luttig and Comstock 2023). Lawyers who engage in lawfare are in danger of 'helping to undermine the very institutions upon which democracy and the rule of law depend' (*The Times* 2023b).

Lawfare, 'as both a concept and a species of political practice, has exploded over the past decades' and it 'proliferates definitions at a giddy rate' (Comaroff 2023). No wonder regulators are paying attention: 'the use or threat of litigation for reasons that are not connected to resolving genuine disputes nor advancing legal rights' (SRA 2022b) constitute abuses in the conduct of disputes. It's 'improper to bring cases or allegations without merit, or to do so in an oppressive, threatening or abusive manner'. For clients who can afford to pay, lawyers 'professionally skilled in casuistry, finding loopholes in rules, exploiting ambiguity and uncertainty, and playing strategic games ... can rapidly exhaust adversaries who cannot, and thus turn the legal system into ... a medium for extortion and oppression of the weak by the strong' (Gordon 1990: 259).

That said, depending on the context, lawfare might be 'virtuous or vicious' (Dressler 2021). So while the word 'lawfare' has been traced back to 1975 (Carlson and Yeomans 1975), 'unnamed, the phenomenon has a deep past' with 'cadres of lawyers' using 'their learned skills' (Comaroff 2023: Preface) for a variety of purposes. Virtuous examples include using legal tactics to constrain political power in the struggle against apartheid in South Africa (Abel 1995b) and litigation to challenge the US government's so-called 'war on terror' tactics – torture, rendition and detention (Hajjar 2018). One vicious example might be using law to silence community groups in Australia (Walters 2003). Either way, '[l]awfare is a species of the politicization of law' (Luban 2010: 2). It's a legal claim 'backed by nothing but the will of the parties' rather than by legal rights as such (Abel 1995b).

Two lawfare strategies will be explored in this chapter: Strategic Lawsuits Against Public Participation (SLAPPs) and Creative Lawyering in Political Systems (CLIPS). Donald Trump's 'a sort of layman's master in law and lawfare' (Kruse 2024), so his use of SLAPPs and CLIPS will be discussed.

I. SLAPPs

SLAPPs are legal actions brought 'with the intention of harassing, intimidating and financially or psychologically exhausting opponents via improper use of the legal system' (GovUK 2023a). They're 'designed to silence criticism' and stifle 'scrutiny and debate on matters of public interest' (FPC 2023: 5). Another key feature, evident from the anti-SLAPP legislation – 33 US States have them – is they're characterised by 'an abuse of process by a plaintiff or excessive claims in matters in which the defendant is exercising a constitutionally protected right' (Borg-Bathet et al 2021: 12).

Concern about SLAPPs 'has been growing globally' (FPC 2023: 5) but it's 'the UK, and more specifically, London, that has been identified as a leading jurisdiction for domestic and trans-national SLAPP cases against media' (ibid; see also Hooper 2023). London has 'earned the reputation of being the "town named Sue"' (*The Times* 2023c); it's a 'global hub for the super-rich, including those enriched through illicit schemes', but 'cases rarely make the public record unless journalists themselves speak out' (FPC 2023: 5). Targets include 'journalists, independent media outlets, academics, civil society and human rights NGOs' (Borg-Bathet, et al 2021: 7). Filers include 'corporations, wealthy individuals, or even governmental bodies in some instances' (ibid), such as 'those oligarchs and kleptocrats who are using "weapons grade" legal action – lawfare – to silence their critics' (Agnew and Hodge 2023).

Four separate libel claims were made by three Russian billionaires, including Roman Abramovich, and Rosneft, a Russian state-controlled oil company, against investigative journalist Catherine Belton and her publisher after the 2020 publication of *Putin's People: How the KGB Took Back Russia and Then Took the West*. After Eliot Higgins named Yevgeny Prigozhin as involved with the mercenary Wagner group, it was 'hard to imagine a more clear-cut example of a Slapp … designed to silence journalists' (*The Times* 2023b). Prigozhin later acknowledged he'd founded the group. Nadhim Zahawi tried to stop *The Independent* newspaper reporting he was negotiating with his own tax authorities – he was Chancellor of the Exchequer (finance minister) – about his tax liability. He 'tried to bully us … by issuing repeated legal threats … and … was using every trick in the book of political dark arts to silence us' (*The Independent* 2023). The warning of legal action by mining company ENRC against journalist Tom Burgis, author of *Kleptopia: How Dirty Money is Conquering the World*, his publisher and others, was described by HarperCollins as 'an egregious case of lawfare' (Garside 2023). The cases were either dismissed or discontinued, but only after a defence costing £340,000.

Lawyers facilitate SLAPPs in several ways. Hooper (2023) points to the 'needlessly aggressive tactics and venality of some law firms'. Tactics entail 'large numbers of pre-action letters, targeting a financially weak defendant and bringing claims simultaneously in multiple jurisdictions' (GovUK 2023a). They're 'a rising problem and amount to abusive proceedings' as 'claimants explore new ways to suppress legitimate reporting (ibid). They include 'making excessive or meritless claims, aggressive and intimidating threats; otherwise acting in a way which fails to meet the wider public interest principles' (SRA 2022b). There's also the '"hidden problem" of UK law firms sending threatening legal communications prior to any official filings' (FPC 2023: 7). Such threats can be 'utilized as a tool for reputation laundering' to 'clean up a client's image and remove unfavourable information in the public domain' and '[t]he availability of highly skilled expensive British law firms, adept at utilizing heavy-handed tactics that are designed to, or have the effect of, intimidating journalists' (ibid). Such firms 'appear to operate in combination with a network of public relations consultants, corporate investigators and private protection agencies' (ibid: 8).

II. CLIPS

The CLIPS strategy also redefines political goals as technical legal issues. The 'torture memos' concealed moral and political choices by presenting them as technical legal analysis. Actions which stretch 'the limits of legality' had been 'laundered by law to serve the purposes of US military "necessity"' (Comaroff 2023). SLAPPs and CLIPS advance client interests but also threaten to undermine the lawyers' role as public professionals acting in the public interest. Both pose an ethical challenge and 'important consideration' for lawyers: 'whether the claim is meritless, or – in light of your understanding of the defences available to your opponent – is bound to fail' (SRA 2022b). Have lawyers given 'a false patina of legal legitimacy to meritless claims' (Joy and McMunigal 2022: 143)? What are the implications of turning the political into the legal for lawyers' ethics, democracy and the rule of law?

III. Trump's SLAPPs

Trump's used 'shotgun pleading designed to serve a political purpose' (*Trump* 2022b: 6, Judge Middlebrooks). It sought 'to advance a political narrative; not to address legal harm caused by any Defendant' (ibid: 7). It was 'a deliberate attempt to harass; to tell a story without regard to facts' (ibid: 10). Trump is a 'prolific and sophisticated litigant who is repeatedly using the courts to seek revenge on political adversaries' (ibid: 6); 'the mastermind of strategic abuse of the judicial process' and has a 'pattern of misusing the courts to serve political purposes' (ibid: 21); and is 'using the courts as a stage set for political theater and grievance. This behavior interferes with the ability of the judiciary to perform its constitutional duty' (ibid: 34).

A. Pattern of Abuse

In a section headed 'A Pattern of Abuse of the Courts', Judge Middlebrooks illustrated Trump's 'misusing the courts to serve political purposes'. In November 2021, his lawyer, Alina Habba, sent a 'Demand Letter, Notice of Potential Litigation and Non-spoliation of Evidence' to the Pulitzer Prize Board demanding they 'take immediate steps to strip *The New York Times* [*NYT*] and *The Washington Post* of the 2018 Pulitzer Prize for National Reporting' (*Trump* 2022b: 22). A series of articles on Trump's 'dubious tax schemes' won the Prize. Nineteen individual members of the board were targeted. In 2024, the New York Supreme Court ordered Trump to pay *NYT* \$392,638 in 'attorneys' fees, legal expenses and costs' having accused the newspaper of an 'insidious plot' to obtain his tax records (Yousif 2024). The decision shows 'how the state's newly amended anti-SLAPP statute can be a powerful force for protecting press freedom' (New York County Supreme Court Judge Robert R Reed, quoted in Woodward 2024).

Another example was a lawsuit in October 2022, filed in Okeechobee, Florida, a location with 'no apparent connection' to Trump or any of the defendants. The complaint 'misrepresented the findings of the Mueller Report'. According to the judge: 'The effort by Mr Trump and his lawyers to use the courts to bully journalists as part of a dishonest and futile attempt to rewrite history is a shameless attack on a freedom essential to democracy' (*Trump* 2022b: 24) Middlebrooks also referred to March 2019, when the New York Office of the Attorney General began investigating Trump and his business. Trump's attempts to quash subpoenas were denied all the way to the highest court, the New York Court of Appeals. In December 2021, Trump and the Trump Organization LLC sued Attorney General Letitia James individually rather than in her official capacity alleging that the investigation infringed his constitutional rights. This 'attempt … was plainly frivolous' (ibid: 28).

In July 2021, Trump and others sued Twitter, YouTube and Facebook, claiming they'd censored his speech. The First Amendment, however, prohibits only governmental abridgment of speech. Therefore, in order to succeed in the claim, Trump had to allege these private companies were so dominated by governmental authorities that they could be considered 'state actors'. In the Twitter legislation, Trump lawyers claimed Democratic members of Congress, Vice President Kamala Harris and First Lady Michelle Obama 'coerced' the company to censor Trump. The claim was dismissed.

In 2019, Charles Harder, 'litigation counsel' for Trump and his campaign, advised CNN: 'my clients intend to file legal action'. His letter claimed violation of the Lanham Act for misrepresentations. In March 2020, Harder sued CNN for libel based on a contributor's article entitled 'Soliciting Dirt on Your Opponents from a Foreign Government is a Crime. Mueller Should Have Charged Trump Campaign Officials with it'. The complaint didn't plead actual malice, as required, and was dismissed. In October 2022, Trump sued CNN for defamation, claiming malice, but also arguing that standard 'does not – and should not – apply where the defendant is not publishing statements to foster debate, critical thinking or [the] "unfettered exchange of ideas" but rather seeks to participate in the political arena by offering propaganda' (*Trump* 2022b: 32).

B. Shotgun Pleading

Middlebrooks found part of the complaint was a 'quintessential shotgun pleading, that its claims were *foreclosed* by existing precedent, and its factual allegations were undermined and contradicted by the public reports and filings upon which it purported to rely' (ibid: 3, emphasis added). Such a pleading was 'an abusive litigation tactic which amounts to an obstruction of justice' (ibid: 6). There are four categories of shotgun pleading: multiple counts where each count adopts the allegations of all preceding counts, causing each successive count to carry all that came before and the last count to be a combination of the entire complaint; one that is replete with conclusory, vague and immaterial facts not obviously connected to any particular cause of action; one that does not separate into a different cause of action or claim of relief; and one that asserts multiple claims against multiple defendants without specifying which are responsible for which acts or omissions, or which of the defendants the claim is brought against (*Trump* 2022a: 7).

C. Sanctions

Middlebrooks said the lawsuit 'should never have been filed, which was completely frivolous, both factually and legally, and which was brought in bad faith for an improper purpose' (*Trump* 2022b: 6). He concluded

> this widespread and persistent conduct points to the need for deterrence ... This is purposeful conduct, some of which occurs beyond the pleadings and even outside of the courtroom ... Trump's deliberate use of a frivolous lawsuit for an improper purpose constitutes bad faith. And the behavior is not unique, but part of a plan, or at least a playbook. The telltale signs: Provocative and boastful rhetoric; A political narrative carried over from rallies; Attacks on political opponents and the news media; Disregard for legal principles and precedent; and Fundraising and payments to lawyers from political action committees. And when a ruling is adverse, accusations of bias on the part of the judges – often while the litigation is ongoing. (ibid: 33)

Trump, his lawyer Alina Habba and her firm Habba Madaio were sanctioned as jointly and severally liable and ordered to pay $937,989.39 in sanctions.

IV. Trump's CLIPS

Trump initiated not just a 'shotgun pleading', but also a 'shotgun lawsuit': 'Thirty one individuals and organizations were summoned to court, forced to hire lawyers to defend frivolous claims. The only common thread was Mr. Trump's animus' (*Trump* 2022c: 14, Judge Middlebrooks). One defendant, Charles Dolan, sought sanctions against Trump's lawyers under FRCP Rule 11. This requires lawyers to certify that to the best of their knowledge, information and belief formed after an inquiry reasonable in the circumstances that a case is not being presented for an improper purpose, the legal contentions are warranted by existing law or by a non-frivolous argument and the factual assertions have evidentiary support, or will have after further investigation or discovery. Judge Middlebrooks' conclusion was damning:

> These were political grievances masquerading as legal claims. This cannot be attributed to incompetent lawyering. It was a deliberate use of the judicial system to pursue a political agenda. ... It is harmful to the rule of law, portrays judges as partisans, and diverts resources that should be directed to real harms and legitimate legal claims. (ibid)

The lawyers were ordered to pay $50,000 into court and $16,274.23 in fees and costs to Dolan. This order was stayed pending an Eleventh Circuit appeal.

However, it's the CLIP plan, hatched in early December 2020 following Trump's election defeat, that's the main focus here. The architect of this 'bold, controversial strategy' was lawyer Kenneth Chesebro (Haberman et al 2023). What the strategy could achieve, Chesebro said, 'is not simply to keep Biden below 270 electoral votes. ... at no point will Trump be behind in the electoral vote count unless and until Biden can obtain a favorable decision from the Supreme Court upholding the Electoral Count Act as constitutional' (ibid). Chesebro acknowledged the Supreme Court was 'likely' to reject the strategy in the end, but it would focus attention on voter fraud and 'buy the Trump campaign more time to win litigation that would deprive Biden of electoral votes and/or add to Trumps' Column' (ibid). The aim was to delay the count on 6 January. The legal 'victory' could pave the way for 'political victory'.

Lawyer John Eastman 'championed the plan' (ibid). First, he attempted to put pressure on Republican-led legislatures to appoint alternate slates of electors. When no state legislature agreed to do so, he sought out Trump-supporting electors to sign documents falsely claiming to be legitimate presidential electors. These false and unauthorised slates of electors would go through the motions of voting as if they had authority to do so (ibid). Eastman then argued the 'false electors presented enough of a controversy for [Vice President Mike] Pence to decide which ones to count – or at the very least to refuse to count Biden's votes and call for a delay in finalizing the election to permit those GOP-run states to revisit the outcome' (Cheney 2023). They were said to be 'alternate' electors who could replace Biden's electors on 6 January. The aim was to persuade or put pressure on Pence unilaterally to throw out the real electors on 6 January and count those false slates of votes rather than the official and certified ones (Haberman et al 2023). In support of this political plan, Eastman prepared two memos: a 'preliminary' two-page memo and a six-page 'legal memo'. One judge called the strategy 'a coup in search of a legal theory' (CBS 2023). In 2024, the 'fake or alternate electors' and some unindicted co-conspirators have been charged with crimes in Arizona, Nevada, Georgia and Michigan.

A. The Eastman 'Coup' Memos

The memos provided the legal backing to the political strategy of disputing the election results and promoting the idea the election was tainted by fraud, disregard of state election law and misconduct by election officials: 'The fact is that the Constitution assigns this power to the Vice President as the ultimate arbiter. We should take all our actions with this in mind' (two-page memo). The strategy was reinforced by his argument that, since the counting of electoral votes at the Joint Session of Congress was a legal proceeding and not a judicial proceeding before a court, those who brought a lawsuit to challenge the unilateral action by Pence 'would have their past position – that these are non-justiciable political questions – thrown back at them, to get the lawsuit dismissed' (*In the Matter of John Charles Eastman* 2023: 17). The memo was 'designed to provide legal support and convince Vice President Pence to carry out' the strategy of declaring Trump as the winner (*In the Matter of John Charles Eastman* 2024: 88–89).

The six-page memo was discussed on 4 January by Eastman, Trump, Pence and two Pence aides, Chief of Staff Marc Short and legal counsel Greg Jacob. Eastman told Pence 'even assuming he had constitutional authority to reject contested electoral votes, it would be "foolish" to exercise any such authority in the absence of the state legislatures actually having certified the alternate Trump slate of electors' (Eastman 2021a). On 5 January, Eastman conceded to Pence's Jacob and Short that the 'positions he was urging Pence to take were contrary to historical practice, violated several provisions of statutory law, and would likely be unanimously rejected by the Supreme Court' (*In the Matter of John Charles Eastman* 2023: 20). So, Eastman 'actually recommended to … Pence … that he accede to requests from numerous state legislators … to delay the proceedings long enough for the legislatures in the contested states to assess the impact of acknowledged illegality in the conduct of the election' (Eastman 2021a).

On 6 January, Pence refused, stating the Constitution constrained him from 'claiming unilateral authority to determine which electoral votes should be counted and which not' (Lee 2023). Jacob said Eastman was 'inventing something without any historical roots or any historical foundations and then desperately trying to find some hook in the constitutional text that neither history, nor structure, nor practice, nor common sense supported' (Marcus 2023); Eastman was a 'serpent in the ear of the President' (CBS 2023). No wonder the memos generated 'enormous controversy' (Bessette 2021).

i. Eastman Disciplinary

Eleven disciplinary charges were brought by the California State Bar (*In the Matter of John Charles Eastman* 2023, 2024): failing to support the US Constitution and laws (Count 1), misleading a court and moral turpitude (Counts 2–11). Judge Yvette D Roland of the State Bar Court (the only independent court dedicated solely to attorney discipline) found him culpable of 10, including Count 1. She found clear and convincing evidence that Eastman and Trump agreed to obstruct the counting of electors on 6 January (2024: 111) and that Eastman's actions were carried out with deceit or dishonesty as he was 'aware his plan was unlawful and lacked any factual or legal support' (ibid: 114).

Eastman argued in his two-page memo: 'There is very solid legal authority, and historical precedent, for the view that [Pence] does the counting, including the resolution of disputed electoral votes … and all Members of Congress do is watch.' Claiming the Electoral Count Act was 'likely unconstitutional', he suggested it 'places the executive of the state above the legislature, contrary to Article II' of the US Constitution, which assigns to legislatures the plenary power to determine the manner for choosing presidential electors. Thus, a state legislative certification could supersede a prior executive branch certification (by election officials).

Judge Roland, however, noted the two-page memo took a position contrary to what Eastman had held for 20 years. Eastman said his change was 'due to a significant amount of additional research' (ibid: 45). The Judge found this incredible, and more likely correlated with the timeframe of his representation of Trump (ibid: fn 54). Eastman claimed 'solid legal authority' for his view that Pence did the counting, but Roland disagreed: 'there was no *solid* legal authority' – he'd relied on four law review articles.

Judge Roland found Eastman culpable because he 'knew, or was grossly negligent in not knowing, that there was no evidence upon which a reasonable attorney would rely of election fraud or illegality that could have affected the outcome of the election' (*In the Matter of John Charles Eastman* 2023: 5, 2024), yet provided legal advice, formulated legal strategies and engaged in litigation on that basis. Also, based on misinterpretations of historical sources and law review articles, and law review articles that he knew or was grossly negligent in not knowing were themselves fundamentally flawed, he provided and proposed actions based on legal advice regarding the unilateral authority of the Vice President to disregard or delay the counting of electoral votes that were unsupported by the historical record and established legal authority and precedent, such that no reasonable attorney with expertise in constitutional or election law would have concluded that the Vice President was legally authorised to take the actions Eastman proposed (ibid: 6; 2024). In short, 'the course of conduct in his memos was factually and legally unsupported' (2024: 108).

V. The Role of Lawyers

The 'key feature of SLAPPs is their tendency to transfer debate from the political to the legal sphere' (Borg-Bathet et al 2021: 7, 8). As Judge Middlebrooks put it, 'the Plaintiff is not attempting to seek redress for any legal harm; instead he is seeking to flaunt a two-hundred-page political manifesto outlining his grievances against those that have opposed him' (*Trump* 2022a: 64). The same is true of CLIPS. Eastman's legal memo's 'way of formulating the point makes it appear what is going on here is a kind of legal exercise' when it was actually 'made to influence the counting of electoral votes on January 6' (Bessette 2021). What Chesebro did was 'to bring the patina of elite law to a Trump campaign struggling to find attorneys who would work on its effort to overturn the election' (Kovensky 2022).

Clearly, the role lawyers play is an essential component of lawfare. Should they employ SLAAPs and CLIPS for clients? If yes, what are the implications for the rule of law, democracy, freedom of speech and other fundamental values? If no, what does it say about professional ethics if lawyers carry on regardless?

The State Bar's allegation assumes Eastman knew, or was grossly negligent in not knowing, the allegations of election fraud were false. But what if clients insist they were true and instruct lawyers to proceed on that basis? Trump consistently, and defiantly, claimed the election was 'stolen'. As Trump lawyer John Lauro said, Trump 'believed in his heart of hearts that he had won that election … he believes he won' (NBC 2023). A section heading of one of the memos read in part, 'this Election was Stolen by a strategic

Democrat plan to Systematically flout existing election laws for partisan advantage; we're no longer playing by Queensbury Rules, therefore' (Karp 2023, quoting Bruce Green). Isn't it the lawyer's job to protect the client's propositions and representations of information, and to challenge contradictory versions? Isn't that version what the client asserts to be the truth?

VI. Ethical Ambiguity

To be ethical, lawfare must fall within the limits of the rule of law and the constraints of ethical rules. But both are remarkably flexible. So, the challenge for lawyers is how to navigate the ethical ambiguities. It's the 'duty' of every lawyer to 'to use legal procedure for the fullest benefit of the client's cause, but also a duty not to abuse legal procedure' (MR 3.1[1]). Judge Middlebrooks decided the filing on behalf of Trump against Hillary Clinton et al was frivolous. However, MR 3.1, Comment [2] states that filing a claim for a client 'is not frivolous merely because the facts have not first been fully substantiated'. What the lawyer is required to do it to 'inform themselves about the facts of their client's causes and the applicable law and determine that they can make good faith arguments in support of their client's cause'. An action is not frivolous 'even though the lawyer believes that the client's position ultimately will not prevail'.

Similarly, the duty not to mislead regarding law and facts doesn't prevent an EW lawyer 'putting forward your client's case simply because you do not believe that the facts are as the client states them to be' (BSB 2024: gC6). That said, a lawyer must not 'recklessly mislead' and recklessly means 'being indifferent to the truth, or not caring whether something is true or false' (ibid: rC9). Lawyers should also consider the prospects of a proposed course of action being unsuccessful or counterproductive (SRA 2022b). If they suspect a client's case is not honestly brought or the context is high-risk, their duty to the administration of justice, the court and the rule of law, 'demand[s] proper checks of the instruction and evidence' (SRA 2018).

In US Federal cases, FRCP Rule 11 applies. Some Trump lawyers have been sanctioned for falling foul of its provisions (Joy and McMunigal 2022). Alina Habba made no apology, despite being sanctioned for 'willful' conduct, a 'shotgun pleading' and a 'shotgun lawsuit' under the Federal rules (*Trump* 2022b). Jenna Ellis did apologise and, after pleading guilty of aiding and abetting false statements in Georgia, told the court: 'I failed to do my due diligence. I relied on others, including lawyers with many more years of experience than I, to provide me with true and reliable information … what I did not do, but should have done … was to make sure that the facts other lawyers alleged to be true were, in fact, true' (Cohen 2023). After admitting that many of her public statements were false, Ellis was censured in Colorado.

Judge Middlebrooks also described claims in Trump's lawsuit as 'foreclosed by existing precedent' (*Trump* 2022b: 3). But the ambiguity is evident: a precedent is a precedent only as long as it exists! It can be changed. As MR 3.1 states, 'the law is not always clear and *never* is static' (Comment [1], emphasis added). It adds: 'in determining the proper scope of advocacy, account must be taken of the law's ambiguities and potential for change'.

Lawyers must uphold the constitutional principle of the rule of law and the proper administration of justice (SRA Principle 1). But they're also told 'Making advice and legal representation available to all is in the public interest' (SRA 2018) and it's 'not in the public interest for false or misleading information to be needlessly published' (SRA 2022b). Indeed, the 'rule of law and our legal system provides that there is a right to advice and representation for all' (SRA 2022a). The right to bring a legal claim in defence of spurious accusations 'is an important part of a democracy and functioning judicial system' (FPC 2023: 11). This includes protecting a client's privacy or reputation – the same objective as a SLAPP. Hugh Tomlinson told the court in the Catherine Belton case that his client Roman Abramovich understood his action could be construed as 'an attack on free speech and public interest journalism' (Sabbagh 2021). However, ultimately, the case was settled; the publisher agreed to make edits to the book and a charitable donation after agreeing some of the information about the oligarchs was incorrect. Legal costs were £1.5 million (Moffatt 2023).

In short, there are genuine as well as meritless cases; strong as well as weak. There are lying clients like Jeffrey Archer and Lance Armstrong. Both won libel cases against newspapers only for the former, 14 years later, to be jailed for perjury, and the latter telling Oprah Winfrey in 2013 that his denial of using banned substances in his Tour de France wins between 1999 and 2005 was 'one big lie'. Trump's been accused of another 'Big Lie', but if lawyers ask 'serious questions' and get 'serious answers', must they proceed on the basis of those instructions? How do they know whether it's a SLAPP or whether the CLIPS argument will succeed? As a specialist in legal malpractice law stated: 'There is a duty not to bring falsehoods to court. There is also a duty to zealously advocate for your client. That balance is probably a moving target' (Samuel C Bellicini, quoted in Karp 2023). In short, how should lawyers strike the balance between prevention while protecting access to justice?

VII. Striking the Balance?

Many would argue that withholding legal arguments from clients – in effect denying them options – constitutes malpractice. The duty is to present all lawful options and let clients decide whether to pursue them. As Chesebro put it: 'It is the duty of any attorney to leave no stone unturned in examining the legal options that exist in a particular situation.' He added, 'If there is a non-frivolous argument concerning the meaning of the Electoral Count Act or its constitutionality, its legitimate to press that and to let the courts decide.' In short: 'Lawyers have an ethical obligation to explore every possible argument that might benefit their clients. In my work for the Trump campaign, I fulfilled that obligation' (Kovensky 2022). There's a spectrum of greys at the boundaries of the law. How can it *not* be ethical if it *is* arguably legal?

The critical question in the Eastman CLIPS is whether

> the arguments and scenarios in the two memos [can] withstand scrutiny. If not, why not? Are they of any value in guiding us as to how to address, through new law or constitutional amendment, the conundrum we face when statewide vote results are disputed in presidential elections – a conundrum likely to bedevil us for many elections to come in our hyper-partisan political environment. (Bessette 2021)

Eastman (2021a) argued the memos were grounded in 'constitutional text and supported by scholarly writings or prior judicial precedent', though he admitted they were 'premised on the assumption of proven electoral fraud or illegality'. However, there's little doubt Eastman and Trump shared the same conviction: the election had been 'stolen'. In his six-page memo, Eastman referred to 'illegal conduct by election officials' and asserted that 'important state election laws were altered or dispensed with altogether in key swing states and/or cities and counties'. Examples included 'signature verification requirements, prohibitions on ballot harvesting, and allowance of observers during ballot counting'. These illegalities 'without question, took place'. He concluded: 'we are facing a constitutional crisis … If the illegality and fraud that demonstrably occurred here is allowed to stand … then the sovereign people no longer control the direction of their government, and we will have ceased to be a self-governing people'. Eastman still feels the US faces 'an existential threat' (CBS 2023).

Eastman and Trump also argued that the law was uncertain. Trump pointed to the Count Reform and Presidential Transition Improvement Act 2022: the 'fact that they had to CLARIFY THE LAW means there was UNCERTAINTY, which means it was open to interpretation. It could have been done!' (Marcus 2023). Edward B Foley, a distinguished election law professor at Ohio State University and author of one of the four law review articles Eastman cited, warned, just two weeks after the November 2020 vote, that the Electoral Count Act was 'riddled with uncertain language and loopholes' (Blum 2021). He 'delineated a process by which Vice President Pence, counting the submitted electoral votes on Jan. 6, might try to point at that vagueness to throw the entire election into a state of uncertainty'. When asked about the 'possibility of competing slates of electors – that is, Trump's chosen electors saying that *their* votes should count', Foley responded: 'There's a version of what you just said that I have not publicly written about because I don't want to invite a scenario that I think is inappropriate in an electoral democracy, which should be based on what the voters want.' Foley clearly 'understood that there was at least enough breathing space within the normally uncontentious process of counting those votes that an actor less interested in upholding the will of the electorate might be empowered'.

Eastman also cited in support of his argument Harvard Law Professor Laurence Tribe. Tribe indicated a vice president has power to reject ungrounded challenges to state certifications, but 'may have other powers'. He refused to discuss them because 'I don't want to lay out a complete road map for the other side' (quoted in Bessette 2021) This hints at a potential 'large assertion of power' with 'only the vice president standing between totalitarianism and us, between bloodless coup and democracy' (ibid). Indeed, Eastman's case to Pence wasn't dismissed until after Pence or his high-level staff consulted with former Vice President Dan Quayle and Michael Luttig, a retired federal appellate judge (for whom Eastman had once clerked).

VIII. Disciplinary Ambiguity

Eastman's lawyer argued that Eastman wasn't looking to 'steal the election' or 'invent ways' to make Trump the winner, but 'engaging in … a serious debate about the vice president's authority regarding election certification' (Lee 2023). This is the ethical dilemma CLIPS pose to lawyers. After all, Trump enjoyed legal victories, suffered narrow defeats and made some non-frivolous claims. Here is a list extracted from Cummings' comprehensive review (2024):

- while first-wave suits focused on technical compliance with state law, some raised constitutional violations which asserted 'aggressive, though not frivolous, interpretations of the Constitution' and some 'did yield some Trump victories';
- many cases advanced independent state legislature (ISL) theory which, despite being 'an aggressive interpretation of the Constitution, it was not without legal plausibility' and one case succeeded;
- 'stopping fraud was the group's animating principle', 59 post-election lawsuits were filed and 'some individual cases … raised legitimate claims of improper voting rules and ballot processing';
- of 11 cases filed between 13 and 21 November, Trump won one case;
- when the Supreme Court denied the petition in a case which used ISL theory and an 'expert' economist evidence that Biden's odds against winning the popular vote in four states was one quadrillion to one, the denial was not unanimous: two justices dissented.

Eastman claimed 'the only thing he's guilty of is giving bold legal advice' (CBS 2023). He argued (2021b) it was 'patently untrue that my statements have "no basis in fact or law"'. So, for regulators too, there's a challenge: 'No disciplinary action should be taken when the lawyer chooses not to act or acts within the bounds of such discretion' (MR Preamble [14]). However, Judge Roland has recommended Eastman be disbarred. The Supreme Court is the ultimate arbiter.

IX. The Rule of Law Re-imagined

Lawfare highlights the gap between the rule of law in theory (books) and the rule of law in action. The rule of law is a double-edged sword: it may constrain arbitrary state power, but it's also a weapon for lawyers and clients. Cummings (2024: 105) details the 'role that lawyers play in contributing to democracy's decline'. He argues there's a 'professional paradox at the center of democratic backsliding': lawyers attack the rule of law (ibid: 106). He's correct that for autocrats seeking to breakdown democracy, 'it is critical to have the law – or at least the appearance of legality – on their side' (ibid): 'the patina of legality' (Joy and McMunigal 2022: 143). This 'must appear to follow legal process, violating the spirit but not the form of liberal constitutionalism' to effectuate change (Cummings 2024: 113). Their strategy is to 'use legal "tactics" to defend changes that undermine the "liberal" dimension of liberal democracy' and 'for this, they need lawyers' (ibid: 114).

But Cummings's conclusion – autocrats 'therefore cloak attacks of the rule of law in the language of law' – hints at why the rule of law requires re-imagining. What autocrats – and other clients – do is not to *attack* the rule of law, but to *use* it to their benefit (McBarnet and Whelan 1991, 1999). This isn't turning the rule of law on itself – unless one views the rule of law as available only to some and not others. It's why the 'spirit of the law' can be 'elusive' or, more importantly, made to be so. In fact, another principle of the rule of law is that it should, unless otherwise justified, be accessible to all. If lawyers decided to whom they would make law available, they would become the dreaded 'oligarchy of lawyers' (Pepper 1986; Wasserstrom 1975). This use of the rule of law is the real professional paradox.

A. The Professional Paradox

Lawyers generally reify law and have an ideology of 'legalism': the ethical attitude that holds moral conduct – what lawyers should do – to be a matter of rule following, and moral relationships to consist of duties and rights determined by rules (Shklar 1964: 1). They have this ideology not only for autocrats and oligarchs but also for most clients, whether liberal or illiberal. Cummings' review actually reveals this 'professional paradox'. Lawyers are indeed 'guardians of formalism' (2024: 106); they learn to 'think like a lawyer' (ibid: 107). No wonder they *rely* on the rule of law not only to legitimise political goals, whether SLAPPs or CLIPS, but also to achieve client goals more broadly. They are, indeed, 'essential enablers' (ibid: 108), but their tool is the *law* and maybe that's the challenge disciplinary authorities must overcome. 'Perfectly legal' equals 'perfectly ethical'. 'Arguably legal' equals 'arguably ethical'.

Cummings acknowledges this: 'As zealous advocates lawyers are *permitted* to make aggressive legal arguments – to "spin" the law in favor of clients' (ibid: 116, emphasis added). He adds: 'In this way, lawyers ensure the viability of the rule of law.' So, how should they do it? He says, rightly, that lawyers have discretion to 'exercise independent legal judgment to align client interests with principles of justice' (ibid: 115). But should *lawyers really* have 'discretion to decide what counts as valid *law*' (ibid: emphasis added) or should they have a more limited discretion: to argue for 'an extension, modification or *reversal* of existing law', even if 'the lawyer believes that the client's position ultimately will not prevail' (MR 3.1 and Comment [2])? Lord Bingham, the former senior UK Supreme Court judge, cited another fundamental principle of the rule of law: that legal questions should be determined 'according to law, not by the exercise of discretion' (Bingham 2011: Chapter 2), least of all, one might add, by lawyers.

It may be true the 'pathway to autocracy relies on law' (Cummings 2024: 140) but is that 'autocratic lawyering' (ibid: 120) or 'creative lawyering'? I would say the latter – as does Cummings: 'Stop the Steal did not reject the law, but rather purported to follow its letter by rationalizing legal grounds for rejecting the election results' (ibid: 114). The campaign 'mobilized *the symbolic power* of law' (ibid: 142, emphasis in original). As with creative compliance, some strategies succeed and some don't. Indeed: 'Ultimately, Stop the Steal was foiled by the decision of judges to systematically reject the campaign's post-election challenges' (ibid: 174). Abel and Cummings are correct: it was politics by other means based on the power of the rule of law. But the paradox wasn't only of professionalism but also of the rule of law.

In 2024 the UK Conservative government supported a Bill to deter SLAPPs via a dismissal mechanism and costs protection scheme. But it's one thing to deter abusive legal proceedings and another not to deter legitimate claims. There's a risk of increased costs, uncertainty about the definition of 'public interest' and concern that ordinary people may be more affected than the 'super-rich and powerful wrongdoers that it is supposed to be targeting' (Hugo Mason, 'reputation specialist' at Simkins, quoted in Cross 2024).

Common to controlling both CLIPS and SLAPPs is the issue of 'law': what's arguable, what's frivolous – indeed, what's facetious? How does a lawyer *know* which is which? Is it really their job to find out and if so how sure must they be? Or should they not leave it to the courts (acknowledging, however, that the goal of many legal proceedings – not just SLAPPs – is to avoid court altogether)? As Cummings (2024: 180) notes: 'Courts wield powerful tools that hold lawyers to account ... they can demand facts, reject unsubstantiated claims, and dismiss frivolous suits. Overall, courts performed these functions well in the 2020 election and US judicial independence has been rightly credited as a central reason for why the Trump election attack failed' (ibid: 192). Law is indeed both a weapon and a shield against authoritarianism (ibid: 205). Lawfare *uses* the rule of law. Law is not 'mobilized *against* legality' (ibid: 193), powerful actors *use* legality to achieve their goals. That said, autocrats seeking power also abuse power, attack expertise (Abel 2024a, b. c) and may lose in the courts, but *not* in the court of public opinion.

X. Conclusions

There are genuine concerns about lawyers and lawfare, but there are also substantial counter-arguments. Were Eastman's memos 'unsupported by law'? If clients have sole responsibility for determining the objectives of legal representation and claim they've been defamed, or want to challenge facts or law, shouldn't lawyers proceed on that basis? At what point is an ethical line crossed when lawyers make legal arguments?

12

The Sword of Truth and the
Dagger of Deceit*

A truth that's told with bad intent beats all the lies you can invent.
— William Blake (cited in Gilchrist (1863))

According to Judge Frankel (1975: 1037): 'The statistical fact remains that the preponderant majority of those brought to trial did substantially what they are charged with.' Dershowitz (1982: xiv) believed 'almost all of my own clients have been guilty', but lawyers 'are no more ethical representing an innocent client than a guilty client, you're just doing an easier job' (WETA 1986). Van Kessel said (1993: 436): 'Pursuing acquittal of the guilty while avoiding presentation of clearly perjured testimony is admired as one of the great achievements of advocates.' The same might be said of winning in a civil trial. It's unethical to mislead courts with information known to be false, but what about misleading by submitting information known to be true? Giving evidence can be a double-edged sword because one way to help clients is, paradoxically, to use one truth to conceal or disguise the 'whole truth'. Can 'lying with the truth' be ethical?

After a husband and wife started legal proceedings, the husband died for an unrelated reason. To enhance the overall amount of compensation, Robert J Forrest advised the wife not to voluntarily reveal his death. At the mandatory automobile arbitration hearing, the arbitrator asked: 'Why's the husband absent?' The lawyer replied: 'He is unavailable.' The arbitrator entered awards for both the husband and wife. At his disciplinary hearing, Forrest admitted it was imprudent but not misrepresentation; he was merely withholding information, 'a negotiation technique he called "bluffing and puffing"' (*In the Matter of Robert J Forrest*: 342).

The District XIII Ethics Committee determined it was professional misconduct. The New Jersey Supreme Court agreed: 'Misrepresentation of a material fact to an adversary or a tribunal in the name of "zealous representation" never has been nor ever will be a permissible litigation tactic' (ibid: 345). It added: 'A misrepresentation to a tribunal is a most serious breach of ethics because it affects directly the administration of justice'. Forrest was suspended for six months. In 2024, the Virginia Supreme Court approved

---

* 'If it falls to me to start a fight to cut out the cancer of bent and twisted journalism in our country with the simple sword of truth and the trusty shield of British fair play, so be it.' Jonathan Aitken, British Member of Parliament 1974–97, 10 April 1995. After the collapse of a libel action against *The Guardian*, Aitken was convicted of perjury in 1999 and Granada Television broadcast a *World in Action* programme: 'The Dagger of Deceit'.

Legal Ethics Opinion 1900 (based on MR 3.3 and 4.1). If clients die during the course of legal representation, lawyers must disclose the death to opposing counsel or litigant and, if pending in a court, must inform the court; concealing would be misrepresentation or deceit. EW courts agree: lawyers are under a duty to inform courts of changed circumstances even after the conclusion of proceedings and even though the information provided during the proceedings was thought to be true (*Vernon*).

I. The Sword of Truth

Freedman argued that lawyers have a duty to take advantage of all opportunities to help clients. Failing to do everything that's not perjurious or illegal would be 'wrong' and a 'violation of the client's confidence'; zealous defence promotes the administration of justice and protects the client's dignity (1966: 1474–75). After all, clients 'disclose' their guilt in confidence; they shouldn't be prejudiced for having done so by lawyers adopting less 'zealous' tactics. Simon (1993: 1726) described Freedman's view as 'implausible'. Perhaps lawyers should never rely on confessions, even if there's corroborating evidence (Silver 1994: 379–90).

Challenging the reliability and credibility of prosecution evidence is clearly part of that duty, regardless of whether clients are known to be factually guilty (Freedman 1966: 1475). However, representing criminal defendants *known* to be guilty *is* the 'nightmare scenario' (Asimow and Weisberg 2009: 258) and a controversial issue in legal ethics (for example, Mitchell 1987; Simon 1993: 1717–19, Subin 1987, 1988). On the one hand, lawyers 'institutionally cannot care about guilt with regard to the degree of their effort or the zealousness of their representation' (Mosteller 2010: 2); on the other, 'clear knowledge of guilt as a result of a client's confidential confession … certainly affects and restricts the way that counsel can defend' (ibid: fn 5).

But should it? Subin (1987: 149) called a false defence a 'truth-defeating' device and this would include introducing mistaken testimony in order to induce false inferences. However, the ABA (2017: Standard 4-1.4(b), emphasis added) stated that: 'It is *not* a false statement for defense counsel to suggest inferences that may reasonably be drawn from the evidence.' But what evidence? Should lawyers take advantage of *any* truthful evidence, even knowing the client is factually guilty?

A. The Defence of David Westerfield

Westerfield abducted, raped and murdered seven-year-old Danielle van Dam. Lead lawyer Steven Feldman and co-counsel Robert Boyce knew of his 'factual' guilt because Westerfield told them where her body was located. It was found before a plea bargain – take the death penalty 'off the table' in exchange for disclosing the location – could be concluded. Westerfield pleaded not guilty.

At the 2002 trial, Feldman, in his opening statement, told the jury:

> We have doubts. We have doubts as to the cause of death. We have doubts as to the identity of Danielle van Dam's killer. We have doubts as to who left her where she resided, where she remained. And we have doubts as to who took her. (Jeralyn 2002)

Two alternative strategies about van Dam's death and Westerfield's link to it were presented. Van Dam's parents led a 'wild, swinging lifestyle' – smoking marijuana and swapping sex partners at their home. They might have unwittingly introduced the killer – one of their 'unsavoury' friends – into their home.

Hodes regarded this as acceptable: it was a false argument but was based on true facts. It was misdirection, but, he argued, false argumentation is ethical – an alternative narrative which the jury could accept or reject. Wendel (2018: 153) agrees: introducing true evidence that supports a false inference is part of persuading a jury the state hasn't proven its case beyond a reasonable doubt, and the only way to do that is by presenting a 'coherent narrative inconsistent with the state's evidence and theory of guilt'. He argues that the role of the criminal defence lawyer is to 'tell stories made up of true evidence that support false inferences of factual innocence'. This is 'justified by political ends such as protecting individuals against state power' (ibid: 154).

I disagree. Throwing suspicion on the parents' friends was a narrative *they knew* was false. In substance it *wasn't* about the parents' lifestyle at all. The argument implied someone else was more likely to have killed van Dam than Westerfield. A jury might conclude 'yes' Westerfield might have done it, but 'yes' so might someone else – we cannot convict beyond a reasonable doubt.

The second strategy was to challenge forensic evidence against Westerfield. The lawyers found experts to estimate a time of death when Westerfield was under 24-hour police surveillance, so Westerfield couldn't be the killer. Again, the argument went, the prosecution evidence was insufficient to prove guilt beyond a reasonable doubt. Hodes regards this as unacceptable because even if the experts believed their estimates, the lawyers *knew* it was false evidence. They were challenging reliable – and accurate – evidence by introducing *knowingly* inaccurate evidence, in contrast to the 'true' evidence about the parents' lifestyle.

I agree with Hodes: adopting this strategy was wrong, though there's a fine line between both strategies. When I present them to law students (in the US and EW), a majority always believe *both* approaches are acceptable. For me, where lawyers *know* their client *is* factually guilty – admittedly an exceptional scenario – they're *both* unethical.

Hodes (2002: 60) agrees with Freedman: defence lawyers are obliged 'to use all lawful means to mount a defense, whether or not the client is known to be factually guilty' – the obligation is rooted in lawyers' ethics and the US Constitution's Sixth Amendment. But is this a proper interpretation of MR 3.1: 'defend so as to require that every element of the case be established'? Defending by introducing irrelevant doubts undermines the mantra: conviction only 'beyond a reasonable doubt'. It substitutes a new mantra: acquit if there is 'unreasonable doubt'. The lawyers knew their evidence was lying with the truth; the jurors didn't. Rather than submitting that it was unsafe to convict because every element hasn't been established, they were suggesting Westerfield may not have committed the crime.

Hodes cites Supreme Court Justice Byron White – defence counsel must defend the client 'whether he is innocent or guilty', can 'confuse a witness, even a truthful one' and that: 'Our interest in not convicting the innocent permits counsel to put the State to its proof, to put the State's case in the worst possible light, regardless of what he thinks or knows to be the truth.' But White added this caveat: 'Undoubtedly there are some limits which defense counsel must observe' (*US v Wade*: 256–58).

I would suggest those limits were ignored. So did outraged members of the public; the defence lawyers 'turned themselves into public enemies' (Asimow and Weisberg 2009: 257). They were subject to so much public criticism that the San Diego Bar Association's answering machine told callers: 'If you want information about the Association, press 1; if you want to complain about Steven Feldman, press 2' (234). As for Westerfield, neither strategy worked; he was sentenced to death in August 2002. In February 2019, the California Supreme Court rejected his appeal (despite a 490-page brief). He's currently in San Quentin.

i. An EW Perspective

Barristers would be misleading courts 'if you were to set up a positive case inconsistent with the confession, as for example by: .1 suggesting to prosecution witnesses, calling your client or your witnesses to show; or submitting to the jury, that your client did not commit the crime; or .2 suggesting that someone else had done so; or .3 putting forward an alibi' (BSB 2024: gC10). It would therefore be unethical to set up 'any positive case' not in accordance with clients' instructions (ibid: gC6). A private confession imposes 'very strong limitations on the conduct of the defence' (Bar Council 1997: 12.3). Both Westerfield strategies were unethical by EW standards. After a client confessed to the crime, a barrister couldn't offer the client's mother as a witness even if she truthfully 'swore' her son was home – he put a mannequin under his bed covers!

Similarly, barristers shouldn't emulate American public defender James Kunen. He invited a jury, in his closing argument, to draw this inference: his client, accused of handling stolen goods, wouldn't have loaded them into the back seat of a borrowed car, rather than the trunk/boot if he'd known they were stolen. In fact, the client did so because he didn't have the key to the trunk/boot (Kunen 1983: 117), a fact the lawyer knew. Luban (2007: Chapter 2) claimed lawyers would be morally right to argue this. In EW, propositions shouldn't be put forward unless evidence has been presented which could be challenged in cross-examination (*R v Farooqi*).

If clients admit factual guilt but wish to plead not guilty, the Code guidance makes clear it's ethical for advocates to *keep* their admission confidential and to *continue* to represent them. It wouldn't be misleading the court to 'test in cross-examination the reliability of the evidence of the prosecution witnesses and then address the jury to the effect that the prosecution had not succeeded in making them sure of your client's guilt' (BSB 2024: gC9.2). Barristers can challenge the courts' jurisdiction and the admissibility of evidence. They may seek not guilty verdicts based on law – by reason of, for example, insanity, self-defence or 'coercive control' (*R v Challen*). They can also challenge prosecution evidence, including expert evidence, even knowing – from clients – the evidence is correct. Similarly, truthful eyewitnesses who correctly identify clients can be challenged on the basis they weren't wearing their prescription glasses or were too far away to be 'certain'. Circumstances may undermine confidence in their testimony. The submission isn't that the witness was wrong, but their evidence isn't reliable or credible enough to meet the burden of proof.

However, this can be a grey area. What if there's a hostile relationship between witness and client? Suggesting this is a motive for the witness's evidence is akin to implying they're lying – when the lawyer knows they're not. In my opinion, this crosses the ethical line, but it's another close call.

ii. A Canadian Perspective

In Canada, admissions by clients impose strict limitations on the conduct of the defence and clients should be made aware of this. If a client

> admits to the lawyer the factual and mental elements necessary to constitute the offence, the lawyer, if convinced that the admissions are true and voluntary, may properly take objection to the jurisdiction of the court, the form of the indictment or the admissibility or sufficiency of the evidence, but must not suggest that some other person committed the offence or call any evidence that, by reason of the admissions, the lawyer believes to be false. Nor may the lawyer set up an affirmative case inconsistent with such admissions … *Such admissions will also impose a limit on the extent to which the lawyer may attack the evidence for the prosecution.* The lawyer is entitled to test the evidence given by each individual witness for the prosecution and argue that the evidence taken as a whole is insufficient to amount to proof that the accused is guilty of the offence charged, but the lawyer *should go no further than that.* (Law Society of Ontario 2019: Rule 5.1-1, Commentary [10], emphasis added; see also Federation of Law Societies of Canada 2019: Rule 5.1-1)

Li confessed to his lawyer he'd robbed a jewellery store (*R v Li*). Two store clerks saw Li and gave evidence about his appearance – hairstyle, fluency and proficiency in English. The lawyer called two independent witnesses to testify truthfully that Li had never worn his hair in the way described, and his level of English proficiency was incompatible with their version. The British Columbia Court of Appeal held the lawyer hadn't breached any ethical rule; the defence was acceptable. The matters raised by the witnesses 'raised a doubt about the reliability of the identification evidence given by the jewelry store clerks'. This doubt 'was the only hope the accused had', yet testing the evidence in this way wasn't asserting that the clerks didn't see him, but rather suggesting that their memory wasn't sufficiently reliable.

B. Strong and Weak Adversarialism

Asimow and Weisberg (2009) discuss different legal 'cultures' operating when the lawyers know clients are guilty: strong and weak adversarialism. All 'adversarialists' agree no one should be convicted unless there's proof beyond a reasonable doubt, and every criminal defendant has the right to a competent and ethical defence. The issue at trial is proving guilt, not innocence. But what constitutes a competent and ethical defence when clients are known to be guilty?

Strong adversarialists emphasise the client and place their interests above all others; weak adversarialists emphasise other values such as substantive justice. Asimow (2004: 2; see also Asimow 2007) asserts strong adversarialism 'is the dominant, usually unquestioned, ideology of the U.S. justice system. As a consequence, the U.S. employs a more extreme version of the adversarial system *than any other country*' (Asimow 2007: 653 fn 10, emphasis added). He argues that its unquestioned dominance, 'despite the unpopularity of lawyers and the practical problems of the adversarial system', is the result of many factors including tradition, ignorance (of alternatives, such as the inquisitorial system), the exalted value placed on personal, individual autonomy, dislike of government power (see also Wills 1999; Hibbing and Theiss-Moose 2001), distrust of judges and the fact that lawyers prefer it (possibly because they control it). Asimow (2004: 4) suggests 'there is another important, though usually overlooked reason': popular culture. This has taught people 'to trust adversarialism and to regard the lawyer as the champion of our personal interests, indeed, our liberty ... that the adversarial system discovers the truth about what really happened'. He concludes: 'By endlessly valorizing the adversary system, but without dwelling on its shortcomings, the media may have reinforced the adversary ideology.'

This ideology may not as strong in EW (Whelan 2001). There may be greater civility in court, symbolised by referring to other counsel as 'My Learned Friend' and supported by the more active, case-managing role of, and deference towards, judges. In 2018 it was reported that in Crown Courts there was a 'trend towards more respectful and considerate treatment of lay people in court – or "sensitivity to the humans involved"' (Hunter et al 2018: 13).

There may be exceptions. Sir Jeremiah Harman's obituary noted he 'gained a reputation as an outstanding, but extremely aggressive, advocate who sometimes antagonised opponents through his win-at-all-costs attitude' (*The Times* 2021a). But the obituary also claimed his 'willingness to go for the jugular set Harman apart from the vast majority of his colleagues at the Chancery Bar, which to this day retains a reputation for gentlemanly behaviour'. Barristers' relationships with clients are less intense than those of attorneys and solicitors. In most cases, barristers are chosen not by lay clients, but by instructing solicitors – their professional clients. Barristers want to impress solicitors who bring repeat work. This doesn't undermine barristers' efforts because solicitors monitor them. But this tripartite structure increases the separation between barristers and clients and reduces pressure to 'win at all costs'.

Barristers' 'cab-rank' duty to accept cases also helps separate barristers from clients and their cause. Whether or not the rule is followed, there's an ideology of independence from clients. In short, little may have changed from what an American observer said: 'Because of his role in the system, the English barrister is an independent, able, and ethical advocate, bringing to the trial a detached, unemotional dedication to justice that is the hallmark of a professional' (Cameron 1981: 992).

C. Tilting at Windfalls

Should lawyers treat truthful errors as windfall opportunities to help clients?

i. *The Alibi*

Schwartz (1988), Hodes (2002: fn 48) and Henning (2006: 275–76) discussed this scenario. A client admitted an armed robbery to his lawyer. The victim correctly identified the client but mistakenly thought the robbery was at 11 am. The robber actually stole the victim's watch and hit him on the head at 2 pm. Two credible friends gave the client a truthful alibi at 11 am. Should lawyers 'lie with the truth' and present the 'windfall' alibi despite knowing of clients' culpability?

The Michigan State Bar Ethics Committee decided it was 'perfectly proper' to subpoena the friends: 'The victim's mistake concerning the precise time of the crime results in this windfall defence to the client' (OP CI-1164 1987). A client is entitled to effective assistance of counsel and, even though the client has confessed, a 'defense lawyer may present any evidence that is truthful'.

The BSB says it would be misleading courts if, inconsistent with a confession, barristers 'put forward an alibi' (2024: gC10). Would this lead to a different answer? I don't think so. The lawyer's using the alibi to challenge *prosecution* evidence that a crime was committed at 11 am. There's no requirement for criminal defence barristers to correct prosecution errors of fact of which they may have knowledge (*Saif Ali*: 200, Lord Diplock; see also Blake and Ashworth 2004, Boon 2014: 644). Arguably, the prosecution is at fault by not enquiring whether the time suggested by the victim might be wrong. In both countries the defence must provide particulars of an alibi in advance of trial (Criminal Procedure and Investigation Act 1996 (Defence Disclosure Time Limits) Regulations 2011; Levine and Miller 2021) Therefore, defence lawyers should be allowed to raise doubts about prosecution evidence.

D. The Lying Client

Another challenging scenario for trial lawyers is when they discover clients are lying.

i. Jeffrey Archer

Archer, formerly an MP and Deputy Conservative Party Chairman, is a best-selling author. In 1987, he won £500,000 in libel damages from *The Star* newspaper which claimed he'd paid to have sex with a prostitute.[1] The newspaper's legal costs were £700,000. Another newspaper, the *News of the World*, also settled with Archer. A few years later, a new witness and other evidence suggested Archer had lied. Charged with perjury and perverting the course of justice, his barrister, Nicholas Purnell QC, informed the court he was encountering 'professional difficulties'. There followed an 'in camera' – closed – session lasting some time (Dyer 2001). Upon the trial re-starting, Purnell announced that Archer wouldn't be giving evidence, thereby leaving the evidence against Archer essentially unchallenged. One KC has said that 'professional difficulties'

> sometimes means that the client, though pleading not guilty, has confessed to his counsel. In that case, the barrister may not put forward an active defence suggesting something he knows to be untrue, but must simply leave it to the prosecution to prove their case. (ibid)

---

[1] One memorable part of this trial was Mr Justice Caulfield's comments about Archer's wife Mary. Instructing the jury, he stated: 'Remember Mary Archer in the witness box. Your vision of her probably will never disappear. Has she elegance? Has she fragrance? Would she have, without the strain of this trial, radiance? How would she appeal? Has she had a happy married life? Has she been able to enjoy, rather than endure, her husband Jeffrey? Is she right when she says to you – you may think with some delicacy – Jeffrey and I lead a full life? Is he in need of cold, unloving, rubber-insulated sex in a seedy hotel?' See: *defamationwatch.com.au/the-classics/number-4-jeffrey-archer-v-daily-star-1987-you-could-write-a-book-about-it/*.

Mr Justice Potts said the charges against Archer 'represent as serious an offence of perjury as I have had experience of, and as I have been able to find in the books' (Kelso 2001). Archer was sentenced to four years. He remained a Member of the House of Lords until retiring in July 2024.

If barristers encounter 'difficulties', they must have a 'substantial reason' to withdraw (BSB 2024: rC26.8). In one case, the client accepted his voice was to be heard on tapes and the defence proceeded on that basis. During the trial he said it wasn't his voice – a complete change of instructions: 'an impossible situation' (*R v Ulcay*: 28). It's for counsel to decide whether they're professionally embarrassed, but withdrawal mid-trial is a 'grave step' (*Daniels*: 77). Counsel should make a clear, full and contemporaneous record, preferably signed by the client, explaining the circumstances that led to the decision. They should also consult with the client and not make a unilateral decision.

ii. Perjury: The Ethical Trilemma

Freedman asked the 'Three Hardest Questions' (1966; see also Freedman and Smith 2010: Chapter 6) to 'provoke a discussion'; instead they provoked a 'firestorm' (Fox 2015, quoting Dershowitz). This is the 'ethical trilemma'. First, lawyers have a duty to provide 'competent representation' (MR 1.1; SRA 2023a: 3.2, 3.3, 3.6; BSB 2024: CD 7). They must inquire into and analyse the factual and legal elements of the problem (MR 1.1, Comment [5]; SRA 2023a: 3.4, 8.6). Secondly, lawyers owe clients a duty of confidentiality, so they mustn't use client information other than for the client's benefit. Thirdly, lawyers have a 'duty of candor' to the court and a duty not to mislead the court. Similarly, in EW, the advocate 'must not knowingly or recklessly mislead or attempt to mislead the court and must not abuse your role as advocate' (BSB 2024: rC3.1, rC3.2). The duty of confidentiality may conflict with the duty to the court (ibid: gC44). How to resolve the trilemma?

Freedman's answer was to prioritise the duty to clients over the duty to the court, to subordinate the latter to the former. If clients give false testimony, 'the lawyer should proceed in the ordinary way'; they wouldn't help clients in preparing to give their testimony and the 'client would take the stand cold' (Gillers 2006: 822). He argued that giving priority to the duty of candour to the court would be more harmful than permitting perjury. Clients wouldn't engage in full and frank disclosure especially if lawyers warned them of their duty to the court, and lawyers might maintain intentional ignorance to avoid triggering the duty of candour. In both cases, the duty of competent representation suffers. If lawyers are required to inform the court clients will lie or have lied, 'the duty of confidentiality is compromised as well (ibid: 823). None of the authorities agreed with Freedman.

iii. Prevent Perjury?

If lawyers know, before giving their evidence, that clients intend to lie, 'it is universally agreed that at a minimum the attorney's first duty … is to attempt to dissuade the client from the unlawful course of conduct' (*Nix*: 169). This may succeed. Lawyers can be persuasive, using ethical, legal and moral arguments. False evidence may increase the likelihood of conviction, and lead to more serious consequences, including a longer sentence. It might be better if clients don't give evidence at all. US Supreme Court Chief Justice Burger said the threat to reveal is ethical and not a breach of clients' right to testify on their own behalf. MR 3.3, Comment [11] points out that 'unless it is clearly understood that the lawyer will act upon the duty to disclose the existence of false evidence, the client can simply reject the lawyer's advice to reveal the false evidence and insist that the lawyer keep silent'. Lawyers might also choose to withdraw. Freedman argued that lawyers should make good faith efforts to dissuade clients from committing perjury and may withdraw as long as withdrawal wouldn't prejudice them.

iv. Rectify/Remedy Perjury?

But what if clients do lie in court? Here there is not 'universal agreement' and it's noteworthy that the ABA gives precedence to the court and the BSB to the client. If there's a risk courts will be misled unless barristers disclose confidential information, they should ask clients for permission to disclose it to the court (BSB 2024: gC11). However, if they know courts will be misled 'unless [the lawyer] disclose confidential information', they 'must not reveal the information to the court' even if this results in courts being misled, unless the client permits it. If clients reject advice to disclose, the BSB requires barristers to cease to act (ibid: rC25.2).

There are contradictions in the BSB rules. Barristers must 'observe [their] duty to the court in the administration of justice [CD1] ... act in the best interests of each client [CD2] [and] ... act with honesty, and with integrity [CD3]'. These core duties are 'in order of precedence'. In other words, 'CD 1 overrides any other core duty, if and to the extent the two are inconsistent' (ibid: gC1.1). The desired outcome is that the 'court is able to rely on information provided to it by those conducting litigation and by advocates appearing before it (ibid: oC1), and the proper administration of justice is served (ibid: oC2). The interests of clients are protected to the extent *compatible* with these outcomes and the Core Duties (ibid: oC3). It's also intended that both those who appear before the court and clients 'understand clearly the extent of the duties owed to the court by advocates and those conducting litigation and the circumstances in which duties owed to clients will be overridden by the duty owed to the court' (ibid: oC4).

But withdrawal doesn't achieve the outcome. The 'duty to act in the best interests of each client [may be] subject to your duty to the court' (ibid: rC4), but the latter duty 'does not require you to act in breach of your duty to keep the affairs of each client confidential' (ibid: rC5). The duty of confidentiality is not overridden and the court is not protected from being misled. So, the EW 'solution' to the trilemma is to keep confidentiality but withdraw. This favours clients rather than the court; revealing the perjury is not mandated (*Sankar*).

The US position favours the court. MR 3.3, Comment [2] 'sets forth the special duties of lawyers as officers of the court to avoid conduct that undermines the integrity of the adjudicative process ... the lawyer must not allow the tribunal to be misled by false statement of law or fact or evidence that the lawyer knows to be false'. Lawyers are obliged 'to prevent the trier of fact from being misled by false evidence' (MR 3.3, Comment [5]).

MR 3.3(a)(3) concerns statements made by the lawyer's client or witness, both in the past and in the future. It states lawyers shall not knowingly

> offer evidence that the lawyer knows to be false. If a lawyer, the lawyer's client, or a witness called by the lawyer, has offered material evidence and the lawyer comes to know of its falsity, the lawyer shall take reasonable remedial measures, including, if necessary, disclosure to the tribunal.

How to rectify this varies from State to State. MR 3.3, Comment [10] states:

> If withdrawal from the representation is not permitted or will not undo the effect of the false evidence, the advocate must make such disclosure to the tribunal as is reasonably necessary to remedy the situation, even if doing so requires the lawyer to reveal information that otherwise would be protected [by the duty of confidentiality].

Remedial measures should be understood as a 'euphemism for "blowing the whistle" one way or another' (Hazard and Hodes 1985: 354).

MR 1.16(a)(1) also provides that lawyers 'shall withdraw from the representation of a client if the representation will result in a violation of the rules of professional conduct or other law' (see, for example, *People v Johnson*). They can choose to withdraw if 'the client persists in a course of action involving the lawyer's services that the lawyer reasonably believes is criminal or fraudulent', as long as withdrawal can be accomplished without material adverse effect on the client's interests (MR 1.16(b)(1), (2)).

Of course, withdrawing and telling a client to seek other representation

> might amount to encouragement by the first advocate to the client to deceive the court by giving evidence as to his innocence, with the aid of the second advocate who commits no breach of professional duty because he is not informed as to his guilt. (Napley 1991: 59)

The client may learn to withhold incriminating evidence from the next lawyer, be less than candid or try to present false evidence with counsel's assistance. This is a 'backdoor' way to deceive the court, because the second lawyer will be given different instructions by the client. The lawyer's lack of knowledge protects the lawyer, but not the court. Attorneys face an additional problem: courts may deny their motion to withdraw (MR 1.16(c)). What happens then?

v. *The Narrative 'Solution'*

Jurisdictions are increasingly approving the 'narrative solution' (see Perrin 2007: 1737–42) – the 'best accommodation of the competing interests of the defendant's right to testify and the attorney's obligation not to participate in the presentation of perjured testimony' (*People v Johnson*). Attorneys are passive and able to 'disassociate … from the false testimony of the accused' (Silver 1994: 419). They'll simply invite clients to tell juries their version of what occurred regarding the allegations against them. This isn't 'ineffective assistance of counsel' because that requires not only deficiency but also prejudice. It remains difficult because lawyers may suspect clients will lie under oath, but, until that happens, they should proceed as normal and turn to the narrative approach only after clients actually lie.

One way of resolving the ethical trilemma which I've not found discussed is for lawyers to treat the perjury as a crime-fraud exception to confidentiality and privilege.

Lawyers could reveal the perjury to the court because clients are not using their services appropriately.

E. Opinion-Shopping

In asbestos cases, claimants had to show that fibrosis in their lungs – the inflammation caused by dust particles – was the result of exposure to asbestos and not, for example, to silica. They needed an expert opinion. Brickman found that some medical experts hired by plaintiff lawyers virtually always found asbestosis, while those hired by defendants rarely did. This is 'opinion-shopping' – looking for and paying for an opinion that supports one 'truth' or another. As one Litigation Associate told us: 'Experienced lawyers and law firms know what experts to use – I guess they've already shopped.' It reflects the adversary system where, in principle, each party presents its own evidence or, as Brickman (2002) called it, 'Asbestos Litigation Land'

EW 'experts' must be agreed by the parties and their duty is to the court, not to either party (Practice Direction accompanying Part 35 of the Civil Procedure Rules). This leads to a non-partisan 'truth'. When a federal district court judge substituted court-appointed medical experts for the parties' experts to examine 65 patients, they found that only 15 per cent had asbestosis and 20 per cent had 'pleural plaques' (the result of exposure to asbestos, but, for the most part, totally benign). The remaining 65 per cent had no identifiable condition (Brickman 1992: 1847, fn 20, referring to Rubin and Ringenbach 1991: 37–38). Between September 1987 and September 1990, the court-appointed experts testified in 16 cases; in only two did they find asbestosis. Jury verdicts 'essentially followed the expert testimony' (ibid: 39–40).

II. The Dagger of Deceit

Solicitors mustn't 'mislead or attempt to mislead … the court or others, either by your own acts or omissions or allowing or being complicit in the acts or omissions of others (including your client)' (SRA 2023a: 1.4). Barristers 'must not knowingly or recklessly mislead or attempt to mislead the court' (BSB 2024: rC3.1, 3.2) – or indeed 'anyone' (ibid: rC9.1) – and 'must not abuse your role as advocate' (ibid: rC3.1, 3.2). The duty includes 'being complicit in another person misleading the court [and] inadvertently misleading the court if you later realise that you have misled the court and you fail to correct the position' (ibid: gC4.1, gC4.2). Recklessly means 'being indifferent to the truth, or not caring whether something is true or false' (ibid: gC4.3). Courts regard misleading them as 'one of the most serious offences that an advocate or litigator can commit. It is not simply a breach of a rule of a game' (*Brett*: 111, Lord Thomas).

However, the duty

> does not prevent you from putting forward your client's case simply because you do not believe that the facts are as your client states them to be (or as you, on your client's behalf, state them to be), as long as any positive case you put forward accords with your instructions and you do not mislead the court. Your role when acting as an advocate or conducting

litigation is to present your client's case, and it is not for you to decide whether your client's case is to be believed. (BSB 2024: gC6)

There's a paradox and a contradiction which ethical lawyers must navigate. Wishing to conceal a truth that would adversely affect a trial's outcome, they may seek to deflect strong arguments in favour of weak ones. The intention may be to mislead the court about the law or facts. Doesn't this contradict the 'rule' not to mislead? The practical issue is how far EW lawyers can go, especially as the Lord Chief Justice states the privilege of conducting litigation and appearing in court 'is granted on terms that the rules are observed not merely in their letter but in their spirit' (*Brett*: 111). However, if lawyers decide to conceal information, the losing party may not know what information was withheld.

According to Lord Diplock, defence lawyers may 'consistently with the rule that the prosecution must prove its case … passively stand by and watch the court being misled by reason of its failure to ascertain facts that are within the barrister's knowledge' (*Saif Ali*: 220). However, interpretation of this 'Diplock' principle seems to vary according to the application of another fundamental principle that's emerged in the cases: what was the lawyer's intention? Here are some cases that illustrate these issues.

A. *Tombling*

At the time a witness was called to help establish the client's case, he was serving a prison sentence. He appeared in court wearing ordinary clothes. He confirmed he lived at what was normally his home address, that he'd previously been a prison governor and what his work was after that. Nothing was said about his current prison sentence. The lawyer asked questions which allowed the witness to avoid that fact. A majority of the Court of Appeal held the lawyer's conduct didn't justify ordering a new trial because awareness of the true position wouldn't have affected the outcome and the questions hadn't been put with the intention to mislead. Also, the prison sentence was for a motoring offence, which didn't impact the witness's credibility in the instant case.

Lord Justice Denning said:

> The duty of counsel to his client … is to make every honest endeavour to succeed. He must not, of course, knowingly mislead the court, either on the facts or on the law, but, short of that he may put such matters in evidence or omit such others as in his discretion he thinks will be most to the advantage of his client … The reason is because he is not the judge of the credibility of the witnesses or of the validity of the arguments. He is only the advocate employed by the client to speak for him and present his case, and he must do it to the best of his ability, without making himself the judge of its correctness, but only of its honesty. (*Tombling*: 297)

B. *Meek*

Fleming, a police officer, arrested Meek, a press photographer, during disturbances in Trafalgar Square. Meek was charged with obstructing a police officer in the execution of his duty. After Meek was acquitted, he accused Fleming of assault and wrongful imprisonment, and claimed damages. At the time of the arrest, Fleming was a Chief Inspector. Before the trial brought by Meek, Fleming, unable to attend another court hearing, had suborned perjury by directing a colleague to say they'd been the arresting officer. Fleming had been demoted to the position of Sergeant as a result. Meek's counsel didn't know of this demotion.

Fleming argued that no excessive force was used on Meek. His lawyer, Victor Durand QC, concealed the demotion by a 'premeditated line of conduct' (*Meek*: 379). Fleming appeared in court without a uniform, although six other police officers testified in uniform. Durand repeatedly referred to him as 'Mr' rather than by rank; in other words, he created the misleading impression that the client was still a chief inspector. This was reinforced by the judge and counsel for Meek repeatedly referring to Fleming as 'Chief Inspector'. When Meek's counsel began cross-examination, he asked Fleming: 'You are a chief inspector, and you have been in the police force since 1938?' Fleming answered 'yes, that is true' (House of Commons Debates, 9 March 1962, vol 655, cols 860–70). Both parts of the answer were true at the time of the incident, but the first part was a lie at the time of the trial. It was a 'he said – he said' case. Clearly the demotion was material to that issue. Had he worn a Sergeant's uniform, it would have aroused suspicion. Unlike the *Tombling* case, what was concealed would have impacted the credibility of the evidence presented.

Fleming won, but after his demotion became known, the Court of Appeal ordered a new trial. Lord Pearce said:

> In every case, it must be a question of degree, weighing one principle against the other. In this case it is clear that the judge and jury were misled on an important matter. I appreciate that it is very hard at times for the advocate to see his path clearly between failure in his duty to the court, and failure in his duty to his client. I accept that in the present case the decision to conceal the facts was not made lightly, but after anxious consideration. But in my judgment the duty to the court was here unwarrantably subordinated to the duty to the client.

Before the re-trial, Meek was paid £2,000. And Mr Durand? He told the Court of Appeal he took

> responsibility for the decision ... the decision not to make disclosure of the defendant's change of status was mine, and mine alone ... Neither my learned junior counsel ... nor my instructing solicitor was responsible for initiating or pursuing that policy, and indeed they expressed their disapproval of it. (ibid: cols 863–64)

Durand was disbarred after a disciplinary hearing at his Inn, Inner Temple. But on appeal to the 'Visitors' (High Court judges), a sentence of suspension was substituted. When Durand reached the age of 75, 'the Inn decided to treat his sin as having been requited, and he was elected as a Bencher' (Leggatt 1998/99: 79).

C. John Francis Bridgwood

Solicitor John Francis Bridgwood was told by a longstanding client with several previous convictions that she'd given the police a false name, address and date of birth when arrested. Bridgwood advised her to disclose the truth – it would be established through fingerprint evidence – but she refused. Instead, she pleaded guilty under the false name hoping that the previous convictions wouldn't come to light. They didn't: the prosecution failed to establish her true identity. Bridgwood represented her at the sentencing hearing after spending a very short time with her beforehand. She told him she intended to appear in court using the false name. Bridgwood spoke in mitigation, but didn't refer to her by any name, false or true, or to her character. He was found to have acted in a manner tending and intending to pervert the course of justice and was fined £2,000 by the SDT (Burleigh 1989).

This case may be distinguished from one where the prosecution fails to get all the facts regarding previous convictions, but there's no client deceit. Under the Diplock principle the defence lawyer wouldn't have to act, even though the court had been misled. This was confirmed by Lord Justice Stuart-Smith: barristers needn't disclose clients' previous convictions, but mustn't assert their good character (*Vernon*). In the case of Bridgwood, by contrast, the information about previous convictions was available but the client's deception – known to the lawyer – meant the prosecution might not associate or connect the client with her criminal record. But there *are* differences of opinion (Blake and Ashworth 2004). Du Cann (1980: 42) argued that it's permissible for counsel to allow an error in any evidence about the client's record given to the court – this isn't 'deceit by equivocation'. Pannick (1992: 35) disagreed: counsel will be participating in 'deception of the court or [furthering] the maladministration of justice on false premises'.

The Bar Code (2024: gC12) supports du Cann in most scenarios: 'if your client tells you that they have previous convictions of which the prosecution is not aware, you may not disclose this to the court without their consent'. It also states that, in these circumstances, the duty not to mislead the court means barristers are constrained in what they say in mitigation, such as advancing clients' good character. Where mandatory sentences apply, or if the court asks the lawyer a direct question and the client refuses to reveal the information, the barrister must withdraw.

D. *Vernon*

The client suffered nervous shock after failing to rescue two of his children. They'd drowned after their car, driven by the defendant (a nanny), crashed into a river. In May 1993, medical experts told the High Court his prospects of recovery were poor. In October, after final submissions had been made, but before final judgment, the client sought a residence order in relation to his surviving children. The same experts told the Family Court the client's mental health had improved. Mr Justice Sedley awarded over £1 million, unaware of the change in prognosis.

By a 2-1 majority, the Court of Appeal reduced the damages award to just over £500,000. It held that a lawyer is under a duty to inform the court of changed material circumstances even after the conclusion of proceedings, and that duty continued until the judge had given judgment, even though the information provided during the proceedings were thought to be true. In some respects, these facts seem not unlike the lawyer passively keeping quiet about a client's record of previous convictions. Here, too, there was no 'active' misleading of the trial court. However, the reasoning of the majority – and the dissent – show how nuanced the choices are.

The Court stated that where a case is conducted on the basis of essential material facts – here the client's medical condition and prognosis – the court was being misled by the failure of the lawyer to correct the information. In dissent, Lord Justice Evans agreed with the lawyer's 'defence': there'd been no intention to mislead – an important factor in some of the cases – and the original evidence was truthful; it was the circumstances that had changed. Lord Justice Stuart-Smith agreed there'd been no deliberate intention to mislead and so counsel would have withdrawn (unless he could persuade the client to reveal the new information). But he didn't think counsel had an obligation to correct the error. Lord Justice Thorpe felt that counsel should have corrected it, either by informing the other side or the court.

E. The 'Nightjack' Case

The Times Newspapers were fighting an injunction to prevent their naming the author of the 'Nightjack' blog, an anonymous account of life as a police officer. A journalist unlawfully hacked the officer's email account to uncover his identity and told the Newspaper's Legal Manager, solicitor Alastair Brett, that he'd done so. This conversation was 'off the record' as the journalist needed legal advice. The hacking was 'unauthorised', but it suggested the officer was using confidential police information in breach of police regulations. There was therefore a 'strong public interest' in exposing him.

Brett told the journalist that what he'd done was 'unacceptable' and the story was 'dead in the water' unless the information could be obtained through publicly available information. The journalist did this via 'jigsaw identification' – putting the pieces together – and then felt able to reveal the name via the practice of 'parallel construction', a form of 'evidence laundering'. The journalist informed the officer who then sought the injunction.

At the injunction hearing, Brett didn't reveal to the court, or to the barristers he instructed, that the journalist had hacked the emails. By the time the injunction application was rejected, and because of what Brett did, the claimants dropped their previous confident assertion that the journalist or someone else *must* have hacked the account since some of the information wasn't in the public domain.

After the injunction application failed, nothing further might have happened. But during a public judicial inquiry – the 'Leveson Inquiry' into the 'culture, practices and ethics of the British press' which followed the hacking scandal in the Milly Dowler case – the Nightjack hack was disclosed. The SDT accused Brett of allowing the journalist to put in a misleading witness statement and then the court to proceed on the basis of the statement and an incorrect assumption. Brett had written to the officer's lawyers with a false denial saying, to the suggestion that the journalist might have accessed the emails, 'I regard this as a baseless allegation'. He admitted at the Leveson Inquiry that the witness statement 'was not entirely accurate' and 'it certainly doesn't give the full story'. He'd instructed the journalist to prepare his statement and reviewed its contents knowing the journalist couldn't deny accessing the emails.

Brett created the impression the journalist *only* used information and documents in the public domain to identify the officer. The SDT found Brett guilty of two breaches of the 2007 Code: failing to act with integrity and 'knowingly allowing the Court to be misled in the conduct of litigation'. He was suspended for six months and paid costs of £30,000. Brett appealed the findings of breach and the award of costs (he'd already served the suspension period).

The High Court considered Brett's defence, noting the SDT made clear the allegation wasn't that he'd been dishonest. Brett argued that this contradicted the finding that he 'knowingly allowed the Court to be misled'. Mr Justice Wilkie agreed: a finding of 'knowingly' is the functional equivalent of a finding of dishonesty. Given the explicit disavowal of Brett being dishonest, the judge substituted the word 'recklessly' for 'knowingly'. He then went on to consider Brett's other defence to see if this new wording changed the seriousness of the conduct.

Brett's defence had been twofold. First, he didn't accept he was under a duty to breach the journalist's confidence. He claimed that LPP was attached to the information about hacking, and he couldn't include that information in the witness statement. Mr Justice Wilkie looked at the scope of privilege as applicable to the journalist. He pointed out the absolute nature of privilege and that the parties had agreed the judge should proceed on the basis the information did invoke a duty of confidentiality as one of LPP. The SDT was therefore wrong to conclude Brett had a duty to disclose.

However, the charge wasn't a failure to disclose, but allowing the court to be misled. It was misled in two ways: allowing the witness statement to be served and relied on, which created a misleading impression as to the facts and matters deposed to in that statement; and allowing the court to proceed on the basis of an incorrect assumption as to the facts and matters set out in the witness statement. Brett's defence was that he'd '*a genuine misunderstanding of the prioritisation of his competing duties and obligations*' (*Brett*: 47, emphasis added). That defence failed. Brett could've reconciled his conflicting duties. One way was to get the journalist to waive privilege. Another was for Brett to correct the witness statement by stating the identity *could* have been revealed through publicly available sources and, in the absence of a waiver, to refuse to say how the identity was discovered. Also, Brett could've informed his counsel of the true position and invite them to correct the record. Finally, he could've abandoned defending the claim.

III.   Economical with the Truth

Words can be carefully chosen to present a version that may not be wholly true. In the OJ Simpson trial, the lead prosecutor, Marcia Clark, used the word 'match' in connection with hair and fibres when examining the FBI's Doug Debrick about DNA. The defence objected, claiming the best that could be said was 'consistent with'. However, Clark repeatedly used the word and in the end Judge Lance Ito warned her she was 'flirting with contempt' (Shapiro with Warren 1996: 301).

Words can be 100 per cent true but 100 per cent misleading. It's 'true' that the average wealth status of every person travelling on a bus is that of a millionaire whenever Jeff Bezos or Bill Gates is one of the passengers – hence the aphorism 'lies, damned lies and statistics' (Huff 1954). There's also a 'number bias' (Blauw 2020). A simple example would be to ask students in the tenth Lawyers' Ethics class: 'How many classes have we had before today's class?' When the first answer given is 'nine', the professor says 'that's true', then asks 'is any other answer true?' After a moment, the creative students will suggest other answers: 'eight', 'seven', 'six' and so on – you cannot have nine classes without having had one to eight beforehand. All answers are literally true even if designed to mislead. And if they're true, not a lie or a false statement of material fact, then shouldn't lawyers advise clients to give answers that assist their cause?

Freedman (2006: 776) discusses 'mental reservation', a strategy of telling the truth and keeping secrets at the same time, or a way of not telling the truth but not lying either. Words can be spoken with concurrent unspoken thoughts. This strategy might be used to avoid answering questions without lying (McGarry 2009).

A. *Bronston*

Samuel Bronston was president of a film production company in Switzerland. The company petitioned for bankruptcy. Creditors wanted to know whether Bronston had assets they could target, and he gave evidence under oath. A referee was to determine how much value remained in the company and where any assets were located. Bronston and his company *both* had Swiss bank accounts in the past. Bronston transferred Swiss money between the company account and his secret account. The secret account was now closed, but Bronston wanted to 'protect' its existence because knowledge of it would expose him to creditors.

Bronston was asked: 'Do you have any bank accounts in Swiss banks, Mr Bronston?' Bronston answered: 'No sir.' This was literally true at that time. He was then asked: 'Have you ever?' He replied: 'The company had an account there for about six months, in Zurich' (*Bronston*: 354). This didn't answer the specific question, but *implied* that he'd never had a personal bank account. The creditor's lawyer didn't follow up Bronston's failure to answer.

When it was discovered Bronston had opened a large personal Swiss bank account and held it for nearly five years, depositing over $180,000, he was convicted of perjury. Bronston appealed and the US Supreme Court unanimously reversed the conviction. The issue was 'whether a witness may be convicted of perjury for an answer, under oath, that is literally true but not responsive to the question asked and arguably misleading by negative implication' (ibid: 353). Bronston hadn't made a false statement, but a true statement that led to a false inference.

This has been called the 'literal truth defense' (Solan 2018: 79). Bronston's answer, the Court said, wasn't responsive and, in casual conversation, might imply there was never a personal bank account, 'But we are not dealing with casual conversation' (*Bronston*: 357–58). Bronston's answer 'was so blatantly unresponsive, the Court reasoned, it was the *questioner* who should be held responsible for the truth not coming out' (Solan 2018: 80, emphasis added). Bronston took advantage of the lawyer's failure to realise he hadn't answered, and to ask the question again. The Supreme Court emphasised:

> It is the responsibility of the lawyer to probe; testimonial interrogation, and cross-examination in particular, is a probing, prying, pressing form of enquiry. If a witness evades, it is the lawyer's responsibility to recognize the evasion and to bring the witness back to the mark, to flush out the whole truth with the tools of adversary examination. (*Bronston*: 358–59)

The Court held 'the perjury statute is not to be loosely construed, nor the statute invoked simply because a wily witness succeeds in derailing the questioner – so long as the witness speaks the literal truth' (ibid: 360). Perjury requires the witness to make a statement the witness themselves believe not to be true. The solution to the problem in this case was therefore not to invoke the perjury law, but to ask a follow-up question.

There's a degree of irony here because it *is* perjury if a witness *believes* they're lying, even if, by accident, what they say is in fact true (*US v DeZarn*).[2] But it's *not* perjury if the witness wilfully uses misleading or deceptive language to avoid having to lie. Yet the effect might be the same as lying since the questioner doesn't know the truth. Suppose a person doesn't want to reveal they have a brother. When asked 'do you have a brother?' or even 'do you have any siblings?', the person might answer 'I have a sister'. The clear implication of this (true) answer is the person doesn't have a brother (untrue) (Tiersma and Solan 2012). Just as in *Bronston*, the 'smoking gun' information is kept hidden and, in Bronston's case, would've remained so had the Swiss bank account not been discovered independently.

---

[2] In *DeZarn*, a person, when asked about attending a fundraising party in 1991, thought he was being asked about attending the party in 1990. There was no fundraising in 1991, but there was in 1990, so his denial that there was fundraising at the party was literally true – 1991 – but constituted perjury – because he was answering about 1990. See 18 USC § 1621(1). Some regard this case as an 'outlier'.

13

The Smoking Gun

[A]s we know, there are known knowns; there are things we know we know. We also
know there are known unknowns; that is to say, we know there are some things we do not
know. But there are also unknown unknowns – the ones we don't know we don't know.
— Donald H Rumsfeld, US Defence Secretary
(Department of Defense News Briefing, 12 February 2012)

The smoking gun metaphor implies that whoever holds the 'smoking gun' is guilty. In
one case, two wrongfully concealed items were described as 'smoking gun documents'
(*Washington State*). Ironically, 'smoking gun' evidence concealed by lawyers occurred,
literally, in a smoking context: the tobacco industry. The scenario can arise in many
ways. One lawyer discovered a sawed-off shotgun (used in an armed robbery) in a
client's safe deposit box and transferred it to his own box, expecting to be able to claim
attorney–client privilege; he couldn't (*In re Ryder*)! But suppose Michael Jackson's
lawyer learnt about his 'triple-locked' secret room at Neverland Ranch alleged to be
full of 'paedophile porn' (Liddle 2016) or in-house lawyers about 'red flag' documents?
What if clients and their lawyers want to hide information, but others want to see it? No
wonder the responsibility of lawyers in smoking gun scenarios is 'complex and far from
settled' (*Wemark*: 816) and 'the legal ethics of real evidence is messy' (Sisk 2014: 79).

If information is withheld, courts might compel disclosure and there are legal and
ethical sanctions for abuse. MR 3.4(a), 'Fairness to Opposing Party and Counsel', states
that lawyers shall not 'unlawfully obstruct another party's access to evidence or unlawfully alter, destroy or conceal a document or other material having potential evidentiary
value. A lawyer shall not counsel or assist another person to do any such act'. In pre-trial
procedure, lawyers shall not 'fail to make reasonably diligent effort to comply with a
legally proper discovery request by an opposing party' (MR 3.4(d)). But 'a lawyer can
be faced with a host of conflicting important obligations to balance, including the duty
to preserve client confidences, investigate the case, and maintain an allegiance to the
system of justice as an officer of the court' (*Wemark*).

I. Resisting Discovery (US)/Disclosure (EW)

Resistance is the obvious way of protecting client information. In the US: 'The widely
shared norm of discovery is ... "make the other side work"' (Sarat 2003: 150). A junior
partner in a large Washington DC law firm told us: 'I'm not going to do the other side's

work for him. I'm not going to do his discovery. I'm not going to give him some fact which is going to help him and hurt my client.' Responses to discovery requests can be narrow or slow. Lawyers may feel they can 'get away with it'. One judge reported: 'There is usually no consequence at all to an attorney for hiding documents. What matters is keeping the client and winning the case' (ibid). However, lawyers and clients sometimes get caught concealing 'smoking guns'.

A. *Qualcomm v Broadcom*

If Qualcomm had participated in the creation of the H.264 video compression standard by the Joint Video Team (JVT) standards-setting organisation, it would have been required to identify its patents and license them royalty-free or under non-discriminatory, reasonable terms. Broadcom claimed Qualcomm had participated, or at least was aware that the standard was being discussed. Qualcomm denied both claims.

Broadcom sought evidence through discovery. Qualcomm agreed to produce non-privileged documents describing its 'participation in the JVT, if any, which can be located after a reasonable search'. None was provided linking Qualcomm to the H.264 standard. 1.2 million pages of marginally relevant documents were disclosed; 46,000 critically important emails and documents were hidden (Fliegel 2008). Magistrate Judge Barbara Major found clear and convincing evidence that Qualcomm's counsel's misleading and false discovery responses constituted misconduct. It was

> likely that … one or more of the retained lawyers chose not to look in the correct locations for the correct documents, to accept the unsubstantiated assurances of an important client that its search was sufficient, to ignore the warning signs that the document search and production were inadequate, not to press Qualcomm employees for the truth, and/or to encourage employees to provide the information (or lack of information) that Qualcomm needed to assert its non-participation argument and to succeed in the lawsuit. These *choices* enabled Qualcomm to withhold hundreds of thousands of pages of relevant discovery and to assert numerous false and misleading arguments to the jury. (Emphasis added)

The result? An order to pay over $8.5 million and six attorneys reported to the California State Bar for ethics violations.

B. Fisons Corporation

A medical malpractice claim was brought against a doctor, who prescribed an asthma drug, Somophyllin Oral Liquid, and Fisons, which manufactured it (*Washington State*). The main ingredient was theophylline. The plaintiff claimed the drug caused permanent brain damage to a two year old. Despite three years of discovery, documents indicating the company knew the drug could be dangerous weren't disclosed. These included two items described by the doctor – counterclaiming against Fisons – as 'smoking gun documents' (ibid: 337). They revealed Fisons was aware of 'life-threatening theophylline toxicity' in children who received the drug while suffering from viral infections. The first item, revealed anonymously, showed Fisons had sent a letter in June 1981 telling a small number of 'influential physicians' they needed to understand theophylline can be a 'capricious drug'. The second was a July 1985 memorandum from Fisons' director of medical communications to the vice president of sales and marketing:

> This 1985 memorandum referred to a dramatic increase in reports of serious toxicity to theophylline in early 1985 and also referred to the current recommended dosage as a significant 'mistake' or 'poor clinical judgment'. The memo alluded to the 'sinister aspect' that the physician who was the 'pope' of theophylline dosage recommendation was a consultant to the pharmaceutical company that was the leading manufacturer of the drug and that the consultant was 'heavily into [that company's] stocks'. The memo also noted that the toxicity reports were not reported to the journal read by those who most often prescribed the drug and concluded that those physicians may not be aware of the 'alarming increase in adverse reactions such as seizures, permanent brain damage and death'. The memo concluded that the 'epidemic of theophylline toxicity provides strong justification for our corporate decision to cease promotional activities with our theophylline line of products'. The record at trial showed that the drug company continued to promote and sell theophylline after the date of this memo. (ibid: 308–09, Chief Justice Andersen)

Fisons knew theophylline posed significant dangers to children. In April 1990, 'shortly after the memo was revealed', Fisons settled the claim for $6.9 million.

Fison's lawyers worked for Bogle & Gates, Washington State's second-largest law firm at the time, with over 200 attorneys. They only handed over documents mentioning the brand name 'Somophyllin Oral Liquid'; they objected to other discovery requests. The firm's managing partner, William F Cronin, claimed: 'The attorneys involved believed what they were doing was appropriate under the rules, and consistent with their obligations to zealously advocate for the client' (Walsh 1993). Washington State attorney Fredric Tausend, a former law school dean, stated in an affidavit that what was done by the lawyers was 'consistent with the practice of many of the best lawyers in this community and throughout the nation', to make the other side 'work to get the documents' (*Washington State*). Withholding information is

> unfortunately, an unremarkable example of a tactic that's used by lawyers all the time ... The dominant culture of discovery in this country is that it's a game ... A litigator's arsenal depends on his ability to define discovery questions as narrowly as possible. It's a skill that's admired and rewarded. (Stephen Gillers, quoted in Walsh 1993)

The Washington Supreme Court found 'discovery abuse' by the lawyers. The two items were crucial to the doctor's defence and the injured child's case. Had the company not been 'persistent in its resistance to discovery requests' (*Washington State*: 346), the smoking gun documents would've been produced (ibid: 350). The responses were 'misleading ... It appears clear that no conceivable discovery request could have been made ... that would have uncovered the relevant documents, given the ... responses of the drug company' (ibid: 352). The responses 'did not comply with either the spirit or the letter of discovery rules'.

The lawyers and Fisons argued: 'Discovery is an adversarial process and good lawyering required the responses made in this case' (ibid). Chief Justice Andersen pointed to the 'conflict between the attorney's duty to represent the client's interest and the attorney's duty as an officer of the court to use, but not abuse the judicial process' (ibid: 354) He concluded:

> Vigorous advocacy is not contingent on lawyers being free to pursue litigation tactics that they cannot justify as legitimate. The lawyer's duty to place his client's interests ahead of all others presupposes that the lawyer will live with the rules that govern the system … He is subject to the correlative obligation to comply with the rules and to conduct himself in a manner consistent with the proper functioning of the system. (ibid: 354–55)

Fisons and their lawyers settled the sanctions claim for $325,000 (Taylor Jr 1994: 5). This amount was dwarfed by the amount paid by DuPont and its law firm, Alston & Bird, for concealing documents suggesting a DuPont fungicide had been contaminated. They settled a criminal investigation by agreeing to pay $2.5 million each to four Georgia law schools to endow a chair in professional ethics, $1 million to endow an annual symposium on legal ethics, and $250,000 to the state bar's professionalism commission (Geyelin 1999: A18).

C. The Post Office Scandal

Between 1999, when the Horizon online accounting system developed by Fujitsu was introduced to 20,000 PO branches, and 2015, around 4300 branch owner-managers were accused of false accounting, fraud or theft as shortfalls were alleged (Wallis 2022). A total of 927 were prosecuted privately by POL. In 2001, the PO dropped an IT expert as a witness after he found the system was 'clearly defective'. This was an early example of the systematic cover-up that, despite mounting concerns, led to around 700 convictions, 236 imprisoned, 2,800 having to pay back money, many sackings and bankruptcies, and at least four suicides: 'the Post Office closed its eyes to the truth' (Moorhead 2021a).

In 2009, after seven postmasters contacted *Computer Weekly* and it published an article on problems with Horizon, the Justice for Subpostmasters Alliance was formed. A total of 555 sued the PO and, after a trial, settled in 2019 for £57.75 million (£46 million went to lawyers and litigation funders). Mr Justice Peter Fraser told the DPP of his 'grave concerns' about what had happened, that the data in the system 'was not reliable' and Fujitsu 'clearly knew' about serious errors with Horizon at an early stage. By April 2024, the Court of Appeal overturned 101 convictions – 'pervasive failures of investigation and disclosure went in each case to the very heart of the prosecution' (Post Office Trial 2019). In 2024, the Post Office (Horizon System) Offences Act automatically quashed all convictions relating to post offices where Horizon was used between 1996 and 2018.

In 2020, an independent public inquiry was established and in 2021 became a statutory inquiry with greater powers, including compelling the production of documents and summoning witnesses on oath. The inquiry Chair, Sir Wyn Williams, said the evidence showed PO lawyers knew about the bugs in 2010. Indeed, a company, Second Sight, had been hired in 2012 by POL to investigate cases linked to Horizon and it identified two bugs in the system. The company's head, Ian Henderson, learnt that Fujitsu could also access PO branch accounts remotely and that 10 PO staff worked at Fujitsu

HQ dealing with Horizon's bugs and errors. He said his company was sacked in 2015 for 'getting too close to the truth' (Ledwith 2024). However, not only was the 'smoking gun' evidence of the systems' unreliability withheld, but Henderson himself was also subject to a 'draconian' NDA and, he claimed, a 'thinly veiled' threat from POL's head of legal (ibid).

In November 2021, the PO waived legal privilege for the purpose of the inquiry and stated it wouldn't seek to enforce NDAs. Ben Foat, POL group general counsel, told the inquiry that 'between four and eight in-house Post Office lawyers, as well as 46 from Herbert Smith Freehills and five from Peters & Peters, are now working on disclosure and remediation issues' (Hyde 2023). The inquiry itself is 'investigating the late or non-provision of disclosure by the Post Office in a series of criminal prosecutions which lasted over a decade, and the non-disclosure of documents in civil proceedings, and the unfairness that such non-disclosure had on parties and on witnesses' (ibid).

At the time of writing, the inquiry is ongoing. However, an email from a solicitor 'proposed to try and *suppress* disclosable evidence ... There were suggestions of routine/systematic attempts to label matters as legally privileged ... evidence of a long-standing practice of structuring documents' to appear privileged 'even when they were not' (Moorhead 2024). We must wait until the inquiry reports to see whether its 'core participants', the SRA or the BSB, take disciplinary action; the SRA had 'more than 20 live investigations' into the lawyers working for POL in June 2024 (Ames 2024). In the meantime, a three-year research project led by Richard Moorhead is examining whether there were professional and ethical failures that enabled and contributed to the scandal. He wondered (2021c) if 'mutually assured irresponsibility' was part of the problem. We shall see.

II. Whistleblowers

'Whistleblowers' are important in the fight against cover-ups. The leak of the 'Panama Papers' – 11.5 million documents – showed how a Panama law firm, Mossack Fonseca, assisted in tax planning for wealthy clients, including celebrities and government personnel all over the world, by using shell companies in various tax havens. Over half the companies cited in the Papers were registered in the British Virgin Islands, where there are 31,000 inhabitants and 366,000 registered companies, 'many of them anonymous shell companies' (Hodge 2024).

While 'lawyers hold special appeal as potential whistleblowers', whistleblowing by lawyers is 'rare, and whistleblowing against client interests, and in order to promote the administration of justice, is even rarer' (Parker et al 2017: 1010). That said, some lawyers have 'blown the whistle', though not all have done so within the ethical rules.

Legal protections for whistleblowers have been introduced, as have significant rewards – 'bounties' (Clark and Moore 2015). There are four primary American government reward programmes: the False Claims Act (combating fraud against the government), the SEC, the Commodities Futures Trading Commission and the IRS. Phillips and Cohen, representing whistleblowers in the US and the UK, has recovered 'more than $12.8 billion' (www.phillipsandcohen.com). Since its inception in 2011, the

SEC's whistleblower office has recovered over $4.6 billion and paid out over $1 billion to whistleblowers, including a record-breaking $279 million in 2023. The SEC has fielded tips from over 114 foreign countries, including the UK. It doesn't name the companies fined, but 'tips' refer to corporate financial disclosures, fraud, manipulation and insider trading.

Whistleblower rewards have included $1 million awarded to a British marine engineer, Christopher Keays, by American courts. He revealed that Princess Cruises, part of the Carnival Corporation, had a 'magic pipe' used to discharge thousands of gallons of waste into British waters (Clatworthy 2017). Bradley Birkenfeld received $104 million in 2012 after providing the IRS with information about the inner workings of tax schemes in which his employer UBS played a role. Wealthy clients could hide millions of dollars in secret bank accounts (Frean 2016). He even claimed to have smuggled diamonds in a tube of toothpaste across the Atlantic (Robertson 2012). UBS paid a penalty of $780 million and agreed to hand over details of 4,500 American citizens with accounts in Switzerland; more than $5 billion in extra taxes and penalties have been raised as a result of Birkenfeld's actions (ibid). John Kochanski, a sales representative, was awarded $51.5 million in 2009 for exposing Pfizer's illegal promotion of an arthritis drug; Cheryl Eckard received $96 million in 2012 after she revealed that Glaxo were knowingly selling contaminated drug products; Keith Edwards was awarded $63.9 million in 2014 for exposing that JP Morgan Chase had defrauded the government into insuring flawed home loans; also in 2014, former Countrywide Financial executive Edward O'Donnell was awarded $57 million for helping reveal Bank of America's role in 'shoddy mortgage and related securities' before the financial crisis – he helped federal prosecutors force the Bank to pay a record $16.65 billion penalty in connection with the mortgages and related securities it provided prior to the 2007–08 financial crisis; Jim Alderson and John Schilling split $100 million in 2000 for helping to expose Medicare fraud by the hospital chain HAS.

III. Strategies

Lawyers have two main smoking gun strategies: 'Removing the Gun', by destroying or otherwise denying its existence; and 'Removing the Smoke', so that privilege can be invoked. Both are subject to ethical constraints. Solicitors mustn't 'misuse or tamper with evidence or attempt to do so' (SRA 2023a: 2.1). ABA guidance, if defence counsel receives physical evidence implicating clients in criminal conduct, is not to disclose it to law enforcement unless required by law or unless the item itself is contraband so that possession of it is a crime (ABA 1993: Standard 4–4.6(d)). If it's contraband, such as hard drugs, lawyers may 'suggest that the client destroy it' where there is no pending case or investigation, as long as such destruction 'is not in violation of any criminal statute' (ibid). However, the MR 3.4 prohibition on the concealment or destruction of potentially relevant material evidence applies to 'evidentiary material generally' (Comment [2]), though it also refers lawyers to their state law which may allow them to 'take temporary possession of physical evidence of client crimes for the purpose of conducting a limited examination that will not alter or destroy material characteristics of the evidence'. If legal proceedings have commenced, the destruction of evidence will be prohibited.

A. Removing the Gun

i. *OJ Simpson's Knife*

Simpson was accused of killing his ex-wife Nicole Brown Simpson, and Ronald Goldman.[1] A 'dream team' of defence lawyers (Hodes 1996) was hired. One of them, Gerald Uelman, a Santa Clara law professor, joined the team three days after the bodies were found and one day after the 'Bronco chase' – Simpson being 'chased' by many police vehicles at low speeds (Uelman 1996).

The store proprietor and a salesman at the Ross Cutlery Store in Los Angeles told the *National Enquirer* they remembered OJ buying a large folding knife. The police became convinced this was the murder weapon (Shapiro with Warren 1996: 78); it became the main prosecution theory. Simpson confirmed he bought the knife and told his lawyers where it was in his Rockingham mansion – the police having missed it in their search. Uelman went to the master bedroom and its built-in dressing table. There were large, hinged mirrors on each side above the table. He pulled open the right one and found the knife, on a shelf, behind the mirror, in its original box. OJ insisted he hadn't used the knife and if true, it would be valuable exculpatory evidence.

There was no ethical obligation to reveal its location, but taking possession makes the lawyer a witness and a lawyer cannot be an advocate and witness in the same case. Uelman asked the presiding judge to appoint a neutral 'special master' to retrieve the knife, return it in a sealed envelope to the court, and then release it for analysis. If incriminating, it would be turned over to the prosecution; if exculpatory, it could be preserved as defence evidence. The judge, Lance Ito, later the trial judge, agreed and appointed a retired Superior Court judge to get the knife. It was examined by Dr Henry Lee. No marks, scratches or traces of blood were found. It appeared to be brand new and pristine. If the prosecution relied on their theory, the defence could rebut. However, Judge Ito ordered disclosure of Lee's report under California's reciprocal discovery law and the prosecution discovered their theory was unsound.

ii. *Robert Wemark's Knife*

Unless the law imposes specific requirements, what *can* lawyers advise clients about 'real evidence' such as OJ's knife? Wemark, accused of murdering his estranged wife, told his two lawyers he'd hidden the knife in a pile of automotive parts under the base-ment steps of his house. A two-day 'inept search' (Sisk 2014: 896) by law enforcement hadn't searched the basement. The lawyers, unsure whether to believe him, found it and left it there. They discussed options with Wemark and told him, incorrectly, that

---

[1] Much of this section is based on *San Jose Mercury News*, 28 April 1996.

the location of the knife must be disclosed. They encouraged him to tell the truth to the state's medical expert psychiatrist, expecting him to do so. He did and the psychiatrist told the police. They searched again and found the knife. It had his wife's blood on it. After conviction, Wemark argued 'ineffective assistance of counsel' because his lawyers had betrayed confidentiality. The court agreed that '[t]actics or strategy cannot support disclosure in this case', but there was no prejudice: the trial result would not have been different but for counsel's errors (*Wemark*: 817).

The location of real evidence, revealed to lawyers by clients, is communication protected by privilege, even if lawyers verify the location: 'the attorney-client privilege protects statements by a client revealing the location of the fruits or instrumentality of a completed crime' (ibid: 812). Sisk notes 'the observation of evidence in its original location by a lawyer pursuant to a client's confidential communication falls *comfortably* within the privilege' (2014: 862, emphasis added). Lawyers may take possession of evidence to examine it. They must adhere to strict standards and be careful not to alter or destroy it.

If after examination the evidence corroborates the prosecution case or undermines the client's case, 'the option of returning the evidence to its source after examination ought to be presumptively and generally available' (ibid: 868). Lawyers are restoring the situation to what it was had they merely been informed of the location. Sisk (2014: 868–89) notes, citing Gillers (2009), '[t]he [ethical] rules don't transform the lawyer for a private client into an arm of the state'. The client's constitutional right against self-incrimination would be compromised if lawyers were required to deliver up evidence to law enforcement. Even though evidence is not in itself a 'communication', the US Supreme Court observed the act of producing evidence has 'communicative aspects of its own, wholly aside from' the nature of the item (*US v Hubbell*: 41–42). To require lawyers to deliver the evidence to law enforcement would provide them with a 'windfall … that it would not have found on its own' (Sisk 2014: 870).

iii. Document Destruction ('Retention') Policy

What if lawyers have information suggesting a product is dangerous? Legal proceedings may not be current, but are always a prospect, especially if that information is revealed. To pre-empt disclosure, a lawyer may advise it be destroyed unless laws prevent it. In the US, if there's a pending legal proceeding, it's a criminal offence for anyone who 'corruptly … influences, obstructs, or impedes, or endeavors to impede, the due administration of justice' (18 USC 1503). This includes persuading, causing or inducing another person to 'alter, destroy, mutilate, or conceal an object with intent to impair the object's integrity or availability for use in an official proceeding' (ibid: 1512(b); see also 1519).

A document destruction policy could be established by the lawyer and given the name: 'Document Retention Policy' (*Brambles*). It might relieve office space, but also manage the risk of 'smoking guns'. While evidence destruction might be unethical, recycling is applauded! There's no obligation on lawyers to preserve sensitive information to help possible future adversaries. The US Supreme Court reversed Arthur Andersen's conviction for obstruction of justice in the Enron case. The firm audited Enron but instructed its employees to destroy documents 'subject to its document retention policy'. The Court reversed because the judge instructed the jury, incorrectly, it didn't need to find the firm acted 'dishonestly', but could convict even if it 'honestly and sincerely believed that its conduct was lawful' (*Arthur Andersen*).

B. Removing the Smoke

If there's 'no smoke without fire', maybe there's 'no fire without smoke'! One way to 'remove the smoke' is to invoke privilege. There's evidence that an Australian law firm, Clayton Utz, working on behalf of British American Tobacco Australia Services Limited (BATAS), 'established a database of scientific material that was intended to "have documents stored offshore, again with the intention of putting them beyond reach of discovery"' (Parker et al 2017: 1002–03, referring to Cameron 2002: 784). A whistle-blowing in-house lawyer claimed Clayton Utz was '"warehousing" 230,000 documents and claiming privilege over them', the copies having been given to the law firm 'ostensibly for legal advice and the originals at BATAS destroyed' (ibid: 1003). Australian lawyers may have 'adjusted to the litigation culture already developed in the United Kingdom ("UK") and USA and firmly entrenched in the defendant's corporate strategy' (Cameron 2002: 781).

Strategies to hide tobacco's health dangers probably began in the US. For over 30 years, while companies' advertisements said smoking tobacco wasn't proven to cause cancer and heart disease – and was not addictive – their own research showed that wasn't true. Indeed:

> The key to the [tobacco] industry's defense strategy – which had been successful for decades – was the concealment of the industry's internal documents, including documents disclosing the industry's secret acknowledgment of the health hazards and addictiveness of smoking, documents disclosing the industry's manipulation of nicotine, and documents disclosing the industry's dependence upon new generations of American youth to preserve the viability of the cigarette market. (Ciresi et al 1999: 479)

The companies hid the truth behind a screen of public relations, political protection and lawyers: 'there is a long history of lawyers assisting tobacco companies to avoid public and legal scrutiny of their responsibility and culpability in relation to the marketing of cigarettes, their addictiveness and the associated harm' (Parker et al 2017: 1002).

In 2006, an American court confirmed the central role lawyers played in concealing the dangers (*US v Philip Morris*). Lawyers oversaw and managed the companies' campaigns. They developed strategies to use the science for, rather than against, companies. They asserted control over scientific research and became intermediaries for the receipt of that research. They based attorney–client privilege – unethically – on two fictions: the materials were 'work-product' in anticipation of litigation; and the lawyers provided the materials to company personnel to assist them in anticipation of litigation. The strategy was to assert privilege, wait for a challenge and let the courts decide (Cavallaro 1997). But plaintiffs couldn't challenge when they didn't know the materials existed or couldn't show enough to challenge privilege claims. Invoking privilege stopped the tobacco papers from being revealed for decades. Judges had to accept what lawyers claimed – that the papers were confidential communications between lawyer and client, or part of work-product immunity. Some companies used overseas subsidiaries to store sensitive documents.

The tactics of the industry and their lawyers were exposed in landmark Minnesota litigation in 1994 which was settled in 1998. Apparently: 'Leading experts on ethics and privilege have been shocked and dismayed by the abuses of privilege uncovered in Minnesota' (Ciresi et al 1999: 499: 500). Privilege was used 'to conceal deception' (Hazard Jr 1998: A22). Judge Kenneth Fitzpatrick, reviewing the 'Cigarette Papers' in the late 1990s, including one that referred to a link between smoking and cancer as early as 1955, said his review revealed 'a conspiracy of silence and suppression of scientific research' (Cavallaro 1997). This suppression was achieved by conducting the research under the close consultation or even management of lawyers (Ciresi et al 1999: 500), and then 'inserting' scientific research into communications between lawyer and client.

The industry argued that research was privileged because documents prepared by scientists were received by in-house counsel, or that the scientists themselves were 'litigation consultants'. This was an attempt to 'launder' corporate information and research, even corporate decisions, through corporate counsel, so that attorney–client privilege could be invoked. Like 'money laundering' cleanses dirty money, corporate information could be cleansed by lawyers manipulating ethical and procedural rules. Their manoeuvres to 'create' privilege held off challenges for years.

Ultimately, they failed. Judge Fitzpatrick ordered cigarette companies to disclose thousands of internal industry documents. These showed that 25 years before Surgeon General C Everett Koop made an official determination that nicotine was addictive, the general counsel for Brown & Williamson Tobacco Corp concluded in a memo to colleagues: 'nicotine is addictive. We are, then, in the business of selling nicotine, an addictive drug effective in the relief of stress mechanisms' (American Council on Science and Health 2000: 9). At the time, the industry was denying cigarettes were addictive or unsafe: 'since the 1950s, the industry had engaged in a systematic effort to keep the public ignorant of the truth' (ibid). Judge Fitzpatrick became the first judge to sanction a tobacco company, Brown & Williamson. In 1997, he imposed a $100,000 fine for 'flagrant' violations of evidentiary discovery rules before trial (Adler 2016). His rulings 'lifted the lid on a trove of damaging scientific and marketing research kept secret for years by the tobacco industry'.

In another case, part of a series of cases against the tobacco industry, the court held that all confidential documents in lawyers' files allegedly showing the tobacco companies knew of the health risks of smoking fell within the 'crime-fraud exception' and were therefore discoverable (*American Tobacco*). The 'discovery battles' had lasted years, but resulted in around 35 million pages of internal documents (Ciresi et al 1999: 479). Just one month after the US Supreme Court refused to stay an order requiring the production of tens of thousands of documents withheld under a claim of privilege (*Philip Morris*), the case was settled.

The defence strategy changed with every 'wave' of litigation. In the first wave, in the 1950s, the industry's claim was 'smoking does not cause cancer'. Yet the statistical link identified in industry documents revealed a cause and effect (Ciresi et al 1999: 484). In the second wave in the 1980s, the industry argued, 'not without a certain audacity' (ibid: 485), 'everybody knows' smoking causes cancer, but it's a freedom of choice issue. Yet the addictiveness of nicotine was well known within the industry (and companies continued to argue it was not proven that cigarettes caused disease) (ibid: 485–86). The third wave began in 1994 and involved states, individual smokers and class action suits. The states were seeking to recover medical costs for injured workers (ibid: 486). They had the resources to take on the industry.

In EW, 'laundering' pre-existing documents, such as scientific research, cannot attract privilege merely by being added – or attached – to privileged communications such as letters or emails (*FRC*). But, as in the US, the onus is on the claimants/plaintiffs to discover the documents.

i. Dalkon Shield

AH Robins Company marketed a contraceptive intrauterine device, Dalkon Shield, in the early 1970s in the US. In the next few years, over two million women used it, but it was defective: it caused uterine perforations, ectopic pregnancies, sterility and pelvic inflammatory disease, amongst other things. Some babies were born deformed or brain damaged (Perry and Dawson 1985). The company delayed disclosure of sensitive documents 'with stalling tactics, such as motions for reconsideration, requests for stays or attempted appeals of discovery orders' (*In re AH Robins Co*: 14). Documents included the company's knowledge of the harm caused by the product. Ten years after Dalkon Shield was taken off the market, a former AH Robins lawyer admitted he knew Robins had destroyed Dalkon Shield documents a decade earlier.

14

A Sporting Chance?

Criminal Trial Tactics

A jury consists of twelve persons chosen to decide who has the better lawyer.
— Robert Frost (attributed)

Criminal justice has 'different social and legal significance from civil justice' for two reasons. It's a 'censuring institution: it allocates blame and censure … and there is a range of other official agencies … dedicated to ensuring that this function is duly carried out'. Also, punishment may be the outcome, and there may be 'deprivations' during the process as well (Blake and Ashworth 2004: 167–68). In short, 'not only is the might of the State ranged against the suspect/defendant, but he or she also stands to lose a number of basic liberties if sentenced' (168).

I. Blackstone, Franklin and Voltaire

This is why defendants and lawyers need heightened protections – despite the consequences. As William Blackstone put it (1769: 352): 'The law holds, that it is better that ten guilty persons escape, than that one innocent suffer.' Benjamin Franklin (1785: 293) claimed 'it is better that 100 guilty Persons should escape than that one innocent Person should suffer is a Maxim that has been long and generally approved'. He was possibly alluding to 'that generous Maxim' of the philosopher Voltaire (whom Minister to France Franklin met in Paris in 1778) that ''tis much more Prudence to acquit two Persons, tho' actually guilty, than to pass Sentence of Condemnation on one that is virtuous and innocent' (Bartleby nd; also translated as: 'It is better to risk sparing a guilty person than to condemn an innocent one'). The US Supreme Court in 1895 stated simply 'it is better to let the crime of a guilty person go unpunished than to condemn the innocent' (cited in *Coffin*).

Clients are therefore entitled to say to lawyers: 'I want your advocacy not your judgment; I prefer that of the court' (*Emerson*: 371). Thomas Paine's book *The Rights of Man* (1791) led to him being charged with seditious libel for challenging the existing order, arguing that the people had the right to replace the government. His 'seditious proposals' included the 'introduction of old age pensions, unemployment benefit, child benefit, and a progressive income tax' (Neuberger 2012: 56). As Lord Neuberger put it: 'Today's heterodoxy is tomorrow's orthodoxy'. Thomas Erskine, defending Paine, said:

I will for ever, at all hazards, assert the dignity, independence and integrity of the English Bar, without which impartial justice, the most valuable part of the English Constitution, can have no existence. From the moment that any advocate can be permitted to say that he will, or will not, stand between the Crown and the subject arraigned in the court where he daily sits to practise, from that moment the liberties of England are at an end. If the advocate refuses to defend, from what he may think of the charge or of the defence, he assumes the character of the Judge; nay, he assumes it before the hour of judgment; and in proportion to his rank and reputation, puts the heavy influence of, perhaps, a mistaken opinion into the scales against the accused, in whose favour the benevolent principle of English law makes all presumptions. (ibid: 52)

Erskine 'lost a lucrative position [as Attorney-General to the Prince of Wales] and could well have lost future work … He only had his conscience and his duty to ensure that justice was done to concern him' (ibid: 54), though Erskine was earning 'around £7 million a year in modern money' (ibid: 48) and when appointed Lord Chancellor in 1806, about £120 million. As Lord Neuberger says: 'It is not a case that an advocate defends the guilty. Guilt is a question for the court, and in important trials, for the jury. It is not for an advocate to presume to determine guilt, to set aside the presumption of innocence' (ibid: 55).

II. Division of Responsibility

The question before a court is not 'guilt or innocence', but has guilt been proved beyond a reasonable doubt? As Viscount Sankey, the Lord Chancellor, put it: 'throughout the web of the English criminal law one golden thread is always to be seen that it is the duty of the prosecution to prove the prisoner's guilt' (*Woolmington*). He added that 'no attempt to whittle it down can be entertained', which is why the duty of EW counsel is 'to promote fearlessly and by all proper and lawful means the client's best interests' (BSB 2024: CD2 and rC15.1), and in the US, in a proceeding that could result in incarceration, the duty is to 'defend so as to require that every element of the case be established' (MR 3.1). Or as one Crown Court judge put it starkly: 'From the defence point of view, the only motivation is to get your client off' (Hunter et al 2018: 16). So: 'In criminal defense, the focus must be on proof not truth' (Smith 2000b: 509, fn 100). That's why a senior barrister can legitimately claim: 'I don't get guilty people off. I try to ensure, along with other barristers, that people who are not guilty are not convicted' (Menkele 2010).

That said: 'Defense counsel is the professional representative of the accused, not the accused's alter-ego' (ABA 2017: 4.1–2(d)). Attorneys are bound to abide by clients' decisions regarding the objectives of representation (MR 1.2(a)), but clients normally defer to lawyers when it comes to strategies to accomplish them (MR 1.2, Comment [1]). Similarly, in EW: 'The client does not conduct the case: that is the responsibility of the trial advocate' (*R v Farooqi*: 107). The advocate 'is not the client's mouthpiece, obliged to conduct the case in accordance with whatever the client … "instructs" him' (ibid: 108). 'Instructions' do 'bind the advocate and … form the basis for the defence case at trial', but the 'foundation for the right to appear as an advocate, with the privileges and responsibilities of advocates and as an advocate, burdened with twin responsibilities, both to the client and the court' is that while 'the advocate is bound to advance the defendant's case on the basis that what his client tells him is the truth ... the advocate, and the advocate alone remains responsible for the forensic decisions and strategy' (ibid).

III. The Sporting Theory of Justice?

Tactics are, however, constrained. In EW, for example, the defence is required, at least to some extent, to cooperate with the prosecution to facilitate a 'full and fair hearing on the issues canvassed at trial' (*R v Gleeson*, Lord Justice Auld). The nature of the defence, any alibi that will be relied upon and what elements of the prosecution case are contested must be provided (section 5 of the Criminal Procedure and Investigations Act 1996). Barristers mustn't abuse their role as advocates (BSB 2024: rC7). This means they mustn't 'make statements or ask questions merely to insult, humiliate or annoy a witness' (rC7.1). MR 4.4(a), 'Respect for Rights of Third Persons', states: 'a lawyer shall not use means that have no substantial purpose other than to embarrass, delay, or burden a third person, or use methods of obtaining evidence that violate the legal rights of such a person'. Lawyers shouldn't use legal procedure 'to harass or intimidate others' (MR Preamble [5]).

Courts have warned lawyers:

> A criminal trial is not a game under which a guilty defendant should be provided with a sporting chance. It is a search for truth in accordance with the twin principles that the prosecution must prove its case and that a defendant is not obliged to inculpate himself, the object being to convict the guilty and acquit the innocent. (*R v Gleeson*, Lord Justice Auld)

> The days of ambushing and taking last-minute technical points are gone. They are not consistent with the overriding objective of deciding cases justly, acquitting the innocent and convicting the guilty. (*R v Chorley*: 26, Lord Justice Thomas)

> [A] criminal trial is not a game. (*US v Chronic*: 657)

> [It is] not yet a poker game in which players enjoy an absolute right always to conceal their cards until played. (*Williams*: 82)

But have these warnings been heeded? Roscoe Pound (1906: 738) believed the 'sporting theory of justice' was 'so rooted in the profession in America that most of us take it as a fundamental legal tenet'. Mark Rowley, then Chief Constable of Surrey Police and now Metropolitan Police Commissioner, said, after the Dowler trial (discussed below), criminal justice seems like a 'legal game in which experts duel elegantly and witnesses and victims are trashed' (Purves 2011). It's 'more of a legal game than a search for truth' (Rowley 2011). Indeed, 'tactical opportunities for creative lawyers to distort the truth are nearly limitless' (Siegel 2006: 34). They can hide the client's factual guilt. Defence counsel may 'often admit to himself that his client will win only if counsel is successful in preventing the truth from being disclosed' (Pye 1978: 928). So, the defence lawyer's role is often 'to work to obscure inconvenient truths and to prevent the truth from coming out' (Hodes 2002: 60–61).

How should criminal defence lawyers wield their power? Dershowitz's answer was a soundbite: 'what criminal defense lawyers "may" do, they *must* do, if it's necessary to defend their clients' (WETA 1986; Dershowitz 1996: 145). It's the duty of barristers to act in clients' interests 'without regard to the consequences to any other person' (BSB 2024: rC15.3). It seems '[m]ost [American] scholars and attorneys agree that criminal defense lawyers ought to be allowed to take advantage of loopholes, trick their opponents and stretch the law to its limits to help their clients' (Roiphe 2011: 204). But so do many judges: '[E]very counsel has a duty to his client fearlessly to raise every issue, advance every argument, and ask every question, however distasteful, which he thinks will help his client's case', unless there is no sufficient basis in the information the barrister has (*Rondel*: 227, Lord Reid) The advocate has significant leeway, and a broad duty, to engage in many courtroom tactics, which may be why '[i]n truth, there is probably no such thing as a "hopeless case"' (General Council of the Bar 1992: 508) and '[y]ou can never predict what will happen in a criminal trial' (The Secret Barrister 2021a).

IV. Excluding Evidence

The job of jurors is not to determine the truth, but whether the *evidence* presented convinces them of guilt beyond a reasonable doubt. So, 'careful decisions will have to be made as to what should and what should not have been placed before the jury. Only relevant and admissible material should be presented before a court of trial' (Wace 2021). Hearsay is generally excluded, as are prior criminal convictions: 'There should be no trial by smear' (ibid). Jurors may be shocked when they hear, after acquittal, the defendant's criminal record.

The more exclusionary rules can be used, the more the client is protected. In the US, 'the scope, complexity, and stringent operation of our exclusionary rules suggests that no other country has so little regard for the accuracy of its criminal trial results' (van Kessel 1993: 451). Indeed: 'The evidence rules are rife with possibilities of loophole lawyering' (Capra 2007). In both countries though:

> The lawyer's job at trial is to assemble the strands of evidence supporting her client's version of things, wrap the useful pieces into a coherent and compelling narrative that hopefully explains and describes the relevant events, and offer that narrative as 'the truth' of what happened. (Siegel 2006: 34)

Clients can protect themselves by not giving evidence. This avoids cross-examination and perjury. If the prosecution lacks sufficient evidence to convict or the defence creates doubts, the client 'wins'. That said, in EW, if a defendant raises a specific defence, such as self-defence or alibi, their failure to give evidence to substantiate it may lead the court to draw an adverse inference (sections 34–35 of the Criminal Justice and Public Order Act 1994). There are exceptions, including if the refusal to testify is justified on the grounds of LPP.

Defence lawyers can challenge the admissibility of unfavourable evidence. In the US, unconstitutional searches are usually excluded despite 'the substantial social costs' of so doing (*US v Leon*: 907). Courts are obliged to suppress even truthful evidence if obtained in violation of the Fourth Amendment (*Mapp*). EW courts may reject prosecution evidence if it appears, having regard to all the circumstances, including how the evidence was obtained, that its admission would 'have such an adverse effect on the fairness of the proceedings that the court ought not to permit it' (section 78 PACE).

V. Challenging Evidence

A. Eyewitness Testimony

Eyewitness testimony is highly influential on a jury's willingness to convict (Simon 2011: 157), and a major factor in wrongful convictions and miscarriages of justice.

i. Picking Cotton

In 1984, a man broke into 22-year-old Jennifer Thompson's apartment in the middle of the night, held a knife to her throat and raped her. She was determined, if she survived, to identify him. So, she studied him and after escaping told police she was certain she could identify him. Three days later, at an identification parade, she picked Ronald Cotton. She was certain because she'd recalled his distinct nose, tall and slender physique, and slouchy posture.

In 1985, based on her confident identification, Cotton, then aged 23, was convicted. In 1987, there was a second trial because an imprisoned felon, Bobby Poole, boasted he'd raped Thompson. At this trial, Poole denied it and then, in a dramatic moment, Thompson told the jury: 'Bobby Poole did not rape me; Ronald Cotton did.' Cotton was sent back to prison to complete his sentence of life plus 54 years. Then, as Thompson put it: 'For 365 days, for years and years, I prayed. I prayed for him to die.' She did this for 10 years, but Cotton didn't die and ... she was wrong. In 1995, DNA evidence proved Cotton's innocence and Poole's guilt. So, after his release, Thompson and Cotton spoke and wrote together about the dangers of eyewitness testimony (Thompson-Cannino et al 2009).

ii. Confidence

Greater witness confidence leads to a higher conviction rate (Brewer and Burke 2002). Jurors are more likely to have an intuitive belief in the testimony of witnesses who display 'richness-in-detail'; 'completely certain' witnesses were three times more likely to be judged accurate by jurors than those 'somewhat uncertain'; and conviction rates were 50 per cent higher when the witness was '100 per cent confident' than when the witness 'could not say that he was 100 per cent confident' (Simon 2011: 165, 157, 158). Witness confidence might be treated by jurors as a 'proxy' for witness 'accuracy', but 'only seventy percent of witnesses who claim to be absolutely certain are in fact correct' (ibid: 158; see also 163). Indeed, 'about one out of every three positive identifications is wrong' (ibid: 153), but juries are not particularly adept at distinguishing accurate from inaccurate identifications. Witnesses are significantly worse at identifying people with characteristics different from their own, especially age, race/ethnic background or gender.

Contested criminal trials typically happen months, or even years, after the crime event itself. Examining how witnesses remember can challenge the jury's confidence in them (POST 2019). The viewing circumstances may undermine an eyewitness' credibility: how far away they were, how long the event lasted, how well-lit the scene and whether there were any visual obstructions. Their 'state' – drunk, tired, scared, stressed – can reduce accuracy. As Simon (2011: 166) notes: 'Savvy attorneys can readily encourage witnesses to include trivial details, and attack opposing witnesses for the failure to recount details or for mentioning mistaken ones.' As for consistency: 'This cue too is susceptible to manipulation at trial, as lawyers can praise witnesses for being consistent, irrespective of their accuracy, and they can catch truthful witnesses in an inconsistency in some detail or other.'

Witnesses may self-report their viewing circumstances and 'state'. However, 'research casts doubt over these self-reports' (ibid: 157). Once an event is experienced, it's 'encoded as a memory that may be retrieved later', but 'memories can alter after they have been encoded' (POST 2019: 2). They can also be influenced by the situation in which the memory is recalled, for example, in an intimidating police interview room.

iii. Contamination

Human memory is 'a powerful cognitive apparatus, but it can be fickle and is vulnerable to error and contamination' (Simon 2011: 161). Although EW police, when interacting with witnesses, follow standardised guidelines (through Codes of Practice), 'witness testimony may still be at risk of contamination from biases during investigations' (POST 2019: 2). This can occur when witnesses discuss the event with others, or see media coverage of it which may be inaccurate, misleading or 'sensational'. Contamination increases with the length of time before they recall the event. Statements, or identifications, made soon after an event are not immune from contamination, but are considered to be more accurate.

In EW, a statement should be read by the judge to the jury if the case depends entirely or substantially on witness identification (CPS 1977). The 'Turnbull Guidelines' aim to improve evaluation of the testimony and debunk some 'memory myths'. Judges generally may choose to warn the jury about witness testimony; defence lawyers could do so as well.

B. Confessions

In EW, a 'confession' is any statement which is wholly or partly adverse to the person making it. If it's an admission of guilt, it's 'probably the most probative and damaging evidence' (*Parker*: 72). However, false confessions have led to wrongful convictions and miscarriages of justice. In the US, the 'Reid Technique' of police interrogation elicits true confessions by guilty people but is '*too* powerful, i.e. can break down the innocent as well as the guilty' (Hirsch 2014: 805; see also Leo 2008). Confessions not 'voluntarily given' (18 US Code § 3501(a), Admissibility of Evidence) shouldn't be admitted.

In EW, tape recording police interrogations is mandatory, but admissibility of confessions can still be challenged on the basis that they were obtained 'by oppression' or 'in consequence of anything said or done which was likely, in the circumstances existing at the time, to render' them unreliable' (section 76(2)(a), (b) PACE). Oppression includes 'torture, inhuman or degrading treatment, and the use or threat of violence'. Incorporated within that is 'the exercise of authority or power in a burdensome, harsh or wrongful manner; unjust or cruel treatment of subjects, inferiors etc; the imposition of unreasonable or unjust burdens' (*R v Fulling*). It also includes 'questioning which by its nature, duration or other circumstances (including the fact of custody) excites hopes (such as the hope of release) or fears, or so affects the mind of the subject that his will crumbles and he speaks when otherwise he would have stayed silent' (*R v Mushtaq*). In other words, the confession was involuntary and the suspect confessed against their will. One oppressive interview lasted 13 hours, during which the police shouted at the suspect what they wanted him to say, but the suspect denied involvement over 300 times (*R v Paris*).

Unreliability means the defendant might have made a confession for reasons other than guilt. Something is said or done – a denial of refreshments or not being given proper rest (*R v Trussler*); a suspect not being cautioned at the start of an interview (*R v Doolan*); the police failing to make a proper record of the interview in breach of the Code of Practice (*R v Delaney*); an inducement such as making the suspect believe confessing would result in more favourable treatment (*R v Matthias*); the strength of the prosecution case being misrepresented; and the suspect being threatened. If oppression or unreliability is shown, the court mustn't allow even a truthful confession to be used, unless the prosecution can prove beyond reasonable doubt it wasn't so obtained (section 76(2) PACE). A confession might also be excluded if obtained by a trick (*R v Mason*) or a 'significant or substantial' breach of PACE and the Codes of Practice.

VI. A Theory of Innocence: SODDI

To achieve not guilty verdicts, defence lawyers 'will almost inevitably have to present at least some suggestion as to who might have done the acts instead' (Hodes 2002: 59, fn 18). They need a '"reasonable" alternative theory that will permit jurors to satisfy their natural human curiosity about dramatic events, and also their sense that real events must have some real-life explanation'. The alternative narrative is important because jurors 'naturally fit trial information into story-like formats' (Simon 2011: 186, referring to Pennington and Hastie 1993), and 'evidence that lends itself to the story format is more likely … *to convince a jury*' (ibid: 186–87, emphasis added) – like the 'SODDI' defence – 'Some Other Dude Did It' (Lubet 1993: 93, fn 17), or 'the Perry Mason defence': 'proving "whodunit"' (McCord 1996).

A. Terry Nichols

Michael Tigar, the lead lawyer defending Terry Nichols, the alleged accomplice of Oklahoma bomber Timothy McVeigh, says the advocate's perspective should be 'presenting a story of the offense that contradicts the prosecution story enough to create a reasonable doubt' (Tigar and Coleman Jr 2014: 4; see also Tigar 2003). Building 'a theory of innocence' has

> two basic principles of advocacy … First, do not make yourself look bad to the jury by deny-
> ing the obvious. Second, employ the theory of minimal contradiction; look for a case theory

that shifts perspective just enough to require a different result. It is never enough in a criminal case, simply to rest on reasonable doubt. Never assume a burden you do not have, but always provide the jurors with a plausible alternative view of events. (Tigar and Coleman Jr 2014: 4)

Tigar said in his opening statement 'we'll show you the hard evidence, the truthful alternatives to their theory' (ibid: 20) that Nichols 'was unlikely to have joined with McVeigh or anyone else to plant a bomb that would kill people indiscriminately' (ibid: 4). The 'plausible alternative reality [was] based on the idea that the government's investigation had been slipshod' (ibid: 15). Tigar pointed to 'errors and omissions in the government's forensic evidence, and on its failure to pursue leads to other conspirators' (ibid: 5). He said:

I'm going to talk about the FBI and its laboratory, its so-called 'expert,' some of whom are going to testify here, how these people ignored vital evidence, used junk science, did sloppy field work, and rushed to a very wrong and quite early judgment (18).

Our 'job,' Tigar repeated, 'is simply to show the reasonable doubts, the truthful alternatives to their theory' (ibid: 20).

After deliberating for 41 hours over six days, the jury convicted Nichols of conspiracy to use a weapon of mass destruction and eight counts of involuntary manslaughter, but acquitted him of first-degree murder. He avoided the death penalty after the federal jury was deadlocked and did so again at his subsequent trial in Oklahoma state court.

B. Levi Bellfield and Milly Dowler

Thirteen-year-old Amanda 'Milly' Dowler went missing in March 2002; her body was discovered in September. Years later, in 2010, Levi Bellfield, already serving life sentences, was charged with Milly's abduction and murder as well as the abduction of 11-year-old Rachel Cowles. For years, Milly's parents had been subjected to suspicion, threats to kill Milly's sister, false claims by an individual to have killed Milly, a person impersonating Milly by telephone to the parents, the school and the police, and someone saying Milly had been trafficked to Poland to work as a prostitute. Bellfield's trial, compounding their grief, was a 'cruel ordeal' (Purves 2011). It led to public outrage – and media hypocrisy: the *News of the World* newspaper 'hacked' Milly's mobile phone when she was missing.

Bellfield pleaded not guilty and 'he instructed his lawyers to show alternative explanations for her disappearance' (Rayment and Leppard 2011). The strategy adopted by Jeffrey Samuels KC was reviewed subsequently by Ali Naseem Bajwa KC (2011). The evidence against Bellfield was 'strong' but 'circumstantial'. Bellfield lived near where Milly was last seen alive; he'd attempted to kidnap a young woman the day before Milly went missing; and two years later, 'in circumstances that bore a striking similarity to Milly's disappearance', Bellfield abducted and murdered two young women and attempted to murder a third. In court, Samuels accused prosecutors of exploiting Bellfield's past convictions as 'an easy opportunity' to bring an end to the nine-year-old 'mystery'. He said: 'The claims do not stand up to scrutiny. No eyewitnesses, no scientific evidence to link him to her or vice versa. No images on CCTV' (Bannerman 2011a).

Bajwa noted:

if Bellfield was not responsible for Milly's murder, there were really only two other possibilities: either a person other than him, with a freakishly similar opportunity and skill at abducting and killing young women, had kidnapped and murdered Milly; or Milly had not been abducted by Bellfield at a location just metres from his flat but had chosen to run away from home, and had met her death in an unknown way and at an unknown place not long thereafter. (Bajwa 2011)

Bajwa concluded: 'Given Bellfield's plea of not guilty and the extreme unlikelihood of the first possibility, *the defence had little choice but to pursue the second one*' (emphasis added).

Adoption of this 'alternative theory' led the defence to cross-examine Milly's parents about 'highly personal and sensitive material – suggesting Milly, months before her disappearance, didn't enjoy a good relationship with her parents, was unhappy at home, and had considered running away' (ibid). Letters in her toybox revealed she'd written: 'I hate myself'; her sister was 'everything I am not, everything I dream to be – pretty, smart, intelligent, wanted, loved'; and her parents should have had her aborted or adopted (Rayment and Leppard 2011). She'd made a 'half-hearted attempt to cut her wrists with a dinner knife' (ibid). This cross-examination was relevant to a key issue – had Milly been abducted? It also followed from Bellfield's plea of not guilty: 'A counsel's duty is always to carry out his client's instructions fiercely, although there is always an element of judgment in how he presents the style and manner in which he presents the defence' (Michael Wolkind KC, quoted in Blake 2011).

To show Milly was troubled, Samuels revealed details of the Dowler family's private life, including Milly's discovery of pornographic magazines, hardcore fetish gear and bondage videos around the family home (Rayment and Leppard 2011). He suggested Milly ran away because she was tormented and unhappy. He claimed her mother favoured Milly's sister (Blake 2011). Letters written by Milly were read out to Milly's father Bob Dowler in which she referred to herself as 'your little disappointment' (ibid). As Bajwa notes: 'Counsel was right, indeed was obliged, to explore an alternative version of events which was based on his instructions, supported by evidence and relevant to his client's defence.' Not surprisingly, however, the parents and the media didn't see it the same way. Bob Dowler told the BBC after the Bellfield conviction:

My family has had to pay too high a price for this conviction. The pain and agony that we have endured as a family since [Milly's disappearance] has been compounded by the devastating effects of this trial … The trial has been a truly mentally scarring experience on an unimaginable scale … [It] has been a truly horrifying ordeal for my family … During our questioning, my wife and I both felt as if *we* were on trial. The questioning of my wife was particularly cruel and inhuman, resulting in her collapse after leaving the stand … [Bellfield] chose … to hide behind his defence QC to challenge the testimony of every witness. Where is the fairness in the system which allows such behaviour? The defence inferences about myself and my wife were hugely distressing. (www.bbc.co.uk/news/av/uk-13908422)

Milly's sister called the day her parents were questioned by Samuels

the worst day of my life. It is hard to believe but it was worse than when I heard that the remains were those of my sister Milly. The way my parents were questioned can only be described as mental torture. (Bannerman 2011b)

The Times (2011) called Bellfield's trial 'a catastrophe'. Bellfield's lawyers 'had a difficult task' because of the evidence against him, so they

> bombarded the jury with irrelevant information, hoping the confusion would cast doubt where there really could not be much. They would have to draw their cards from the bottom of the deck, because that was all Bellfield had left them. And so they did.

Chief Constable Rowley echoed the view of the Association of Chief Police Officers: the criminal justice system is a 'playground for lawyers' and 'too often tactics come before truth' (Purves 2011).

But are these criticisms justified? When Milly disappeared, information caused the police to be suspicious of Milly's father and the cross-examination was based on this. It upset Bob Dowler, but was consistent with the 'SODDI' approach. As Chairman of the Bar, now Judge Peter Lodder KC (2011), put it: 'Mark Rowley ... must be aware of the importance of testing in court the points that his police force's investigation raised.' Bellfield's instructions required his counsel to show there were other reasons why Milly might have disappeared, as police originally suspected. The judge agreed this evidence was 'relevant and legitimate' and the cross-examination was 'skilfully and sensitively' done. Bajwa described it as 'firm but fair'.

The jury heard this evidence and rejected it. Bellfield was sentenced to an unprecedented second whole-life term. As Lodder put it: 'Justice was done' Bajwa (2011) concluded 'no radical changes need to be made to the Criminal Justice System'. Justice White of the US Supreme Court showed why:

> Our interest in not convicting the innocent permits counsel to put the State to its proof, to put the State's case in the worst possible light, regardless of what he thinks or knows to be the truth. Undoubtedly there are some limits which defense counsel must observe but more often than not, defense counsel will cross-examine a prosecution witness, and impeach him if he can, even if he thinks the witness is telling the truth, just as he will attempt to destroy a witness who he thinks is lying. In this respect, as part of our modified adversary system and as part of the duty imposed on the most honorable defense counsel, we countenance or require conduct which in many instances has little, if any, relation to the search for the truth. (*US v Wade*: 1948)

VII. The 'Cockroach' Defence: Trial by Ordeal

Trial by 'ordeal' determined guilt via several methods, including the accused carrying a hot iron or putting their hand into boiling water (see Lowell 1897: 290). If they didn't burn, they were innocent (Bartlett 1986). Pope Innocent III abolished such trials in 1215 when he and the Lateran Council forbade priests from officiating. It was replaced, at least in part, by jury trial.

The modern meaning of ordeal has changed. Wigmore (1905) famously claimed that cross-examination is 'the greatest legal engine ever invented for the discovery of truth'. Defence lawyers may view it instead as the greatest engine for *concealing* the truth. It's no longer the *accused* who suffers the 'cruel ordeal', but those on the receiving end of lawyers' efforts to convince juries. On the one hand: 'The art of cross-examination is not the art of examining crossly. It's the art of leading the witness through a line of propositions he agrees to until he's forced to agree to the *one fatal question*' (Clifford Mortimer, quoted in Mortimer 1982). On the other hand: 'Being cross-examined by an effective advocate can be a bruising and chastening experience' (Boon 2014: 702). Wigmore acknowledged (1905: 1697): 'It may be that in more than one sense [cross-examination] takes the place in our system which torture occupied in the mediaeval system.'

McElhaney (2005: 21) described 'the cockroach defense ... there is no real defense, and all advocates can do is act like cockroaches and crawl all over the other side'. By challenging witnesses: 'The slightest slip or inconsistency can be fatal to the credibility of a witness in the eyes of a jury' (The Secret Barrister 2021a), no matter how truthful or vulnerable they might be. The witness box is now the 'pulpit of human despair' (ibid 2018: 133).

A. The Truthful Witness

Freedman and Smith (2010: 206; see also Pepper 1986) claim 'almost every ... commentator on lawyers' ethics' agrees that it's 'proper for a lawyer to cross-examine an adverse witness who has testified accurately and truthfully in order to make the witness appear to be mistaken or lying'. Freedman (1975) even had a chapter entitled 'Cross-Examination: Destroying the Truthful Witness'. The ABA is milder: 'Defense counsel's belief or knowledge that a witness is telling the truth does not preclude vigorous cross-examination, even though defense counsel's cross-examination may *cast doubt* on the testimony' (2017: Standard 4-7.7(b)). The aim is to make witnesses appear incredible, uncertain or unreliable; the hope is that witnesses withdraw their evidence, or even themselves.

B. 'Brutal' Cross-Examination

In general, intrusive questions or calling someone a liar would be regarded as harassment and bullying. However, lawyers are duty-bound to present clients' cases in court: 'it is not for you to decide whether your client's case is to be believed' (BSB 2024 gC6). Cross-examination can feel – and maybe is – 'brutal', but the 'brutal rituals of adversarial adjudication' (Fan 2014: 14) may achieve clients' goals.

New York attorney Michael Mullen was praised by Reginald Sharpe, who represented a co-defendant in the trial: 'He is an excellent trial lawyer. I have witnessed him in action first hand. He is the real deal. The jury loved him even as he was tearing apart the prosecution witnesses in cross-examination' (www.criminaldefenselawyerbrooklyn.com). Lawyers mustn't 'use means that have no substantial purpose other than to embarrass ... or burden a third person' (MR 4.4). But they already have a substantial purpose, 'namely winning the case at hand' (Hazard and Hodes 2001: §40.3). After 'brutal cross-examination' the case might collapse, the victim get blamed or their evidence undermined, or confusion created.

In 2004 in EW, a 36-year-old man was accused of raping a 39-year-old colleague at a 'get-to-know-you party' after she rejected his advances. He was cleared because the case collapsed. The alleged victim said she'd kill herself if she continued giving evidence. She'd fallen ill after being cross-examination on the defendant's insistence that she'd consented. On the second day, she collapsed in the witness box. The trial was adjourned for two weeks, but she was too fragile to return. She had a history of mental problems including several suicide attempts and claimed she'd been abused by her father as a child.

No wonder fear of cross-examination, not to mention the investigation and prosecution process generally, has deterred genuine rape victims from pursuing justice (Topping 2020). This is why there's been a debate as to whether a defence lawyer should vigorously, even brutally, cross-examine a rape victim (see Mitchell 1987; Subin 1987; Lawry 1996; Schwartz 1988; Subin 1988), even one known to be truthful (see Freedman and Smith 2010: 207–13; see also Selinger 1993). Lininger (2005: 1354) 'explored the darker side of cross-examination', especially in rape and sexual assault cases. He found 'the best defense is to vilify the accuser' (ibid: 1356); in other words, 'Try the accuser' (ibid: 1355). Should – or must – a lawyer take advantage of a victim's 'fragility' as a 'windfall' defence? Their mental state might have been discovered by the lawyer's private investigator.

i. Lindsay Armstrong

In EW, Lindsay Armstrong, a teenage rape victim, committed suicide, but not because she feared giving evidence – she'd done so and the 14-year-old rapist was convicted. Armstrong had been subjected to 'a horrific time in court'. As she gave her evidence, the defence lawyer got her to hold up her thong underwear, which bore the words 'Little Devil' – she claimed they'd been 'ripped'. According to her mother, Lindsay burst out crying and put them down; then 'the defence lawyer would shout at her to hold them up again. She was disgusted and humiliated. She felt raped all over again' (Record View 2018). She held them up three times. Two weeks after the trial, aged 17, she took a fatal overdose. After a similar courtroom experience for a rape victim in an Irish court, an Irish MP, Ruth Coppinger, held up a lace thong to 'highlight routine victim-blaming' (ibid).

C. Vulnerable Witnesses

The EW Crime Survey estimated that 1.4 million people experienced domestic abuse in the year ending March 2023 (ONS 2023). Despite seeking to protect victims from trauma and fear, the critical role they play compels the prosecution and police to go to extraordinary lengths to ensure their allegations are presented in court. In one month alone, 140 victims of domestic violence were given 'witness orders' – an enforceable obligation to testify (section 97(2) of the Magistrates' Court Act 1980). Failure to do so would be in contempt of court and expose them to punishment, including prison.

In 2012, a 17-year-old girl was held in a California juvenile detention centre to ensure she appeared at the trial of a man accused of raping her. She'd twice missed Frank Rackley's trial after she ran away from the foster home. Her lawyer, Amina Merritt, said the girl refused to testify because she felt – and was – at risk from Rackley. The

DA's response: 'It's really the last thing we want to do, but we do feel there is a public danger that has to be balanced here.' The girl was held for nearly one month, but gave her evidence. She admitted portions of her original story were a lie. Initially she told investigators she'd been kidnapped by Rackley. On the witness stand she said she'd been prostituting and voluntarily got into Rackley's truck. She claimed that was when it all went wrong. He raped her before she could escape the truck. Rackley was convicted.

In EW, there are 40,000 child witnesses every year. Lord Judge argued they should give video-recorded evidence rather than appear in person. Some have said the same should happen for victims of sexual offences. Lord Judge pointed to 'bullying' cross-examination of children, 'comment posing as cross-examination' and '[c]omplicated tagged questions, double and triple negatives and comment, along with the accompanying paraphernalia for all of them' (Gibb 2013b). Apparently, 90 per cent of children under 10 don't understand the questions they're asked in court (Gibb 2013a). Barristers should be 'stopped from manipulating vulnerable child witnesses' and there should be an end to the 'brutality' of cross-examination in courts (ibid). Since 2020, vulnerable alleged victims and witnesses can pre-record cross-examination evidence 'to avoid the stress of a full courtroom' (Slingo 2020). The aim is to ensure vulnerable witnesses were 'protected and able to give their best possible evidence, without reducing a defendant's right to a fair trial' (Ames 2020, quoting Alex Chalk MP).

A report in 2023 found the process 'less intimidating and yields better evidence' (GovUK 2023b). However, a study in 2024 suggested there was 'a significant' decline in convictions where the testimony was recorded. Lady Chief Justice Dame Sue Carr called for a 'pause' in the scheme (Bentham 2024). That said, as former DPP Lord Macdonald put it: 'it is the judge's job to protect witnesses' (Blake 2011). In EW, there's been 'diminishing tolerance, on the part of the judges and juries, for "aggressive" treatment of witnesses during cross-examination' (Hunter et al 2018: 12). An investigation of judicial perceptions of the quality of criminal advocacy in the Crown Court reported that 'advocates' skills in dealing with young and vulnerable witnesses' had been 'largely improving' (ibid: iv). If the major onus is indeed on the *judge*, defence lawyers may be able 'play them' to the advantage of their clients.

VIII. Playing the Judge

The role of judges in EW and US trials has similarities and differences. After the evidence is presented and closing arguments made, they instruct the jury on the law and burden of proof. This acts as 'a counterbalance to arguments of counsel' (van Kessel 1992: 434) and 'rescuing the case from the false glosses of powerful advocates' (Wolchover 1989: 788). EW judges go further though: they comment on the credibility of witnesses and the weight of the evidence; summarise the issues of fact and arguments on both sides; and state the inferences which the jury is entitled to draw from the facts. It's been suggested that '[h]ints from the judge are very likely to have a powerful influence on jury verdicts' (Lloyd-Bostock and Thomas 1999: 34).

In EW, evidence or questions about a complainant's sexual history or sexual behaviour are restricted (section 41(2) of the Youth and Criminal Evidence Act 1989). However, 'with the leave of the court' it is clear that evidence of a complainant's past sexual history could be admitted where that evidence and the questions it raised was so relevant to the issue of consent that to omit it might prejudice the fairness of the trial. The relevance of the previous sexual experience was a matter for the trial judge to determine (*R v A*).

It's a sensitive issue with arguments on both sides. In EW, the *legal* question in a rape trial is not only 'did the alleged victim consent?' but also whether the accused reasonably believed there was consent (section 1(1)(c) of the Sexual Offences Act 2003). If there's a reasonable belief the 'victim' consented, then it's not rape, regardless of what the victim believed. In this context, it's not surprising that judges might view the alleged victim's behaviour – and, indeed, sexual history – as a matter for juries to hear about. Juries may conclude the 'victim' consented because of their behaviour – regardless of what the defendant truly believed. Perhaps it's not so much the ethics of lawyers that matters as the wisdom – or otherwise – of the law itself. In one case sexual history might be relevant, but in another not, making an absolute rule impractical.

However, there's 'a suspiciously high level of cases where victims' sexual history was admitted into evidence' (Kelly et al 2006, cited in Boon 2014: 699). A study of 550 EW trials over two years by Limeculture, a sexual violence training organisation, found victims of alleged rape or sexual assault cases were being questioned about their sexual history in nearly three out of every four cases (Gibb 2017). Another study found lawyers sought to introduce sexual history in almost one-quarter of cases, and were successful in two-thirds of them. It also found lawyers failed to put in written application to use sexual history prior to the trial and that delaying notice put pressure on victims. Some of the tactics were 'devious' (ibid).

Judges can be 'played' in other ways too: 'There is a terrific importance in the trial court, never equaled in any appellate court, of knowing who is the judge' (Wyzanski Jr 1973). In 1924, Roger Baldwin, founder of the ACLU, was arrested in New Jersey, charged under a 1796 statute and convicted. He spent six months in jail. A New York lawyer, Samuel Untermyer, volunteered to take an appeal to the New Jersey Supreme Court. After a delay of two years, the conviction was affirmed. However, a final appeal was possible to the Court of Errors and Appeals, the highest New Jersey court at the time. Untermeyer was replaced for that hearing because:

> They all said, including our Jewish lawyers, that a New Yorker, a rich Jew like Untermeyer, would certainly get licked pleading before the Court of Errors in New Jersey ... we wouldn't use a New York lawyer in Alabama; and we wouldn't use a southern lawyer, particularly one with a strong accent, in a northern court. (Gillers 2018: 183)

In 2018, the female barrister Rehana Popal, an Afghan national, was removed from a case because the solicitor's client wanted a 'white' man to represent him. He thought English judges would be more likely to believe and respect 'white male' barristers. She lost six similar instructions in two years (Ames 2018).

Knowing judges' 'views' offers another strategy. Judge Edward Sutcliffe QC in 1976, summing up to the jury in a rape trial, told them: 'It is well-known that women in particular and small boys are liable to be untruthful and invent stories' (Slapper 2013). In 1998, Mr Justice Harman declared, after a witness said her title was 'Ms': 'I've always thought there were only three kinds of women: wives, whores and mistresses. Which are you?' (ibid; see also Obituary 2021a) A judge who'd complimented a barrister's appearance asked a male barrister whether he was 'enjoying the view' (*The Times*, 24 March 2018). To tackle prejudices, cases involving the 'sex-grooming' of young people will be tried by judges drawn from a panel of elite specialists who have undergone 'bespoke training from the Judicial College' (Norfolk 2013b).

A. Tory Bowen

In 2005 in Nebraska, Bowen claimed a man she met in a bar raped her in a hotel room while she was too drunk to consent. His defence lawyer argued that certain words were legal conclusions and not, until the client was proven guilty, facts. The judge agreed; she was prevented using words such as 'rape, sexual assault, sexual assault kit, victim, assailant'. She was allowed to say 'sex, sexual intercourse, intercourse' and that 'he had sex with me' but not 'he raped me'. In the first trial, in 2006, there was a hung jury, after 13 hours of her testifying. At the second in 2007, a mistrial was declared because of street protests about the judge's ban on those words. The judge said the protests interfered with the jury selection. Bowen sued the judge on 1st Amendment grounds, but the suit was dismissed. There was no third trial and therefore no conviction.

B. Paul Manafort

In Manafort's tax evasion and bank fraud trial in 2018, US District Court Judge TS Ellis III prevented the prosecution from using the word 'oligarch' to describe the Ukrainian businessmen with whom Manafort was associated: 'We're not going to have a case tried that [Manafort] was associated with despicable people and, therefore, he's despicable. That's not the American way' (Gerstein and Samuelsohn 2018). Manafort, a lawyer as well as President Trump's campaign chairman in 2016, pleaded guilty and was sentenced to 73 months in prison. He was released after one year because of COVID-19 health fears.

C. Mamma Mia

These kinds of tactics can hardly be an abuse of legal procedure if judicially approved – despite the consequences. A top Italian appeals court in 1998 agreed that women wearing tight jeans cannot be raped or sexually molested because removal of the jeans requires 'collaboration and consent'. The 'rule' was reversed only in 2008 where the court declared: 'Jeans cannot be compared to a chastity belt' (Swaine 2008).

IX. Victim-Blaming

The strategy of 'victim-blaming' is controversial; there are special laws to protect alleged victims. The EW Victims' Commissioner, created in 2004 (under the Domestic Violence, Crime and Victims Act), promotes the interests of victims and witnesses of crime and encourages good practice in their treatment. There's also a regularly updated Code of

Practice for Victims (2024). US rape shield laws seek to prevent defence lawyers 'smearing' the reputation of alleged victims in front of juries. There are different categories of laws 'distinguishable by the manner and degree to which they admit evidence of a woman's sexual history' (Anderson 2004). Most try to prevent juries making decisions based on stereotypes about victims' sexual histories; some prevent the naming of alleged victims in court. FRE 412 was enacted to 'protect rape victims from degrading and embarrassing disclosure of intimate details' without 'sacrificing any constitutional right possessed by the defendant' (124 Cong Rec 34,913 (1978), statement of Rep Mann). The aim is to protect victims without ignoring the accused's rights. Rape complainants' 'other sexual behavior' or 'sexual predisposition' is inadmissible, except when it's offered 'to prove that a person other than the accused was the source of semen, injury or other physical evidence', when it's offered to prove consent and it consists of 'specific instances of sexual behavior by the alleged victim with respect to the person accused', or when exclusion would 'violate the constitutional rights of the defendant'.

Despite these protections, blaming victims is a strategy used particularly in sexual assault cases, including rape (Lininger 2005). It plays into prejudices or beliefs held by jurors that reflect similar prejudices in a society or culture (Temkin and Krahe 2008; Temkin 2002; Stuart et al 2016; Angelone et al 2020). They include 'rape myths' (Franiuk et al 2008) – the idea that 'real rape' involves a violent stranger – so what the defendant is accused of is something less than rape (Gurnham 2016). Juries acquit accused rapists 'by importing the tort doctrines of assumption of risk and contributory negligence, although neither is a defense to a criminal charge of rape' (Anderson 2002: 106). Blame might attach to a woman for many reasons: putting herself in circumstances in which 'rape happens', wearing clothes that are 'asking for it', being drunk, failing to say no, or being a sex worker or prostitute.

In a 'sex grooming' trial in 2015, six girls aged between 13 and 16 were accused by Michael Magarian QC of claiming serial abuse 'because it is better to be a victim than a slag' (Norfolk 2015). Peter Sutcliffe, the 'Yorkshire Ripper', killed 13 women and committed nine assaults on women between 1975 and 1980. One police officer talked about 'innocent' women among the victims, implying other victims were not. Sir Michael Havers, prosecuting Sutcliffe in 1981, said in court that while some of the women were prostitutes, 'perhaps the saddest part of the case is that some were not. The last six attacks were on totally respectable women' (Purves 2020). As Purves notes: 'Victim-blaming is one of the less creditable human instincts: who could fail to notice how much less coverage there is when a young man, stabbed or shot, is found to have been a gang member?'

A. Kobe Bryant

Bryant was charged in 2003 in Colorado with sexual assault of a 19-year-old resort worker. He claimed the sex was consensual. The case came down to two words: yes or no (Shapiro and Stevens 2004)? Colorado's rape shield laws were 'a protection of the truth-seeking process' (ibid, quoting Michelle Anderson), so the trial should focus on relevant and material facts, and not prejudices. However: 'Too often, legal shields function as sieves' (Anderson 2002). Bryant's lawyer, Pamela Mackey, named the victim five times, saying she turned up at the post-rape hospital examination wearing a pair of yellow knickers containing a sample of blood and semen from someone other than Bryant, and pubic hair from a 'white' man. The alleged victim admitted having consensual sex in the days before Bryant's alleged attack, adding that was not a crime. But Bryant's lawyer argued her genital injuries could have come from having sex with three different men in three days.

Victim-blaming uses sexual history to portray the alleged victim as a 'slut' – both in court and the 'court of public opinion'. The case exploited every myth about women: 'That women are mentally ill, and vindictive, and lie for sport. That false allegations are common, and women like men to force themselves on them because they're not allowed to be sexually aggressive' (Paulson 2004, quoting Wendy Murphy, adjunct professor of sexual violence law at New England Law/Boston). The suggestion is that certain women 'had it coming to them' (ibid). Mackey said it was 'necessary to use every strategy available': Bryant was facing a life sentence.

After 15 months, the case was dropped during jury selection because the accuser refused to testify. Private investigators discovered she'd attempted suicide on two occasions and had been hospitalised for mental illness. As Mark Shaw, an attorney and author who covered the case for ESPN and *USA Today*, wrote: 'with her identity known, her past sex life revealed, her mental state common knowledge, and her life in shambles due to constant anguish about the motive behind the charges, it is no wonder that she threw in the towel' (quoted in Gibbs 2016).

A civil case settled with the terms kept confidential. Did the criminal case collapse because of the tactics of Mackey? Although it wasn't abuse – the 'letter' of the rape shield laws didn't apply to preliminary hearings – some might argue Mackey's conduct was against the 'spirit' of those laws. Even Bryant seemed to recant slightly after the charges were dropped:

> Although I truly believe this encounter between us was consensual, I recognize now that she did not and does not view this incident the same way I did. After months of reviewing discovery, listening to her attorney, and even her testimony in person, I now understand how she feels that she did not consent to this encounter. (ibid)

Some argue that the impact of these tactics deters women from filing rape charges against high-profile athletes:

> [A]lleged victims have been smeared in a similar way. In the [Patrick] Kane case, it was leaked that traces of DNA from other men were found in the alleged victim's underwear. [Greg] Hardy's alleged victim had her drug use and relationship with rapper Nelly dragged through the media. One of the two women who accused [Ben] Roethlisberger of rape was said to have a 'history of using sex and lies to get what she wanted.' None of these women decided to cooperate with or pursue criminal charges. (Mark Shaw, quoted in ibid)

A survey by the EW Victims' Commissioner of 491 rape survivors (including 37 men) found about a third didn't report what happened to police, the vast majority of whom because 'they did not think they would be believed' (Topping 2020). Generally, only about 1.5 per cent of rape reports proceeded to trial, and of those that did, nearly two-thirds were questioned about their sexual history, despite the legal protections (ibid). American judges have sought to protect victims of serious violent crime and sexual assault from 'strategies of intimidation' (Fan 2014: 14), but then convictions have been reversed because defendants' rights had been undermined (ibid).

B. Harvey Weinstein – Again

Weinstein's 'attack-dog' defence lawyer Donna Rotunno – whose 'specialty is defending people accused of rape – she has lost only one out of 40 sex-crime cases' – 'grilled the women who have accused the disgraced movie producer of sex crimes' (Pullman 2020). After 'hours of ruthless cross-examination this month, one of Weinstein's alleged rape victims collapsed into uncontrollable sobs on the witness stand' (ibid). The 'victim' was accused of manipulating Weinstein and eventually conceded: 'yeah, I guess you could say it was manipulation' (ibid). Rotunno makes no bones about what makes her so effective: she can get away with 'ferocious grillings of accusers that would land any male lawyer in dangerous territory' (ibid). Weinstein was found guilty, but in 2024 successfully appealed his 23-year sentence in New York for rape and sexual assault The judge had allowed three women to testify to testify about separate allegations. Weinstein was convicted in 2023 in California of another rape and sentenced to an additional 16 years. That case will be appealed too, though both could be re-tried.

There's no doubt that rape and sexual assault cases, where the alleged victim is claimed to have consented, illustrate the difficulty striking a balance between the rights of clients, victims and, indeed, the public in need of protection – because false allegations of rape are made.

C. False Allegations

In EW, between '2009 and 2014 more than a hundred women were prosecuted for perverting the course of justice or for the lesser charge of wasting police time, and a handful of them jailed' (Purves 2015). Seventeen-year-old victim Lindsay Armstrong committed suicide, but so did falsely-accused 17-year-old Jay Cheshire in 2015 (ibid). In 2020, a female prison officer, Victoria Hoynes, accused a taxi driver of raping her (Wace 2020). Two drivers were arrested. One had an alibi; the other had driven Hoynes but his dashcam video proved his innocence. The drivers, both married, told the court the devastating effect the allegations had on their livelihood and family life. Hoynes, in court, accepted 'full responsibility for the false allegations and wishes to make it clear through [her counsel] that the two drivers are totally innocent'. She was jailed for 20 months for perverting the course of justice. Judge James Adkin said: 'This type of offence can affect the prospects at trial of cases where it may be finely balanced as to whether the women get the justice they deserve' (ibid).

X. Ethical or Not?

An advocate is bound to follow clients' instructions, so their duty 'depends on what he is told' (Stone 1995: 2). However, barristers 'must exercise personal judgment upon the substance and purpose of statements and questions asked' (Bar Council 1997: 5.10). The BSB puts it like this:

you are personally responsible for your own conduct and for your professional work. You must use your own professional judgment in relation to those matters on which you have been instructed and be able to justify your decisions. You must do so notwithstanding the views of your client, employer or any other person. (2024: rC20)

It's a fine line though. In EW, the victim of a gang rape – meaning several defendants and several advocates – was questioned over a period of 12 days. Mr Justice Boal said: 'For over thirty hours this girl had to relive the ordeal in public court in front of total strangers. Outrageous suggestions were put to her.' Who did Boal blame? The defendants. The suggestions were put to her 'on your instructions. You, *not your counsel*, added insult to injury and heaped further humiliation on her' (Boon 2023: 227, emphasis added). The lawyers hadn't abused legal procedure. When similar 'outrageous' suggestions were made to female victims in the US in a civil case, the judge came to a different conclusion.

A. Dalkon Shield – Again

This intra-uterine device caused thousands of injuries, including stillbirth, hysterectomies, sterility or even death (see generally Mintz 1985; Perry and Dawson 1985; Wendel 1999: 12–13). At least 20 deaths were linked to it. Children were born with serious birth defects; there were also ectopic pregnancies, miscarriages and hundreds of spontaneous abortions. In 1992, *USA Today* commented on Dalkon Shield: 'If intra-uterine devices were automobiles, the Dalkon Shield would have been a Pinto' – a reference to the Ford Pinto car whose design led to many deaths and injuries and, in 1978, the then largest-ever jury damages award of $127.8 million.

Over two million American women used the device between 1971 and 1974, when AH Robins withdrew it from the American (but not the foreign) market. Around 800,000 women in other countries used it. There's little doubt that the product's unsafe design could allow bacteria to accumulate in the uterus, causing injury. However, pelvic inflammatory disease – a serious gynaecological disorder – could be caused by some sexually transmitted diseases associated with multiple sex partners. This wasn't likely in most cases, but possible in some. The company was faced with around 300,000 lawsuits; there was a class action suit against the company; it was the largest tort liability case since the asbestos litigation.

At the request of Robins' lawyers, the judge supervising the pre-trial litigation allowed inquiry into the women claimants' sexual histories, as long as the questions were 'reasonably likely to lead to the discovery of admissible evidence'. The practice had been to settle valid claims for a fair amount, but contest vigorously doubtful ones. In the course of defending, however, it became clear that questioning women about their sexual practices tended to motivate many to settle early and for comparatively small amounts. In cases that the company lawyers judged to be without merit, the company directed lawyers to probe the sexual histories of women. As a result, some women were asked about their sexual relations before marrying, up to 10 years before they used Dalkon Shield. They were asked about the kind of fabric they used in their pantyhose, about whether they had intercourse or used sexual aids – and, if so, how often.

Who did the Judge Miles W Lord of the US District Court for the District of Minnesota blame? Addressing the company's Chief Executive Officer and the General Counsel, he said:

> When the time came for these women to make their claims against your company, you attacked their characters; you inquired into their sexual practices and into the identity of their sexual partners. You exposed these women and ruined families and reputations and careers in order to intimidate those who would raise their voices against you. (Quoted in Luban 1988: 152)

The judge continued: 'You introduced issues that had no relationship whatsoever to the fact that you planted in the bodies of these women instruments of death, of mutilation, of disease' (ibid). He concluded that this was 'corporate irresponsibility at its meanest' (Cherry 1985).

B. Mohammed Tayyab Khan

Perhaps the ethics of courtroom tactics depend on the relationship between the questions being put and the case being presented. In an EW 'sex-grooming' trial in 2011, seven men were accused of turning young women into 'sexual commodities, trafficked and sold to dozens of men' (Norfolk 2013c; see also Norfolk 2011, 2013a, 2013b, 2013d). One alleged victim spent 15 days in the witness box, 12 being cross-examination by defence counsel including Khan, who represented one defendant. He accused her of 'telling lies', 'giving false evidence', 'being a very dishonest girl', 'making a false allegation' and giving 'phoney evidence'. Another alleged victim, cross-examined by Khan, was accused of 'telling lies', making 'false and malicious allegations' and being 'very wicked'. The prosecuting counsel, Deborah Gould, said in court: 'I've never been in a trial where a young witness has been in the witness box for so long. There must come a point at which the questioning ceases. She's been called a liar for day upon day upon day.' The trial lasted four months.

These suggestions may have been justified by client instructions. However, Khan asked one witness about an incident that had nothing to do with the case against any of the accused. When she was 13 years old, she confided to her mother she'd been sexually abused by her stepfather. Her mother telephoned the police and she gave them a statement. One day later, she withdrew it. At Khan's trial, she told the jury she'd been abused but withdrew the statement because she was concerned about the impact of the allegations on her mother. In the police record, however, the incident was listed as a false rape allegation and Khan used it to challenge her credibility. He accused her of being 'very good at making up stories'. He asked her to read out the original police statement, including her initial account of what her stepfather had done. The judge asked Khan if that was necessary; he said it was, but then agreed to read out lines from the statement himself. The witness was upset. Khan put to her 'you are a compulsive liar' and asked: 'You have told lies about my client, also?' She broke down more than once.

Was that ethical? One lawyer walked out in disgust, but Judge Robin Onions allowed Khan to proceed. The trial collapsed after four months and was split into a series of re-trials. When Khan's client was retried, Judge Patrick Thomas QC said: 'The way things went last time is just so wrong that we should all be ashamed that our justice system allowed it.' Judge Thomas specifically informed Khan that he should not delve into the incident involving the stepfather. When Khan asked questions about the girl's family, Judge Thomas intervened and asked:

> How does this relate to the case? She does not want to talk about her family and I do not see why she should. She finds it distressing. Is it difficult for you to understand that she finds all this troublesome and embarrassing and it has nothing to do with the case?

The client was found guilty and jailed for 18 years. Khan claimed he was doing his 'professional duty … If I hadn't cross-examined the girl in the way I did then I would have been negligent'. Khan sought leave to appeal the sentence and the conviction, and in the grounds for appeal criticised Judge Thomas, saying 'he has undermined [the] defence and that as a result [the client] did not receive a fair trial'.

XI. The Twilight Zone

Criminal defence lawyers have to prove 'reasonable doubt' not innocence. F Lee Bailey – 'the theatrical criminal lawyer who invited juries into the twilight zone of reasonable doubt' – was

> a riveting courtroom performer … He had the ventriloquist's trick of directing questions at the witness box but throwing his points at the jury box. He had an actor's voice, by turns bullying, cajoling, sarcastic or sympathetic, searching for *seams of doubt*. Under his reductions, a prosecutor's *'fact'* could be whittled down to a *probability*, then to a mere *possibility* or just a *silly idea*. (McFadden 2021, emphasis added)

As far as OJ Simpson was concerned, Bailey was 'man of the match' in his trial (Obituary 2021b).

Criminal trial tactics may differ somewhat between the US and EW. Dershowitz (1982: 384) observed (jokingly and in rhyme) that 'England and the United States treat their criminal lawyers differently: in England they are apt to knight them; in the United States they are apt to indict them'. He pointed out that many criminal attorneys have become criminal defendants, and half of his clients have been lawyers, many of them criminal lawyers. But he was right to observe that in both countries: 'Sometimes the public has to be reminded the word criminal in criminal lawyer – like the word baby in baby doctor – is a description not of the professional, but rather the clientele.' Finally, Dershowitz notes that while the Supreme Court Justice Felix Frankfurter once commented that he knew of no title 'more honorable than that of Professor of the Harvard Law School. I [Dershowitz, a Harvard Law Professor] know of none more honorable than defense attorney'.

15

Effective Advocacy

> Words are, of course, the most powerful drug used by mankind.
>
> — Rudyard Kipling (quoted in *The Times*, 15 February 1923)

Robert Jackson, Nuremberg prosecutor and Supreme Court Justice, admitted when US Solicitor-General:

> I made three arguments of every case. First came the one that I planned – as I thought, logical, coherent, complete. Second was the one actually presented – interrupted, incoherent, disjointed, disappointing. The third was the utterly devastating argument that I thought of after going to bed that night. (Jackson 1951: 6)

By contrast, Sir Hartley Shawcross QC told Lord Goddard, the Lord Chief Justice, he was making 'three points in this appeal. One is hopeless, one is arguable and one is unanswerable'. Lord Goddard told him: 'just give us your best point'. 'Oh no', said Sir Hartley, 'I don't propose to tell your Lordship which is which' (Kentridge 2003).

Some lawyers are natural advocates; others improve through training and experience. But 'the question of honesty and dishonesty in advocacy is a question that troubles most laymen and a lot of beginners in the legal profession' (Evans 1983). Which is why Supreme Court Justice Stevens said: 'The canons of professional ethics impose limits on permissible advocacy' (*McCoy*: 438). But what is effective – and ethical – advocacy?

I. Playing the Jury

In the US there's an elaborate process of jury selection and vetting; in EW, by contrast, little is known about juries. Research is proscribed (section 8 of the Contempt of Court Act 1981); it's a crime to obtain, disclose or solicit any details of statements made, opinions expressed, arguments advanced or votes cast by members of a jury in the course of their deliberations in any legal proceedings (section 20D of the Juries Act 1974). So

> American trial lawyers are far more attuned to how juries approach their task ... Their understanding of the psychology of jury decision making is profound and they adapt their advocacy accordingly. It is questionable how many barristers think about the psychology of how to influence jurors, or study the American research. (Henry 2019)

Well, here's their chance!

A. Vetting

In EW, determining who sits on juries is difficult. Historically, the defence were allowed 25 peremptory challenges – challenges without cause. The number was reduced over time and abolished in the Criminal Justice Act 1988 (see Sprack 2006). Removing jurors requires a challenge for cause (Criminal Procedure Rules October 2020: 25.8). However: 'Whilst the common law power of challenges … is preserved by the Juries Act 1974, it is now almost inoperative and is of historical significance only' (CPS 2018c). That's because the defence have little or no information about individual jurors.

The US, by contrast, stands 'virtually alone in the world in [its] extensive use of peremptory challenges' (van Kessel 1993: 537), although Arizona in 2022 became the first to eliminate them. There are also challenges for cause. During the process of 'voir dire', potential jurors are asked questions by the judge and attorneys. All say they want 'a fair and impartial jury. In actuality, one side wanted a convicting jury, the other an acquitting jury' (Shapiro with Warren 1996: 174). No wonder jury selection can take so long – five weeks in the Simpson and three in the Nichols trials.

The system varies between States but is 'an opportunity to develop rapport … to provide a basis for exercising peremptory challenges, as well as establishing the basis for cause challenges' (Tigar and Coleman Jr 2014: 11). Clemens (2008: 12) believes: 'Rapport-building is not a separate segment of the jury selection process, it begins with everything you do and say to create a good impression with the jury.' Much has been written about voir dire (Herbig 2021; Suggs and Sales 1978). Advice includes: 'If there are "bad facts" which you know will likely be offered into evidence, try to condition the jurors to hear those bad facts by discussing them in general terms in voir dire' (Clemens 2008: 12). Essentially, voir dire is a process of jury de-selection, designed to eliminate those individuals who the lawyer believes will be unfavourable to the client.

Does vetting make a difference? A study of 2,500 EW cases showed challenges were not associated with an increased likelihood of acquittal (Vennard and Riley 1988). In the US, the same is true, except it appears that African-American defendants are more at risk of conviction when there are no African-American jurors (Anwar et al 2012). Defence lawyers tend to seek to remove 'white' jurors in case of prejudice (Wright et al 2018).

B. Prejudice

Defence counsel shouldn't 'make arguments calculated to appeal to improper prejudices of the jury' (ABA 2017: 4-7.8(c)) or 'knowingly misstate the evidence in the record, or argue inferences that counsel knows have no good faith support in the record' (ibid: 4-7.8(a)). Practitioners circumvent this by introducing evidence rather than arguments (Smith 2000a: 931). Appealing to prejudice may win sympathy for the client, or their argument.

i. Ivan Milat: The 'Backpacker' Killer

Milat was charged with armed robbery and John Marsden, a solicitor and former President of the Law Society of New South Wales, represented him. After Marsden told

Milat he had no chance of acquittal – and was facing 16 or 17 years (the other armed robbers got 17 years) – Milat faked his suicide and fled to New Zealand. Lured back to Australia by his mother suffering a heart attack, Milat was captured in 1974. Amazingly, Marsden got Milat bail, but while awaiting trial, Milat was accused of abducting two women and raping one of them.

Even more amazingly, Milat was acquitted of both the armed robbery and abduction/rape charges. On the robbery charge, Marsden showed that several of the detectives had serious corruption allegations against them. On the abduction/rape charges, Marsden had to respond to the two women and their positive identification of Milat. One night during the trial, Marsden went with a friend to a 'gay bar' and saw the two alleged victims 'holding hands and sharing a lot of intimacy' (Marsden 2004). The next day, during cross-examination, Marsden asked one of them where she was last night. She said at home with her parents. Marsden responded: 'Of course, you wouldn't have gone to a gay and lesbian bar, would you?' (ibid) She denied it, but when pressed admitted she had and broke down. Marsden then suggested that her 'sexuality may have had something to do with what had occurred with Ivan Milat'. As Marsden later described it: 'Crying and under stress, she ended up agreeing – and in that moment, I knew we had won' (ibid). Juries, he said, were 'extremely prejudiced against gays and lesbians'; he'd also intimated the sex was consensual.

After acquittal, Milat was involved in a spate of serial killings between 1989 and 1993 – the 'Backpacker' killings. He was convicted and died in prison in 2019. Marsden 'was plagued by his decision to represent Milat on rape charges in the 1970s, saying the back-packers might be alive today if Milat had not been acquitted' (McClymont and Miller 2006). But, he insisted he 'had no choice but to go down this path. I had to act *according to the ethics of the profession*' (Marsden 2004, emphasis added).

C. Playing the 'Race Card'

It appears, by inserting the issue of race into a case, 'whites and blacks play the race card as a litigation tactic for obtaining a favorable outcome' (Murray 2004: 20). The 1995 OJ Simpson trial introduced many to this expression, but it was not first to 'play' it.

i. John Adams

Adams defended eight British soldiers who fired upon, and killed, five colonists in March 1770. Adams faced anti-British propaganda; Paul Revere produced an etching showing the soldiers – portrayed as vicious men, 'callously murdering American colonists' – portrayed as gentlemen (History.Com 2020). Adams convinced the judge the jury should be non-Bostonians. He told them the mob was 'a motley crew of saucy boys, negroes and molattoes, Irish teagues and outlandish Jack Tarrs' (Peterson 2018; see also: Zobel 1970: 269). He then stated:

> And why we should scruple to call such a set of people a mob, I can't conceive, unless the name is too respectable for them. The sun is not about to stand still or go out, nor the rivers to dry up because there was a mob in Boston on the 5th of March that attacked a party of soldiers.

One of those killed was Crispus Attucks, who was of mixed heritage. Adams told the jury 'his very look was enough to terrify any person ... with one hand [he] took hold of a bayonet, and with the other knocked the man down' (Peterson 2018). Adams blamed Attucks 'in all probability' for 'the dreadful carnage of that night'. According to Peterson: 'A critical part of Adams's strategy was to convince the jury that his clients had only killed a black man and his cronies and that they didn't deserve to hang for it.' His conclusion after taking 'an honest look at the transcript' was that it showed how 'racial prejudice contributed to the outcome'. Was Adams, after all, a hero or a hired gun (see Chapter 1)?

ii. OJ Simpson

Detective Mark Fuhrman was accused of racial bias. Johnnie Cochran (Cochran and Fisher 2002: 31) explained:

> The most important evidence against OJ Simpson had supposedly been found in unusual places by a thoroughly racist LAPD detective – a detective who had been caught on audio-tapes made years earlier admitting the LAPD planted evidence – a detective who for some unknown reason had been present in places he had no legitimate reason to be.

F Lee Bailey cross-examined Fuhrman and put to him that he'd planted a bloody glove matching one left at the murder scene. Fuhrman admitted there'd been no search warrant, but denied the accusation. Bailey couldn't prove it, but got Fuhrman to deny he'd used racist language in the past. Bailey challenged that denial with evidence of recordings made by Fuhrman and four witnesses who said he'd used such language. Fuhrman's credibility was undermined and he later pleaded no contest to perjury.

Simpson was portrayed as the 'victim of a wide-ranging conspiracy of racist law enforcement officials who had fabricated and planted evidence in order to frame him for a crime he did not commit' (Toobin 1996: 11). Cochran's co-counsel, Robert Shapiro, disapproved: 'not only did we play the race card, we played it from the bottom of the deck' (UPI Archives 1995; see also Shapiro with Warren 1996: 349). One prosecutor, Christopher Darden, an African American, argued that 'playing the race card', and especially the effort by the defence team to reveal Mr Fuhrman's use of a racial epithet (the 'n' word), was unfair. He told Judge Ito:

> If you allow Mr Cochran to use this word and play the race card, the direction and focus of the case changes: it is a race case now. It becomes an issue of color ... It's the filthiest, dirtiest, nastiest word in the English language. It will do one thing. It will upset the black jurors. It will say, whose side are you on, the 'man' or 'the brothers'? ... There's a mountain of evidence pointing to the man's guilt, but when you mention that word to the jury, or any African-American, it blinds people. It'll blind the jury. *It'll blind the truth. They won't be able to discern what's true and what's not.* (Noble 1995: 7, emphasis added)

Cochran, also African American, responded:

> It is demeaning to our jury to say that African-Americans who've lived under oppression for 200 plus years in this country cannot work with offensive words, offensive looks, offensive treatment every day of their lives. And yet they still believe in this country. (ibid)

After a four-month trial, the jury took just three hours to find Simpson not guilty. Shapiro, asked if the verdict was correct, answered:

> There's two types of justice that we deal with in America: There's moral justice and there's legal justice. If you look at it from a moral point of view, a lot of people would say he absolutely did it. I deal in legal justice ... and that's proof beyond a reasonable doubt. And there's no question in my mind that any fair juror who saw that case from the beginning to the end would conclude there was reasonable doubt. (Parker 2016, referring to the Megyn Kelly interview on *Fox News*)

Another member of OJ's 'Dream Team', Alan Dershowitz (1996: 16), agreed. He tried to 'explain why even jurors who thought that Simpson "did it" as a matter of fact could reasonably have found him not guilty as a matter of law – and of justice'. Hodes (1996) also approved of the 'ethics and professionalism' of the defence team. In serious criminal cases, playing the race card may be the defence lawyer's main way of responding to the emotional evidence presented by the prosecution.

D. Emotion

Appealing to jurors' emotions is ethical (Murphy 2002: 123). To persuade jurors, trial lawyers must 'target the dominant emotion of the case' with a 'simple slogan' or 'a few words that will stick in the juror's minds' (Dodd 1990: 38). It's been stressed 'how important it is to simulate, impress, and sometimes entertain during the trial of a case. This is the TV generation, and mere words from the witness may no longer be enough to persuade or convince' (ibid). Former Supreme Court Justice Lord Sumption (2021) agrees: 'Never underestimate the importance of entertainment as a tool of advocacy.'

The 'belief that emotions undercut rational decision-making is widely shared today, particularly within the American legal community' (Pettys 2007: 1609). Barrister Mohsin Zaida agrees: 'Pathos is the hook: it now comes first before logic in cases arousing strong feelings. Logic is not abandoned, but emotion underpins the functional logic that juries so often apply' (Henry 2019). Lord Alexander (1991: 9), former Chairman of the English Bar, said: 'lurking below the surface is almost invariably an attempt to persuade people not just in their heads but in their hearts. Indeed, sometimes the attempt is to persuade them in their hearts when they are wholly unpersuaded in the head'. As a result: 'Too often, to capture a jury's emotions is to win the case' (Lilly 2001: 57).

i. Sir Edward Marshall Hall KC

One famous example was the 1894 trial of 47-year-old Austrian prostitute Marie Herman, who was accused of murdering a client. At the end of his closing speech, as he was about to sit down, Hall, the great defence advocate, noticed the client sitting hunched in the dock (where she was held), added these words: 'Look at her, gentlemen of the jury. Look at her. God never gave her a chance – won't you? Won't you?' Although she was found guilty, it was of manslaughter not murder, and the jury strongly recommended her to mercy. She was sentenced to six years' penal servitude (imprisonment with hard labour) which, for the times, was relatively lenient.[1] Hall was proud to insist 'I am an advocate, not a lawyer' (Magrath 2016, reviewing Smith 2016). It was appealing 'to the sentiments of jurors, rather than his argument over finer points of law or procedure that won him cases' (Magrath 2016). Smith's (2016) biography of Hall is 'a must-read for anyone interested in the psychology of jury advocacy' (Noble 2016).

ii. Here's Johnny

The American defence lawyer Clarence Darrow said: 'The main work of a trial lawyer is to make a jury like his client, or, at least to feel sympathy for him; facts regarding the crime are relatively unimportant' (quoted in Levenson 2008: 575). Some prosecutors have the opposite aim. 'Here's Johnny' – spoken as 'Heeeere's Johnny' – were the words used for decades to introduce *Tonight Show* host Johnny Carson. The catchphrase was used in the horror film *The Shining* by the killer, a violent psychopath played by Jack Nicholson. Nicholson hacked a hole through a bathroom door with an axe, poked his head through, and imitating the catchphrase, said: 'Here's Johnny!' It was possibly 'the most terrifying scene' in the film, which 'surely caused its share of nightmares' (Shanahan 2021).

In 2014, Damon Williams handed a bank clerk a note demanding money. It read: 'Please, all the money, 100, 50, 20, 10. Thank you.' He didn't have a gun, nor did he threaten the clerk in any other way. He left with $4,600. The question was whether this constituted a robbery – a crime invoking force or the threat of it – or theft – a lesser offence. In closing arguments, the prosecutor showed the jury a PowerPoint image of Nicholson's face as he poked his head through the bedroom door. The image was presented under an all-capitals heading: 'ACTIONS SPEAK LOUDER THAN WORDS'. She told the jury 'we've all seen this, right? This guy [Nicholson] looks creepy and he's saying some very unthreatening words, "Here's Johnny"'. The jury found Williams guilty of second-degree robbery, which carried a 14-year jail sentence.

The appeal court upheld the conviction, but the New Jersey Supreme Court ordered a re-trial. The prosecutor 'went far beyond the evidence at trial to draw a parallel between defendant's conduct and that of a horror-movie villain'. In short: 'The use of a sensational and provocative image in service of such a comparison, even when purportedly metaphorical, heightens the risk of an improper prejudicial effect on the jury' (*State v Damon Williams*, Justice Lee Solomon). The public defender's office celebrated the appeal by posting on Facebook: 'Heeeere's a new trial!' (Pavia 2021). Careless words can also lead to acquittal.

iii. Lady Chatterley's Lover

DH Lawrence's *Lady Chatterley's Lover*, published in 1928, was banned in the UK and the US. In 1959 the New York Court of Appeals overturned the ban, and the

---

[1] The blood-stained trunk in which the victim was found was later sold to Madame Tussauds waxworks in London.

UK passed the Obscene Publications Act. This made publishers of books which might have 'a tendency to deprave and corrupt those whose minds are open to such immoral influences' liable to imprisonment. In 1960, Penguin Books published it and was prosecuted (*R v Penguin Books*). Mervyn Griffith-Jones probably lost the jury when he asked them, with total sincerity, this question:

> Would you approve of your sons, young daughters – because girls can read as well as boys – reading this book? Is it a book you would have lying around your house? Is it a book which you would even wish your wife or servants to read? (Rolph 1961: 17)

Penguin was acquitted and three million books were sold in the months after the verdict.

iv. Stress

Research has found that 'juries in serious criminal cases suffer stress symptoms as a result of jury service' (Kelley 1994: 115; see also Bornstein et al 2005). Symptoms 'are similar to the stress experienced by actual crime victims' (Miller and Bornstein 2004: 241). In an EW murder trial, one juror had to be discharged because of the effect of the trial on her mental health (Humphries 2020). At the 1995 Rosemary West murder trial, jurors were offered counselling and a free telephone helpline to deal with their exposure to the horrific and gruesome murders of young women committed by Rosemary and Fred West (Conn 1996; see also Grove 1998). The British Psychological Society has called for counselling services to be provided as part of jury duty as they are for judges (Ames 2023). As jurors weigh the evidence, the evidence may weigh on them.

Pettys identified three ways emotions can influence jurors' decisions: those that relate to their efforts to make demeanour-based assessments of witness credibility; their efforts to construct coherent narratives that account for all the credible evidence to which they've been exposed; and their willingness to render a verdict that's faithful to the facts they believe the evidence has established (Pettys 2007: 1625–26).

E. Demeanour

In the Anglo-American legal system, many see demeanour as a critical factor in deciding whether witnesses are telling the truth (ibid; see also Uviller 1993: 825). It's 'one of the standard (and oldest) justifications for appellate deference to lower court fact finding' (Minzner 2008: 2559). It's also why allowing vulnerable witnesses to pre-record evidence or use a video-link is controversial (Poulin 2004).

Clarence Darrow illustrated the potential significance of witness demeanour in a case in which he was defending, but called a key *prosecution* witness to testify. The witness was a

> squat, heavy-set man of medium height … His swollen face, his bleary eyes, puffy eyelids, and reddish-purple nose marked the habitual drunkard. His shaggy hair had been stranger to brush or comb for so long as to have become tangled and matted. His clothes … were covered with dirt and grease. His huge hands … were covered with grime. (Imwinkelried 1985: 226–27)

Darrow didn't ask questions. Instead, he told the witness to stand up and turn round for the jury. Darrow then addressed them: 'That's all. I just wanted the jury to get a good look at you' (quoted in ibid).

Judges frequently advise jurors they should consider witnesses' demeanour in making their determination. They're told it's often not *what* witnesses says, but *how* they say it that will help them decide whether it's believable (Timothy 2000). There's extensive psychological research too on the significance of non-verbal communications, including when defendants are not testifying, that may influence juries' verdicts (see references in Levenson 2008).

However, empirical evidence suggests people aren't very good at distinguishing true statements from lies (Vrij 2000, 2008). People do a better job of determining truth by reading written transcripts rather than hearing witnesses (Wellborn III 1991). Coaching can also affect a witness's demeanour and mask whether they're telling the truth (ibid: 1079 and fn 13). Some liars may give evidence convincingly and truthful witnesses unconvincingly. So it's not clear that either judges or juries are good at 'deception detection' (Minzner 2008: 2578). Indeed: 'There remains a great deal that we do not know about lie detection that should matter to the legal system' (ibid). The Court of Appeal in 2018, citing Minzner, observed the growing recognition that it's usually unreliable and dangerous to draw a conclusion from a witness' demeanour as to whether the witness is telling the truth:

> No doubt it is impossible, and perhaps undesirable, to ignore altogether the impression created by the demeanour of a witness giving evidence. But to attach any significant weight to such impressions in assessing credibility risks making judgments which at best have no rational basis and at worst reflect conscious or unconscious biases and prejudices. (*Sri Lanka*: 41, Lord Justice Leggatt)

But while some judges downplay the role of demeanour in the courtroom, juries seem to regard it as critical: 'witnesses' demeanour seemingly determines the outcome of a large percentage of trials' (Imwinkelried 1985: 186).

How defendants appear in court may also affect juries. Placing EW criminal defendants in the 'dock' may make them look guilty. But so does stabbing Michael Dellastritto, representing Joseph Danks in the penalty phase of his murder trial in 1993, then approaching the jury box! Danks was sentenced to death (*People v Danks*: fn 3). The defendant's 'demeanor and appearance in the courtroom continues to influence jurors' decisions ... jurors readily consider all conduct in the courtroom, not just the testimony of witnesses, in reaching their decision' (Levenson 2008: 592). Defence lawyers know appearances matter and, in a criminal trial especially, the client is the 'star' of the show.

This is why witness preparation is so important and includes 'effective courtroom demeanor' (Wydick 1995: 5). Advising clients – and witnesses – on what to wear is important. The 'Hell's Angel' may be told to shop at 'Country Casuals' because 'if you come to court looking like a football hooligan, what do you expect the jury to think?'[2] Similarly, defendants wearing prison clothes or in shackles may adversely affect the jury (Levenson 2008: 584). The vision of well-dressed defendants may help lawyers construct the alternative narrative. Criminal defence lawyer David Feige had in his office a 'closet full of secondhand suits and ties to share with my clients' (Feige 2001).

---

[2] Advice from the late Michael Beresford-West QC, known as 'Grumpole of the Bailey', in a 1980s television programme *Hypotheticals: A Case of Rape*.

Lawyers' demeanour may matter too. Attorneys who move around the courtroom may find it easier to appeal to emotion than static EW counterparts. New York defence lawyer William F Howe would change his appearance as the trial wore on. At the start he'd appear 'wearing his full complement of diamonds and an ensemble featuring green, purple, or rose'. Later, he changed to 'richly subdued blues and browns'. On the final day, he'd appear 'in a dark grey sack suit, adorned with not so much as a single diamond to brighten the grim proceedings' (Rovere 1947: 83–84).

F. The Coherent Narrative

According to Edelman (2005: 113): 'In contrast to the traditional view of trials as inquests into the objective truth of some set of historical facts, this scholarship suggests that story-telling – which constructs facts rather than documenting preexisting facts – permeates the trial process at all levels.' Lubet argued there are three 'structural devices that add great power to the stories of trial lawyers: theory, theme, and frame' (2001: Introduction). 'Story-telling' establishes a 'theory of the case' – a plausible and reasonable explanation of what happened. It develops the 'trial theme' – adding moral force to the desired outcome. Third, and most importantly, it provides a coherent 'story frame' – organising all the facts into an easily understandable narrative context.

i. 'Script' Theory

This social psychology theory suggests there are sets of rules which individuals learn through experience (Tomkins 1979). The idea is human behaviour falls into patterns – 'scripts' which act as 'a shorthand for understanding events based on past experiences' (Zdrojeski 2005: 181). These experiences give individuals not only a kind of 'memory bank' to make sense of events but also 'a structured set of expectations based on those memories' (Blasi 1995: 337). The stored scripts – or scenes – make 'events meaningful and intelligible' (ibid). Scripts are the structures within which scenes are stored (Nathanson 1996: 3).

If jurors are indeed 'pre-loaded' with scripts, 'it is far more economical for the mind to distort a new experience to make it fit this or another of [their] already-existing scripts' (ibid: 4). Jurors understand what they're hearing 'by reference to prototypes' (Blasi 1995: 338) which will already tell jurors how, for example, crimes are committed: 'People who say "Don't confuse me with facts – my mind is made up" are telling the truth at a far deeper level than they might have known' (Nathanson 1996: 4). Can trial lawyers take advantage of jurors having 'inherited cultural knowledge at [their] fingertips [which are] shaped and informed by the images, scripts, and familiar scenarios' (Sherwin 1994: 689–90)? The Rodney King trial in 1992 suggests they can.

ii. Rodney King

In 1991, two California Highway Patrol Officers attempted to stop a car. A high-speed chase ensued, and the officers called for back-up. The driver ignored repeated signals to pull over. When the car eventually stopped, there were five officers present. The two passengers lay down on the ground. The driver, King, then got out of the car slowly but refused orders to lie down. He resisted initial attempts to apprehend him physically even after two darts from a taser gun (Edelman 2005: 107–08), but 'then endured forty-five baton blows from Powell, dozens of baton blows and kicks from Wind, and one kick to the upper body by Briseno before the police finally handcuffed and arrested him' (ibid: 108).

These facts were not in dispute; a Los Angeles resident surreptitiously made an 81-second videotape of King's arrest (ibid: 107). Four officers stood trial on charges of using excessive force and

> the prosecution's evidence included a videotape of the defendants *in flagrante delicto*, beating Mr King with an apparent savagery that glued prime time television viewers to their screens in horrified fascination and completely convinced the national viewing public of the defendants' guilt before and even after the jury declined to convict them. (Amsterdam et al 2005: 3)

Prior to the trial, a 'large portion of the millions of Americans who had repeatedly viewed segments of that tape ... viewed the jury's task as the mere transformation of the brutal "reality" displayed on their television screens into a formal guilty verdict' (Edelman 2005: 107). The prosecution 'staked its case on the propositions that seeing is believing, that vidcams do not lie, that the images on the videotape of the defendants beating Rodney King showed What Happened, what counted as Reality'. In other words, 'the videotape represented an accurate, unbiased recording of past events and that, as a piece of evidence, it "speaks for itself", obviating the need for any interpretation' (ibid: 121). So why were all found not guilty? The 'prevailing wisdom' was the prosecutors lost because of the racial make-up of the jury (Amsterdam et al 2005: 4). However, it turns out that the case – even the videotape – wasn't 'black and white' (Loftus and Rosenwald 1993).

Alper et al (2005) examined the entire trial to conduct an 'in-depth examination of the lawyers' strategies and performances' to see whether 'they had more influence on the verdict than the prevailing wisdom declared'. 'Particularly relevant' were the 'scripts and stories about the police, especially those that feature encounters between white police officers and African-American civilians in an urban setting like Los Angeles' (Amsterdam et al 2005). They noted that

> jurors come to their task equipped not only with the narrative process as a mode of thought but with a store of specific narratives channeling that process. Stock scripts and stock stories accreted from exposure to the accountings and recounting that continually bombard us ... provide all of us with walk-through models of how life is lived, how crimes are committed, how reality unfolds. When a juror perceives the familiar lineaments of one or another of these narratives emerging from the evidence, s/he 'recognizes' what is afoot and s/he is cued to interpret other pieces of evidence and eventually the whole of it consistently with the familiar story line. (ibid: 7)

When 'facts' aren't in dispute, 'trials of "the facts" tend to turn into story-telling contests' (ibid: 8). Where the 'seemingly incontrovertible' evidence 'cease to "tell the whole story", the story-telling competition begins'. The storytelling is a 'vital means to expand or change the audience's understanding of the human scene'. According to their analysis, 'the collective defense mounted by the lawyers' for three of the officers illustrated a particular tactic. The 'ultimate task' of a jury is not only to decide what happened but 'also to *interpret and categorize the actions and mental states as understandable human behavior* susceptible to legal and moral judgment' (ibid: 16). Therefore, a litigator 'who taps into stock narratives familiar to jurors ... can thus shape the jury's understanding of "what really happened" and what it means'.

The defence lawyers 'drew upon the stock story of the heroic team of roving police officers defending civilized society against rampaging hordes of wild inner-city barbarians and barely holding their own by a combination of courage, discipline, skill, strength and teamwork'. In the years preceding the trial, 'the driving force in national criminal justice policy was the so-called "War on Drugs ... generating an ever-growing number of arrests of African-Americans in the inner city and an ever-increasing over-representation of African-American men in prisons"' (ibid: 38–39). The inner city was portrayed by politicians 'as a dangerous war zone that could be pacified only by expanding the police force, arresting more drug dealers, lengthening prison sentences, and building more prisons' (ibid: 39). The 'mainstream media' propagated these images. The authors conclude that 'the defense case derived much of its force from a resourceful exploitation of stock stories' (ibid: 49).

Critically important for twenty-first-century readers is that it was unusual then to present the world through the eyes of African-Americans harassed by abusive police officers. Six days of rioting in Los Angeles followed the not guilty verdicts. Sixty-three were killed and 2,383 injured (Wikipedia nd). A federal civil rights case followed, and two of the four officers were convicted and sentenced, leniently, to 30-month prison terms. King was awarded $3.8 million from the city of Los Angeles. The King incident may have spawned 'virtually all of the movies and television shows that have made [police harassment] part of their cultural experience' (Amsterdam et al 2005: 40). The King case contrasts with the 2020–21 case of George Floyd, who died while under the control of police officers. Video recordings and the trial were televised and the prosecution also told jurors to 'believe your eyes ... What you saw, you saw ... the defendant pressing down on George Floyd so his lungs did not have room to breathe' (Charter 2021). In contrast to the King police officers, officer Derek Chauvin was convicted of all charges.

II. Cross-Examination

Crown (criminal) Court judges have observed there's 'considerable skill to cross-examining in such a way that the jury and the judge are fully absorbed by what they said' (Hunter et al 2018: 7). Many guidebooks help lawyers, with Wellman's *The Art of Cross-Examination* being the 'classic' (1903; see also Wellman 1924). Others include Mount (1980) and F Lee Bailey's review of his cases (1971). The skills of Norman Birkett were presented in a book of memoirs by his clerk (Bowker 1949).

There are many 'tips' too, such as never ask a question to which you don't know the answer. Lord Neuberger advised that 'the best barristers give the impression that the judge or jury is hearing a first class point from a third class advocate'. In other words, '[c]ontrary to popular belief, an obviously brilliant advocate is not always the best person to persuade a judge, or even a jury', because they might think the point sounds good only because it came 'from the mouth of a brilliant advocate' (Neuberger 2012: 64). What can make the difference is when a lawyer asks 'loaded' questions incorporating the key legal elements which support the case and gets the witness to agree (Coulthard and Johnson 2008).

A. Pozner and Dodd

There is 'a common feeling … that aspects that make an advocate perform and persuade are shared across jurisdictions' (Bedejo 2021). Some in the US and EW regard *Cross-Examination Science and Techniques* by Pozner and Dodd (2018) as 'quite simply the greatest book on cross-examination' (Scott 2019). They see the widely used Hempel method as risky (Hempel et al 2008) – preparing a closing speech first so the advocate can select the most important and relevant areas for cross-examination – because opposing counsel may present a theory and evidence undermining that speech. Instead, they propose the advocate have a series of topics and chapters. Chapters are the facts that need to be established for each witness with the aim of extracting as much favourable testimony from that witness as possible. They're a 'series of small stories that introduce and place into context the best facts' upon which the outcome of the case depends (Henry 2019). The 'alternative narrative' theory can thus be 'taught' to the judge or jury.

This approach means there are only three rules of cross-examination: leading questions only; one new fact per question; and breaking cross-examination into a series of logical progressions to each specific goal. Each chapter – the establishment of facts – must be completed before continuing with the next chapter. Once the order of chapters and order of questions within each chapter have been determined, the whole cross-examination comes across as coherent and persuasive. Their book also looks at case preparation, provides systems for developing the alternative narrative, and offers techniques for controlling the witness. In short, as English criminal court judges confirmed, advocacy is about effective 'story-telling', and about eliciting a story from a witness (Hunter et al 2018: 7).

III. Tools of Persuasion

Advocacy is 'all about persuasion … it is an "art of persuasion"' (Hunter et al 2018). Tigar (1999) calls it 'The Litigator's Art'. There are guidebooks here too. The Inns of Court School of Law's training manual on *Advocacy* (1996: 9) places 'considerable reliance' on du Cann (1980). Some are based on experience, anecdote and/or 'best guesses' (Napley 1991; Pirie 2006; Heinrichs 2007). Others appear to guarantee victory. Gerry Spence 'has never lost a criminal case' either as a prosecutor or defence counsel in over 50 years and 'never lost a jury trial since 1969'. Two of his books are entitled *How to Argue and Win Every Time* and *Win Your Case: How to Present, Persuade and Prevail – Every Place, Every Time* (Spence 1996, 2006).

A. Lend Me Your Ears

It's been claimed that: 'The advanced study of advocacy and persuasion in legal writing and communication requires an understanding of rhetoric' (Murray and DeSanctis 2013: Chapter 2). Rhetoric is 'the art of speaking and writing effectively and persuasively'

(*Cambridge Dictionary*). This begs 'the biggest question of all' – how to put the art into practice? In setting out techniques 'to inspire, persuade and enthuse' an audience, Atkinson noted they're the same as those originally identified by ancient Greeks and formed their schools of rhetoric, the first institutionalised education. Rhetorical techniques are 'the indispensable building blocks of the language of persuasion' (Atkinson 2004: 179). Three techniques can work effectively for trial lawyers (Atkinson 1979, 1992; Atkinson and Drew 1979; Pomerantz and Atkinson 1984): contrasts, questions and puzzles, lists of three.

i. Contrasts

Contrasts take many forms. One is 'contradiction': 'not this but that'. The applause following Tony Blair's first Labour Party Conference speech as leader is an example: 'We are not going to win despite our beliefs. We will only win because of our beliefs.' In court, this might translate into: 'Your duty is to determine guilt not by asking whether you believe X is guilty but whether you believe the prosecution has proved it beyond a reasonable doubt.' Another is 'comparison': 'more this than that' – for example, 'better to find X not guilty than to condemn an innocent person to prison'. A third is 'opposites' such as Martin Luther King Jr's statement (1963: 1) that 'injustice anywhere is a threat to justice everywhere'. So powerful is this that it's prominently displayed in the private library of UK Supreme Court Justices. Fourthly, there are 'phrase reversals'. The words in the first part of the contrast are used in the second part in reverse order. One example would be a variation on the words of Sir Edward Marshall Hall discussed earlier: 'God never gave her a chance, but here is your chance to give it. Won't you? Won't you?' Another example is, instead of this opening statement, 'my client has suffered from severe back pain for six months', this one: 'Every day for ten years, my client woke up in the morning and enjoyed a simple game of tennis with his wife of 25 years. After the accident, most of his days are spent in bed' (Wiener and Zdrojeski 2015: 189).

ii. Questions and Puzzles

Question/puzzles essentially invite the audience to anticipate the solution and to focus on a more serious message – for example, 'what does it mean to make a mistake, to get the verdict wrong? It means you could be next'. 'Rhetorical questions' allow the lawyer themselves to answer – for example, 'what will we show?' or 'what is our aim?' The answers will emphasise the message being delivered. Again, Wiener and Zdrojeski provide an example which I shall amend: 'three years ago, X and Y signed a one-year contract and afterward Y sent X an email congratulating X on the deal. Today, three years later, Y claims no such contract exists. Why would Y deny the contract existed?' (ibid: 191)

iii. Lists of Three

Many famous quotations confirm the power in lists of three. Atkinson showed how lists of two are too short – listeners expect more – whereas lists of four are too long; the speaker is more likely to be interrupted or to lose listeners' attention. Even better is to have the third item longer than the first two, especially when it's the most important – the advocate can emphasise that point by declaring it to be so.

iv. Combinations

Combining these techniques is 'one of the most important weapons in the speaker's armoury ... the combined format, in its various permutations, is indeed the most powerful rhetorical technique of them all' (Atkinson 2004: 198, 199). Atkinson invited readers to rewrite a boring statement:

> Recent years have seen a widespread proliferation in the incidence of medical negligence cases, in which Health Authorities have incurred increased costs as a result of the greater legal sophistication with which cases are being argued. (ibid: 249)

By posing a puzzle, developing a contrast and providing a three-part solution, this is the new version:

> Health Authorities are faced with a new kind of epidemic. A once-rare disease has turned into a plague of litigation.
>
> Medical negligence cases are now more frequent, more expensive and more expertly argued than ever before. (ibid: 249–50)

Atkinson's books (1984, 2004), full of valuable advice, are highly recommended.

IV. Spin-Doctoring

Lawyers' work is 'founded upon the use of language. Words and their nuances and subtleties, and their shades of composition, are all important' (Alexander 1991: 10). Prosecutors describe people as 'victims'; defence lawyers call them 'accusers'.

A. The Illusory Truth Effect

The 'illusory truth effect' (Hasher et al 1977) is the tendency of an audience repeatedly hearing false information to come to believe it. This has potential implications both in court and in the court of public opinion. The effect is best understood as a 'cognitive shortcut', a way of dealing with uncertainty and complexity (Fazio et al 2015).

B. The Innuendo Effect

Statements or questions which are ambiguous but suggest a 'truth' have the 'innuendo effect' (Wegner et al 1981) – for example: 'Is X a paedophile?' By smearing a person – witness, police or victim – the listener may believe there is 'no smoke without fire'.

C. 'Doublespeak'

George Orwell's classic *1984* introduced the concepts of 'doublethink' and 'newspeak'. Today, based on Orwell, we have 'doublespeak': 'language used to deceive usually through concealment or misrepresentation of truth' (*Merriam-Webster Dictionary*). A fictional story illustrates its potential. A researcher discovered the great-great uncle of X, Remus X, was hanged for horse stealing and train robbery in Montana in 1889. On the back of the only known photograph of Remus, showing him standing on the gallows about to be hanged, an inscription reads: 'Remus X, horse thief, sent to Montana Territorial Prison 1885, escaped 1887, robbed the Montana Flyer six times. Caught by Pinkerton detectives, convicted and hanged in 1889'.

The researcher emailed X for information about the great-great uncle. X's staff sent back the following biographical sketch:

> Remus X was a famous cowboy in the Montana Territory. His business empire grew to include acquisition of valuable equestrian assets and intimate dealings with the Montana railroad. Beginning in 1883, he devoted several years of his life to government service, finally taking leave to resume his dealings with the railroad. In 1887, he was a key player in a vital investigation run by the renowned Pinkerton Detective Agency. In 1889, Remus passed away during an important civic function held in his honor when the platform upon which he was standing collapsed.

V. Challenging the Expert

Expert evidence can be significant: 'widespread use of forensic science is an integral part of convicting the guilty and acquitting the innocent; providing everybody involved understands their role and the necessary processes support them in this' (Goldsmith P 2007). After all, what expert witnesses do is not say what they saw or heard but what they think. Their opinion is supposed to inform and guide judges and juries about technical matters. But an opinion is only as good as the expert. No wonder the 'modern expert is essential to modern justice', but 'has been so controversial' (ibid). Challenging the expert is, however, easier said than done which is why 'The cross-examination of an expert witness is often the key to the whole case' (Inns of Court School of Law 1996: 175).

A. Damilola Taylor

In 2000, Taylor, a 10-year-old boy, was stabbed and murdered in London. In 2002, four youths were charged with his murder but not convicted. The defence used cell site analysis – which reveals where a person (or their phone) is located when calls, SMS messages or data are sent or received – to assert there was 'unshakeable' evidence the defendants were too far away from the stabbing. Although no evidence was adduced to provide proof that any particular defendant was in possession of the phone at the material time (and none gave evidence in court), the judge directed that 'the jury could not convict a particular defendant unless they could be sure that defendant was *not using* the particular telephone' (Report of the Oversight Panel 2002: 5.5.3).

B. Sir Bernard Spilsbury

The pioneer of modern forensic science was Spilsbury, the senior pathologist at the UK Home Office. Spilsbury carried out around 25,000 autopsies and meticulously studied and recorded all forms of death. He helped introduce the 'murder bag', the kit containing equipment which detectives carry to scenes of suspicious deaths. Spilsbury gave evidence at many of the most famous early twentieth-century murder trials. These included the American Dr Hawley Harvey Crippen. Spilsbury identified the remains buried in Crippen's cellar as that of his wife Cora through a scar tissue on a small piece of skin. In the 'Brides in the Bath' murders, George Joseph Smith was accused of killing at least three of his wives, each one being found in the bath. One was holding a bar of soap which, according to Spilsbury, meant she'd been murdered. Crippen and Smith were hanged.

In court, Spilsbury was dominant: 'He formed his opinion; expressed it in the clearest, most succinct manner possible; then stuck to it come hell or high water' (Evans 2009: 27). Out of court, his role was crucial too: 'He could achieve single-handed all the legal consequence of homicide – arrest, prosecution, conviction and final postmortem – requiring only the brief assistance of the hangman' (ibid: 122). In 1938, the *Washington Post* 'hailed him as "England's Sherlock Holmes"' (quoted in Macintyre 2010: 40). Spilsbury's success, however, met with some criticism. He was 'aloof, arrogant, and utterly convinced of his own infallibility' (ibid). A contemporary of Spilsbury expressed 'profound disquiet' at one conviction and referred to the 'more than Papal infallibility with which Sir Bernard Spilsbury is rapidly being invested by juries' (*The Law Journal*, 18 April 1925). Spilsbury's evidence, according to forensic pathologist Keith Simpson, 'doubtless led to conviction at trials that might have ended with sufficient doubt for acquittal' (Simpson 1979: 26).

This illustrates how important 'the charisma of a particular expert could have on his influence with a jury' (Goldsmith P 2007). Juries were in 'awe' of Spilsbury and 'he was considered invincible in court' (ibid). In retrospect, however, 'even his evidence in the Crippen case is open to doubt' (Macintyre 2010: 53). A hundred men were sent to the gallows, '[h]elped by Spilsbury', and some 'with hindsight, were plainly innocent' (ibid). His 'theories and opinions had increasingly taken precedence over the facts' (ibid).

C. Sir Roy Meadow

Expert evidence can be so damning that, in effect, the burden of proof is reversed – the defendant has to prove innocence. Meadow was a leading British paediatrician and expert in child abuse. However, his work, and the evidence he presented in court, became controversial. The cases involved 'sudden infant death syndrome', 'cot death' or 'shaken baby syndrome' (SBS), now termed 'Non-accidental Head Injury Cases' to avoid the emotional connotations of SBS. His evidence in several trials contributed to convictions.

i. Sally Clark

Two of Sally Clark's babies died, one at 11 weeks and the other at eight weeks. In 1997, Meadow testified the chance of two cot deaths in the same family was approximately one in 73 million; that such an event would likely occur only once every 100 years in Great Britain; and it would be like an 80-1 outsider winning the Grand National horse race four years in a row. Clark was convicted by a 10-2 majority. At her first appeal, Meadow's evidence was called 'grossly misleading' and 'manifestly wrong'. At a further appeal, evidence indicated one baby could have died due to natural causes. She was released in 2003, but died in 2007 aged 42.

ii. Angela Cannings

Proving innocence in the face of expert evidence can be *Against All Odds*, as the book title by Cannings (2006) implies. She lost three infant children in the space of 10 years. Soon after the third death, she was charged with murder. She was convicted on the basis of a medical theory known as 'Meadow's Law': 'one sudden infant death is a tragedy, two is suspicious and three is murder until proven otherwise' (Meadow 1997). At her appeal, Michael Mansfield QC stated: 'Without Meadow, this case would not have got off the ground. The Crown's case was fundamentally to depend on Meadow. At the trial, we saw the jury must have been impressed by this particular witness' (Frith 2003). The Court agreed: 'The expert evidence was absolutely critical to these convictions' (*R v Angela Cannings*) As Lord Justice Judge said:

> We must reflect on the likely impact on the verdict in the present case if Mr Mansfield had been able to cross-examine Professor Meadow, and undermine the weight the jury would inevitably attach to his evidence, by exposing that, notwithstanding his pre-eminence, at least part of his evidence in the Sally Clark case was flawed in an important respect. To some extent at least, Professor Meadow's standing as a witness would have been reduced. Therefore the flawed evidence he gave at Sally Clark's trial serves to undermine his high reputation and authority as a witness in the forensic process. It also demonstrates that even the most distinguished expert can be wrong and provides a salutary warning against the possible dangers of an over-dogmatic expert approach.

He added: 'In cases like the present, if the outcome of the trial depends exclusively or almost exclusively on a serious disagreement between distinguished and reputable experts, it will often be unwise, and therefore unsafe to proceed'.

In non-SBS cases, however, the Court of Appeal has rejected this suggestion (*R v Kai-Whitewind*; see also CPS 2018b), so '[o]ften a case may turn on a well-argued difference of opinion between Prosecution and Defence experts' (CPS 2019). In these circumstances, the Court of Appeal has emphasised repeatedly it's for the jury to choose between them (*R v Dawson*). However, Lord Justice Judge made it clear that the lawyer – and the judge summing up for the jury – should emphasise:

> In a criminal case, it is simply not enough to be able to establish even a high probability of guilt. Unless we are sure of guilt the dreadful possibility always remains that a mother, already brutally scarred by the unexplained death or deaths of her babies, may find herself in prison for life for killing them when she should not be there at all. In our community, and in any civilised community, that is abhorrent. (ibid)

After two years in prison, Cannings was released unconditionally.

D. Junk Science

The NAS reported in 2009 about the validity of methods used routinely for many years to convict people (National Research Council 2009). Methods they cast serious doubt upon included bite marks, footprints, hair, handwriting, tyre tracks and voice patterns. Many were scientifically unsound, which is why Keith Harward spent 33 years in prison. He was convicted in 1983 of murder and rape after a forensic dentistry expert testified to a 'very, very, very, very high degree of probability' that he was the source of a bite mark on a victim and it was 'a practical impossibility that someone else would have all these characteristics' in his dentition (Stern et al 2019). DNA evidence exonerated him when it showed another man was the rapist. The NAS report concluded that the forensic methods they examined didn't 'have the capacity to consistently, and with a high degree of certainty, demonstrate a connection between evidence and a specific individual or source'. These examples show how 'shifted science [is] potentially calling into question hundreds or thousands of convictions that occurred over the past few decades' (Ram 2016).

Two particular problems with expert evidence are overstating and oversimplifying its reliability. A research study asked 17 experienced examiners to analyse DNA from an alleged gang rape and determine whether one particular individual might have been involved. There were widely divergent conclusions and only one of the 17 agreed with the analyst whose evidence at the trial led to the conviction (Murphy 2015: 5). But how does a lawyer, probably lacking scientific expertise, challenge the expert? Wing it?

E. The AA Rouse Murder Trial

Around 2 am on 6 November 1930, near Northampton, two men, walking home after 'Guy Fawkes Fireworks Night', saw Rouse climb out of a ditch carrying an attaché case. One of them noticed a glow a few hundred yards away and asked Rouse what it was. 'It looks like someone had a bonfire down there' he answered. While the two men ran towards the glow, Rouse walked away and eventually hitched a lift to London. The two men found a Morris Minor car on fire. It was Rouse's car and there was a body inside.

Rouse was charged with murder. The prosecution couldn't suggest a motive and nor could the body be identified. However, there was circumstantial evidence based partly on Rouse's suspicious responses to the two men and to others subsequently. He'd told people his car had been stolen. There was also his lifestyle – relationships with numerous women everywhere he travelled as a salesman, none of them aware of the others.

One key issue was how did the car fire start? An examination showed the petrol cap was on, but loose, the top of the carburettor (which mixes air and fuel for internal combustion) was missing, and a junction nut in the petrol line was loose. Norman Birkett KC suggested Rouse had loosened the nut to douse the car with petrol before igniting it. Rouse's barrister, DL Finnemore, suggested the fire could have been started accidentally – the junction nut might have been loosened by the passenger's foot. Finnemore called Arthur Isaacs, 'an engineer and fire assessor with very vast experience as regards fires in motor cars'. Isaacs theorised – with great confidence – the junction in the fuel line became loose as a result of the heat generated by the fire itself. In other words, the fire was accidental and Rouse's guilt couldn't be beyond a reasonable doubt.

Birkett rose to cross-examine Isaacs:

Birkett: What is the coefficient of the expansion of brass?

Isaacs: I beg your pardon.

Birkett: Did you not catch the question?

Isaacs: I did not quite hear you.

Birkett: What is the coefficient of the expansion of brass?

Isaacs: I am afraid I cannot answer that question off-hand.

Birkett: What is it? If you do not know, say so. What is the coefficient of the expansion of brass?

Isaacs: You want to know what is the expansion of the metal under heat?

Birkett: I asked you: What is the coefficient of the expansion of brass? Do you know what it means?

Isaacs: Put that way, probably I do not.

Birkett: You are an engineer?

Isaacs: I dare say I am.

Birkett: Let me understand what you are. You are not a doctor?

Isaacs: No.

Birkett: Not a crime investigator?

Isaacs: No.

Birkett: Nor an amateur detective?

Isaacs: No.

Birkett: But an engineer?

Isaacs: Yes.

Birkett: What is the coefficient of the expansion of brass? You do not know?

Isaacs: No; not put that way.

The defence collapsed; Rouse was found guilty and, after his appeal failed, hanged. In 2002, in a class action trial after the 1998 Longford Gas Plant Explosion in Australia, the same question was asked, word for word. As Julian Burnside (nd), an Australian barrister, noted: 'Some in court were mystified by the question; some who read the account of it in the Bar News were mystified by it.' What Birkett had done was to move the expert away from his field of expertise to reduce the impact of his evidence. Or as Wooding (2010), a solicitor, put it, Birkett was going 'for the jugular: the expert status itself'.

Without saying as much, the expert was conceding the alternative explanation was possible – he'd admitted he didn't know.

Birkett later said he'd no idea what he was going to ask the expert: 'I simply couldn't think what to ask him. It was the first thing that came into my head' (quoted in Evans 2011: 164). So much for preparation! In a way, Birkett's question was a trick, of which possibly the best-known example (in England) was the questions asked by barrister FE Smith, a formidable advocate. In a personal injury case, he represented the insurance company. The claimant wanted damages for an injured arm which he claimed, after the accident, he could no longer raise above his head. Smith asked him a series of straightforward questions in the witness box and then this one: 'How high could you raise your arm before the accident?' The man showed the court and ... promptly lost the case!

F. Admission of Expert Evidence

FRE 702 allows experts to give evidence only when 'the testimony is based on sufficient facts or data' and 'is the product of reliable principles and methods ... reliably applied ... to the facts of the case'; to be admissible, the testimony must qualify as reliable 'scientific ... knowledge' (*Daubert*). Lawyers can ask judges to look at the 'principles and methodology' used to 'generate' experts' conclusions to see whether they were 'derived by the scientific method' (ibid: 595, 590). In EW, experts should testify only in matters within their knowledge, and those matters which are likely to be outside judges or juror's knowledge and experience. It must also be evidence which gives courts the help they need in forming their conclusions. As a result, challenges to admissibility based on lack of expertise rarely succeed – whether by the prosecution (*R (Doughty)*) or the defence (*R v Hodges*). Since 2008, there's also an independent UK 'Forensic Science Regulator' whose role is to ensure the forensic science services across the criminal justice system are subject to an appropriate regime of scientific quality standards. Since 2006, under the CPR 33.2, experts give 'objective, unbiased opinion on matters within [their] expertise'. This duty overrides any other obligation. The 'key point is that the expert is not a hired gun' (Goldsmith P 2007).

It's possible to make an application to exclude evidence because experts lack the requisite knowledge or are attempting to give evidence beyond their expertise or experience, or their methodology is suspect. As the CPS (2019) points out:

> Some experts will seek to reach conclusions based upon an incomplete reading of the evidence choosing to disregard accepted facts which do not assist their conclusions, or who demonstrates in their reports that they have not understood the facts. They may also take into account irrelevant matters or matters not adduced in evidence upon which they form an opinion.

G. Challenging DNA

In EW, there's a 'primer for courts' on DNA analysis to assist the judiciary when handling scientific evidence in the courtroom (Royal Society 2017). The US Supreme Court has noted, 'Given the persuasiveness of such evidence in the eyes of the jury, it is important that it be presented in a fair and reliable manner' (*McDaniel*). Challenging DNA evidence is possible on several grounds (Murphy 2015), the most common perhaps being contamination.

i. Adam Scott

In 2011, Scott was charged with rape and spent several months on remand. The sole evidence was DNA believed to have been taken from the victim. But the tray containing Scott's DNA, taken from an unconnected incident, was, instead of being disposed of, re-used in the analysis from the rape victim (Forensic Science Regulator 2012).

ii. Lukis Anderson

In 2012, Anderson's DNA was found on the fingernails of a murder victim – a seemingly 'open and shut' case. Anderson spent six months in prison, despite a cast-iron alibi – at the time of the murder, he was comatose in a drunken stupor at the local hospital. The paramedics who treated Anderson at a liquor store had taken him to hospital, then rushed to aid the victim – where they transferred Anderson's DNA (Smith 2016).

If DNA matches the client, the client might claim the DNA was deposited innocently on a moveable object such as a balaclava (*R v Grant*) or a scarf (*R v Ogden*) and left at the scene by someone else. Even when uncontaminated personal DNA, such as saliva, is left at a crime scene and the client is a match for it, that shouldn't be enough to prove guilt beyond a reasonable doubt.

iii. The Prosecutor's Fallacy

Statisticians Thompson and Schumann (1987) were first to identify 'The Prosecutor's Fallacy':

> It is easy, if one eschews rigorous analysis, to draw the following conclusion:
> 1. Only one person in a million will have a DNA profile which matches that of the crime stain.
> 2. The defendant has a DNA profile which matches the crime stain.
> 3. Ergo there is a million to one probability that the defendant left the crime stain and is guilty of the crime.
>
> Such reasoning has been commended to juries in a number of cases by prosecuting counsel, by judges and sometimes by expert witnesses. It is fallacious and it has earned the title of 'The Prosecutor's Fallacy'. (*R v Doheny*: 373–74)

It's overstating the probability of guilt. If the defendant male is indeed one in a million, but there are, let's say, 26 million men, then there will be 26 men who share that DNA profile. Hence the importance of supporting evidence:

> If no fact is known about the Defendant, other than that he was in the United Kingdom at the time of the crime the DNA evidence tells us no more than that there is a statistical probability

that he was the criminal of 1 in 26. The significance of the DNA evidence will depend critically upon what else is known about the suspect. If he has a convincing alibi at the other end of England at the time of the crime, it will appear highly improbable that he can have been responsible for the crime, despite his matching DNA profile. If, however, he was near the scene of the crime when it was committed, or has been identified as a suspect because of other evidence which suggests that he may have been responsible for the crime, the DNA evidence becomes very significant. The possibility that two of the only 26 men in the United Kingdom with the matching DNA should have been in the vicinity of the crime will seem almost incredible and a comparatively slight nexus between the defendant and the crime, independent of the DNA, is likely to suffice to present an overall picture to the jury that satisfies them of the defendant's guilt. (ibid)

This description is reflected in detailed legal guidance that is useful for all lawyers on expert evidence (CPS 2019, also referring to *R v Doheny*: 372):

expert evidence is merely one tool to be used in proving a case ... The Court of Appeal has emphasised that expert evidence can only be judged in the light of other evidence in the case. In these cases, the absence of any other evidence, however limited, should have been fatal to the case being charged.

In *R v Lashley*, the DNA could've originated from 7–10 males in the UK. There was no other evidence against the defendant. When interviewed the defendant made no comment. The Court of Appeal said this was neither an indication nor supporting evidence of guilt as there was no compelling case for him to answer. If the defendant had a connection to the crime scene, gave inconsistent explanations in interview for the presence of DNA at the scene, a history of drug use, or an admission that the suspect needed cash urgently, that might make a difference. The individual might also be at a crime scene for a legitimate or innocent reason prior to the offence being committed.

That said, there's no principle that says juries cannot consider a case solely on DNA evidence (*R v Tsekiri*); it depends on the facts. In the US too, there's been 'a growing number of cases prosecuted based on a DNA match alone' (Murphy 2015: 110), and a growing trend: using databases to search for a match (ibid: 144–45). In short, 'As the art of analysis progresses', a DNA match in future might be so comprehensive and unique that it alone proves guilt, but '[s]o far as we are aware that stage has not yet been reached' (*R v Doheny*).

H. Impartiality

Experts' impartiality may be suspect. One American expert was unusually frank. The plaintiff's lawyer asked: 'Is your conclusion this man is a malingerer?' The response: 'I wouldn't be testifying if I didn't think so, unless I was on the other side, then it would be a post traumatic condition.' Judge Regan referred to 'these pearls of wisdom' as 'of vast significance' when rejecting the defendant's appeal (*Ladner*). If experts only ever give evidence for one side, can they be impartial? Or to put it another way, you wouldn't ask a football manager – albeit a football expert – to decide if his player won a penalty or not (Mitchell 2015).

i. Vernon – *Again*

Vernon was discussed in Chapter 12. In May 1993, medical experts testified in a personal injury case that the plaintiff's prospects of recovery were poor. In October, in the Family Court, they reached a more positive prognosis. A letter from the lawyer had told them: 'we need to show that his mental health has improved dramatically since the date of your report in May 1993 and moreover that it has improved again since the conclusion of his big personal injury case'.

A survey in 2014 suggested nearly a third of expert witnesses felt pressure from lawyers and others to make changes to their reports in a way that harmed their impartiality (Bond Solon 2014). The SRA believes this figure should be treated with care as some of the requests may have reflected a desire for clarification. However, it added (2015: 10): 'Others, such as requests to alter doctors' notes, may represent misconduct'. As a last resort, defence lawyers can ask prosecution experts to agree there can be legitimate differences of opinion, they're not uncommon, and they reflect the fallibility of expert evidence.

VI. Opening and Closing Speeches

A. Opening Speech

According to Pozner and Dodd (quoted in Henry 2019), 'trying to win through force of personality and rhetorical fireworks are out-of-date techniques'. But there's 'an exception to every rule' (Henry 2019), such as Ben Brafman, a New York 'defender' and his

> opening salvo in his successful defence of Sean 'Puff Daddy (now Diddy?) Combs on firearms charges:
>
> [Mr Combs stands]
>
> Ladies and Gentlemen, this is Sean 'Puff Daddy' Combs. You can call him Sean, you can call him Mr Combs, you can call him Puff Daddy, or even just plain call him Puffy, but what you cannot do in this case, you cannot call him guilty, because from the facts, from the evidence, from the Law, you will conclude that he is not guilty.

Experienced American litigators 'often describe a trial as a competition between two stories with the jury as the ultimate arbiter' (Wiener and Zdrojeski 2005: 181). The opening statement, one of the rare opportunities for the lawyer to address the jury directly, is the first chapter in this story.

B. Closing Speech

Evans (2011: 67) suggests there are three objectives in a closing speech. First, make juries realise what their duty is. They've a grave responsibility: sitting in judgment on the liberty of other human beings; they should be made aware of the consequences of wrongful convictions and miscarriages of justice. There's a presumption of innocence, and the burden of proof is on the prosecution. However, that's only one element. Tigar and Coleman Jr (2014: 4) argued: 'It is never enough, in a criminal case, simply to rest on reasonable doubt.'

Secondly, face the difficulties raised by the prosecution evidence and concede good points, but claim, if possible, they don't necessarily mean the client should be found guilty. Tigar and Coleman warned 'do not make yourself look bad to the jury by denying the obvious' (ibid). Evans gives an example of how to say good things before, as it were, sticking the knife in: 'Brutus was an honourable man', says Mark Anthony no fewer than seven times. Brutus understands what's happening and 'by the fifth time Brutus has taken to his heels' (Evans 2011: 77).

Thirdly, show jurors how they may rightly and sensibly acquit. In other words, 'show them the way home'. There needs to be an alternative narrative for the jury to adopt rather than a direct challenge to them to decide – for example, are the police lying? Tigar and Coleman (2014: 4) agree: 'employ the theory of minimal contradiction; look for a case theory that shifts perspective just enough to require a different result ... always provide the jurors with a plausible alternative view of events' – the 'theory of innocence'. The closing argument should be presented 'in a way that demonstrates your total conviction in your case and your unwavering commitment to your side' (Mauet 2007: 398).

VII. Jury Nullification (US)/Jury Equity (EW)

A 'last straw' defence strategy is to invite juries to deliver not-guilty verdicts *despite* the law and evidence: the 'jury has the power to bring in a verdict in the teeth of both law and facts' (*Morisette*: 275, Justice Oliver Wendell Holmes). There's a 'long-standing tradition' that 'legitimates' jury nullification (Simon 1993: 1724), dating from the famous seventeenth-century acquittal of the Quakers, William Penn and William Mead. Prior to this case, courts such as the '"Star Chamber" had been known to punish jurors who refused to convict by seizing their land and possessions' (Lloyd-Bostock and Thomas 1999: 9). Penn and Mead were prosecuted for holding a religious assembly of more than five people (unlawful unless under the auspices of the Church of England) – there were about 300. In court, Penn interrupted proceedings:

> **Penn:** I desire you would let me know by what law it is you prosecute me, and upon what law you ground my indictment.
>
> **Mr Justice Thomas Howel:** Upon the common-law.
>
> **Penn:** Where is that common-law?
>
> **Judge Howel:** You must not think that I am able to run up so many years, and over so many adjudged cases, which we call common-law, to answer your curiosity. You are a saucy fellow, speak to the Indictment.
>
> **Penn:** This answer I am sure is very short of my question, for if it be common, it should not be so hard to produce ... The question is not, whether I am guilty of this Indictment, but whether this Indictment is legal. It is too general and imperfect an answer, to say it is the common-law, unless we knew both where and what it is. For where there is no law, there is no transgression; and that law which is not in being, is so far from being common, that it is no law at all.

Judge Howel: Sir, you are a troublesome fellow, and it is not for the honour of the court to suffer you to go on … Take him away. My lord, if you take not some course with this pestilent fellow, to stop his mouth, we shall not be able to do any thing to night. (American University nd; see Phillips and Thompson 1986)

Penn was removed from the court, leaving Mead alone to defend. The jury were unable to reach a verdict when four of the 12, including Bushell, the foreman, refused to return to court. Judge Howel accused Bushell of being 'the cause of this disturbance, and manifestly shew yourself an abettor of faction; I shall set a mark upon you, Sir'. Judge John Robinson addressed Bushell: 'I tell you, you deserve to be indicted more than any man that hath been brought to the bar this day'. Judge Bloodworth called Bushell 'an impudent fellow, I will put a mark upon you'.

After the jury came back with two exculpatory verdicts, including 'guilty of speaking in Gracechurch street', Judge Howel said: 'Gentlemen, you shall not be dismissed till we have a verdict that the court will accept; and you shall be locked up, without meat, drink, fire, and tobacco' (*Bushell's Case*: 1007); he went on: 'you shall not think thus to abuse the court; we will have a verdict, by the help of God, or you will starve for it'. Penn responded:

My jury, who are my judges, ought not to be thus menaced; their verdict should be free, and not compelled; the bench ought to wait upon them, but not forestall them … You are Englishmen, mind your privilege, give not away your right.

Judge Howel responded: 'Stop that prating fellow's mouth, or put him out of the court.'

The jury refused to find them guilty despite being locked up without a chamber-pot for two nights. The judge then fined the jurors and said they would be imprisoned until they paid. Bushell appealed on a writ of habeas corpus to the Court of Common Pleas. Chief Justice John Vaughan cleared all the jurors and set the rule for the future: 'The jury must be independently and indisputably responsible for its verdict free from any threats from the court.' There's a plaque at the Old Bailey about *Bushell's Case*. It 'commemorates the courage and the endurance of the jury'. It says the case 'established the right of juries to give their verdicts according to their convictions'.

In the US, examples include refusing to convict sellers of alcohol during the Prohibition era and Vietnam War 'draft-dodgers'. Hodes (1996) argues that the acquittal of OJ Simpson was a 'jury nullification of the third kind'. In EW, examples include the acquittal of Alan Blythe, who was charged in 1998 with cultivating cannabis with intent to supply, an imprisonable offence. He supplied his wife, a terminally ill multiple sclerosis patient. The judge told the jury not only that duress was no defence, but also instructed them to find Blythe guilty. They returned a verdict of not guilty on all charges except possession, for which the sentence was a fine. In 1985, Clive Ponting, a senior British civil servant, was acquitted despite admitting passing secret information to an MP about the sinking of the Argentinian warship *General Belgrano* during the Falklands War – a clear violation of the Official Secrets Act. The crime writer Ian Rankin (1998: ix) recounted his experience on an Old Bailey jury where another juror told him 'I think he done it, but I don't want him going to prison for it', and voted not guilty. Similarly, one former juror reported acquitting a rape suspect because of 'fear of the likely disproportionate prison sentence' (Simpson 2021).

Lord Neuberger (2012: 64) told a 'sad little story' about a man refused planning permission to replace a dangerous wall (at his own expense). After his son was killed because of the wall, he replaced it without permission and was prosecuted. The judge summed up as follows:

> Members of the jury, my role is to direct you as to the law, and your role is to give a verdict. There are only two directions I will give you as to the law. The first is that the defendant has no defence to this charge. The second is that there is no appeal against a jury's verdict of not guilty.

The jury accepted the judge's veiled invitation to acquit despite the lack of defence.

A more likely judicial approach is to discourage jury nullification as 'lawless and arbitrary' (*Strickland*: 695). In the US, some argue that 'to prevent misuse of the power, juries must not be told they possess such power' (Horowitz et al 2001: 1217). A demonstrator who held up a sign outside a London criminal court in 2023 saying 'JURORS YOU HAVE AN ABSOLUTE RIGHT TO ACQUIT A DEFENDANT ACCORDING TO YOUR CONSCIENCE' is being prosecuted with contempt of court (Kaminski 2024). She was protesting against judicial restrictions preventing climate activist defendants mentioning in court 'climate change, insulation or fuel poverty'. Several demonstrators have been similarly arrested. Another judge said jurors cannot 'acquit by their conscience if by that it is meant that they can disregard the evidence and directions given by the judge and decide on their own beliefs' (Quakers in Britain 2023).

The question for lawyers is what they can legitimately tell juries about nullification/ equity. Hodes (1996: 1081) argues that 'coaxing a nullification vote ... must be counted as one of criminal defense attorney's built-in arsenal of tactical weapons'. Lawyers are obliged to uphold the law and not undermine the proper administration of justice. But, in that sentence, the issue is revealed – upholding the 'law' might not equate with 'justice', as in Lord Neuberger's 'sad little story'. As Zander (2007: 527) put it: 'The right to return a perverse verdict in defiance of the law or the evidence is an important safeguard against unjust laws, oppressive prosecutions or harsh sentences.' Lord Devlin regarded the jury's right to be perverse as 'our proudest constitutional achievement' (quoted in Rozenberg 2020; see also Devlin 1956).

VIII. Preparation: The 'Dream Team'

Effective advocacy often depends on adequate preparation and lawyer competence. While some lawyers lack resources, there are also 'Dream Teams', so-called after the Simpson case (see Shapiro with Warren (1996) for a comprehensive description). As Rhode (2000a: 8) put it: 'For many [criminal] defendants, it is better to be rich and guilty than poor and innocent.'

Michael Tigar's team, defending Terry Nichols, included 'five lawyers, five paralegals, and five investigators, with contract services from experts in several key subjects, and the help of a dozen law students at various times' (Tigar and Coleman Jr 2014: 5). A computer expert scanned the materials so they could be searched electronically. The team worked full-time from April 1995 until the trial in September 1997. Without such a large team they couldn't have sifted through a discovery process that gave the defence 'access to more than 40,000 witness statements collected by the FBI, 100,000 items of physical evidence, and dozens of expert reports'.

16

Courting the Court of Public Opinion

> Justice must be seen on TV to be done.
> — Newman (cartoonist, referring to *Bates*, *The Times*, 14 January 2024)

There were 350 further stories in *Computer Weekly* after its 2009 report and investigation into the Horizon system – the heart of the UK PO Scandal; 383 in *The Times*, 343 in the *Daily Mail*, 234 in the *Daily Telegraph*, 152 in the *Sunday Times*; and a BBC exposé in 2015 (despite being threatened with legal action) (*The Times*, 2024b). *Channel 4 News* reported on it in 2010 and *Private Eye* investigated in 2012. However, it was an ITV drama, *Mr Bates vs The Post Office*, that 'catapulted' the scandal 'into the national consciousness' (ibid). One headline read: 'The Post Office Scandal Has Revealed the Country's True Leader – Prime-Time TV' (Sitwell 2024).

Lawyers know the public can become fascinated by certain cases, especially in 'big trials' (Brown 2004). Robert Shapiro (Shapiro with Warren 1996: xvii), one of OJ Simpson's lawyers, noted: 'There's a natural symbiosis between big trials and the media, with both getting caught up in the playing-field drama of game plans, strategy, key players, winning and losing'. Another OJ lawyer, F. Lee Bailey, 'believed it was part of the job to defend his clients in the court of public opinion' (Obituary 2021b), which may be why, in 1971, he was suspended for violating pre-trial publicity rules (*New York Times* 1971).[1] The lawyer representing the family of George Floyd, killed by a Minneapolis police officer in 2020, was 'very honest about what I'm using the media for. We can't just win in the courtroom, we need to change narratives – hearts and minds – first. If we win in the court of public opinion, then we might just prevail in the court of law' (Glancy 2020). Or not need to if there is no trial.

I. Kobe Bryant – Again

Bryant's lawyer, Pamela Mackey, was 'fighting two battles … The first is in the media; the second is in the courtroom. Strategic arguments in pretrial motions and in the press have largely won her the first battle' (Anderson 2004). She 'won' by default because, after 15 months, the case was dropped during jury selection after the accuser refused to testify. Even before a trial date was set or a plea entered, Americans following the

---

[1] Bailey was disbarred subsequently in Florida and Massachusetts for misappropriating stock left with him in escrow by an imprisoned drug trafficker.

alleged rape case in 2003 became 'well-versed in rumors of his accuser's "American Idol" aspirations, suicide attempts, drug abuse, and sexual history' (Paulson 2004). They – and, potentially, jurors –would have known about her underwear and whose semen it contained, that she'd been briefly hospitalised for mental illness, and the defence lawyers' claim that she was an unstable attention-seeker. They would hear from a pre-hearing Mackey's 'bombshell question': could the accuser's injuries 'be consistent with a person who had sex with three different men in three days?' (ibid). Mackey also asked the police detective at the preliminary hearing: 'The accuser arrived at the hospital wearing panties with someone else's semen and sperm in them, not that of Mr Bryant, correct?' (Anderson 2004)

Much of this 'evidence' would've either *not* been admitted in court or would've been tested in pretrial hearings (in private) to determine admissibility. All of it, however, could be heard by the public. In other words, 'the battle for public opinion has been under way for eight months' (Paulson 2004) and '[t]his will be a trial both by public opinion and by a set of jurors' (Michelle Anderson, quoted in ibid). As Paulson notes: 'Most jurors will hear allegations about the victim's past whether or not a judge deems them admissible in court.'

A study of 156 articles about Bryant's case found 65 mentioned at least one rape myth (Franiuk et al 2008). Rape myths are 'generalized and widely held beliefs about sexual assault that serve to trivialize the sexual assault or suggest that a sexual assault did not actually occur' (ibid). Only 13 of the 156 countered such myths by mentioning how rarely women lie about rape, or how entering a hotel room with a man is not the same as consenting to sex. It found those exposed to myth-endorsing articles were more likely to believe Bryant was not guilty and the alleged victim lying. The study also focused on the headlines and their use of words. 'Accuser' was used nearly a quarter of the time, whereas 'alleged victim' or 'victim' only in two per cent of cases.

There've been attempts to help American journalists 'navigate the charged terrain of reporting on sexual assault and domestic violence' (Fitts 2013). In the 1969 trial of the infamous London gangsters the Kray Twins, the trial judge indicated he would exclude any juror who'd read some of the 'lurid newspaper reporting' (*R v Kray*). But for lawyers, trial publicity is an opportunity to help clients by exploiting the media's willingness to try the case in the 'court of public opinion'. Supreme Court Justice Kennedy endorsed as a lawful strategy 'an attempt to demonstrate in the court of public opinion that the client does not deserve to be tried' (*Gentile*: 1043).

II. Public Opinion

Some cases create 'moral panics' – a feeling of fear which spreads like wildfire when people perceive an evil that threatens them. They're 'usually the work of moral entrepreneurs and the mass media' (Scott 2014: 492), but often have a real-world cause. In the Oklahoma bombing case 'the grief and anger of the victims ... their cry for vengeance' was why Michael Tigar sought a change the trial venue from Oklahoma to Colorado in order to construct 'a sanctuary in the jungle' (Tigar and Coleman Jr 2014). But the jungle is ever-present in high-profile cases, especially if these are televised.

A. The Media Jungle

The first-ever televised trial was that of Nazi war criminal Adolf Eichmann in Israel. In the UK currently, only Supreme Court proceedings are televised, and these are a world apart from the famous American televised criminal trials. Ted Bundy's trial in 1979 was first to be televised nationally. Others include OJ Simpson – the 'Media Trial of the Century' (Shapiro with Warren 1996: 357), William Kennedy Smith, Jeffrey Dahmer, the Menendez Brothers' first trial and Casey Anthony. There are US TV channels devoted to analysing current trials. Two trials where the 'Court of Public Opinion' delivered a unanimous verdict – guilty – well before they began involved Lindy Chamberlain and Casey Anthony. These show the complexity of the relationship between the two courts – public opinion and law.

B. Lindy Chamberlain

Chamberlain's trial was not only the most publicised trial in Australian history, but also received worldwide attention. In 1980, Lindy and Michael Chamberlain were camping at Ayers Rock – now Uluru – with their nine-week-old daughter Azaria. Lindy heard a scream coming from the tent, followed by silence. The question that gripped the world – and the jury in 1982 – did a dingo drag Azaria away and kill her or did Lindy? In the two years between the disappearance and trial, everybody had an opinion: 'The intensity of the witch-hunt that followed' was 'compelling' (Jackson 2020). The case showed

> the disturbing mass behaviour that can occur when the public get stirred up by a media sensation – one on to which they project their psychological fears, pain or revulsions – it also offers a classic example of what Malcolm Gladwell calls the 'mismatch paradox'. Mum Lindy and Dad's body language outside the court was not in accord with the stereotypical notion of how they were supposed to act as grieving parents. She was too hard-faced; he was far too calm. They must have dunnit. (ibid)

During the trial, women came to the court to spit at the Chamberlains and wore T-shirts emblazoned with 'The dingo is innocent' (ibid; see also Richardson 2002). The jury was told about blood in the family car; that the tears in Azaria's clothing were more likely the result of scissors than a dingo; and that the parents were 'acting strange'. So, lacking a body, weapon, eyewitness or motive, the prosecutor relied on emotional arguments and prejudice. Prosecutor Jim Brown's final address to the jury was along these lines:

> Ladies and gentlemen. Thank you for your patience; it's been many weeks of evidence; you've heard lots of it. But the simple thing is, we as Northern Territorians know that dingoes don't take babies; we know that crocodiles do, but dingoes don't take babies. And these people, from down south, come up here and try and tell us what's happening in our territory. (Channel 5 (UK) 2020)

Lindy's conviction confirmed her as the most hated mother in Australia; protesters said she should be hanged. Her sentence of life imprisonment with hard labour began just days after she'd given birth to another daughter – who was taken away after just one hour. Lindy's family could visit her in prison only three times per year. That would've been an end to the story had it not been for another Uluru tragedy. In 1986, six years after Azaria disappeared, a tourist, David Brett, fell to his death. During the search for him, Azaria's jacket was found near a dingo den. Lindy, having spent 1,035 days in jail, was immediately released and pardoned. In 1988, her conviction was quashed and the case was portrayed in the film *A Cry in the Dark*. It turned out the blood in the car was paint emulsion. Then in 2001, a nine year old was killed by a dingo and in 2019 a four-month-old baby was dragged from his bed in a camper van by a dingo.

It wasn't until 2012, over 30 years after the event, that a coroner issued a death certificate: Azaria had been killed by a dingo. The Chamberlain case illustrates most vividly the dangers of miscarriages of justice. Lindy lost one daughter, had another taken away, lost her husband and her freedom.

C. Casey Anthony

Time magazine called Anthony's trial 'the first major murder trial of the social-media age' (Cloud 2011). A UCLA forensic psychiatrist, Dr Carole Lieberman, called it 'a soap opera … a very captivating murder-mystery' (Conley 2011). Anthony, a 22-year-old single mother, was charged in October 2008 with killing her two-year old daughter Caylee, despite the lack of a body. The US media described her as a 'murdering monster'; she was 'subjected to what all sides agree was probably the most prejudiced media bombardment in history' (Allen-Mills 2011). That said, the media had circumstantial information to report. Anthony repeatedly lied to police after Caylee's grandmother reported her missing – 31 days after she disappeared in June 2008. Anthony invented a babysitter who, she claimed, kidnapped Caylee. Caylee's remains were found, six months after she went missing, in December 2008.

Despite the media coverage, however, the jury took only 11 hours to find Anthony not guilty. They found her guilty of misdemeanours: lying to, and wasting the time of, the police. There was a public outcry at the verdict; the main reason, according to Dr Lieberman, 'is that the media convicted Casey before the jury decided' (Conley 2011). Lieberman noted that she was not aware of a single news story that questioned whether Anthony could be innocent.

III. Trial Publicity Rules

Trial publicity is regulated in both the US and EW, but the scope for influencing public opinion is greater in the US. MR 3.6 provides that:

> A lawyer who is participating or has participated in the investigation or litigation of a matter shall not make an extrajudicial statement that the lawyer knows or reasonably should know will be disseminated by means of public communication and will have a substantial likelihood of materially prejudicing an adjudicative proceeding in the matter. (See also ABA 2017: Standard 4-1.10(c)).

The aims are clear: public opinion can be affected by what's said and heard in the media about a forthcoming trial. Indeed, 'the subject matter of legal proceedings is often of direct significance in debate and deliberation over questions of public policy' (MR 3.6, Comment [1]). It's possible public opinion may affect the trial outcome. That's why there are limits: 'If there were no such limits, the result would be the practical nullification of the protective effect of the rules of forensic decorum and the exclusionary rules of evidence' (ibid).

The MR therefore seek to 'strike a balance between protecting the right to a fair trial and safeguarding the right of free expression'. MR 3.6, Comment [5] points out there are 'certain subjects that are more likely than not to have a material prejudicial effect on a proceeding' particularly when there is a jury or incarceration might result. Those subjects relate to:

(1)   the character, credibility, reputation or criminal record of a party, suspect in a criminal investigation or witness, or the identity of a witness or the expected testimony of a party or witness;

...

(3)   the performance or results of any examination or test ... or the identity or nature of physical evidence expected to be presented;

...

(5)   information that the lawyer knows or reasonably should now is likely to be inadmissible in a trial and that would, if disclosed, create a substantial risk of prejudicing the impartial trial.

But is MR 3.6 honoured more in the breach than in the observance? According to Dershowitz (1982: 396): 'It is perfectly proper for a lawyer to use the press – if done to further his client's interests (and if not in violation of any legal or ethical rules).' But one reason to defy the rules is if they all do it! Anecdotally, that seems to be the case. Repercussions are rare, and then only in the most egregious cases such as the 'Public Branding' of the Duke lacrosse team by Michael Nifong, who was disbarred (Matthews III 2008).

Barristers used to be warned to be cautious when expressing personal opinions in the media to ensure their comments don't undermine, or are not reasonably seen as undermining, their independence. That includes expressing a personal opinion to the press or other media or in any other public statement upon the facts or issues arising in the proceedings. There are also strong legal deterrents to prejudicing a fair trial by broadcast (see CPS 2018). There's strict liability if proceedings are 'active' and the publication 'creates a substantial risk that the course of justice ... will be seriously impeded or prejudiced' (section 2(2) of the Contempt of Court Act 1981). 'Publication' is defined to include any speech, writing, programme or other communication in whatever form which is addressed to the public at large, once proceedings are 'active' (see generally Corker and Levi (1996), though there have been significant changes since 1996).

There are three specific defences under the Act: 'a fair and accurate report of legal proceedings held in public, published contemporaneously and in good faith'; publications relating to discussions in good faith of public affairs or matters of general public interest, providing that the risk of prejudice to particular legal proceedings is incidental to the discussion; or that the publishers and distributors can show they took reasonable care and didn't know or have reason to suspect proceedings were active (publishers) or that a publication contained matters in breach of the strict liability rule (distributors) (sections 4, 5 and 3 respectively). However, the media is 'in jeopardy of being in contempt of court when reporting criminal proceedings unless the reporting is fair and accurate and published in good faith' (Judicial College 2015: 11).

A. Joanna Yeates

In the murder case of Joanna Yeates in 2010, the *Daily Mirror* and *The Sun* newspapers were found guilty of contempt of court: 'the vilification of a suspect under arrest is a potential impediment to the course of justice' (*Attorney General v MGN*, Lord Judge,) There were two unusual aspects to this case. First, the person vilified, Christopher Jefferies, was not only 'presumed in law to be innocent of the killing ... [he] was innocent' (ibid) – Vincent Tabak confessed and was convicted (see Clegg (2018: Chapter 23) for an account by Tabak's counsel). Secondly, even more 'unusual' is that the articles published 'did not have and could not have had any impact whatsoever on the trial ... just because ... there will never be one' (ibid).

Defending the newspapers, Jonathan Caplan KC and Adrienne Page KC contended that the memory of anything read by someone who would become a jury member would have faded by the time of trial and, together with appropriate judicial directions, it would have proceeded in the usual way, with the jury returning unbiased verdicts in accordance with the evidence. This is the 'fade factor'. However, Lord Judge agreed with the Attorney General that the contempt law not only dealt with the substantial risk of serious prejudice to the course of justice, but that it would be 'seriously impeded' (section 2(2) of the Contempt of Court Act 1981). As Lord Justice Oliver observed, the 'course of justice' includes the freedom of the accused to elect the mode of trial – jury or not – and to conduct their defence in the way that seems best to them and their lawyers (*Attorney General v Times*). External pressure might impede or restrict that freedom. The course of the defence might be diverted by publicity; witnesses might be influenced or fail to come forward. In other words, the evidence subsequently heard by the jury might *already* be incomplete. The risk to the preparation of the defence means vilification of a suspect under arrest is, as a matter of principle, in contempt of court.

B. Reporting Restrictions

In the US, the constitutional protection afforded to press freedom makes the scope for publicity wider than in EW. Section 4(2) of the Contempt of Court Act 1981 empowers judges, where it appears to be necessary for avoiding a substantial risk of prejudice to the administration of justice in those proceedings, to order that the publication of any report of any part of the proceedings be postponed for such period as the court thinks necessary (Practice Direction Contempt of Court Act 1981 (1983) 76 Cr App R 78; Judicial College 2015). Some reporting restrictions are automatic – the identity of child victims of sexual offence, or teachers who are alleged by pupils at the same school (or someone on their behalf) to have committed a criminal offence against them. In addition, reports of pre-trial hearings in the Crown Court cannot generally be published until the trial is over.

Discretionary reporting restrictions might be imposed to protect victims and witnesses (section 46 of the Youth and Criminal Evidence Act 1989). A witness is eligible for protection if the quality of their evidence or their cooperation with the preparation of a case is likely to be diminished by reason of fear or distress if they were to be publicly identified as a witness. Quality here refers to completeness, coherence and accuracy. When reporting restrictions are in place, they impose potential criminal liability on media organisations, journalists or editors who breach them and they face unlimited fines (section 85 of the Legal Aid, Sentencing and Punishment of Offenders Act 2012).

IV. Injunctions

Another way to protect EW clients is to seek an injunction preventing disclosure. A court's power to grant one is unlimited, and breaching it is contempt. Injunctions don't normally prevent the naming of the parties, but may prevent the disclosure of underlying facts. However, a super-injunction, a 'term unknown to [EW] law' until recently has now become 'well-known' (Neuberger 2011: 2.1). A super-injunction prevents publication of private or confidential information about a person and, more importantly (hence the term 'super-'), prevents publicising or informing others of the existence of the injunction and the proceedings to which it relates (ibid: 2.12). The super-injunction may also restrict access to court documents known (not entirely accurately) as 'sealing the court file' (ibid).

An anonymised injunction differs from the super-injunction, although the two are sometimes confused. It restrains a person from publishing confidential or private information where the names of either or both of the parties are not stated (ibid: 2.14). There's a perception that the use and application of super-injunctions has grown and there's an increasing frequency with which proceedings are being anonymised. A 'hyper-injunction' prohibits individuals from discussing the topic covered by a super-injunction with journalists, lawyers, or MPs (ibid: 6.19). They can discuss it with their lawyer. Finally, there's a privacy order where publicity would undermine the efficacy of the legal process (CPR 39.4). While the parties' identity and the proceeding's existence remain public, certain personal privacy or confidential information can remain private.

These injunctions take information relating to legal proceedings out of the 'court of public opinion'. Their purpose is *not* to protect the client – although that may be the reason to seek one – but to ensure the purpose of the proceedings is not frustrated pending trial. They're granted 'to facilitate the administration of justice at the trial' (*Snell's Equity* 2020; *Smith v Peters*: 513). That said, these orders are not easily obtained and usually involve matters such as blackmail rather than merely protecting confidential or personal information.

PART III

The Final Verdict

There comes a point when a man must refuse to answer to his leader
if he is also to answer to his own conscience.

— Sir Hartley Shawcross
(Chief Prosecutor, Nuremberg Trials, 4 December 1945)

17

The Ethical Compass

> Art, like morality, consists in drawing the line somewhere.
>
> GK Chesterton (1928)

This book began with a conundrum: 'Lawyers are generally unpopular ... but aren't they necessary for justice?' Its aims have been to get a better understanding of the nature – and complexity – of lawyers' professional responsibility, to put lawyers on trial and to invite you to decide: hired guns or heroes? So, it would be wrong of me to answer that question for you. But I will anyway! That's because it's a false dichotomy. Some lawyers are hired guns, some heroes, some both, and some neither!

No wonder this and other fundamental questions about lawyers, what they should and shouldn't do, what they must and mustn't do, have been debated, some would say *ad nauseam*. And they have. But that reinforces the point: the questions won't go away. They're important, complex and nuanced, and there can be honest – repeat honest – differences of opinion – as well as dishonest or at least not disinterested ones. That's why I proposed, in the first edition of this book, a modified conception of the lawyer's role.

I. A Modified Conception

I argued that it's essential the standard conception of lawyers' ethics should begin with the axiom, 'lawyer first; client second'. This isn't an endorsement of an 'oligarchy of lawyers' or a denial that lawyers are clients' agents who should act in their interests. It's an acknowledgment of reality: there already *is* an 'oligarchy of bodyguards'. Clients are not downgraded, loyalty is still required. Professional responsibility means lawyers can, and often should, act as 'amoral technicians'. But the power to protect clients' truths, construct a false reality and significantly influence the operation of law, the legal system and the administration of justice places *them* – lawyers – as principals, not agents, in terms of ethics.

But this second edition asks about hired guns and heroes and if it's a false dichotomy, have you wasted time reading hundreds of pages, only to be told the correct answer is 'yes'? Instead of responding (please), here's another question which only *you* can answer: 'has your better understanding of the (complex) role and (conflicting) responsibilities of lawyers and of the "tragic choices" they have to make [the aim of this book], improved your image of lawyers – or made it worse?' Let's sum up before your final verdict.

II. Lawyers' Ethics: An Oxymoron?

The ethical choices and scenarios reviewed in this book are, for lawyers, 'true dilemmas' (Greenebaum 1977: 628–29). It means: 'Practitioners are inevitably left with discretion, which requires a choice or judgement to be made' (Blake and Ashworth 2004: 187). Dilemmas are the result of a conflict – or potential conflict – between lawyers' duties to clients and to the legal system as officers of the court. Regulators acknowledge that: 'Virtually all difficult ethical problems arise from conflict between' these responsibilities (MR Preamble [9]). No wonder they will not – and should not – take disciplinary action 'when the lawyer chooses not to act or acts within the bounds of such discretion' (ibid: [14]).

That's why 'Lawyers' Ethics' really *is* an oxymoron, not because lawyers have no ethics, but because ethical codes 'institutionalise a basic conflict of rules' (Blake and Ashworth 2004: 169). The divided loyalty is real. So there's another, ethical, oxymoron: 'core duty'. There are several core duties, some of which conflict with the duty to clients.

A. Ethical Pluralism

Lawyers practise in a wide and diverse variety of settings. They perform a wide and diverse variety of roles too. The values and cultures pervading these contexts of legal practice reflect those of clients, the legal system and third parties – so much so that any expectation that all lawyers adhere to a single, standard conception of legal ethics is misconceived both empirically and theoretically (Schneyer 1984). Lawyers have 'multiple functions, and conflicting obligations, that cannot be resolved simply' (Zacharias 2008: 511). Lawyers can choose to be hired guns and/or heroes. 'Ethical pluralism' is playing out everywhere – in academia, in 'Bar Politics' and in the practice of law itself (Schneyer 1989). The ethical rules themselves reflect very different 'images' of lawyers, both good and bad (Zacharias 2007). So is there a framework for better understanding professional responsibilities and evaluating their performance? Perhaps.

B. First-Class Lawyering

A model of 'first-class lawyering' might help. It's based on several fundamental propositions. First, lawyers play a key role in protecting the law and institutions of society – or not! Secondly, lawyers' use (or non-use) of the 'tricks of the trade' illustrates the enormous potential power they possess. Thirdly, lawyer deference or blind loyalty – to the client, law, system or whatever – inappropriately outsources their power; it's an abdication of professional responsibility. Fourthly, exercising professional judgment/ discretion is inevitable in the practice of law. Finally, it means the critical ethical question is not 'hired guns or heroes?', but 'integrity or iniquity?'

III. Lawyers, Law and Society

The starting point is to acknowledge 'there is no such thing as a "client" without a legal system within which the words "lawyer" and "client" have meaning' and 'the lawyer is the client's "champion only within the realm"' of the legal system (Lawry 1990: 319, 320). The law (and access to it thorough lawyers) can give (and take away) power and rights. The importance of law is reinforced by the ideological rhetoric – and practical reality – of the 'Rule of Law'. That's why we also need to acknowledge the ideological and practical reality – and implications – of what might be called the 'Rule of Lawyers'. As Rhode (2000a: vii) put it: 'Attorneys play a central role in the structure of legal, economic, and political institutions. The principles that guide professional practice have crucial social consequences.'

IV. The Power of Tricks

The fundamental duty of lawyers is to achieve the lawful objectives of clients. In so doing, however, they wield power independently of the client. This power derives from the law and their freedom to choose whether – and how – to employ the tricks of the trade. Ewen Montagu QC described the deception tactics in 'Operation Mincemeat' as 'a crooked lawyer's dream of heaven' (Macintyre 2010: 95), but this book has shown tactics may or may not be 'crooked'. They may be 'good', 'bad' or 'ugly' and it's lawyers who have the exclusive responsibility to make – and justify – their choices.

A. Kurt Hughes: The Good

In 2004, Isaac Turnbaugh was accused of murdering a friend and co-worker. He allegedly confessed to friends, but denied the killing during police questioning. The FBI couldn't establish that Turnbaugh's rifle was the murder weapon and there was no motive for the crime. He pleaded not guilty, was represented by Hughes, and acquitted. Vermont Attorney General William Sorrell was 'surprised by the verdict'. He said: 'We had these admissions from him, but he had a very good lawyer who was able to raise reasonable doubt' (Lohr 2017). In 2011, Turnbaugh contacted the police, confessed and 'gave some details this time that were consistent with evidence in the case'. Whether or not this confession was true, the ancient rule of 'double jeopardy' prevented a re-trial with the new evidence being presented. (Exceptions to the rule were introduced in the EW Criminal Justice Act 2003.)

Few would doubt that Hughes was partly responsible for the outcome, but he was 'right' to act with integrity and deserved to be praised by Sorrell as a 'very good lawyer'. Hughes should be proud of what he did as a lawyer – despite the consequences. But this concept of 'responsibility' is the precondition *both* for awarding praise *and* attributing blame.

B. Andy Prince: The Bad

Shakespeare wrote 'Let's Kill All the Lawyers', but how about 'Let Lawyers Kill'? Prince gave ineffective legal assistance to Robert Wayne Holsey at his murder trial in Georgia in 1997. Prince, an alcoholic, consumed a quart of vodka every night of the trial. At the sentencing hearing, he failed to refer to the US Supreme Court's ban on executing intellectually disabled people. Holsey had an IQ of 70, a level of functioning equivalent to a nine year old. Significant mitigating evidence was also not presented to the jury which might have persuaded them to spare his life. An affidavit by one juror at the 1998 appeal stated: 'I was left to assume Mr Holsey was one of the "worst of the worst" in our society … even a small part of the wealth of information … would have made a difference' (Bookman 2014). Prince also admitted to the appeal court: 'I shouldn't have been representing anybody in any case' (Pilkington 2014). Holsey was executed in December 2014, an example perhaps of getting the death sentence not for the worst crime, but for the worst lawyer (Bright 1994).

C. John Marsden: The Ugly

Marsden was 'plagued by his decision' to represent Ivan Milat on rape charges in the 1970s. Milat subsequently killed seven Australian and international backpackers in the 1990s. Marsden said 'the backpackers might be alive today if Milat had not been acquitted' (McClymont and Miller 2006). Yet it wasn't *representing* Milat that led to his acquittal, but the *tactic* he credited it with – exploiting the prejudices of the jury. Recall what he said: he 'had no choice but to go down this path. I had to act *according to the ethics of the profession*' (Marsden 2004, emphasis added). That's what I dispute.

Lawyers have enormous responsibilities because *they* make 'tragic choices'. King Solomon had to make a judgment – whether to lie (bad) to produce justice (good), or not lie (good) and let the true mother lose her child (bad). Lawyers are the judge and jury in *their* domain, deciding whether and how to use 'tricks of the trade'. But, to return to the wartime metaphor, lawyers are a well-trained army wielding real power with cutting-edge weapons. Like Solomon, their choices influence and may even determine outcomes, good, bad or ugly.

V. Partisanship and Deference

It's not surprising lawyers feel 'partisan' and want genuinely to do their best for clients; they should. The 'partisan problem' though is *how* to be *both* partisan *and* offer candid, independent and *objective* advice? It's called 'partisanship's distorting influence' (Perlman 2015: 1640). Perlman questions the assumption that lawyers 'are capable of acting as partisans – representing one side of a matter – and actually *identifying* the line between permissible and impermissible behavior' (ibid: 1644). He suggests partisan lawyers may not be able to 'consistently and accurately locate that line'. But if lawyers have trouble locating the line, how can *we* tell if they've crossed it or not? Understanding *why* they might cross it is a starting point.

A. Crossing the Line

Crossing the ethical line is not inevitable, but Luban, writing from personal experience, warns prospective lawyers:

> if you think that you will not have any trouble practicing law ethically – you are wrong. Dead wrong. In fact, particularly if you go to work for a big firm, you will probably begin to practice law unethically in at least some respects within your first year or two in practice. (1999: 906)

Langevoort claimed that 'ethical apathy' can overtake a corporate lawyer's professional responsibilities. He suggested corporate lawyers are susceptible to the 'slippery slope': their awareness may slip, and small transgressions lead to newly defined baselines (2020: 1689). In addition, with a client-centred focus, they may be incentivised to rationalise their conduct, and downplay the existence and significance of ethical dilemmas. As each step is justified, turning back becomes harder.

It's as Primo Levi (1995), a Holocaust survivor, warned: 'Monsters exist, but they are too few in number to be truly dangerous. No: more dangerous are the common men, the functionaries ready to believe and to act without asking questions.' Arendt's (1963) study of Adolf Eichmann, perhaps the main Holocaust organiser, revealed he was 'neither a monster nor an ideologue' (Luban 2000: 104). She concluded that Eichmann became an organisation man, a careerist, a functionary who could 'never understand why doing a responsible job well might be regarded as a crime against humanity' (ibid). As a result, 'Eichmann's inability to think from another's point of view deprived him of the ability to think from his own point of view' (ibid), perhaps even the capacity to *have* a point of view of his own. Eichmann's superiors defined the situation he was in and so 'an average, "normal" person, neither feeble-minded nor indoctrinated nor cynical, could be *perfectly incapable of telling right from wrong*' (Arendt 1963: 26, quoted by Luban 2000: 104, emphasis added).

Most lawyers are also so busy, they 'are going to have to act almost instinctively' (Schlitz 1999: 911). As Economides points out, lawyers

> are so much absorbed in their day-to-day lives … with the business of communicating and applying rules, or handling disputes and whatever other managerial pressures govern modern professionals, that there really isn't time, space, energy or inclination for deep reflection on concepts such as justice. (Symposium 2008: 46)

Using the tricks of the trade – whether ethical or unethical – can become routine. Potential violations then are not recognised so steps cannot be taken to avoid them (Valdez 2011). This danger isn't because they're a 'bad' person, but because they believe they're a good lawyer performing a noble role: serving clients' interests and goals. Ethical dilemmas pervade the practice of law, but repeated exposure to them can produce a form of 'ethical numbing' or 'fading' (Tenbrunsel and Messick 2004: 228).

i. The Rainmaker

In the film of Grisham's *The Rainmaker* (1995), Leo Drummond is a lawyer who uses unscrupulous tactics to win cases. The 'hero', Rudy Baylor, asks Drummond: 'Do you remember when you sold out?' Drummond doesn't even *understand* the question.

However, another lawyer comes to realise that he had sold out. He explained: 'Clients expect some magic nothing less and I could probably give it to them if it didn't matter how I did it. And then one morning I'd wake up and find I'd become Leo Drummond.'

He went on:

> Every lawyer, at least once in every case, feels himself crossing a line he doesn't really mean to cross: it just happens. And if you cross it enough times, it disappears forever. And then you're nothing but another lawyer joke. Just another shark in the dirty water.

Like Watergate.

ii. Watergate

In 1972, the Democratic National Committee headquarters in Washington DC, the 'Watergate building', was broken into. It was one of many illegal activities which led to President Richard Nixon's resignation in 1974. When Nixon's lawyer, John Dean, drew up a list of people he thought had violated the law, his first reaction was 'there certainly are an awful lot of lawyers involved here' (Dean III 1973). He asked 'how in God's name could so many lawyers get involved in something like this?' Dean added together the names of other lawyers involved in illegal activities during the Nixon presidency; the total was 21 (Dean 2000: 611–12). Some were disciplined, some imprisoned. Watergate is

> the story of people who crossed the moral and legal line so easily and so quickly and so often that they hardly appreciated that they were doing so. They were, many of them, startled when they appreciated that they had broken the law and even resisted the idea that they had done so. They had completely lost their way. (Finkelstein 2019)

B. Blind Loyalty

One of Dean's 'thoughts on how so many lawyers got on the wrong side of the law during Watergate' (2000: 610) seems apposite. Some of the loyalty Nixon received from lawyers was 'blind loyalty … They never doubted the propriety of the activity because it was in the service of the President, or at his direct request' (ibid: 622).

i. Michael Cohen

Cohen was Donald Trump's personal lawyer from 2006 to 2018. At his sentencing hearing in 2018, after pleading guilty to several charges including campaign finance violations, he blamed his 'weakness and a blind loyalty' to Trump 'that led me to choose a path of darkness over light' (*NBC News* 2018). It appears that '[l]oyalty often drives corruption' (Hildreth et al 2016; see also Hildreth and Anderson 2018).

ii. Lemmings?

Dean stated, probably correctly: 'Lawyers are not known to be lemmings' (Dean 2000: 622). But blind loyalty, partisanship and deference put them at risk of becoming them.

So, how can the role of lawyers, 'as professionals', be distinguished 'from technicians who merely deliver the service clients pay for' (Boon 2015: 128)? Rhode (2000b: 213) believes:

> Individual clients' concerns are entitled to deference, but not to the exalted position they now occupy in the professional's moral universe. Lawyer's primary responsibility should be to the core values of honesty, fairness, and good faith that sustain it.

Hodes (2002, emphasis added) warns lawyers: 'Legal ethics is hard. You must try to find the line between what is permitted and what is not, and then get as close to that line as you can *without crossing over to the bad side.*' But Rhode also notes, her vision of professionalism 'is much easier to defend in principle than to realise in practice' (2000b: 213). If *lawyers* struggle to tell if they've crossed a line, how on earth can *we* locate it?

VI.   Ethical Discretion

Ethical codes emphasise the importance of independent professional judgment in representing clients (MR 2.1; BSB 2024 rC20). They reject the exclusively legalist, client-first and client-last approach. Before 2002, MR 1.2, Comment [1] stated that 'a lawyer is *not* required to … employ means simply because a client may wish that the lawyer do so' (emphasis added). MR 1.2, Comment [2] now states that if there is disagreement, the rules 'do not prescribe how [they] are to be resolved', it's up to lawyers and clients to work it out. However, the ABA Commission on Professionalism (ABA 1986: 30) was clearer: 'where the two conflict, the [lawyer's] duty to the system of justice must transcend the [lawyer's] duty to the client'.

The BSB (2024, rC20) also says lawyers must use their 'own professional judgment … [and] must do this *notwithstanding the views of your client*' (emphasis added). Barristers' duty to the court in the administration of justice overrides any inconsistent duty to act in the best interests of clients. In short, the advocate's professional judgment and independence may be 'more powerful than any duty to represent the client's wishes' (Blake and Ashworth 2004: 183).

A.   The Fox and the Hedgehog

Isaiah Berlin (1953) contrasted two kinds of thinker: the hedgehog and the fox. The hedgehog – like the zealous, amoral, legalist lawyer – has one big idea, and reduces the resolution of tragic choices by reference to this idea: 'if you may do, you must do'. It has the attraction of simplicity and universality and allows lawyers to proceed at full speed. Conflicting duties and moral concerns are filtered out and, if challenged, a process of cognitive dissonance provides confidence to justify the choice.

The fox, by contrast, is open to ideas, sees a broader context, and seeks further and better information. 'Overzealous representation' reduces the lawyer to thinking like a hedgehog. Indeed, overzealousness lawyers have little need to think at all! So, what *should* 'thinking like a lawyer' really mean?

B. Thinking Like a Lawyer

The answer is that lawyers must look beyond the law and clients to make their own professional choices.

i. A Rejection of Legalism

Exercising ethical discretion requires the rejection of 'legalism' – the ideology that legal rules alone determine what conduct should take place, or what limits should apply. This may not be easy because it's 'the operative outlook of the legal profession, both bench and bar' (Shklar 1964: 1). Legalist lawyers

> will fight to the death to defend legal rights against persuasive arguments based on expediency or the public interest or the public good … [The legalist lawyer] distrusts them … [and] believes, as part of his mental habits, that they are dangerous and too easily used as cloaks for arbitrary action. (ibid: 1–2)

But the law is not the be all and end all of everything – far from it. Nor should it be. As Martin Luther King Jr (1963) warned: 'Never forget that everything Hitler did in Germany was legal.' Not only that, but the development of 'equity' in common law systems was also founded on a rejection of legalism and the distinction between law and conscience.

ii. Equity, Conscience and Justice

The common law system, although 'very fully developed' by the early fifteenth century (Simpson 1988: 76), was 'defective' (ibid: 77) because it didn't necessarily achieve 'justice'. For example, common law courts didn't recognise trusts. If a person transferred landed property to two trusted friends with instructions to look after it for the benefit of his son – while the person was 'off to battle in Agincourt' – the courts took the view that since ownership had been transferred, the two friends had legal rights to the property. The remedy for the son lay with a petition to the Lord Chancellor, who could make a decree ordering the two friends to carry out the trust. He was not administering the law as such, but '*conscience*' (ibid: 78).

In the sixteenth century, a new theory was developing. The Chancellors were administering not conscience, but equity (ibid: 79). The idea, Simpson notes, derived from Aristotle who argued in *Nichomachean Ethics* that law is 'inevitably imperfect' in pursuit of justice. Law cannot formulate a general rule that can cope with all the circumstances which might arise. So, 'if justice is to be done we need not just rules, but a power to depart from them when they produce unjust results' (ibid: 79–80). This 'power, not itself governed by any rule, to depart from the rule' was called equity (ibid: 80).

Simpson notes the activities of the 'equity' court, the Court of Chancery, appeared to be in conflict with the common law. The conflict, however, was 'settled, after some controversy, that equity prevailed over law, and this rule is now statutory'. In 1876, the institutional distinction between law and equity was abolished. The 'orthodox theory' is there's no conflict, but the law 'shall be modified so as to achieve the end of law, which is justice'.

This history undermines strict adherence to legalism. Lawyers are in danger of reifying law just as common law courts had done, sometimes at the expense of justice. But we've seen in Part II an everyday reality in legal practice: lawyers have discretion to make choices; they have to exercise professional judgment. To depart from a rule, therefore, isn't necessarily a violation. Allowing ethical discretion to prevail over a rule or law reflects the development of the common law system. MR 2.1 acknowledges that while lawyers, in representing clients, 'shall exercise independent professional judgment and render candid advice', they 'may refer not only to law but to other considerations such as moral, economic, social and political factors, that may be relevant to the client's situation'. This is because 'moral and ethical considerations impinge on most legal questions and may decisively influence how the law will be applied' (MR 2.1, Comment [2]). It's also because: 'Rules do not ... exhaust the moral and ethical considerations that should inform a lawyer, for no worthwhile human activity can be completely defined by legal rules' (MR Preamble [16]). There are therefore few, if any, constraints on the exercise of discretion, and lawyers have many professional options available.

VII. Integrity or Iniquity?

'[A]n enduring feature of professional codes of conduct' (*Wingate*: 62, Rupert Jackson LJ) is that professionals should adhere to higher standards than the general norms of society. This is a justification for the principle of self-regulation. It means lawyers must not only avoid acting dishonestly, but 'should discharge their professional duties with integrity, probity and complete trustworthiness' (*Bolton*: 518A–D, Sir Thomas Bingham). Lord Thomas of Cwmgiedd explained the reasons in the context of a lawyer misleading the court:

> our system for the administration of justice relies so heavily upon the *integrity* of the profession and the full discharge of the profession's duties and in part because the privilege of conducting litigation or appearing in court is granted on terms that the rules are observed *not merely in their letter but in their spirit*. Indeed, the reputation of the system of the administration of justice in England and Wales and the standing of the profession depends particularly upon the discharge of the duties owed to the court. (*Brett*: 111, emphasis added)

While dishonesty is the most serious lapse, falling 'below the required standards of integrity, probity and trustworthiness ... remains very serious indeed in a member of a profession whose reputation depends on trust' (*Bolton*: 518A–D). Solicitors' and barristers' codes both name 'integrity' as a core principle and duty (SRA 2019d: 5; BSB 2024: CD3). It's 'one of the fundamental tenets of ethical behaviour' (SRA 2019d: Introduction).

Integrity is a 'broader' and 'more nebulous concept than honesty ... [and] less easy to define' (*Wingate*: 95–96). It's 'a useful shorthand to express the higher standards which society expects from professional persons and which the professions expect from their own members' (ibid: 97). The duty doesn't require lawyers to be 'paragons of virtue' (ibid: 102). But: 'In every instance, professional integrity is linked to the manner in which that particular profession professes to serve the public' (ibid).

As Sir Brian Leveson put it: 'Professional standards … rightly impose on those who aspire to them a higher obligation to demonstrate integrity in all of their work' (*Williams*: 130).

The SRA (2018: 3, 5) acknowledges that the need to effectively balance all their duties – to clients, the court, third parties and to the public interest – depends on the facts of each case. But it also states solicitors' 'best guides' in maintaining the balance 'are their integrity and independence' (ibid: 17). The question, however, is how can 'integrity' be operationalised and put into practice? As Lord Justice Rupert Jackson says, 'it is a counsel of despair to say: "Well you can always recognise it, but you can never describe it"' (*Wingate*: 98). That's why there may be honest differences of opinion about what is the 'right' choice, and why a lawyer must apply *their* ethical discretion.

The proper yardstick to assess how lawyers represent clients is how they behave, not as 'partisan advocates' but as 'professional representatives' (Kentridge 2003). Some lawyers may think because they're 'obliged to follow the instructions of their client [they] bear no moral or other responsibility for the outcome' (Moorhead 2021b). But Dr Johnson was right: 'a lawyer is to do for his client all that his client might *fairly* do for himself, if he could' (*Three Rivers*: 114, emphasis added). In short,

> the arms which an advocate wields he ought to use as a warrior, not as an assassin. He ought to uphold the interests of his clients *per fas* [by fair means] not *per nefas* [unfair means]. He ought to know how to reconcile the interests of his clients with the eternal interests of truth and justice. (Lord Chief Justice Alexander Cockburn, quoted in *The Times*, 9 November 1864)

The emphasis though, is on the word that identifies the lawyer's *professional* responsibility: 'fairly' (or *per fas*). That requires thought and reflection.

A.   The Application of Ethical Discretion

In Florida in July 2012, lifeguards were subject to a rule designed to prevent potential liability: they shouldn't leave the marked beach zone without waiting for a supervisor to cover their station. A lifeguard saw a person in difficulties in the sea outside the marked zone, there was no supervisor to cover, but there was another lifeguard present. Their choice was to save the person and break the rule or … who knows? The lifeguard decided to rescue the person – and was fired for doing so.

Should a lifeguard break a 'small' rule – the risk of liability was low – to follow a big 'rule' – saving swimmers in danger of drowning? Should the reason they were employed – the legal liability, not 'altruism' – make a difference? The lifeguard thought not: 'I wasn't going to choose my job over someone in danger. My job is to help people in distress. It was a moronic rule … I understand the liability issues, but …' (Alvarez 2012).

There was a public outcry; the lifeguard was offered his job back. He refused and three other lifeguards quit in protest. All said they would've made the same choice. But what's the 'correct' answer? Some – legalists – might believe the potential legal liability means the lifeguard should follow the rule; others' instincts might tell them in this scenario the rule shouldn't be followed. The fact that 'there is no final or objective answer to ethical problems' doesn't mean 'there are no answers' (Hutchinson 1998: 176). It means lawyers have to find them.

There's another way rules can be drafted that might help even the legalist lawyer. An EW coastguard rescue crew decided to rescue a teenage girl swept out to sea by strong currents. They did so despite being ordered not to launch the rescue boat because of safety concerns over the hull. They broke the order and literal rule and were disciplined by the Maritime and Coastguard Agency. However, Rule 2B of the International Maritime Organisation Regulations states: 'In construing and complying with these Rules due regard shall be had to … any special circumstances … which may make a departure from these Rules necessary …'.

Note the word 'departure' rather than 'break' or 'breach'. Another example is section 393 of the UK Companies Act, an overriding requirement of which is that accounts should give a 'true and fair view' of a company's financial performance. Normally, companies present a true and fair view by following accounting standards for measurement, presentation and disclosure. The 'override', however, envisages directors *departing* from provisions if in special circumstances compliance with those standards is inconsistent with a true and fair view. This is a *legal* requirement: 'where directors and auditors do not believe that following a particular accounting policy will give a true and fair view, they are legally required to adopt a more appropriate policy, *even if this requires a departure from a particular standard*' (ACCA 2014, emphasis added). The critical point is that applying the true and fair override 'relies heavily on professional judgement' (Ho 2017) – like lifeguards and 'bodyguards of lies'.

VIII. The Verdict?

The word 'ethics' is 'derived from the Greek *ethike*, which was used to denote the science of character' (Hutchinson 1998). This was not 'solely or even mainly a matter of rule forming, but involved the development of a personal faculty of good judgment' (ibid: 4). We've seen how professional codes assume lawyers can apply rules 'wisely and appropriately. This is the idea of professionalism' (ibid). Hutchinson's definition of professionalism is 'an approach or attitude that embodies a justification for a particular course of conduct within a wider account of a morally defensible *modus vivendi*'. In other words, when there's a tragic choice to be made, or an ethical dilemma to be resolved, lawyers are able to make a feasible or practical compromise. But Hutchinson also emphasises that it's the lawyer's individual responsibility, as does the MR (Preamble [7]): 'a lawyer is guided by personal conscience and the approbation of professional peers' – hence the need for a 'context-sensitive sense of applied judgment' (Luban and Milleman 1995).

Making 'tragic choices' isn't easy: the

> obvious virtue of ethical principles is often belied by the complexity of practical situations; obligation and duty are not on/off concepts, but vary in weight and force depending on the context. Moreover, 'doing the right thing' will not always be apparent or persuasive to others. (Hutchinson 1998: 173)

Hutchinson rejects the standard conception of the lawyers' ethics and the 'legalistic mentality': 'To read most codes of professional conduct is to encounter a series of pronouncements that are long on righteous assumptions and vague generalities, but short on serious instruction and concrete guidance' (ibid: 174) Instead, 'what counts as acting ethically will always be a contextual question'. To the claim that this leads to irrational or arbitrary decision-making, Hutchinson responds that what operates as reason 'is never outside of its informing context'. Even if the ethical rules permit certain conduct, lawyers still have a choice whether to do it.

A.   The Ethical Trick of the Trade

There's another false dichotomy though: debating whether lawyers should be *either* hired guns – clients' mercenaries – *or* moral imperialists – deciding for themselves what's right and just. Instead, there's an alternative conception which acknowledges what we've seen in this book: law is uncertain, ethical rules conflict and lawyers' loyalties are divided. So the 'ethical "trick"' of the trade is exercising 'professional conscience' (Zacharias and Green 2005), not personal conscience, and not deferring their decision-making. Ethical 'compliance' by lawyers is 'the obedience … to that which [they] cannot be forced to obey. [They] are the enforcer of the law upon [themselves]' (Moulton 1924). Making tragic choices means lawyers having to 'judge between competing priorities when none are wholly satisfactory' and then having 'the courage to act consistently with the judgment' (Evans 2011: 72). Isn't *that* how we should evaluate whether lawyers have been professionally responsible and 'ethical'?

Let's leave the final words – fictional but wise – to the Law School Dean congratulating law students on graduation day (Queens Counsel cartoon, 29 June 1999):

> Three years ago, when asked a legal question, you could answer in all honesty: 'I don't know'.
>
> Now you can say with all the authority you can muster … 'It Depends!'

When lawyers confront ethical questions, the honest answer is: 'it depends on you!' That's *my* final verdict. What's *yours*?

REFERENCES

ABA (1908) *Canons of Professional Ethics*
—— (1971) *Project on Standards for Criminal Justice: Standards Relating to the Prosecution Function and the Defense Function*
—— (1979) *Model Code of Professional Responsibility*
—— (1986) *In the Spirit of Public Service* (Chicago, ABA Commission on Professionalism)
—— (1993) *Standards for Criminal Justice* (3rd edn)
—— (2002) Task Force on Corporate Responsibility, Preliminary Report (2002), reprinted in 58 *Business Law* 189
—— (2005) *Committee on Ethics and Professional Responsibility*, Formal Opinion 437
—— (2017) *Criminal Justice Standards for the Defense Function* (4th edn, 2017)
—— (2019) *Model Rules of Professional Conduct*
—— (2023) 'The Ethics of Witness Preparation' *Formal Opinion 508*
Abel RL (1979) 'Socializing the Legal Profession: Can Redistributing Lawyers' Services Achieve Social Justice?' 1 *Law and Policy* 5
—— (1989) *American Lawyers* (Oxford, Oxford University Press)
—— (1995a) *Revisioning Lawyers*, in Abel and Lewis (1995)
—— (1995b) *Politics by Other Means: Law in the Struggle against Apartheid 1980–1994* (London, Routledge)
—— (ed) (1997) *Lawyers: A Critical Reader* (New York, The New Press)
—— (2011) *Lawyers on Trial: Understanding Ethical Misconduct* (Oxford, Oxford University Press)
—— (2024a) *How Autocrats Seek Power* (Abingdon, Routledge)
—— (2024b) *How Autocrats Abuse Power* (Abingdon, Routledge)
—— (2024c) *How Autocrats Attack Expertise* (Abingdon, Routledge)
Abel RL and Lewis PSC (eds) (1995) *Lawyers in Society: An Overview* (Berkeley, University of California Press)
ACCA (2014) True and Fair Statement Published by the FRC
Ackerman S (2010) 'Mystery Merc Group Is Blackwater's 34th Front Company' *Wired*, 4 October
Adams J and Butterfield LH (eds) (1962) *Diary and Autobiography of John Adams*, vol 2 (Cambridge, MA, Harvard University Press)
Adler E (2016) 'Obituary: Kenneth Fitzpatrick, Judge Who Ruled in Landmark Cigarette Industry Case, Dies at 80' *Star Tribune*, 8 October
Agnew T and Hodge M (2023) 'We Must Hit Back against Oligarchs' *The Times*, 7 February
Alexander R (1991) 'The Art of Advocacy' *Journal of the New South Wales Bar Association Bar News*, Summer, 9
Alibrandi T with Armani FH (1984) *Privileged Information* (New York, Dodd, Mead)
Allen-Mills T (2011) 'Justice Sees off the Net's Howling Lynch Mob' *Sunday Times*, 10 July
Alper T, Amsterdam AG, Edelman TE, Hertz R, Janger RS, McAllister-Nevins J, Rudenstine and Walker-Sterling R (2005) 'Stories Told and Untold: Lawyering Theory Analyses of the First Rodney King Assault Trial' 12 *Clinical LRev* 1
Alschuler AW (1975) 'The Defense Attorney's Role in Plea Bargaining' 84 *Yale LJ* 179
Alvarez L (2012) 'Lifeguard Says He Chose Saving Man over Saving Job' *New York Times*, 5 July
American Council on Science and Health (2000) *Bridging the Ideological Divide: An Analysis of Views on Tobacco Policy across the Political Spectrum* (New York, American Council on Science and Health)
American University (nd) fs2.american.edu/dfagel/www/BushellsCase_Case%20of%20William%20Penn%20and%20William%20Mead%20(1670).pdf

Ames J (2018) 'Ditched Asian lawyer Had Been Stripped of Six Cases' *The Times*, 10 November

—— (2019) 'Driver Who Shot Crash Video on His Phone Saved by Loophole' *The Times*, 6 April

—— (2020) 'Rape Victims to Pre-record Trial Evidence' *The Times*, 26 October

—— (2021) 'Weinstein Victim's Fury at Solicitors' Watchdog' *The Times*, 25 January

—— (2023) 'Abuse Trial Juries "Need Mental Health Support"' *The Times*, 18 October

—— (2024) 'Watchdog Investigates More Than 20 Law Firms in Post Office Scandal' *The Times*, 21 June

Ames J and Baksi C (2021) 'Weinstein Victim's Fury at Solicitors' Watchdog' *The Times*, 25 January

Ames J and Ellery B (2024) 'Calls for Whistleblower Payment' *The Times*, 22 February

Amsterdam AG, Hertz R and Walker-Sterling R (2005) 'Introduction' in Alper et al (2005)

Anderson MJ (2002) 'From Chastity Requirement to Sexual License: Sexual Consent and a New Rape Shield Law' 70 *George Washington LRev* 51

—— (2004) 'Time to Reform Rape Shield Laws' 19 *Criminal Justice* 14

Andrews CR (2009) 'The Lawyer's Oath: Both Ancient and Modern' 22 *GJLE* 3

Angelone DJ, Cantor N, Marcantonio T and Joppa M (2020) 'Does Sexism Mediate the Gender and Rape Myth Acceptance Relationship?' 27 *Violence against Women* 748

Anwar S, Bayer P and Hjalmarsson R (2012) 'The Impact of Jury Race on Criminal Trials' 127 *Quarterly Journal of Economics* 1017

Applegate JS (1989) 'Witness Preparation' 68 *Texas LRev* 277

Arendt H (1963) *Eichmann in Jerusalem: A Report on the Banality of Evil* (New York, Viking, 1963)

Aristotle, 'The Epilogue' in Cooper L (ed) (1932) *The Rhetoric of Aristotle 3* (New York, D Appleton & Co)

Asimow A (2004) 'Popular Culture and the American Adversarial Ideology' in Freeman M (ed), *Law and Popular Culture, Current Legal Issues* (Oxford, Oxford University Press)

Asimow M (2007) 'Popular Culture and the Adversary System' 40 *Loyola LRev* 653

Asimow M and Weisberg R (2009) 'When the Lawyer Knows the Client is Guilty: Client Confessions in Legal Ethics, Popular Culture, and Literature' 18 *Southern California Interdisciplinary LJ* 229

Association of Chartered Certified Accountants (2014) *True and Fair Statement Published by the FRC* (June)

Atkinson JM (1979) 'Sequencing and Shared Attentiveness to Court Proceedings' in Psathas G (ed) *Everyday Language: Studies in Ethnomethodology* (New York, Irvington Publishers)

—— (1984) *Our Masters' Voices: The Language and Body Language of Politics* (London, Methuen)

—— (1992) 'Displaying Neutrality: Formal Aspects of Informal Court Proceedings' in Drew P and Heritage J (eds), *In Talk at Work: Interaction in Institutional Settings* Cambridge, Cambridge University Press)

—— (2004) *Lend Me Your Ears* (London, Vermilion)

Atkinson JM and Drew P (1979) *Order in Court: The Organisation of Verbal Interaction in Judicial Settings* (Oxford, Macmillan)

Bailey FL with Aronson H (1971) *The Defense Never Rests: The Art of Cross-Examination* (Ann Arbor, University of Michigan Press)

Bajwa AN (2011) 'Trial by Ordeal' *Counsel*, 31 August

Baksi C (2021) 'Has the Wig Finally Had its Day?' *The Times*, 22 April

—— (2023a) 'Should Lawyers Work on Fossil Fuel Projects?' *The Times*, 25 May

—— (2023b) 'Cab Rank Rule "Should Be Scrapped"' *The Times*, 6 April

—— (2024) 'We Must Stand with Iran Lawyers' *The Times*, 1 February

Ball T (2021) 'Record £90m Fine for Dumping Sewage' *The Times*, 10 July

Bannerman L (2011a) '"No Evidence" That Bellfield Killed Milly' *The Times*, 21 June

—— (2011b) 'Day after Harrowing Day, This Has Been Truly Awful for Us' *The Times*, 25 June

Bar Council (1997) *Written Standards for the Conduct of Professional Work*

—— (2024) *Money Laundering and Terrorist Financing*

Barnhizer DR (2015) 'The Moral Lawyer and the Machiavellian Nature of Law Practice' *Cleveland State University Research Paper 15-288*

Bartleby (nd) www.bartleby.com/73/953.html

Bartlett R (1986) *Trial by Fire and Water: The Medieval Judicial Ordeal* (Oxford, Clarendon Press)

Bassetti V (2018) 'The Curious History of "What Did the President Know and When Did He Know it?"' Brennan Center for Justice

Basu T (2014) 'Timeline: A History of GM's Ignition Switch Defect' *NPR*, www.npr.org/2014/03/31/297158876

Bauer J (2008) 'Buying Witness Silence: Evidence-Suppressing Settlements and Lawyers' Ethics' 87 *Oregon LRev* 481

BBC (2019) 'Dutch Gangster Case: Shock at Murder of Lawyer Derk Wiersum' 18 September

BBC News (2017) 'Thames Water Fined £20m for Sewage Spill', 22 March

—— (2023) 'Thames Water Fined £3.3m over River Sewage', 4 July

Bedejo B (2021) 'An Advocate is Never Too Experienced to Work on Their Technique' *The Bar Council*, guest blog, 11 February

Beioley K (2022) 'Slapp-Happy Law Firms Come under Pressure from Regulator' *Financial Times*, 2 December

Bellow G and Moulton B (1981) *The Lawyering Process: Ethics and Professional Responsibility* (Mineola, Foundation Press)

Beloff M (2017) 'The Bar and the Way We Were' *The Times*, 21 December

Bentham J (1843) *The Works of Jeremy Bentham* (London, Simpkin Marshall, published under the superintendence of his executor John Bowring, vol 10)

Bentham M (2024) 'Rape Victims' Pre-recorded Evidence "Very Problematic" and Impacts "Guilty Verdicts" Top Judge Tells MPs' *Evening Standard*, 17 January

Berg D (1987) 'Preparing Witnesses' 13(2) *Litigation*

Berle AA (1933) 'The Legal Profession and Legal Education' *Encyclopedia of Social Sciences* vol 9

Berlin I (1953) *The Hedgehog and the Fox: An Essay on Tolstoy's View of History* (New York, Simon & Schuster)

Bernabe A (2017) 'Through the Looking Glass in Indiana: Mandatory Reporting of Child Abuse and the Duty of Confidentiality' 92 *Notre Dame LRev Online* 22

Bessette JM (2021) 'A Critique of the Eastman Memos' *Claremont Review of Books*

Biederman C, Korosec T, Lyons J and Williams P (1998) 'Toxic Justice' *Dallas Observer*, 13 August

Bierce A (1906) *The Cynic's Word Book* (London, AF Bird)

Bingham T (2011) *The Rule of Law* (London, Penguin)

Blackstone D (2006) 'A Criminal Defence Attorney in a Murder Case Defines His Position' 4 *New York State Bar Association Criminal Law Newsletter*

Blackstone W (1769) 4 *Commentaries on the Laws of England* (Oxford, Clarendon Press)

Blake M (2011) 'Villified QC in Bellfield Case "Just Doing His Job"' *The Independent*, 27 June

Blake M and Ashworth A (2004) 'Ethics and the Criminal Defence Lawyer' 7 *Legal Ethics* 168

Blakely R (2014) 'Landmark $3m Payout for Family Made Ill by Fracking' *The Times*, 29 April

Blank J and Jensen E (2005) *Living Justice: Love, Freedom, and the Making of the Exonerated* (New York, Atria Books)

Blasi GL (1995) 'What Lawyers Know: Lawyering Expertise, Cognitive Science and the Functions of Theory' 45 *Journal of Legal Education* 313

Blauw S (2020) *The Number Bias* (London, Sceptre)

Blum P (2021) 'By Memo or by Mob, Trump and His Team Positioned the Country for Chaos' *Washington Post*, 21 September

Bond Solon (2014) *Annual Expert Witness Survey* (London, Bond Solon)

Borg-Bathet J, Lobina B and Zabrocka M (2021) *The Use of SLAPPs to Silence Journalists, NGOs and Civil Society* (European Parliament's Committee on Legal Affairs)

Bok S (1979) *Lying: Moral Choice in Public and Private Life* (New York, Pantheon Books)

—— (1983) *Secrets: On the Ethics of Concealment and Revelation* (New York, Pantheon Books)

Bolt R (1960) *A Man for All Seasons* (London, Heinemann Educational Books)

Bookman M (2014) '10 Ways to Blow a Death Penalty Case' *Mother Jones*, 22 April

Boon A (1999) *The Ethics and Conduct of Lawyers in England and Wales* (Oxford, Hart Publishing, 1st edn)

—— (2014) *The Ethics and Conduct of Lawyers in England and Wales* (Oxford, Hart Publishing, 3rd edn)

—— (2015) *Lawyers' Ethics and Professional Responsibility* (Oxford, Hart Publishing)

—— (2023) *The Ethics and Conduct of Lawyers in England and Wales* (Oxford, Hart Publishing, 4th edn)

Boon A and Levin J (1999) *The Ethics and Conduct of Lawyers in England and Wales* (Oxford, Hart Publishing)

—— (2008) *The Ethics and Conduct of Lawyers in England and Wales* (Oxford, Hart Publishing, 2nd edn)

Bornstein BH, Miller MK, Nemeth RJ, Page GL, Musil S (2005) 'Juror Reactions to Jury Duty: Perceptions of the System and Potential Stressor' 23 *Behavioral Sciences and the Law* 321

Botsford P (2018) 'Awkward! Allen & Overy Partner Stumbles in Face of Grilling by MPs over Non-disclosure Agreements' *Legal Cheek*, 28 March

Bowker AE (1949) *Memoirs: Behind the Bar* (London, Staples Press)

Boyd C (1998) 'Black's Magic', www.Royblack.com/files/news/general?Blacks_Magic_UM_Spring_1988.pdf

Boyd W (2010) 'Operation Mincemeat by Ben Macintyre' *The Times*, 16 January

Brattleboro Reformer (2007) 'Failed Sting against Lawyer Draws Protests', 26 February

Brewer N and Burke A (2002) 'Effects of Testimonial Inconsistencies and Eyewitness Confidence on Mock-Juror Judgments' 26 *Law and Human Behavior* 353

Brickman L (1992) 'The Asbestos Litigation Crisis: Is There a Need for an Administrative Alternative?' 13 *Cardozo LRev* 1819

—— (2002) 'Asbestos Litigation: Malignancy in the Courts?' 40 *Civil Justice Forum* 1

Bright SB (1994) 'Counsel for the Poor: The Death Sentence Not for the Worst Crime But for the Worst Lawyer' 103 *Yale LJ* 1835

Brill S (1979) *Esquire* 23–24 (19 December)

Brodeur P (1985) *Outrageous Misconduct: The Asbestos Industry on Trial* (New York, Pantheon)

Broggan S (2006) 'Call Him Mr Loophole' *The Guardian*, 27 January

Brougham H (Lord) (1871) *The Life and Times of Henry Lord Brougham Written by Himself, Vol II* (New York, Harper and Brothers Publishing)

Brown D (2023) 'Lottery Winner's Husband Jailed for Attacking Lawyers' *The Times*, 23 September

Brown LT (2004) '"May it Please the Camera … I mean the Court": An Intrajudicial Solution to an Extra-judicial Problem' 39 *Georgia LRev* 83

Brudney J and Leib EJ (2023) 'Any' 49 *Brigham Young University LRev* 2

Bryden DP and Lengnick S (1996–97) 'Rape in the Criminal Justice System' 87 *Journal of Criminal Law and Criminology* 1194

BSB (2014) *Handbook*

—— (2024) *Handbook, Version 4.8, Code of Conduct*, 21 May

Buffington MH (2018) *A Conspiracy of Silence: The Murder of Solicitor-General Floyd Hoard* (Scotts Valley, CreateSpace Publishing)

Burger W (1971) 'Address to the American Law Institute' 52 *Federal Rules Decision* 211

Burgess, K (2021) 'Justin Welby Demands Ban on NDAs in Church of England after Racist Abuse Exposed' *The Times*, 21 April

Burleigh D (1989) 'John Francis Bridgwood and Solicitors Duty to Client and Court' 26 *Law Society Gazette* 86

Burnside J (nd) 'R v AA Rouse', copy on file with the author

Callahan MS and Pitkow HC (1980) 'The Propriety of the Attorneys' Actions in the Lake Pleasant Case' in A Gerson (ed) *Lawyers' Ethics* (Piscataway, NJ, Transaction Books)

Cameron C (2002) 'Hired Guns and Smoking Guns: McCabe v British American Tobacco Australia Ltd' 25 *University of New South Wales LJ* 768

Cameron JD (1981) 'The English Barrister System and the American Criminal Law: A Proposal for Experimentation' 23 *Arizona LRev* 991

Cannings A (2006) *Against All Odds: A Mother's Fight to Prove Her Innocence* (London, Time Warner)

Capra DJ (2007) 'Symposium, Ethics and Evidence, Introduction' 76 *Fordham LRev* 1225

Carlson J and Yeomans N (1975) 'Whither Goeth the Law – Humanity or Barbarity?' in Smith and Crossley

Carroll L (1871) *Through the Looking-Glass* (Oxford, Macmillan)

Cavallaro R (1997) Associate Professor of Legal Ethics, Suffolk Law School, quoted in *The Boston Globe*, 28 December

Cave Brown A (1975) *Bodyguard of Lies* (London, WH Allen)

CBS (2019) 'Inside the Mind of Eric Williams: "One of the Most Notorious Texas Killers"', www.cbsnews.com/texas/news/inside-mind-eric-williams-notorious-texas-killers

—— (2023) *60 Minutes*, 5 November

Centre for Ethics and Law (2018) *Ethics and NDAs* (London, University College London)

Chambliss E and Wilkins DB (2003) 'A New Framework for Law Firm Discipline' 16 *GJLE* 335

Channel 5 (UK) (2020) *Trial in the Outback*, 8 and 9 December

Chao V (2021) 'Hyperlexis and the Rule of Law' 27 *Legal Theory* 126

Charter D (2021) 'Believe Your Eyes, Floyd Jurors Told as Trial Concludes' *The Times*, 20 April

Cheney K (2023) 'He Devised a Fringe Legal Theory to Try to Keep Trump in Power: Now He's on the Verge of Being Disbarred' *Politico*, 6 November

Cherry R (1985) 'Chronicle of a Scandal' *New York Times*, 22 September

Chesterton GK (1928) 'Our Note Book' *Illustrated London News*, 5 May

Churchill WS (1956) *A History of the English-Speaking Peoples* (New York, Dodd, Mead & Company)

Cimini CN (2008) 'Ask, Don't Tell: Ethical Issues Surrounding Undocumented Workers' Status in Employment Litigation' 61 *Stanford LRev* 355

Ciresi MV, Walburn RB and Sutton TD (1999) 'Decades of Deceit: Document Discovery in the Minnesota Tobacco Litigation' 25 *William Mitchell LRev* 477

Clark B (1978) *Whose Life is it Anyway?* (Charlbury, Amber Lane Press)

Clark K and Moore NJ (2015) 'Financial Rewards for Whistleblowing Lawyers' 56 *Boston College LRev* 1697

Class Action Reporter (2000) 1 May, vol 2, no 83

Clatworthy B (2017) 'Engineer Wins $1 Million for Exposing Ship's Pollution' *The Times*, 25 April

Clegg W (2018) *Under the Wig: A Lawyer's Stories of Murder, Guilt and Innocence* (Kingston, Canbury Press)

Clemens RB (2008) 'Voir Dire in Civil Cases' *Trials & Tribulations* Fall

Cloud J (2011) 'How the Casey Anthony Murder Trial Became the Social-Media Trial of the Century' *Time*, 16 June

Cochran J and Fisher D (2002) *A Lawyer's Life* (New York, Thomas Dunne Books/St Martin's Press)

Cochran RF Jr and Collett TS (1996) *Cases and Materials on the Rules of the Legal Profession* (St Paul, West Publishing Company)

Code of Practice for Victims of Crime in England and Wales (2024) (London, HMSO)

Cohen M (2023) 'Former Trump Campaign Lawyer Jenna Ellis Pleads Guilty in Georgia Case' *CNN*, 24 October

Cohn A and Chisholm J (1934) *Take the Witness* (New York, Frederick A Stoles Co)

Coleman L and Kay P (1981) 'Prototype Semantics: The English Word *Lie*' 57(1) *Language* 26

Comaroff JL (2023) 'Preface' in Martins CZ, Martins VTZ and Valim R (eds) *Lawfare: Waging War through Law* (Abingdon, Routledge)

Conley M (2011) 'Public Irate over Casey Anthony Verdict; Social Media Sites Explode With Opinions' *ABC News*, 5 July

Conn D (1996) 'Counselling for Counsel' *The Times*, 2 January

Conway G, Luttig M and Comstock B (2023) 'The Trump Threat is Growing: Lawyers Must Rise to Meet This Moment' *New York Times*, 21 November

Corbin A (1923) 'Hard Cases Make Good Law' 33 *Yale LJ* 78

Corker D and Levi M (1996) 'Pre-trial Publicity and its Treatment in the English Courts'

Coulthard M and Johnson A (2008) *An Introduction to Forensic Linguistics: Language in Evidence* (Abingdon, Routledge)

CPS (1977) *The Turnbull Guidelines, based on R v Turnbull [1977] QB 224*

—— (2018a) *Contempt of Court, Reporting Restrictions and Restrictions on Public Access to Hearings*, 11 May

—— (2018b) *Non-accidental Head Injury Cases – Prosecution Approach*, 21 June

—— (2018c) *Jury Vetting: Legal Guidance*

—— (2019) *Expert Evidence*, updated 9 October

—— (2022) *Prosecution Guidance*

Cramton RC (1978) 'The Ordinary Religion of the Law School Classroom' 29 *Journal of Legal Education* 247

—— (2005) '*Spaulding v Zimmerman*: Confidentiality and its Exceptions' in Rhode and Luban (eds) (2005)

Cramton RC and Knowles LP (1998) 'Professional Secrecy and its Exceptions: *Spaulding v Zimmerman* Revisited' 83 *Minnesota LRev* 63

Craver CB ((2010) 'Negotiation Ethics for Real World Interactions' 25 *Ohio State Journal on Dispute Resolution* 299

—— (1997) 'Negotiation Ethics: How to Be Deceptive without Being Dishonest/How to Be Assertive without Being Offensive' 38 *South Texas LRev* 713

Cross M (2024) 'Government Backs SLAPPs Legislation' *Law Society Gazette*, 23 February

Cross R (1973) 'The Lawyer and Justice', Presidential Address to the Holdsworth Club, University of Birmingham

—— (1976) *Statutory Interpretation* (London, Butterworths)

Cummings SL (2024) 'Lawyers in Backsliding Democracy' 112 *California LRev* 101

Curtis CP (1951) 'The Ethics of Advocacy' 4 *Stanford LRev* 3

Daly MC and Goebbel R (eds) (1995) *Rights, Liability and Ethics in International Legal Practice* (Amsterdam, Kluwer)

Dare T (2001) 'Lawyers, Ethics and *To Kill a Mockingbird*' 25 *Philosophy and Literature* 127

—— (2004) 'Mere-Zeal, Hyper-zeal and the Ethical Obligation of Lawyers' 7 *Legal Ethics* 24

Dathan M (2023) 'Professional Migration Cheats Risk Life in Jail' *The Times*, 8 August

—— (2024) 'Priest "was Told to Make up Evidence for Asylum Claims"' *The Times*, 13 March

Davey M (2007) 'Kevorkian Speaks after His Release from Prison' *New York Times*, 4 June

Davidson D (1996) 'The Folly of Trying to Define Truth' 93 *Journal of Philosophy* 263

Dean JW III (1973) 3 Hearings before the Senate Select Comm on Watergate (93d Cong 1053–54)

—— (2000) 'Watergate: What was it?' *51 Hastings LJ* 609

Dean M (2018) 'Contracts of Silence' *Columbia Journalism Review* Winter

DeMott D (1998) 'The Lawyer as Agent' 67 *Fordham LRev* 301

Department for Business, Energy & Industrial Strategy (2019) *Confidentiality Clauses: Response to the Government Consultation on Proposals to Prevent Misuse in Situations of Workplace Harassment or Discrimination*

Dershowitz AM (1982) *The Best Defense* (New York, Random House)

—— (1996) *Reasonable Doubts: The OJ Simpson Case and the Criminal Justice System* (New York, Simon & Schuster)

Devlin P (1956) *Trial by Jury* (London, Stevens, 1956)

Dickens C (1841) *The Old Curiosity Shop* (London, Chapman & Hall)

Dillon P and Cannon C (2011) *Circle of Greed: The Spectacular Rise and Fall of the Lawyer Who Brought Corporate America to its Knees* (New York, Penguin/Random House)

Dodd RJ (1990) 'Innovative Techniques: Parlor Tricks for the Courtroom' Trial April

Dolnick S (2011) 'Immigrants May Be Fed False Stories to Bolster Asylum Pleas' *New York Times*, 11 July

Donegan M (2021) '"Women are Capable of Doing This": The Doctor Defying Laws to Provide Abortions by Sea or Mail' *The Guardian*, 12 December

Drahozal CR and Hines LJ (2006) 'Secret Settlement Restrictions and Unintended Consequences' 54 *Kansas LRev* 1457

Dressler M (2021) 'Lawfare: Both an Existential Threat to the International Rule of Law And an Indispensable Tool of American Foreign Policy in the Twenty-First Century' *Penn State LRev Blog*, 6 March

Du Cann R (1980) *The Art of the Advocate* (London, Penguin)

Dyer C (2001) 'QC's "Difficulties" Suggest Client May Have Changed His Story' *The Guardian*, 21 July

Eastman JC (2021a) 'Trying to Prevent Illegal Conduct from Deciding an Election Is Not Endorsing a "Coup"', 30 September, copy on file with the author

—— (2021b) 'John Eastman's Statement on His Retirement from Chapman University's Fowler School of Law' *The American Mind*, 14 January

Economides K (2007) 'Lawyers Take a Stand: Lawyers Must Make Some Kind of Hippocratic Oath' Letter to *The Times*, 15 November

Edelman TE (2005) 'Cross-Examination as Story Telling' in Alper et al (2005)

Edman I (ed) (1928) *The Works of Plato* (New York, Modern Library)

Eekelaar J, Maclean M and Beinart S (2000) *Family Lawyers: The Divorce Work of Solicitors* (Oxford, Hart Publishing)

Ekman P (1985) *Telling Lies: Clues to Deceit in the Marketplace, Politics and Marriage* (London, WW Norton, 1985)

Ellery B and Ames J (2020) 'Bogus Claim Lawyers Still Active' *The Times*, 17 October

Enloe C (2023) 'ACLU Stands by Decision to Represent NRA for Critical First Amendment Case at Supreme Court' *Blazemedia*, 11 December

Ervin Jr SJ (1980) 'The Role of the Lawyer in America' in Gerson 1980b

Eskridge Jr WN (1988) 'Overriding Statutory Precedents' 76 *Georgetown LJ* 1361

Evans A (2011) *Assessing Lawyers' Ethics: A Practitioner's Guide* (Cambridge, Cambridge University Press)

Evans C (2009) *The Father of Forensics: How Sir Bernard Spilsbury Invented Modern CSI* (Thriplow, Icon Books)

Evans K (1983) *Advocacy at the Bar: A Beginner's Guide* (London, Financial Training Publications)

Facher JP (1999) 'The Power of Procedure: Reflections on "A Civil Action"' in Grossman LA and Vaughn RG (eds) *A Documentary Companion to a Civil Action* (New York, Foundation Press)

Fallis D (2009) 'What is Lying?' 106(1) *Journal of Philosophy* 29

Fan M (2014) 'Adversarial Justice's Casualties: Defending Witness-Victim Protections' 55 *Boston College LRev* 1

Faulkner RR (2011) *Corporate Wrongdoing and the Art of Accusation* (London, Anthem Press)

Fazio LK, Brashier NM, Payne BK and Marsh EJ (2015) 'Knowledge Does Not Protect against Illusory Truth' 144 *Journal of Experimental Psychology* 993

FBI (2009) New York Field Office, Press Release, 3 April

Federation of Law Societies of Canada (2019) *Model Code of Professional Conduct*

Feige D (2001) 'How to Defend Someone You Know is Guilty' *New York Times*, 8 April

Ferran H (2022) 'Hard Proof: Trump was Never a Business Genius' *Sunday Times*, 1 October

Finkelstein D (2019) 'Burglary and Perjury in Nixon's Name' *The Times*, 31 August

Fischel DR (1998) 'Lawyers and Confidentiality' 65 *University of Chicago LRev* 1

Fitts AS (2013) 'The Right Way to Write about Rape' *Columbia Journalism Review*, 18 July

Fliegel J (2008) '*Qualcomm* Court Imposes Multi-million Dollar Sanctions for Electronic Discovery Failures' 12(2) *Wall Street Lawyer*, February

Foreign Policy Centre (2023) *London Calling: The Issue of Legal Intimidation and SLAPPs against Media Emanating from the United Kingdom* (London, Foreign Policy Centre)

Forensic Science Regulator (2012) 'Report into the circumstances of a complaint received from the Greater Manchester Police on 7 March 2012 regarding DNA evidence provided by LGC'

Forsyth W (1875) *The History of Lawyers Ancient and Modern* (Boston, Estes & Lauriat)

Fowler G (1931) *The Great Mouthpiece: A Life Story of William J Fallon* (New York, Grosset & Dunlap)

Fox M (2015) 'Monroe Freedman, Influential Voice on Legal Ethics, Dies at 86' *New York Times*, 2 March

Franiuk R, Seefelt JL, Cepress SL and Vandello JA (2008) 'Prevalence and Effects of Rape Myths in Print Journalism: The Kobe Bryant Case' 14 *Violence against Women* 287

Frankel ME (1975) 'The Search for Truth: An Umpireal View' 123 *University of Pennsylvania LRev* 1031

—— (1980) *Partisan Justice* (New York, Hill & Wang)

Franklin B (1785) 'Letter to Benjamin Vaughan, March 14, 1785' in Smyth AH (ed) *The Writings of Benjamin Franklin*, vol 9 (New York, Macmillan)

Frean A (2016) 'Pfizer Whistleblower Triumphs to Tune of $100m' *The Times*, 18 February

Freedman MH (1966) 'Professional Responsibility of the Criminal Defense Lawyer: The Three Hardest Questions' 64 *Michigan LRev* 1469

—— (1975) *Lawyers' Ethics in an Adversary System* (New York, Bobbs-Merrill)

—— (1990) *Understanding Lawyers' Ethics* (New York, Matthew Bender)

—— (1993) 'The Morality of Lawyering' *Legal Times*, 20 September 22

—— (1994) 'Must You Be the Devil's Advocate?' *Legal Times*, 23 August 19

—— (1995) 'The Lawyer's Moral Obligation of Justification' 74 *Texas LRev* 111

—— (1998) 'The Ethical Danger of "Civility" and "Professionalism"' 6 *Criminal Justice Journal* 17

—— (2006) 'In Praise of Overzealous Representation: Lying to Judges, Deceiving Third Parties, and Other Ethical Conduct' 34 *Hofstra LRev* 771

—— (2008) 'Getting Honest about Client Perjury' 21 *GJLE* 133

—— (2011) 'Henry Lord Brougham and Resolute Lawyering' 37 *Advocates' Quarterly* 403

Freedman MH and Smith A (2010) *Understanding Lawyers' Ethics* (New York, Matthew Bender, 4th edn)

Freeman N (2018) 'They're Unpopular, But "Loopholes" are the Letter of the Law' *The Times*, 18 November

Frith M (2003) 'Scientist's Claim on Cot Death is Flawed, Appeal Court Hears' *The Independent*, 5 December

From B (2001) 'Bringing Settlement out of the Shadows: Information about Settlement in an Age of Confidentiality' 48 *UCLA LRev* 663

Galanter M (1974) 'Why the "Haves" Come out Ahead: Speculations on the Limits of Legal Change' 9 *Law and Society Review* 95

—— (2005) *Lowering the Bar: Lawyer Jokes and Legal Culture* (Madison, University of Wisconsin Press)

Galanter M and Cahill M (1994) '"Most Cases Settle": Judicial Promotion and the Regulation of Settlements' 46 *Stanford LRev* 1339

Galanter M and Palay T (1991) *Tournament of Lawyers: The Transformation of the Big Law Firm* (Chicago, University of Chicago Press)

Garrahan M (2017) 'Harvey Weinstein: How Lawyers Kept the Lid on Sexual Harassment' *Financial Times*, 23 October

Garside J (2023) 'Designed to Distress and Deter: The Impact of Slapp Lawsuits on Journalists and Free Speech' *The Guardian*, 3 November

Geiger D (2019) 'What Happened to John Demjanjuk's Lawyer Yoram Sheftel from Netflix's "The Devil Next Door"?' *Oxygen*, True Crime Buzz, 6 November

General Council of the Bar of England and Wale (1981) *Code of Conduct*

—— (1992) *The Efficient Disposal of Business in the Crown Court: Report of [the Seabrooke] Working Party*

Gerson A (1980a) 'Introduction' in Gerson 1980b

—— (ed) (1980b) *Lawyers' Ethics* (Piscataway, NJ, Transaction Books)

Gerstein J and Samuelsohn D (2018) 'Manafort Trial Day 2: Judge Reins in Mention of Oligarchs' *Politico*, 1 August

Geyelin M (1999) 'DuPont, Atlanta Law Firm Agree to Pay Nearly $113 Million in Benlate Matter' *Wall Street Journal*, 4 January

Gibb F (2013a) 'Call for a Change to Protect Child Witnesses' *The Times*, 12 September

—— (2013b) 'Remove All Child Witnesses from Courts, Says Judge' *The Times*, 22 November

—— (2017) 'Sexual History of Rape Victims Still Being Put on Trial' *The Times*, 25 September

—— (2023) 'Review of Hooper' *The Times*, 20 December

Gibbs L (2016) 'The Legacy of the Kobe Bryant Rape Case', 13 April, https://archive.thinkprogress.org/the-legacy-of-the-kobe-bryant-rape-case-6a42f159be7b/

Gilchrist A (1863) *Life of William Blake* (London, Macmillan)

Gillers S (2006) 'Monroe Freedman's Solution to the Criminal Defense Lawyer's Trilemma is Wrong as a Matter of Policy and Constitutional Law' 34 *Hofstra LRev* 821

—— (2009) *Essentials: Regulation of the Legal Profession* (New York, Aspen)

—— (2012) *Regulation of Lawyers* (New York, Aspen Publishers, 9th edn)

—— (2018) *Regulation of Lawyers: Problems in Law and Ethics* (Philadelphia, Wolters Kluwer, 11th edn)

Givelbar DJ and Robbins A (2006) 'Public Health versus Court-Sponsored Secrecy' 69 *Law and Contemporary Problems* 134

Glancy J (2020) 'The Justice Warrior' *Sunday Times*, 27 December

Gloppen S (2023) 'Foreword', in Pinos JC and Hau MF (eds) *Lawfare: New Trajectories in Law* (Abingdon, Routledge)

Goldberger D (1995) 'Clients Everyone Hates' 21 *Litigation* 10

Goldsmith J (2007) *The Terror Presidency: Law and Judgment Inside the Bush Administration* (New York, WW Norton)

Goldsmith P (2007) 'Expert Evidence – The Problem or the Solution? The Role of Expert Evidence and its Regulation' Academy of Expert Witnesses, *John Bolton Memorial Lecture*, 25 January

Goodman LS (1967) 'The Historic Role of the Oath of Admission' 11 *American Journal of Legal History* 404

Gordon RW (1990) 'Corporate Law Practice as a Public Calling' 49 *Maryland LRev* 255

—— (1998) 'A Collective Failure of Nerve: The Bar's Response to Kaye Scholer' 23 *Law & Social Inquiry* 315

GovUK (2023a) *Factsheet: Strategic Lawsuits against Public Participation (SLAPPs)*

—— (2023b) 'Pre-recorded Evidence Improves Rape Victims' Experience of Court', 3 April.

Graff GM (2022) *Watergate: A New History* (New York, Simon & Schuster)

Graham MH (2010) 'The "English" Approach to Criminal Jury Trials: Stacking the Deck in Favor of the Prosecution' 46 *Criminal Law Bulletin* 1021

Green B and Roiphe R (2021) 'Lawyers and the Lies They Tell' 69 *Washington University Journal of Law and Policy* 37

Greenebaum EH (1977) 'Attorneys' Problems in Making Ethical Decisions' 52 *Indiana LRev* 627

Grey Jr R (2018) 'There is No Justice as Long as Millions Lack Meaningful Access to it' *ABA Journal*, 30 August

Griffin N and Nardell G (2021) 'RIP Legal Professional Privilege?' *Counsel*, 30 May

Griffiths I (1986) *Creative Accounting: How to Make Your Profits What You Want Them to Be* (London, Sidgwick & Jackson)

Grisham J (1989) *A Time to Kill* (New York, Wynwood Press)

—— (1995) *The Rainmaker* (New York, Doubleday)

Grove T (1998) *The Juryman's Tale* (London, Bloomsbury)

Gudjonsson GH (2018) *The Psychology of False Confessions: Forty Years of Science and Practice* (Chichester, Wiley)

Gurnham D (2016) 'Victim-Blame as a Symptom of Rape Myth Acceptance? Another Look at How Young People in England Understand Sexual Consent' 36(2) *Legal Studies* 258

Haberman M, Savage C and Broadwater L (2023) 'Previously Secret Memo Laid out Strategy for Trump to Overturn Biden's Win' *New York Times*, 8 August

Hajjar L (2018) '*In Defense of Lawfare: The Value of Litigation in Challenging Torture*' in Anderson SA and Nussbaum MC (eds) *Confronting Torture* (Chicago, University of Chicago Press)

Hake T (2015) *Operation Greylord: The True Story of an Untrained Undercover Agent and America's Biggest Corruption Bust* (Chicago, American Bar Association)

Hamilton F (2023) 'Lawyers Face Threats from China for Defending Hong Kong Mogul' *The Times*, 30 September

Hanratty J (2020) *The Making of an Immigration Judge* (London, Quartet Books, 2nd edn)

Harris G (2008) 'Half of Doctors Routinely Prescribe Placebos' *New York Times*, 23 October

Harry Prince (2023) *Spare* (London, Penguin)

Harry T and Edwards HT (1988) 'The Role of Legal Education in Shaping the Profession' 38 *Journal of Legal Education* 285

Hart HLA (1961) *The Concept of Law* (Oxford, Oxford University Press)

Hart-Davis D (2012) *Man of War: The Secret Life of Captain Alan Hillgarth, Officer, Adventurer, Agent* (London, Century)

Hasher L, Goldstein D and Toppino T (1977) 'Frequency and the Conference of Referential Validity' 16 *Journal of Verbal Learning and Verbal Behavior* 107

Haskell PG (1998) *Why Lawyers Behave as They Do* (New York, Routledge)

Haskins PA (ed) (2013) *Essential Qualities of the Professional Lawyer* (Chicago, ABA)

Hays KE and Tulle JL (2000) 'State Bar of Texas, Ultimate Trial Notebook: Family Law' 7–8 December

Hazard Jr GC (1997) 'The Client Fraud Problem as a Justinian Quartet: An Extended Analysis' 25 *Hofstra LRev* 1041

—— (2000) '*Law Practice and the Limits of Moral Philosophy*' in Rhode 2000a

Hazard Jr and Hodes WW (1985) *The Law of Lawyering: A Handbook on the Model Rules of Professional Conduct* (Clifton, Prentice Hall)

—— (1998) 'Tobacco Lawyers Shame the Entire Profession' *National Law Journal*, 18 May 18

—— (2001) *The Law of Lawyering* (New York, Wolters Kluwer Law, 3rd edn)

—— (2008) *The Law of Lawyering* (New York, Wolters Kluwer 3rd edn Supp)

Heinrichs J (2007) *Winning Arguments* (Harmondsworth, Penguin)

Helm RK, Reyna VR, Franz AA, Novick RZ, Dincin S and Cort AE (2018) 'Limitations on the Ability to Negotiate Justice: Attorney Perspectives on Guilt, Innocence, and Legal Advice in the Current Plea System' 24 *Psychology, Crime and Law* 915

Hempel G, Brimer E and Kune R (2008) *Advocacy Manual* (Melbourne, Australian Advocacy Institute)

Henning PJ (2006) 'Lawyers, Truth, and Honesty in Representing Clients' 20 *Notre Dame Journal of Law, Ethics and Public Policy* 209

Henry E (2019) 'What the Bar Can Learn from US Trial Lawyers' *Counsel*, March

Herbig RS (2021) 'Don't Judge a Book by its Cover: The Challenges of De-selection in Voir Dire' *Ted Dalton Inns of Court*, 26 March

Hibbing JR and Theiss-Morse E (eds) (2001) *What is it about Government That Americans Dislike?* (Cambridge, Cambridge University Press)

Hildreth JAD Gino F and Bazerman M (2016) 'Blind Loyalty? When Group Loyalty Makes Us See Evil or Engage in it' 132 *Organizational Behavior and Human Decision Processes* 16

Hildreth JAD and Anderson C (2018) 'Does Loyalty Trump Honesty? Moral Judgments of Loyalty-Driven Deceit' 79 *Journal of Experimental Social Psychology* 87

Hinshaw A (2019) 'On Professional Practice: Ethics and Negotiation' *Dispute Resolution Magazine*, 12 September

Hirsch A (2014) 'Going to the Source: The "New" Reid Method and False Confessions' 11 *Ohio State Journal of Criminal Law* 803

HistoryCom (2020) 'Boston Massacre' 23 September

Hitler A (1925) *Mein Kampf* (Munich, Hr Ebre Karbl)

HMRC (2020) *General Anti-abuse Rule (GAAR) Guidance*, 11 September

Ho H (2017) 'Case Study of True and Fair Override in Financial Reporting' *Nang Yan Business Journal*, 15 January

Hobin T and Jensen DJ (1980) '*The Attorney's Duty to Disclose the Commission of Criminal Acts – Two Views on the Lake Pleasant Case*' in Gerson 1980b

Hodes WW (1996) 'Lord Brougham, the Dream Team, and Jury Nullification of the Third Kind' 67 *University of Colorado LRev* 675

—— (1999) 'The Professional Duty to Horseshed Witnesses Zealously – within the Bounds of the Law' 30 *Texas Tech LRev* 1343

—— (2000) 'Accepting and Rejecting Clients – The Moral Autonomy of the Second-to-the-Last Lawyer in Town' 48 *University of Kansas LRev* 977

—— (2002) 'Seeking the Truth versus Telling the Truth at the Boundaries of the Law: Misdirection, Lying, and "Lying with an Explanation"' 44 *South Texas LRev* 53

—— (2010) Legal Ethics Discussion List (Washburn University), 26 January

Hodge M (2024) 'Offshore Tax Havens Must Be Forced to Open Public Registers' *The Times*, 15 April

Holmes OW (1897) 'The Path of the Law' 10 *Harvard LRev* 457

Holmes V and Bartlett F (2023) *Parker and Evans's Inside Lawyers' Ethics* (Cambridge, Cambridge University Press)

Hooper D (2023) *Buying Silence* (Hull, Biteback)

Horowitz IA, Kerr NL and Niedermeier KE (2001) 'Jury Nullification: Legal and Psychological Perspectives' 66 *Brooklyn LRev* 1207

Howick J (2013) 'Placebos Work. Is That Hard to Swallow?' *The Times*, 21 March

Huff D (1954) *How to Lie with Statistics* (London, WW Norton)

Humphries W (2020) 'Policeman Who Broke Lover's Neck is Cleared of Murder' *The Times*, 28 October

Hunter G, Jacobson J and Kirby A (2018) *Judicial Perceptions of the Quality of Criminal Advocacy* (Institute for Criminal Policy Research, Birkbeck College, University of London)

Hutchinson AC (1998) 'Taking it Personally: Legal Ethics and Client Selection' 12 *Legal Ethics* 168

Hyde J (2021) 'Court Dismisses 28 Separate Divorce Petitions with Identical Wording' *Law Society Gazette*, 12 October.

—— (2023) 'Post Office Inquiry Hearing Aborted over Disclosure Failure' *Law Society Gazette*, 6 July

—— (2024) 'Post Office Scandal Expert Moorhead Predicts Solicitor Strike-offs' *Law Society Gazette*, 9 February

Hyde J and Castro B (2024) 'Clyde & Co Fined £500,000 after Admitting Due Diligence Failure' *Law Society Gazette*, 11 January

Hyman A and Nombembe P (2019) 'Legal Fraternity under Siege in Cape, as Another Murdered Lawyer Mourned' *TimesLive*, 30 May

Imwinkelried EJ (1985) 'Demeanor Impeachment: Law and Tactics' 9 *American Journal of Trial Advocacy* 183

The Independent (2023) 'How We Exposed Nadhim Zahawi's Tax Affairs – and Why it Matters' 23 January

Indictment of Margaret Sanger (1914) 021;Records of the District Courts of the United States National Archives at New York City, 25 September

Inns of Court School of Law (1996) *Advocacy* (London, Blackstone)

Ipp DA (1998) 'Lawyers' Duties to the Court' 114 *Law Quarterly Review* 63

IRS (nd) *Understand Taxes, Worksheet Solutions, The Difference between Tax Avoidance and Tax Evasion*

Isbell DB and Salvi LN (1995) 'Ethical Responsibility of Lawyers for Deception by Undercover Investigators and Discrimination Testers: An Analysis of the Provisions Prohibiting Misrepresentation under the Model Rules of Professional Conduct' 8 *GJLE* 791

Jackson B (1995) *Making Sense in Law: Linguistic, Psychological and Semiotic Perspectives* (Liverpool, Deborah Charles)

Jackson J (2020) 'Review of "Accused: Trial in the Outback"' *The Times*, 9 December

Jackson RH (1951) 'Advocacy before the United States Supreme Court' 37 *Cornell Law Quarterly* 1

Jackson S (2022) *Love Me to Death: The Chilling True Story of William 'Wild Bill Cody' Neal: The Vicious Denver Lady-Killer* (New York, Kensington Publishing; Denver, WildBlue Press, revised edn)

Jeralyn (2002) 'On Westerfield's Lawyers' Conduct, Talk Left: The Politics of Crime' 19 September, talkleft.com/story/2002/09/19/723/24550/crimenews/On-Westerfield-s-Lawyers-Conduct

Jessup HW (1922) 'The Ethics of the Professions and of Business' 101 *Annals of the American Academy of Political and Social Science* 16

Johnson D (2007) 'Look at This Ad, But Don't Get Any Ideas' *New York Times*, 13 May

Johnson S (1759) *Rasselas* (London, R and J Dodsley, W Johnston)

Johnson T (2022) 'Lying at Plea Bargaining' 38 *Georgia State University LRev* 673

Joy PA (2004) '*Spaulding v Zimmerman*: Exploring the Ethics and Morality of Lawyers and Physicians in Practice' 1277 *JURISUTO* 80

Joy PA and McMunigal KC (2020) 'Post-Conviction Relief after a Guilty Plea?' 35 *ABA Criminal Justice* 53

—— (2022) 'The Ethics of Trump's Shadow Lawyers? 69 *Washington University Journal of Law and Policy* 127

Judicial College (2015) *Reporting Restrictions in the Criminal Courts, April* (London, Judicial College, revised May 2016)

Kaminski I (2024) 'Solicitor General Urged to Drop Prosecutions of Jury Rights Activists' *The Guardian*, 5 February

Kant I (1799) *On a Supposed Right to Lie from Altruistic Motives*, translated and edited by LW Beck (Chicago, University of Chicago Press, revised May 2016)

—— (1959) *Foundations of the Metaphysics of Morals* (London, Macmillan, [1785])

Kantor J and Twohey M (2000) *She Said: Breaking the Sexual Harassment Story That Helped Ignite a Movement* (New York, Penguin)

Kaplan DA (1988) 'Death Row Dilemma' *The National LJ*, 25 January, 35–38

Karp J (2023) 'Eastman's Ethics Case Tangled up in Attorney Speech "Tightrope"' *Law 360*, 16 June

Kassin SM and Gudjonsson GH (2004) 'The Psychology of Confessions: A Review of the Literature and Issues' 5 *Psychological Science in the Public Interest* 33

Kavanagh J and Rich MD (2018) *Truth Decay: An Examination of the Diminishing Role of Facts and Analysis in American Public Life* (Santa Monica, Rand Corporation)

Kelley JE (1994) 'Addressing Juror Stress: A Trial Judge's Perspective' 43 *Drake LRev* 97

Kelly L, Temkin J and Griffiths S (2006) *Section 41: An Evaluation of New Legislation Limiting Sexual History in Rape Trials* (London, Home Office)

Kelso P (2021) 'A Liar's Moment of Truth' *The Guardian*, 20 July

Kenton W (2020) 'Repo 105' *Investopedia*, 6 May

Kentridge S (2003) 'The Ethics of Advocacy' *South Eastern Circuit of the Bar of EW*

Kershaw D and Moorhead R (2013) 'Consequential Responsibility for Client Wrongs: Lehman Brothers and the Regulation of the Legal Profession' 76 *Modern LRev* 26

Kevorkian J (nd) 'Famous Trials by Professor Dougals O Linder', https://famous-trials.com/drkevorkian/2431-kevorkian-s-decision-to-represent-himself

Kim Sung Hui (2023) 'Legal Ethics after #MeToo: Autonomy, Domination, and Nondisclosure Agreements' 73 *Duke LJ* 463

King Jr ML (1963) 'Letter from Birmingham City Jail' 16 April 16

Kipling R (1923) Speech made to the Royal College of Surgeons, quoted in *The Times*, 15 February

Klein R (2012) 'The Role of Defense Counsel in Ensuring a Fair Justice System' *The Champion*, June, Issue 38

Knake Jefferson R (2024) *Law Democratized: A Blueprint for Solving the Justice Crisis* (Berlin, De Gruyter)

Kotkin MJ (2007) 'Outing Outcomes: An Empirical Study of Confidential Employment Discrimination Settlements' 64 *Washington & Lee LRev* 111

Kovensky J (2022) 'Exclusive: Trump Lawyer Kenneth Chesebro Talks about His Role in the Runup to Jan 6' *Talking Points Memo*, 16 June

Kronman A (1993) *The Lost Lawyer* (Cambridge, MA, Harvard University Press)

Kruse M (2024) 'This to Him is the Grand Finale: Donald Trump's 50-Year Mission to Discredit the Justice System' *Politico*, 12 January

Kunen JS (1983) *How Can You Defend These People?: The Making of a Criminal Lawyer* (New York, Random House)

Lacey M (2009) 'Mexico Lawyer Who Defended Drug Traffickers Is Shot Dead' *New York Times*, 9 August

Lagan B (2020) 'Mob Lawyer Slept with Police While Informing on Clients' *The Times*, 5 February

Lakhani N and Milman O (2022) 'US Fracking Boom Could Tip World to Edge of Climate Disaster' *The Guardian*, 11 May

Langevoort DC (2020) 'Gatekeepers, Cultural Captives, or Knaves? Corporate Lawyers through Different Lenses' 88 *Fordham LRev* 1683

Law Commission (2010) Consultation Paper No 195, Criminal Liability in Regulatory Contexts

Lawfare Institute (2021) 'Lebanon and the Increasing Risk of Lawfare' 25 June

Lawry RP (1990) 'The Central Moral Tradition of Lawyering' 19 *Hofstra LRev* 311

—— (1996) 'Cross-Examining the Truthful Witness: The Ideal within the Central Moral Tradition of Lawyering' 100 *Dickinson LRev* 563

Law Society (2015) *Criminal Procedure Rules*

—— (2020) *Suspicious Activity Reports*

Law Society Gazette (2010) 'ASA Ditches Complaint', 21 September

Law Society of Ontario (2019) *Rules of Professional Conduct*

LawCare (2020/21) *Life in the Law* (lawcare.org.uk)

Ledwith, M (2024) 'Post Office Bosses Accused of Running "Criminal Conspiracy"' *The Times*, June 19

Lee E (2023) 'Ex-Trump lawyer Who Led Scheme to Overturn the 2020 Presidential Election Could Be Disbarred' *USA Today*, 8 August

Lee H (1960) *To Kill a Mockingbird* (Philadelphia, JB Lippincott)

Lee Myers A and Christie B (2011) 'Police: Arizona Man Kills 5, Including Ex-wife's Lawyer, before Taking Own Life' *Mass*, 3 June

Legal Sector Affinity Group (2018) *Anti-money Laundering: Guidance for the Legal Sector*

Leggatt A (1998/99) 'The Morality of the Practising Barrister' *Inner Temple Yearbook* 76

Leo R (2008) *Police Interrogation and American Justice* (Cambridge, MA, Harvard University Press)

Lerman LG, Armani FH, Morgan TD and Freedman MH (2007) 'The Buried Bodies Case: Alive and Well after Thirty Years' *The Professional Lawyer* 19

Letter to Judge Cooper from Thomas Youk's Wife, famous-trials.com/drkevorkian/2426-letter-to-judge-cooper-from-thomas-youk-s-wife

Letter to *The Times* (2010) 14 January

Levenson LL (2008) 'The Theater of the Courtroom' 92 *Minnesota LRev* 573

Levi P (1995) *If This is a Man/Survival in Auschwitz, Afterword* (New York, Simon & Schuster)

Levin DL (2004) 'Definition of Torture under 18 USC §§2340-2340A: Memorandum for the Deputy Attorney General', 30 December

Levin LC (1994) 'Testing the Radical Experiment: A Study of Lawyer Response to Clients Who Intend to Harm Others' 47 *Rutgers LRev* 81

—— (2022) '"This is Not Normal": The Role of Lawyer Organizations in Protecting Constitutional Norms and Values' 69 *Washington University Journal of Law and Policy* 173

Levine K and Miller C (2021) 'The Strategic Use of Alibi Defenses', ssrn.com/abstract= 3798769

Levine TR (2014) *Encyclopedia of Deception* (New York, Sage Publications)

Lewis A (2004) 'Making Torture Legal' *New York Review of Books*, 15 July

Lilly GC (2001) 'The Decline of the American Jury' 72 *University of Colorado LRev* 53

Lincoln A (1850) 'Notes for a Law Lecture', www.abrahamlincolnonline.org/lincoln/speeches/lawlect.htm?

Lininger T (2005) 'Bearing the Cross' 74 *Fordham LRev* 1353

Llewellyn JT (2014) 'Operation Mincemeat' in Levine

Llewellyn K (1952) 'The Adventures of Rollo' 2 *University of Chicago Law School Record* 3

Lloyd-Bostock S and Thomas C (1999) 'Decline of the "Little Parliament": Juries and Jury Reform in England and Wales' 62 *Law and Contemporary Problems* 7

Lobel O (2018) 'NDAs are out of Control: Here's What Needs to Change' *Harvard Business Review*, 30 January

Lodder P (2011) 'We May Despise Bellfield But Justice was Done' *The Times*, 26 June

Loftus EF and Ketcham K (2013) *The Myth of Repressed Memory: False Memories and Allegations of Sexual Abuse* (New York, St Martin's Griffin)

Loftus EF and Rosenwald LA (1993) 'The Rodney King Videotape: Why the Case was Not Black and White' 66 *Southern California LRev* 1637

Lohr D (2017) 'Isaac Turnbaugh: Man Acquitted of Friend's Murder Confesses to Police, Walks Free' *Huffington Post*

Lord Chancellor's Department (1995) *Access to Justice: Interim Report*

Lorenz L (nd) Cartoonstock.com/directory/l/legal_professions.asp

Los Angeles Times Archives (1986) 'Marin Deaths Convict's Visit Fulfils Fears of Prosecutor', 20 November

Lowell A (1897) 'The Judicial Use of Torture, Part I' 11 *Harvard LRev* 220; Part II, at 290

LS4CA (2023) *The Law Firm Climate Scorecard*

LSAG (2023) *Anti-Money Laundering Guidance for the Legal Sector*

LSB (2024) *The Misuse of Non-disclosure Agreements: Call for Evidence Themes and Summary of Evidence*

Luban DJ (1983a) 'The Adversary System Excuse' in Luban DJ (ed) *The Good Lawyer: Lawyers' Roles and Lawyers' Ethics* (Lanham, MD, Rowman and Allenheld)

—— (1983b) 'Epistemology and Moral Education' 33 *Journal of Legal Education* 636

—— (1984) 'The Sources of Legal Ethics' *Rabels Zitschift* 262

—— (1988) *Lawyers and Justice: An Ethical Study* (Princeton, Princeton University Press)

—— (1999) 'Contrived Ignorance' 87 *Georgetown LJ* 957

—— (2000) 'The Ethics of Wrongful Obedience in Rhode 2000a: 94

—— (2006) 'Introduction' in Rhode and Luban

—— (2007) *Legal Ethics and Human Dignity* (Cambridge, Cambridge University Press)

—— (2010) 'Carl Schmitt and the Critique of Lawfare' 43 *Case Western Reserve Journal of International Law* 457

—— (2012) 'Misplaced Fidelity' 90 *Texas LRev* 673

—— (2020) 'Fiduciary Legal Ethics, Zeal and Moral Activism' 33 *GJLE* 275

Luban DJ and Milleman P (1995) 'Good Judgment: Teaching Ethics in Dark Times' 9 *GJLE* 31

Lubet S (1993) *Modern Trial Advocacy Analysis and Practice* (Notre Dame, National Institute for Trial Advocacy)

—— (2001) *Nothing But the Truth: Why Trial Lawyers Don't, Can't and Shouldn't Have to Tell the Whole Truth* (New York, New York University Press)

Macintyre B (2019) 'At Last, a Lie Detector That Tells the Truth' *The Times*, 29 June

—— (2010) *Operation Mincemeat: The True Spy Story That Changed the Course of World War II* (London, Bloomsbury)

Magrath P (2016) *Book Review – Marshall Hall: A Law unto Himself* (London, Incorporated Council of Law Reporting, 25 June)

Marcus J (2023) 'Trump Falsely Claims "60 Minutes" Proves Pence Could Flip Election' *The Independent*, 7 November

Margaret Sanger Papers Project (2011) 'Tracing *One Package* – The Case that Legalized Birth Control' Newsletter #59, Winter

Markham JW (2006) *A Financial History of Modern US Corporate Scandals: From Enron to Reform* (New York, Routledge)

Markkula Center for Applied Ethics (nd) 'Corporate Wrongdoing, Articles on Corruption, Bribery, Scandals, and Whistleblowers', scu.edu/ethics/focus-areas/business-ethics/resources/articles/corporate-wrongdoing

Markovits D (2008) *A Modern Legal Ethics: Adversary Ethics in a Democratic Age* (Princeton, Princeton University Press)

Marsden J (2004) 'I was Sacked by a Serial Killer' *Sydney Morning Herald*, 4 September

Mason III CT (1997) *Lawyers' Duties of Candor toward the Arbitral Tribunal* (New York, Practising Law Institute)

Matthews III RT (2008) 'The Duke Lacrosse Rape Case – A Public Branding, is There a Remedy?' 52 *St Louis University LJ* 669

Mauet TA (2007) *Trial Techniques* (Austin, Wolters Kluwer)

Mayhew L (1975) 'Institutions of Representation: Civil Justice and the Public' 9 *Law and Society Review* 401

Maynard R (2020) 'Gangsters May Go Free over Lawyer Who was Police Spy' *Sunday Times*, 9 February

McBarnet D (1981) *Conviction: Law, the State and the Construction of Justice* (Basingstoke, Palgrave)

—— (1991) 'Whiter Than White Collar Crime: Tax, Fraud Insurance and the Management of Stigma' 42 *British Journal of Sociology* 323

McBarnet D and Whelan C (1991) 'The Elusive Spirit of the Law: Formalism and the Struggle for Legal Control' 54 *Modern LRev* 848

—— (1992) 'International Corporate Finance and the Challenge of Creative Compliance' in Fingleton J (ed) *The Internationalisation of Capital Markets and the Regulatory Response* (Graham & Trotman, London, 1992) 129–46, reprinted in Wheeler S (ed) (1994) *Law and the Business Enterprise* (Clarendon Press, Oxford) 403

—— (1997a) 'Challenging the Regulators: Strategies for Resisting Control' in McCrudden JC (ed) *Regulation and Deregulation: Policy and Practice* (Oxford, Clarendon Press)

—— (1997b) 'Creative Compliance and the Defeat of Legal Control' in Hawkins K (ed) *The Human Face of Law* (Oxford, Clarendon Press)

—— (1998) 'Challenging the Regulators: Strategies for Resisting Control in McCrudden JC (ed) *Regulation and Deregulation: Policy and Practice* (Oxford, Clarendon Press)

—— (1999) *Creative Accounting and the Cross-Eyed Javelin Thrower* (Chichester, John Wiley)

McClymont K and Miller S (2006) 'Milat Lawyer Dies' *The Age*, 16 May

McConville M (1998) 'Plea Bargaining: Ethics and Politics' 25 *Journal of Law and Society* 562

McConville M, Hodgson J, Bridges L and Pavlovic A (1994) *Standing Accused: The Organisation and Practices of Criminal Defence Lawyers in Britain* (Oxford, Oxford University Press)

McCord D (1996) '"But Perry Mason Made it Look So Easy!": The Admissibility of Evidence Offered by a Criminal Defendant to Suggest That Someone Else is Guilty' 63 *Tennessee LRev* 917

McElhaney JW (2005) *Trial Note* (Chicago, ABA, 4th edn)

McFadden RD (2021) 'F Lee Bailey, Lawyer for Patty Hearst and OJ Simpson, Dies at 87' *New York Times*, 3 June

McGarry P (2009) 'Church "Lied without Lying"' *Irish Times*, 26 November

McNeill SC (1999) 'The History of the Lawyer's Oath' 5 *Massachusetts Legal History* 91

Meadow R (1997) *ABC of Child Abuse* (London, BMJ Books)

Meet the Press with Chuck Todd (2023) 6 August

Memo (2002a) 'Memorandum for Alberto R Gonzales, Counsel to the President, and William J Haynes II, General Counsel of the Department of Defense', 22 January

—— (2002b) 'Memorandum from Assistant Attorney General Jay S Bybee to John Rizzo, Acting General Counsel of the CIA', 1 August

—— (2002c) 'Memorandum for Alberto R Gonzales, Counsel to the President'

—— (2003) 'Memorandum from Assistant Attorney General Jay S Bybee to William J Haynes II, General Counsel of the Department of Defense', 14 March

Memorandum (2002) from Jay S Bybee, Assistant Attorney General to Alberto Gonzales, Counsel to the President, and William J Haynes II, General Counsel of the Department of Defense, 22 January

Menkele P (2010) *The Times*, 28 January

Menkel-Meadow C (2000) 'The Limits of Adversarial Ethics' in Rhode D (ed), *Ethics in Practice* (Oxford, Oxford University Press)

Menkel-Meadow C and Wheeler M (eds) (2004) *What's Fair? Ethics for Negotiators* (Hoboken, Wiley)

Mill JS (1978) *On Liberty* (Indianapolis, Hackett Publishing)

Miller MK and Bornstein BH (2004) 'Juror Stress: Cases and Interventions' 30 *Thurgood Marshall LRev* 237

Mintz M (1985) *At Any Cost: Corporate Greed, Women and the Dalkon Shield* (New York, Pantheon)

Minzner M (2008) 'Detecting Lies Using Demeanor, Bias, and Context' 29 *Cardozo LRev* 2557

Mishcon de Reya (2018) *Non-disclosure Agreements: Ethics and Enforceability* 3 August

Mitchell J (1987) 'Reasonable Doubts are Where You Find Them: A Response to Professor Subin's Position on the Criminal Lawyer's "Different Mission"' 1 *GJLE* 339

Mitchell R (2015) 'Taking on the Expert' *Law Society of Scotland*, 16 March

Moffatt V (2023) 'SLAPPs and Reputational Risks' Law Society, 27 June

Montagu, E (1978) *Beyond Top Secret Ultra* (New York, Coward, McCann & Geoghegan, 1978)

Moorhead R (2018) *Ethics and NDAs* (Centre for Ethics and Law, University College London Faculty of Laws)

—— (2021a) 'The Post Office "Where were the Lawyers?" Post' *Lawyer Watch*, 23 April

—— (2021b) 'Accountability is Key to Unravelling Post Office Scandal' *The Times*, 9 September

—— (2021c) 'Mutually Assured Irresponsibility: An Example from the Post Office' *Lawyer Watch*, 18 September

—— (2024) substack.com, 22 April

Morigiwa Y, Stolleis M and Halperin J-L (eds) (2011) 'Interpretation of Law in the Age of Enlightenment' ssrn.com/abstract=1963882

Morin R and Cohen D (2018) 'Giuliani: "Truth isn't Truth"' *Politico*, 19 August

Mortimer J (1982) *Clinging to the Wreckage* (London, Orion)

Mosteller RP (2010) 'Why Defense Attorneys Cannot, But Do, Care about Innocence' 50 *Santa Clara LRev* 1

Moulton (Lord) (1924) The lecture was reprinted after Moulton's death in *The Atlantic*

Mount TA (1980) *Fundamentals of Trial Technique* (New York, Aspen)

Murphy EE (2015) *Inside the Cell: The Dark Side of Forensic DNA* (New York, Nation Books)

Murphy PW (2002) '"There's No Business Like …?": Some Thoughts on Acting in the Courtroom' 44 *South Texas LRev* 111

Murray JM (2004) 'White Ritual & Black Magic: Playing the Race Card' 31(1) *Litigation* 13

Murray MD and DeSanctis CH (2013) *Advanced Legal Writing and Oral Advocacy: Trials, Appeals and Moot Court* (St Paul, Foundation Press, 2nd edn)

Napley D (1991) *The Technique of Persuasion* (London, Sweet & Maxwell, 4th edn)

Nathanson DL (1996) 'What's a Script?' 3 *Bulletin of the Tomkins Institute* 1

National Commission on Terrorist Attacks upon the United States (nd) (govinfo.library.unt.edu/911/report/911Report_Ch7.htm)

National Council of the Bar Association (1986) *Bar Association Rules (Professional Ethics)*

National Research Council (2009) *Strengthening Forensic Science in the United States: A Path Forward* (Washington DC)

National Registry of Exonerations (nd) 'Darrel Parker'

NBC (2023) *Meet the Press*, 6 August

NBC News (2018) 'Read Michael Cohen's Full Sentencing Statement and Why "Blind Loyalty" to Trump was the Biggest Mistake of His Life', 12 December

NCA (2020) *SAR Online User Guidance*

—— (nd) *Suspicious Activity Reports*

Nebo-lit (nd) 'Lawyers', nebo-lit.com/topic-areas/Justice/lawyers.html

Neuberger D (2011) *Report of the Committee on Super-Injunctions: Super-Injunctions, Anonymised Injunctions and Open Justice*, 20 May

—— (2012) 'Lord Erskine and Trial by Jury', First Annual Seckford Lecture at Woodbridge School, 18 October, www.supremecourt.uk/docs/speech-121018.pdf

New York Times (1971) 'Jersey Suspends F Lee Bailey from Practice', 21 June

New Zealand Law Commission (1998) 'Preliminary Paper 31, Compensation for Wrongful Conviction or Prosecution: A Discussion Paper'

Nicolson D (2005) 'Making Lawyers Moral? Ethical Codes and Moral Character' (2005) *Legal Studies* 601

Nicolson D and Webb J (1999) *Professional Legal Ethics: Critical Interrogations* (Oxford, Oxford University Press)

Nightingale J (ed) (1821) *Trial of Queen Caroline* (London, Albion Press)

Noble KB (1995) 'Issue of Racism Erupts in Simpson Trial' *New York Times*, 14 January

Noble P (2016) 'Book Review – Marshall Hall: A Law unto Himself' *Counsel*, September

Norfolk A (2011) 'Witness in Sex Grooming Trial in Tears as She is Forced to Read out Details of Abuse' *The Times*, 4 August

—— (2013a) 'Abuse Trial That Shamed the British Legal System' *The Times*, 23 May

—— (2013b) 'Humiliation in Court: How the Law Treated Abuse Victims' *The Times*, 23 May

—— (2013c) '"Trial That Shamed British Justice" Led to Changes in Child Abuse Cases' *The Times*, 7 August

—— (2013d) 'Child Abuse Victims Get Handpicked Trial Judges' *The Times*, August 7

—— (2015) 'They are Slags, Not Victims, Lawyer Tells Grooming Trial' *The Times*, 7 March

Norris F (2014) *International New York Times*, 6 June

Noth P (2020) Cartoonist, *New Yorker Calendar*, 19 November

Obituary (2021a) 'Sir Jeremiah Harman' *The Times*, 13 March

—— (2021b) 'F Lee Bailey' *The Times*, 5 June

O'Connor P (2023) 'Is it Time to Reassess the Cab Rank Rule?' *Counsel*, July

ONS (2023) *Domestic Abuse in England and Wales Overview: November*

O'Mara M (2000) *The World's Stupidest Laws* (London, Michael O'Mara Books)

O'Neill J (2020) 'Pat Finucane; A Murder with "Collusion at its Heart"' *BBC News*, 30 November

Olive ME (2014) 'The Daryl Atkins Story' 23 *William & Mary Bill of Rights Journal* 363

OP CI-1164 (1987) 23 January, reported in ABA/BNA, 3 *Laws Manual Prof'l Conduct* 44 (4 March 1987), www.michbar.org/opinions/ethics/numbered_opinions/ci-1164.html

Opinion No 2002-01, 2002 WL 1040180 (NYC Assn B Comm Prof Jud Eth

Orwell G (1949) *1984* (London, Secker & Warburg)

Pannick D (1992) *Advocates* (Oxford, Oxford University Press)

—— (1996) 'You Be the Judge' *The Times*, 2 January, reprinted in Pannick 2008: 109

—— (1997) 'When Counsel Should Come Clean' *The Times*, 14 January

—— (2008) *I Have to Move My Car: Tales of Unpersuasive Advocates and Injudicious Judges* (Oxford, Hart Publishing)

—— (2015) 'How Do We Maintain the Quality of Advocacy?' *The Times*, 15 October

—— (2021) Letter to *The Times*, 3 February

—— (2023) *Advocacy* (Cambridge, Cambridge University Press)

Pardi P (2019) 'What is Truth?' *Philosophy News*, 22 March

Parker C and Evans A (2018) *Inside Lawyers' Ethics* (Cambridge, Cambridge University Press)

Parker C, Le Mire S and Mackay A (2017) 'Lawyers, Confidentiality and Whistleblowing: Lessons from the McCabe Tobacco Litigation' 40 *Melbourne LRev* 999

Parker R (2016) 'Robert Shapiro Reveals What OJ Simpson Said to Him Right after the Verdict' *Hollywood Reporter*, 17 May

Parrock J (2024) 'Europe's King of Cocaine and Killing Finally Brought Down' *The Times*, 28 February

Passas N (2005) 'Lawful But Awful: "Legal Corporate Crimes"' 34 *Journal of Socio-Economics* 771

Paulson A (2004) 'Is the Rape-Shield Law Working?' *Christian Science Monitor*, 25 March

Pavia W (2021) 'Conviction axed over Shining Reference' *The Times*, 22 January

PBS (1988) *Ethics on Trial*, WETA Television Station, Washington DC

Pennington N and Hastie R (1993) 'The Story Model for Jury Decision Making' in Hastie R (ed), *Inside the Juror: The Psychology of Juror Decision Making* (Cambridge, Cambridge University Press)

Pepper S (1986) 'The Lawyer's Amoral Role: A Defense, a Problem, and Some Possibilities' 11 *American Bar Foundation Research Journal* 613

—— (1995) 'Counseling at the Limits of the Law: An Exercise in the Jurisprudence and Ethics of Lawyering' 104 *Yale LJ* 1545

Perkins GD et al (2018) 'A Randomized Trial of Epinephrine in Out-of-Hospital Cardiac Arrest', 379 *New England Journal of Medicine* 711

Perlman AM (2005) 'Untangling Ethics Theory from Attorney Conduct Rules: The Case of Inadvertent Disclosures' 13 *George Mason LRev* 767

—— (2015) 'A Behavioral Theory of Legal Ethics' 90 *Indiana LJ* 1639

Perrin T (2007) 'The Perplexing Problem of Client Perjury' 76 *Fordham LRev* 1707

Perry S and Dawson J (1985) *Nightmare: Women and the Dalkon Shield* (New York, Macmillan)

Peterson F (2018) 'Black Lives Matter and the Boston Massacre' *American Scholar*, 3 December

Pettys TE (2007) 'The Emotional Juror' 76 *Fordham LRev* 1609

Phillips JA and Thompson TC (1986) 'Jurors v Judges in Later Stuart England: The Penn/Mead Trial and Bushell's Case' 4 *Minnesota Journal of Law and Inequality* 189

Pilkington E (2014) 'Georgia Man Executed Despite Lawyer Being Impaired by Alcohol at Trial' *The Guardian*, 10 December

Pirie M (2006) *How to Win Every Argument* (London, Bloomsbury)

Pollman E and Barry JM (2017) 'Regulatory Entrepreneurship' 90 *Southern California LRev* 383

Pomerantz A and Atkinson JM (1984) 'Ethnomethodology, Conversation Analysis and the Study of Court-room Interaction' in Müller DJ, Blackman DE and Chapman AJ (eds) *Psychology and Law: Topics from an International Conference* (Chichester, Wiley)

Posner E and Vermeule A (2004) 'A "Torture" Memo and its Tortuous Critics' *Wall Street Journal*, 6 July

Possley M (2014) 'Operation Greylord' *Chicago Tribune*, 16 September

POST (2019) *Improving Witness Testimony* (- Parliamentary Office of Science and Technology, POSTNOTE No 607 July)

Postema G (1980) 'Moral Responsibility in Professional Ethics' 55 *New York University LRev* 63

Post Office Trial (2019) 'All the Judgments', 23 August, www.postofficetrial.com

Poulin AB (2004) 'Criminal Justice and Videoconferencing Technology: The Remote Defendant' 78 *Tulane LRev* 1089

Pound R (1906) 'The Causes of Popular Dissatisfaction with the Administration of Justice' 40 *American LRev* 729

Pozner LS and Dodd R (2018) *Cross-Examination Science and Techniques* (New York, LexisNexis, 3rd edn)

Preston J (2005) 'Radical Lawyer's Defense Claims Lack of Evidence' *New York Times*, 6 January

Puett M and Gross-Loh C (2016) *The Path: A New Way to Think about Everything* (London, Penguin)

Pullman L (2019) 'El Chapo's Lawyer Goes Silent under My Cross-Examination' *Sunday Times*, 17 February

—— (2020) 'Witnesses Falter as Weinstein's "Bulldog" Goes for the Throat' *Sunday Times*, 16 February

Purves L (2011) 'Why Couldn't the Judge Protect the Dowlers' Privacy?' *The Times*, 27 June

—— (2015) 'Women Who Lie about Rape are Criminals Too' *The Times*, 5 October

—— (2020) 'Sexist Attitudes of the Sutcliffe Era Live on' *The Times*, 16 November

Pye AK (1978) 'The Role of Counsel in the Suppression of Truth' 4 *Duke LJ* 921

Quakers in Britain (2023) 'Quakers Stand up for the Vital Legal Precedent Established in 1670 Quaker Trial', 17 May

Ram N (2016) 'Book Review: *Inside the Cell: The Dark Side of Forensic DNA* by Erin E Murphy (Nation Books, 2015)' 3 *Journal of Law and Biosciences* 1

Rankin I (1998) *Tooth & Nail* (London, Orion Books)

Rayment T and Leppard D (2011) 'Call This Justice?' *Sunday Times*, 26 June

Rayner J (2009) 'Hundreds of Colombian Lawyers Murdered But No One Prosecuted, Report Reveals' *Law Society Gazette*, 30 April

Raz J (1986) *The Morality of Freedom* (Oxford, Clarendon Press)

Record View (2018) 'Court Rape Shame in #ThisIsNotConsent Underwear Scandal is a Relic of the Past' *Daily Record*, 18 November

Reed B (1980) *The Verdict* (New York, Simon & Schuster)

Report of the Oversight Panel (2002) *The Damilola Taylor Murder Investigation Review*

Restatement of the Law Third (2000) *The Law Governing Lawyers*

Rhode DL (2000a) *Ethics in Practice: Lawyers' Roles, Responsibilities and Regulation* (Oxford, Oxford University Press)

—— (2000b) *In the Interests of Justice: Reforming the Legal Profession* (Oxford, Oxford University Press)

—— (2003) 'Ethics in Practice' in Rhode DL (ed) *Ethics in Practice: Lawyers' Roles, Responsibilities, and Regulation*, revised edn (Oxford, Oxford University Press, 2003)

Rhode DL and Luban DJ (eds) (2005) *Legal Ethics: Law Stories* (St Paul, Foundation Press)

Richardson B (2002) *Dingo Innocent: The Azaria Chamberlain Mystery* (Kuranda, Leap Frog Press)

Robertson D (2012) 'Whistleblowers' $104m Reason to Tell All' *The Times*, 13 September

Rogers S (1899) 'The Ethics of Advocacy' 15 *Law Quarterly Review* 259

Roiphe R (2011) 'The Ethics of Willful Ignorance' 24 *GJLE* 187

Rolph CH (ed) (1961) *The Trial of Lady Chatterley* (Harmondsworth, Penguin)

Roscoe LA, Malphurs JE, Dragovic LJ and Cohen D (2000) 'Dr Jack Kevorkian and Cases of Euthanasia in Oakland County, Michigan, 1990–1998' 343(23) *New England Journal of Medicine* 1735

Rose N (2021) 'Prosecution of A&O Partner over Weinstein NDA Stayed' *legalfutures*, 14 January

Rosen J (2007) 'Conscience of a Conservative' *New York Times*, 9 September

Rosman K (2021) 'This is Rachel Uchitel, Representing Herself' *New York Times*, 9 August

Rovere RH (1947) *The Magnificent Shysters: The True and Scandalous History of Howe and Hummel* (New York, Farrar Straus)

Rowley M (2011) 'It's Vital, Public Must Remain Confident to Give Evidence' *The Times*, 25 June

Royal Commission into the Management of Police Informants (2020) *Final Report: Summary and Recommendations, PP No 175, Session 2018–20* (Victoria Government Printer, November)

Royal Commission on Legal Services (1979) *Final Report*

Royal Society (2017) *Forensic DNA Analysis* (London, Royal Society)

Royal Society and Royal Academy of Engineering (2012) *Shale Gas Extraction in the UK: A Review of Hydraulic Fracturing* (London, Royal Society)

Rozenberg J (2020) 'Trial by Jury' *The Critic*, October

Rubin AR (1975) 'A Causerie of Lawyers' Ethics in Negotiation' 35 *Louisiana LRev* 577

Rubin CB and Ringenbach L (1991) 'The Use of Court Experts in Asbestos Litigation' 17 *Federal Rules Decisions* 35

Rubin MH (1995) 'The Ethics of Negotiations: Are There Any?' 56 *Louisiana LRev* 447

Rumbelow H (2014) 'The Woman Who Offers Abortions on the High Seas' *The Times*, 22 October

—— (2021) 'Weinstein was Allowed to Do His Worst' *The Times*, 14 September

Sabbagh D (2021) 'High Court Hears Opening Salvos in Libel Case Brought by Roman Abramovich' *The Guardian*, 30 July

Saks MJ (1987) 'Accuracy v Advocacy: Expert Testimony before the Bench' *Technology LRev* 43, August/September

Salmi L (1999) 'Don't Walk the Line: Ethical Considerations in Preparing Witnesses for Depositions and Trial' 18 *Review of Litigation* 135

Sandefur RL (2019) 'Access to What?' 148 *Daedalus* 49

Sarat A (2003) 'Ethics in Litigation' in Rhode DL (ed) *Ethics in Practice: Lawyers' Roles, Responsibilities, and Regulation*, revised edn (Oxford, Oxford University Press, 2003)

Scahill J (2007) *Blackwater: The Rise of the World's Most Powerful Mercenary Army* (New York, Nation Books)

Scalia A (2018) *A Matter of Interpretation* (Princeton, Princeton University Press)

Schlitz PJ (1999) 'On Being a Happy, Healthy, and Ethical Member of an Unhappy, Unhealthy, and Unethical Profession' 52 *Vanderbilt LRev* 871

Schneyer T (1984) 'Moral Philosophy's Standard Misconception of Legal Ethics' *Wisconsin LRev* 1529

—— (1989) 'Professionalism as Bar Politics: The Making of the Model Rules of Professional Conduct' 14 *Law and Social Inquiry* 677

—— (1991) 'Professional Discipline for Law Firms?' 77 *Cornell LRev* 1

Schulenburg R (2021) 'The Rise of "Lawfare" in the UK Examined: How Parliament Turned the Law into a Battleground' *AOAVorguk*, 5 April

Schwartz ML (1983) 'The Zeal of the Civil Advocate' *American Bar Foundation Research Journal* 543

—— (1988) 'On Making the True Look False and the False Look True' 41 *Southwestern Law Journal* 1135

Scott J (ed) (2014) *M: Moral Panic, A Dictionary of Sociology* (Oxford, Oxford University Press)

Scott M (2019) *BarristerBlogger*, 16 May

Sears N (2017) 'Lawyer Who Passed on Crucial Information That Helped Catch a Killer Nearly 20 years after He Murdered a Schoolgirl is Forced to Resign for Breaching Client Confidentiality' *MailOnline*, 30 June

The Secret Barrister (2018) *Stories of the Law and How it's Broken* (London, Macmillan)

—— (2021a) 'All Rise! This Trial Won't Be Starting until 2023' *Sunday Times*, 24 January

—— (2021b) 'The Hillsborough Judgment: What Just Happened?', 26 May

Sedley S (2008) in Symposium (2008: 52)

Seely A (2020) '*Tax avoidance: A General Anti-Abuse Rule*' House of Commons Library Briefing Paper No 6265

—— (2021) '*Tax avoidance and tax evasion*' House of Commons Library Briefing Paper No 7948

Sefarian AH and Wakley JT (2003) 'Secrecy Clauses in Sexual Molestation Settlements: Should Courts Agree to Seal Documents in Cases Involving the Catholic Church?' 16 *GJLE* 801

Seldon A, Ilersic AR, Bracewell-Milnes B (1979) *Tax Avoision: The Economic, Legal Modal Inter-relationship between Avoidance and Evasion* (London, Institute of Economic Affairs)

Selinger C (1993) 'The "Law" on Lawyer Efforts to Discredit Truthful Testimony' 46 *Oklahoma LRev* 99

Shanahan E (2021) 'The Shining' Scene, Stuff of Nightmares, Turns a Criminal Case Upside Down' *New York Times*, 20 January

Shapiro JS and Stevens J (2004) *Kobe Bryant: The Game of His Life* (New York, Revolution Publishing)

Shapiro R with Warren L (1996) *The Search for Justice: A Defense Attorney's Brief on the OJ Simpson Case* (Burbank, Warner Books)

Shargel GL (2007) 'Federal Evidence Rule 608(b): Gateway to the Minefield of Witness Preparation' 76 *Fordham LRev* 1229

Shavell S (1988) 'Legal Advice about Contemplated Acts: The Decision to Obtain Advice, its Social Desirability, and Protection of Confidentiality' 17 *Journal of Legal Studies* 123

Sherwin R (1994) 'The Narrative Construction of Legal Reality' 18 *Vermont LRev* 681

Shklar J (1964) *Legalism* (Cambridge, MA, Harvard University Press)

Siegel B (1988a) 'Georgia Man's Trials: When One Man's Rights Made a Wrong' *LA Times*, 22 December

—— (1988b) 'Parole Board Frees Man Courts Wouldn't: Lawyers Played by Rules as Justice Failed Inmate' *LA Times*, 23 December

Siegel MJ (2006) 'Zealous Advocacy vs Truth' 31(1) *Litigation* 31

Silver JS (1994) 'Truth, Justice and the American Way: The Case against Client Perjury Rules' 47 *Vanderbilt LRev* 339

Simon D (2011) 'The Limits of Diagnosticity of Criminal Trials' 64 *Vanderbilt LRev* 143

Simon WH (1988) 'Ethical Discretion in Lawyering' 101 *Harvard LRev* 1083

—— (1993) 'The Ethics of Criminal Defense' 91 *Michigan LRev* 1703

—— (1996) 'Should Lawyers Obey the Law?' 38 *William and Mary LRev* 217

—— (1999) 'Virtuous Lying: A Critique of Quasi-categorical Moralism' 12 *GJLE* 433

—— (1998) *The Practice of Justice: A Theory of Lawyers' Ethics* (Cambridge, MA, Harvard University Press)

—— (2000) *The Practice of Justice: A Theory of Lawyers' Ethics* (Cambridge, MA, Harvard University Press, revised edn)

Simon's Taxes (1988) (Oxford, Butterworths, 3rd edn)

Simpson AWB (1988) *An Invitation to Law* (Oxford, Blackwell)

Simpson J (2021) 'Fears over Jail Terms Led to Acquittals' *The Times*, 13 November

Simpson K (1979) *40 Years of Murder* (London, Harrap)

Singer JW (1988) 'Legal Realism Now' 76 *California LRev* 467

Sisk GC (2014) 'The Legal Ethics of Real Evidence: Of Child Porn on the Choirmaster's Computer and Bloody Knives under the Stairs' 89 *Washington LRev* 819

Sitwell W (2024) 'The Post Office Scandal Has Revealed the Country's True Leader – Prime-Time TV' *The Telegraph*, 13 January

Slapper G (2013) 'Classic Judicial Clangers' *The Times*, May 23

Slingo J (2020) 'Pre-recorded Evidence Now an Option across England and Wales' *Law Society Gazette*, 23 November

Smith A (2000a) 'Defending Defending: The Case for Unlimited Zeal on Behalf of People Who Do Terrible Things' 28 *Hofstra LRev* 925

—— (2000b) 'Defending the Innocent' 32 *Connecticut LRev* 485

Smith C (2021) 'What is Litigation Privilege?', Mondaq.com/uk/disclosure-electronic-discovery-privilege/1098158/qbit-what-is-litigation-privilege-video?email_access=on

Smith EK (2021) 'Postmasters Take Ministers to Court over Inquiry Failure' *Sunday Times*, 9 May

Smith M and Crossley D (eds) (1975) *The Way out: Radical Alternatives in Australia* (Melbourne, Lansdowne)

Smith MA (2010) 'Advice and Complicity' 60 *Duke LJ* 499

Smith PA (2016) 'When DNA Implicates the Innocent' *Scientific American*, 1 June

Smith S (2016) *Marshall Hall: A Law unto Himself* (London, Wildy, Simmons & Hill)

Snell's Equity (2020) (McGee J and Elliott S eds) (London, Sweet & Maxwell)

Snow RF (1987) 'Counsel for the Indefensible' 38(2) *American Heritage Magazine*

Solan LM (2012) 'Lawyers as Insincere (But Truthful) Actors' 36 *Journal of the Legal Profession* 487

—— (2018) 'Lies, Deceit, and Bullshit in Law' 56 *Duquesne LRev* 73

Spence G (1996) *How to Argue and Win Every Time* (New York, Macmillan)

—— (2006) *Win Your Case: How to Present, Persuade and Prevail – Every Place, Every Time* (New York, Macmillan, 2006)

Sprack J (2006) *A Practical Approach to Criminal Procedure* (Oxford, Oxford University Press)

SRA (2007) *Solicitors' Code of Conduct 2007*

—— (2011) *Handbook*

—— (2015) *Walking the Line: The Balancing of Duties in Litigation*

—— (2018) *Balancing Duties in Litigation*

—— (2019c) *Guidance, Confidentiality of Client Information*

—— (2019d) *Principles*

—— (2019e) *What You Need to Know about Standards and Regulations*

—— (2019f) *Warning Notice, Tax Avoidance and Your Duties* (published 21 September 2017, updated 25 November 2019)

—— (2020) *Use of Non-disclosure Agreements (NDAs)*

—— (2022a) *Guidance, Conduct in Disputes*

—— (2022b) *Warning notice, Strategic Lawsuits against Public Participation (SLAPPs)*

—— (2023a) *Code of Conduct for Solicitors RELs and RFLs*

—— (2023b) *Code of Conduct for Firms*

—— (2023c) *Thematic Review: The Use of Non-disclosure Agreements in Workplace Complaints*

Stafford D (1999) *Roosevelt and Churchill: Men of Secrets* (New York, Overlook Press)

Starr Report: Narrative (2004) 'Nature of President Clinton's Relationship with Monica Lewinsky' (Washington, DC, US Government Printing Office, 19 May, archived from the original on December 3, 2000 President Bill Clinton, Referral from Independent Counsel Kenneth W Starr in Conformity with the Requirement of Title 28, US Code, Section 595(c), n 1,128)

Steinberg MI (2020) 'Foreword: Corporate Lawyers: Ethical and Practical Lawyering with Vanishing Gatekeeper Liability' 88 *Fordham LRev* 1575

Stern HS, Cuellar M and Kaye D (2019) 'Reliability and Validity of Forensic Science Evidence' 16 *Significance* 21

Stevenson D (2014) 'against Confidentiality' 48 *University of California Davis LRev* 337

Stevenson RL (1881) *Virginibus Puerisque* (London, Kegan Paul & Co)

Stone M (1995) *Cross-Examination in Criminal Trials* (London, Butterworths, 2nd edn)

Stuart S, McKimmie BK and Masser B (2016) 'Rape Perpetrators on Trial: The Effect of Sexual Assault-Related Schemas on Attributions of Blame' 34 *Journal of Interpersonal Violence* 310

Subin HI (1987) 'The Criminal Lawyer's 'Different Mission': Reflections on "the Right" to Present a False Case' 1 *GJLE* 125

—— (1988) 'Is This Lie Necessary? Further Reflections on the Right to Present a False Defense' 1 *GJLE* 689

Suggs D and Sales BD (1978) 'The Art and Science of Conducting the Voir Dire' 9 *Professional Psychology* 367

Sullivan WM, Colby A, Welch Wegner J, Bond L, Shulman LS (2007) *Educating Lawyers: Preparation for the Profession of Law* (San Francisco, Jossey-Bass/Wiley)

Sumption J (2021) *Law in a Time of Crisis* (London, Profile Books)

Sun Tzu/Sun Zi [c 400–320BC] (1910) *SunTzu on the Art of War* (Translated by Lionel Giles London, Luzac and Company)

Sward EF (1989) 'Values, Ideology and the Evolution of the Adversary System' 64 *Indiana LJ* 301

Swaine J (2008) 'Italy Overturns Ruling That a Woman Wearing Tight Jeans "Cannot Be Raped"' *The Telegraph*, 23 July

Symposium (1993–94) 'To Kill a Mockingbird' 45(2) *Alabama LRev* 563

—— (1996) 'The Wrong Man is about to Be Executed for a Crime He Did Not Commit' 29 *Loyola of Los Angeles LRev* 1543

—— (2008) 'A Hippocratic Oath for Lawyers?' 11 *Legal Ethics* 41

—— (2014) '*Atkins v Virginia*: A Dozen Years Later – A Report Card' 23(2) *William and Mary Bill of Rights Journal* 487

Tanford JA (2002) 'The Ethics of Evidence' 25 *American Journal of Trial Advocacy* 487

Taylor Jr S (1994) 'Sleazy in Seattle' *American Law*, April

Temkin BR (2008) 'Deception in Undercover Investigations: Conduct-Based vs Status-Based Ethical Analysis' 32 *Seattle LRev* 123

Temkin J (2002) *Rape and the Legal Process* (Oxford, Oxford University Press)

Temkin J and Krahe B (2008) *Sexual Assault and the Justice Gap: A Question of Attitude* (Oxford, Hart Publishing)

Tenbrunsel AE and Messick DM (2004) 'Ethical Fading: The Role of Self-Deception in Unethical Behavior' 17 *Social Science Research* 223

Thanki B (ed) (2018) *The Law of Privilege* (Oxford, Oxford University Press)

Thompson WC and Schumann EL (1987) 'Interpretation of Statistical Evidence in Criminal Trials: The Prosecutor's Fallacy and the Defense Attorney's Fallacy' 11 *Law and Human Behavior* 167

Thompson-Cannino J, Cotton R with Torneo E (2009) *Picking Cotton: Our Memoir of Injustice and Redemption* (New York, St Martin's Press)

Tiersma PM and LM Solan (2012) 'The Language of Crime' in Tiersma PM and Solan LM (eds) *The Oxford Handbook of Language and Law* (Oxford, Oxford University Press)

Tigar ME (1993) 'Setting the Record Straight on the Defense of John Demjanjuk' *Legal Times*, 6 September

—— (1995) 'Defending' 74 *Texas LRev* 101

—— (1999) *Persuasion: The Litigator's Art* (Chicago, ABA)

—— (2003) *Examining Witnesses* (Chicago, ABA, 2nd edn)

Tigar ME and Coleman Jr JE (2014) 'A Sanctuary in the Jungle: Terry Lynn Nichols and the Oklahoma City Bombing Trial', https://law.utexas.edu/wp-content/uploads/sites/34/2016/09/15NicholsFinal.pdf

The Times (2011) 'Trial and Error', 25 June

—— (2021a) Sir Jeremiah Harman obituary, 13 March

—— (2021b) 'Justice at Last', 24 April

—— (2023a) 'Unjust Trials', 19 December

—— (2023b) 'Slapp Down', 27 January

—— (2023c) 'Slapp Down', 12 September

—— (2023d) Morland cartoon, 7 June

—— (2024a) 'A Warning to Vocal Lawyers', 11 January

—— (2024b) 'Post Office and the Press', 13 January

Times Argus (2007) 23 February

Timothy JP (2000) 'Demeanor Credibility' 49 *Catholic LRev* 903

Tolson R (2008) in Symposium (2008: 54)

Tomkins SS (1979) 'Script theory: Differential Magnification of Affects' in Dienstbier RA, *26 Nebraska Symposium on Motivation* (Lincoln, NE, University of Nebraska Press)

Toobin J (1996) *The Run of His Life: The People v OJ Simpson* (New York, Random House)

Topping A (2020) 'Just One in Seven Rape Survivors Expect Justice in England and Wales' *The Guardian*, 20 October

Traver R (1958) *Anatomy of a Murder* (New York, St Martin's Press)

Trope ML (2001) *Once upon a Time in Los Angeles: The Trials of Earl Rogers* (Spokane, Arthur H Clark Company)

TUC (2013a) *The Deficiencies in the General Anti-Abuse Rule*

—— (2013b) 'New Anti-abuse Rule Will Allow 99% of Tax Avoidance to Continue, Says the TUC' tax briefing, 2 December

Turow S (1999) *Personal Injuries* (New York, Farrar, Straus & Giroux)

Twain M (1897) *More Tramps Abroad* (London, Chatto & Windus)

Twining W (2006) *Rethinking Evidence: Exploratory Essays* (Cambridge, Cambridge University Press)

Uelman GF (1996) 'The Disappearing Knife' *San Jose Mercury News*, 28 April

—— (1991) 'Ethics in the Horseshed: Guidelines for Interviewing and Preparing Witnesses' 4(3) *California Litigation* 16

UPI Archives (1995) 'Shapiro Disagrees with "Race Card", 3 October

Uviller HR (1993) 'Credence, Character, and the Rules of Evidence: Seeing through the Liar's Tale' 42 *Duke LJ* 776

Valdez E (2011) 'Practical Ethics for the Professional Prosecutor' 1 *St Mary's Journal on Legal Malpractice and Ethics* 250

Van Kessel G (1993) 'Adversary Excesses in the American Criminal Trial' 67 *Notre Dame LRev* 403

Vaughan S (2023) 'Existential Ethics: Thinking Hard about Lawyer Responsibility for Clients' Environmental Harms' 76 *Current Legal Problems* 1

Vennard J and Riley D (1988) 'The Use of Peremptory Challenge and Stand by of Jurors and Their Relationship to Trial Outcome' *Criminal LRev* 731

Vile JR (2001) *Great American Lawyers: An Encyclopedia* (Santa Barbara, ABC-CLIO)

Vineall N (2023a) 'The Cab Rank Rule is a Bedrock Obligation' *The Bar Council*, 28 April

—— (2023b) 'Lawyers Must Feel Free to Act for Unsavoury Clients' *The Times*, 5 October

Vlasic B (2014a), 'Inquiry by General Motors is Said to Focus on its Lawyers' *New York Times*, 17 May

—— (2014b) 'GM Lawyers Hid Fatal Flaw, from Critics and One Another' *New York Times*, June 6

Vrij A (2000) *Detecting Lies and Deceit: The Psychology of Lying and Implications for Professional Practice* (Oxford, Wiley)

—— (2008) *Detecting Lies and Deceit: Pitfalls and Opportunities* (Oxford, Wiley, 2nd edn)

Wace C (2020) 'Prison Officer Jailed for Fake Claim She was Raped in Taxi' *The Times*, 10 June

—— (2021) 'Donald McPherson Trial: Secretive Husband "Killed Our Daughter"' *The Times*, April 3

Wallach E (2007) 'Drop by Drop: Forgetting the History of Water Torture in US Courts' 45 *Columbia Journal of Transnational Law* 486

Wallis N (2022) *The Great Post Office Scandal* (Bath, Bath Publishing)

Walsh S (1993) 'State Court Sanctions Firm for Failure to Disclose' *Washington Post*, 29 November

Walters B (2003) *Slapping on the Writs: Defamation, Development and Community Action* (Sydney, University of New South Wales Press)

Wartolowska K et al (2014) 'Use of Placebo Controls in the Evaluation of Surgery: Systematic Review' *British Medical Journal* 348

Wasserstrom R (1975) 'Lawyers as Professionals: Some Moral Issues' 5 *Human Rights* 1

Watergate (1973) Senate Hearings

Watson I (2010) 'Human Rights lawyer Who Fled Iran is Reunited with His Family' *CNN*, 3 September

Way P (2013) 'The Role of Law, Tax Avoidance and the GAAR' XII(I) *GITC Review* 79

—— (2021) 'The Rule of Law, Tax Avoidance and the GAAR' XII *GITC Review*, June

Wegner DM, Wenzlaff R, Kercher RM and Beattie AE (1981) 'Incrimination through Innuendo: Can Media Questions become Public Answers?' 40 *Journal of Personality and Social Psychology* 822

Weinstein JB (1994) 'Ethical Dilemmas in Mass Tort Litigation' 88 *Northwestern LRev* 469

Wellborn OG III (1991) 'Demeanor' 76 *Cornell LRev* 1075

Wellman FL (1903) *The Art of Cross-Examination* (New York, Macmillan)

—— (1924) *Gentlemen of the Jury* (New York, Macmillan)

Wendel WB (1999) 'Public Values and Professional Responsibility' 75 *Notre Dame LRev* 1

—— (2004) *Professional Responsibility* (New York, Aspen)

—— (2010) *Lawyers and Fidelity to Law* (Princeton, Princeton University Press)

—— (2011) 'The Craft of Legal Interpretation' in Morigiwa et al

—— (2012) 'Legal Ethics is about the Law, Not Morality or Justice: A Reply to Critics' 90 *Texas LRev* 727

—— (2018) 'Truthfulness as an Ethical Form of Life' 56 *Duquesne LRev* 141

WETA (1986) Video: Ethics on Trial

—— (1988) 'Ethics on Trial: Law School Guide', Washington DC

Wetlaufer GB (1990) 'The Ethics of Lying in Negotiations' 76 *Iowa LRev* 1219

Whelan CJ (2001) 'Ethical Conflicts in Legal Practice: Creating Professional Responsibility' 52 *South Carolina LRev* 697

—— (2007) 'Some Realism about Professionalism: Core Values, Legality, and Corporate Law Practice' 55 *Buffalo LRev* 1067, reprinted in Rapaport NB, van Niel JD and Dharan BG (eds) (2009) *Enron and Other Corporate Fiascos: The Corporate Scandal Reader* (New York, Foundation Press)

—— (2022) *The Bodyguards of Lies: Lawyers' Power and Professional Responsibility* (Oxford, Hart Publishing)

White JJ (1980) 'Machiavelli and the Bar: Ethical Limitations on Lying in Negotiations' 1980 *American Bar Foundation Research Journal* 926

Wiener LS and Zdrojeski RW (2015) 'The Art of the Persuasive Opening Statement: Finding Your Inner Storyteller' in Worden (2005)

Wiggins K and Browning J (2019) 'How Corporate Britain Hides Thousands of Sex Discrimination Cases' *Bloomberg*, 6 September

Wigmore JH (1905) *4 A Treatise on the System of Evidence at Common Law* (New York, Little Brown)

Wikipedia (nd) 'Rodney King', https://en.wikipedia.org/wiki/Rodney_King

Wilkie C (2011) *The Fall of the House of Zeus: The Rise and Fall of America's Most Powerful Lawyer* (New York, Broadway)

Wilkins DB (1990) 'Legal Realism for Lawyers' 104 *Harvard LRev* 468

Williams B (2002) *Truth and Truthfulness* (Princeton, Princeton University Press)

Wills G (1999) *A Necessary Evil: A History of American Distrust of Government* (New York, Simon & Schuster)

Wishman S (1981) *Confessions of a Criminal Defense Lawyer* (New York, Times Books)

Witherow (2024) 'Vennels Wanted to Brand Horizon Bug an "Exception"' *The Times*, 24 April

Wolchover D (1989) 'Should Judges Sum up on the Facts?' 1989 *Criminal LRev* 781

Wolfram C (1995) 'The US Law of Client Confidentiality: Framework for an International Perspective' in Daly and Goebbel (1995)

Woo I (2010) 'Breaking Up Is Hard to Do' *Wall Street Journal*, 13 August

Wooding A (2010) 'Legal Eagle, the Art of Cross-Examination', http://legaleagleipswich.blogspot.com/2010/01/art-of-cross-examination.html

Woodward A (2024) 'Donald Trump Ordered to Pay Nearly $400,000 to the *New York Times*' *The Independent*, 13 January

Worden JS (ed) (2005) *From the Trenches: Strategies and Tips from 21 of the Nation's Top Trial Lawyers* (Chicago, ABA)

Wright RF, Chavis K, Parks GS (2018) 'The Jury Sunshine Project: Jury Selection Data as a Political Issue' *Illinois LRev* 1407

Wydick RC (1995) 'The Ethics of Witness Coaching' 17(1) *Cardozo LRev* 1

Wyzanski CE Jr (1973) 'An Activist Judge: Mea Maxima Culpa Apologia Pro Vita Mea' 7 *Georgia LRev* 202

Yablon CM (2019) 'The Lawyer as Accomplice: Cannabis, Uber, Airbnb, and the Ethics of Advising' Cardozo School of Law, Faculty Research Paper No 580

Yoo J (2005) *The Powers of War and Peace* (Chicago, University of Chicago Press, 2005)

—— (2006) *War by Other Means: An Insider's Account of the War on Terror* (New York, Atlantic Monthly Press)

Youk MH (nd) 'Letter to Judge Cooper from Thomas Youk's Wife', famous-trials.com/drkevorkian/2426-letter-to-judge-cooper-from-thomas-youk-s-wife

Yousif N (2024) 'Donald Trump Ordered to Pay *New York Times* Nearly $400,000 in Legal Costs' *BBC News*, 13 January

Zacharias FC (1989) 'Rethinking Confidentiality' 74 *Iowa LRev* 351

—— (2002) 'What Lawyers Do When Nobody's Watching: Legal Advertising as a Case Study of the Impact of Underenforced Professional Rules' 87 *Iowa LRev* 971

—— (2007) 'The Images of Lawyers' 20 *GJLE* 73

—— (2008) 'Fitting Lying to the Court into the Central Moral Tradition of Lawyering' 58 *Case Western Reserve LRev* 491

Zacharias FC and Green BA (2005) 'Reconceptualizing Advocacy Ethics' 74 *George Washington LRev* 1

Zacharias FC and Martin S (1999) 'Coaching Witnesses' 87 *Kentucky LJ* 1001

Zander M (2007) *Cases and Materials on the English Legal System* (Cambridge, Cambridge University Press, 10th edn)

Zander M and Henderson P (1993) *The Crown Court Study* (Royal Commission on Justice Study No 19, London, HMSO)

Zdrojeski RW (2005) 'The Art of the Persuasive Opening Statement: Finding Your Inner Storyteller' in Worden (2005)

Zitrin R (1999) 'The Case against Secret Settlement (or, What You Don't Know *Can* Hurt You)' 2 *Journal of the Institute for the Study of Legal Ethics* 115

Zitrin R and Langford C (1999a), 'Buried Bodies: Robert Garrow and His Lawyers' in Zitrin and Langford (1999b)

—— (1999b) *The Moral Compass of the American Lawyer: Truth, Justice, Power and Greed* (New York, Ballantine Books)

Zmina (2016) 'Amnesty International Urges to Secure Ukrainian lawyers', 4 April

Zobel HB (1970) *The Boston Massacre* (London, WW Norton)

INDEX

www.ingramcontent.com/pod-product-compliance
Lightning Source LLC
Chambersburg PA
CBHW061140220326
41599CB00025B/4304